From Bondage to Liberation

From Bondage to Liberation

EAST ASIA 1860—1952

Nigel Cameron

HONG KONG
OXFORD UNIVERSITY PRESS 1975
KUALA LUMPUR SINGAPORE JAKARTA TOKYO

Oxford University Press

OXFORD LONDON GLASGOW NEW YORK
TORONTO MELBOURNE WELLINGTON CAPE TOWN
DELHI BOMBAY CALCUTTA MADRAS KARACHI DACCA
KUALA LUMPUR SINGAPORE JAKARTA HONG KONG TOKYO
NAIROBI DAR ES SALAAM LUSAKA ADDIS ABABA
IBADAN ZARIA ACCRA BEIRUT

© *Oxford University Press 1975*

ISBN 0 19 580735 9

Printed by Dai Nippon Printing Co. (H.K.) Ltd., I Pat Tai Street, Kowloon, Hong Kong
Published by Oxford University Press, News Building, North Point, Hong Kong

Contents

THE CHINESE DYNASTIES

Shang (later called Yin) kingdom　商   c.1520–c.1030 B.C.

Chou 周 dynasty (Feudal Age)
 - Early Chou   c.1030–722 B.C.
 - Spring and Autumn period　春秋   722–480 B.C.
 - Warring States　戰國   480–221 B.C.

FIRST UNIFICATION
Ch'in dynasty　秦   221–207 B.C.
Han dynasty　漢   202 B.C.–A.D.220

FIRST PARTITION
Three Kingdoms　三國   A.D.221–280

SECOND UNIFICATION
Chin dynasty　晉   A.D.265–420
Liu Sung dynasty　劉宋   A.D.420–479

SECOND PARTITION
Northern and Southern Dynasties　南北朝   A.D.479–581

THIRD UNIFICATION
Sui dynasty　隋   A.D.581–618
T'ang dynasty　唐   A.D.618–906

THIRD PARTITION
Five Dynasties period (three of which were non-Chinese)　五代   A.D.907–960
Liao (non-Chinese)　遼   A.D.937–1125
West Liao (non-Chinese)　西遼   A.D.1125–1211
Hsi Hsia (non-Chinese)　西夏   A.D.990–1227

FOURTH UNIFICATION

Sung dynasty { Northern 北宋		A.D.960–1126
{ Southern 南宋		A.D.1127–1279
Chin dynasty (non-Chinese) 金		A.D.1115–1234
Yüan (Mongol) dynasty 元		A.D.1260–1368
Ming dynasty 明		A.D.1368–1644
Ch'ing (Manchu) dynasty 清		A.D.1644–1911
Republic 民國		A.D.1912
People's Republic 中華人民共和國		A.D.1949

EMPERORS OF THE CH'ING (清) DYNASTY, 1644–1911

REIGN TITLE

Shun-chih	順治	1644–1661
K'ang hsi	康熙	1661–1722
Yung-chêng	雍正	1722–1735
Ch'ien-lung	乾隆	1735–1796
Chia-ch'ing	嘉慶	1796–1820
Tao-kuang	道光	1820–1850
Hsien-fêng	咸豐	1850–1862
Tung-ch'ih	同治	1862–1875
Kuang-hsü	光緒	1875–1908
Hsüan-t'ung	宣統	1908–(abdicated 1912)

NOTE: The Dowager Empress Tz'u-hsi was regent during the Kuang-hsü reign except for the period between March 4, 1889 and September 19, 1898.

PART ONE

EAST AND WEST COLLIDE

1 Traditional China

IN any study of the history of East Asia there can be no escaping the dominant fact of China. The earliest and the most important civilization of the whole area is Chinese. The civilization of all the other territories in the area is derived in part at least from the profound and powerful influence of Chinese culture. It is also worth remembering that the territory and the people of China are all but unique in East Asia in that they have never at any time been subjected to the rule of Western man.

The history of East Asia in the nineteenth and twentieth centuries has been shaped in large part by the activities of Western men, and by Western governments and their activities—trading, colonizing, and trying to spread their foreign religion, Christianity. While it would be quite inaccurate to imagine that all events in East Asian history during that time were the result of Western influences of one kind and another, it is true that many important changes took place because of them, especially as we come nearer to the twentieth century.

To understand the way in which such changes took place and what were the results, and to understand the internal events in China, Japan, and in other countries of the area, we have to look briefly at what the civilization of these countries was like before the modern period, before the West intruded in the East.

To the West, China has always been a remote land far away in the East, so remote that what might be happening there generally seemed of very little importance. Roman and Greek writers about the time of Christ were slightly interested because of the silk that arrived in Mediterranean countries from the land of the Seres (as the East was vaguely termed). At one time silk caused concern because of the drain of gold from the treasuries of Rome in order to pay for it. But no one had any precise idea of where the silk people or their country were, or what they were like. A great many fables were told about them, because no one can for long picture the people of a place without attaching some characteristics to them, even if these are largely imaginary.

In China, much the same story is true. The West was a series of countries in the 'Western Ocean' of very little interest because they were supposed to be small and were certainly far away. They produced nothing that could possibly interest the Chinese because, first, the Chinese had everything they wanted; and second, if the West had produced anything of use to China, the Chinese would have obtained it—just as they obtained spices from India and Southeast Asia and furs from the cold mountainous and forested lands north and northwest of the main mass of their own country. The Chinese had just as many and just as strange fables about Western peoples and countries as the West had about them, some of them remarkably similar.

Even from the earliest times, however, there were fundamental differences between the civilization of China and that of the West. Perhaps the main difference arose from the fact that the West never (even under Greek and Roman Empires) consisted of a single country with a single language and a homogeneous people. At its most united under the Roman Empire, it was an area of different peoples with different traditions and languages owing, at that time, allegiance to the Romans, but mostly not really partaking of Roman civilization in any very full way.

China, on the other hand, contained a people who (although of mixed stock) shared a profound heritage in the shape of one written language and one moral and governmental code. The nature and history of Chinese civilization are unlike that of any other surviving culture in that basically the same language and way of writing have survived since the earliest times down to the present; and that a system of ethics based on the teachings of Confucius (K'ung Fu-tzŭ, 559–479 B.C.) formed the basis of official and private conduct, and of the system of government, for over two thousand years until the fall of the last dynasty in 1911. On the official side, this is rather as if we were to discover that England had had a parliamentary democracy since before the time of Christ.

The unified nature of Chinese civilization as evidenced in its one written form of language which meant that all Chinese could communicate with each other if they could write, and in its governmental and ethical aspects, should be considered in the light of Western civilization. The West, when it first came into close contact with China in the eighteenth and early nineteenth centuries, had no such unity. The West consisted of several countries which sent ships and men to China. The men of these countries spoke mutually incomprehensible languages, their sole common factor being a belief in Christianity. But Western governments were not run according to Christian ethics, and the various forms of Christian belief were in any case rather different. Moreover, the nations represented by the first Western arrivals in China were mutually antagonistic, sometimes even at war with each other.

The principal mass of China inhabited by Chinese people was broadly defined in the brief Ch'in dynasty (221–207 B.C.) when the first unification of the area took place. It was consolidated in the following Han dynasty (202 B.C.–A.D. 220). The exact place where the border of China might lie at any given time, was determined always by the relative strength of the Chinese, and that of the 'barbarians' who lived on those borders and beyond. China as a unit and as a unitary civilization was always in the end stronger than her neighbours. Even when China was conquered and ruled by various of those neighbours (which happened several times), she eventually threw the conquerors out. And her civilization remained stubbornly Chinese, absorbing other influences.

Many of China's neighbours, the peoples Chinese knew best, were nomads with no towns, villages, or settled places to live. Many had no written language, and most were keepers of flocks of sheep, goats, yaks, and other cattle, their communities in a comparatively primitive stage of development in comparison to the Chinese way of life. The Chinese, therefore, never encountered any people whose civilization in any way compared to their own in refinement, in literary, artistic, or technical development, until the technical side of Western civilization (in the form of superior ships and devastating guns) hit them between the eyes.

An early Chou dynasty bronze ritual vessel. The Chinese technical mastery of casting is evident in this intricate and large vessel over 40 inches high

This pottery horse, almost forty inches high, came from a Han dynasty tomb. The tall Western breed of horse was introduced to China in the first century B.C. The Chinese called them 'celestial horses'

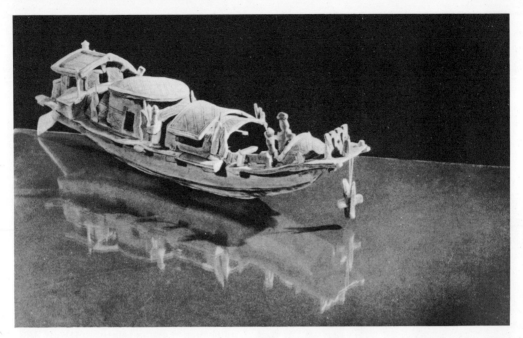

A Han dynasty pottery model of a boat of the period shows the development of various shipbuilding and navigating techniques well in advance of those in the West at the same time (over two thousand years ago)

A recently excavated Han dynasty bronze lamp in the form of a kneeling servant. The light, placed inside the lamp she is holding, can be directed by moving the shutters, while the smoke from the wick travels up through the hollow left arm into the hollow body of the servant figure

China's relations with her immediate neighbours and with peoples who lived a little further away were based on the fact of Chinese superiority in terms of civilization. Neighbouring peoples were encouraged to send representatives at regular intervals to the Chinese capital to present tribute to the emperor. Tribute varied from valuable furs and jade rocks, and the other important products of the tributary area, to trivial things. The envoys, housed in the capital city in places specially set aside for them, their expenses paid while in China, were eventually summoned at dawn to one of the imperial audiences. The emperor, seated in all his magnificence, surrounded by the highest dignitaries of the Chinese state in their rich robes of office, and guarded by thousands of soldiers equipped with flashing halberds, swords, and dressed in armour and uniforms of great brilliance, surveyed the assembled hundreds of envoys—all on their knees—who had come to pay tribute to the might and majesty and undeniable superiority of Chinese civilization. There can have been little doubt in the minds of the envoys about China's greatness and their own smallness. And there can have been little doubt in the imperial and official Chinese minds of the same thing. The situation is a little reminiscent of the great days of British power in various African colonies, with the exception that now and then over the centuries the Chinese were reminded by the tributary peoples (such as those who established the Yuan or Mongol dynasty) that all men are at least potentially equal, and some of them may manage to conquer even the most sophisticated of civilizations for a time.

A Chinese drawing of envoys from countries surrounding China presenting their tribute goods at the department of central administration where details were recorded

Having performed the *kowtow*, the three kneelings and nine knockings of their heads on the hard stone of the palace ground, the envoys of the tributary states were sent back home loaded with Chinese produce—silk, porcelain, and many other goods. The system served several useful purposes. First, it made quite clear who was master. Second, it was a means of barter trade and also stimulated more trade because all embassies to China were accompanied by merchants with caravans of goods for sale, and who, at the end of their time in China, bought there what they thought would sell at home. Third, it spread by slow degrees some elements of Chinese civilization to distant areas where life became slowly less barbarous and primitive. Fourth, it was useful in cementing understanding and in showing how Chinese protection was extended to smaller neighbours if they in turn remained loyal to China and did not form aggressive alliances. In what would now be called a paternalistic way, the system worked quite well. There were occasional rebellious children in the Chinese tributary-nation family but (when we look at how long it lasted and how many states were involved) not too many.

China, therefore, was in theory and generally in practice buffered on her long landward frontiers. She had found that the only people coming by sea were traders

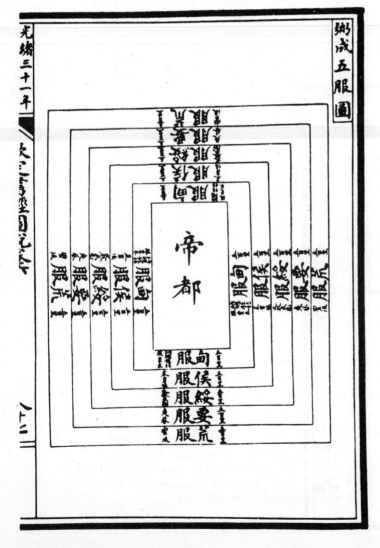

This graphic diagram shows how the Chinese considered their culture radiated from the capital outward. It comes from the *Imperial Illustrated Edition of Historic Classics*. The central rectangle has the characters meaning 'imperial capital', and this is surrounded by five bands: 'imperial domains' (China itself); 'regions of feudal princes tributary to the emperor'; the 'zone of pacification' (meaning the border regions where Chinese influence was dominant); the zone of 'barbarians' allied to China; and finally the Chinese equivalent of the Western concept of 'outer darkness' where total savagery reigned in small boats from as far away as Arabia and India, bringing spices and other luxury and exotic goods, and these were not in the least aggressive. Indeed from very early days—before the T'ang dynasty (A.D. 618–906) there were large communities of Arabs in coastal areas of China, living peacefully. So China was effectively insulated from contact with the outer world. She was certainly much more insulated than was any state or group of states in the West.

Internally, the government of China was run by a class of scholar-officials recruited, for the most part, by competitive examinations held in many parts of the country. The subjects of these imperial examinations were principally the Five Classics, consisting of works supposed to have been compiled by Confucius, and the Four Commentaries, containing the opinions of Confucius. The means to acquire the education sufficient to enter for such examinations was only within the reach of the well-to-do classes, and although some poor scholars obtained help in education, the system largely preserved the functions of government and positions in office for those who were rich. This was entirely in line with Confucian philosophy with its aim to preserve just such a state of affairs, and to teach obedience—obedience to parents and elders, and to all those higher up the social or financial ladder. Wealth was the basic but not the exclusive means to acquire power.

The governmental structure of China broadly reflected these values. The emperor was regarded as the recipient of Heaven's mandate to rule. He was the intermediary between Heaven and the Chinese people. He owed obedience to Heaven, his sole master. The highest officials gathered together the reports of lower officials and of others governing provinces and presented them to the emperor for his consideration, making what comments they felt necessary.

So, from the emperor downward, a pyramid of power widened and at the same time diminished in strength, until in the case of the most minor provincial officials power was slight. This system, unchanged in any important detail over two thousand years, made for a stable form of society when it was honestly worked by those concerned, and for an extortionate and unstable one when officials were corrupt or when the emperor was careless of the needs of the people or was not correctly informed by his officials.

The outlook of the ordinary Chinese, and of officials too, was narrowed by this system which was constructed to look unkindly on change and on innovation. But no study of Chinese history should overlook the fact that there were two strands of human behaviour within it. One was the conforming normal standard, and the other the irrepressible streak of brilliance that runs through all mankind and has produced in the outcome the greatest of men's achievements. Perhaps because of their vast numbers, perhaps because of the vast and not very fertile land they had to cultivate, perhaps because of the side effects of Taoist beliefs encouraging magical investigations, and perhaps because of a combination of all three factors, the Chinese are among the most prolific of the world's inventors, and also among the world's most prolific poets and writers and painters.

Two or three decades ago most scholars, Chinese and Western alike, would have been surprised at the idea of the Chinese as great inventors. But recent research has brought to light many features that the predominantly literary values of Chinese scholarship have ignored. A few examples demonstrate the point, and show how long it was before individual Chinese inventions reached the West.

Model of an astronomical clock-tower. The original was built at K'aifeng on the lower
reaches of the Yellow River by Su Sung and his co-workers in A.D. 1090. On top is a mechanized armillary sphere (a skeleton celestial globe, consisting merely of metal rings representing the equator, ecliptic, tropics, arctic, and antarctic circles) thirty-five feet above
the ground. Inside the top storey is a mechanized celestial globe, and below, surrounding
the water-driven clockwork machinery, are many openings in the revolving pagoda-like
building, in which the time may be told

Invention	Delay in reaching the West
Wheelbarrow	900–1000 years
Crossbow	1300 ”
Kite	about 1200 ”
Deep drilling	1100 ”
Cast iron	1000–1200 ”
Suspension bridge (two types)	800–1200 ”
Canal lock-gates	700–1700 ”
Gunpowder	400 ”
Magnetic compass (lodestone spoon)	1100 ”
Magnetic compass (with needle)	400 ”
Printing (with blocks)	600 ”
Printing (movable type)	400 ”
Paper	1000 ”
Porcelain	1100–1300 ”
Clockwork (the escapement mechanism)	400 ”

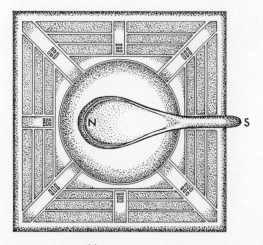

Above, paper-making by the ancient method of dipping a fine bamboo mesh screen into liquid paper pulp. The screen, covered by a layer of pulp, is allowed to dry, and a sheet of paper forms on its surface

Right, the earliest forms of Chinese compass consisted of naturally magnetic stone (lodestone) carved in various shapes such as this spoon-like object, and floated on liquid. In a Swiss museum there is a stone relief dating from A.D. 114, which shows such an instrument in use

In the hundreds of caves hollowed out of cliffs at Tunhuang in Kansu province over a period of centuries, much of the life of the Chinese people at that time may be seen. This scene describing a Buddhist legend gives a clear view of the structure of a Buddhist pavilion and shows also the walls and roof of an important building, together with the costume worn by various types of people. A hermit sits in his tent-like retreat (lower right) with a sacred deer near by. Lotus blossoms cover the ground as riders return to the palatial building (top right). Other people seem to be on their way to the pavilion where a Buddha flanked by two Bodhisattvas can be seen under the complex eaves of the building

The Chinese as a whole never showed signs of being converted to a religion. State Confucianism was not a religion but a code of behaviour and a guide to right conduct. Taoism, another ancient Chinese set of beliefs and philosophical attitudes came to embody, on the popular level, more magic and superstition than any profound belief. Buddhism, the sole religion to penetrate China and to retain any great influence, first arrived from India at the time of Christ, and became powerful for a time in the T'ang dynasty before its suppression together with other minor foreign creeds. Buddhism lasted in China because it was able to adapt to local needs, and to absorb Chinese factors. Yet it could never be said that China was a Buddhist country as can be said of Ceylon or Thailand.

Right, this T'ang ewer has an inscription on the shoulder under a transparent brown glaze. The characters possibly mean 'Why not have some wine?'

Below, a flute of fine white porcelain, perhaps dating from the sixteenth century

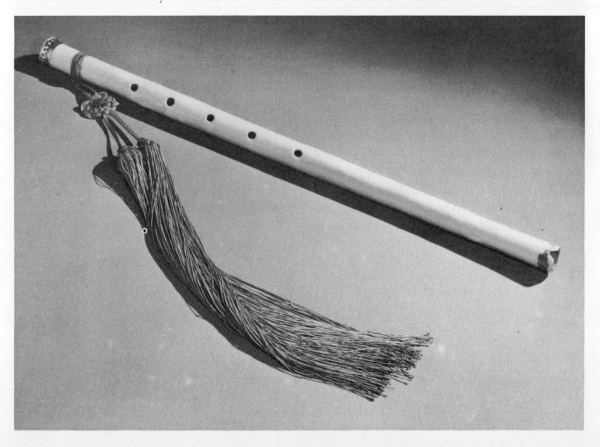

A blue and white large dish of the early Ming dynasty, diameter 13½ in. The delicate pattern of flowers and tendrils that fills the base is matched by a slightly heavier pattern in the surrounding band. The rim of the plate has a design of breaking waves. By this time Chinese craftsmen had perfected the use and control of imported cobalt for the blue colour

Traditional China was isolationist in outlook. Ming and Ch'ing dynasty laws forbade emigration, and also the introduction of foreigners into China. Foreign trade was not considered a natural part of man's existence, and merchants, like soldiers and actors, were looked down on as occupying a low position in society. The population was classified in four categories: *shih*—the scholar-gentry, *nung*—the peasantry, *kung*—the artisans, and *shang*—the merchants.

The vast population of China, much denser than populations in Western countries, lived and worked on the land, farming in the way it had always done. Industry was small. Internal wars as one dynasty succeeded another, invasions as some group of the surrounding peoples joined ranks and became strong enough to make a bid for the rich lands of China—such disturbances had left China largely unchanged for centuries. Each Chinese had from birth a definite place in the scheme of society, and although the success of a popular rebellion such as that against the foreign rule of the Mongols of the Yüan dynasty (1260–1368), could carry a man who began life as a peasant to the position of first emperor of the new Ming dynasty (1368–1644), such a wild leap up the ladder was rare. It was rather more common, perhaps, for girls taken by the emperor or by high officials as concubines and secondary wives to intrigue their way to positions of power from which they managed to elevate their male relations in the social scale.

Informed and educated opinion in China regarded Chinese civilization as the only worthwhile one existing, and the Chinese manner of government and way of life as far superior to those of any other people. In technology this was true until some time in the seventeenth century. Certainly the achievement of China in the arts is the equal of that in any other civilization. But the important fact that the Chinese did not discover for a long time until after it was too late, was that the countries of the Western world were militarily developed to a degree that China had never had any need to be.

The great civilization of China, a way of life that could well have developed in its own way, foundered on its total unpreparedness to defend its coasts against ships and armaments that were a hundred times more powerful than anything constructed in China. The failure was not at first surprising, for nothing had happened in all its history that resembled the threat coming by sea from the West.

2 Traditional Japan

THE racial origins of the Japanese people are mixed and uncertain. The original inhabitants were probably the Ainu people, remnants of whom still live in the northernmost island, Hokkaido, a less desirable terrain into which they were gradually pushed by the incursion and expansion of an aggressive race of Mongol type, starting about two thousand years ago. Most probably this race arrived in the Japanese islands from the Mongolian and Manchurian areas of Asia, through Korea. There seems also to have been an admixture of settlers from southern China and perhaps Southeast Asia. The stone age in Japan persisted in much of the country until around the time of Christ and later, and the different elements in the racial make-up of the population did not become completely blended until about one thousand years ago. Around the tenth century, therefore, the Japanese more or less as they are today came into being. But much had happened before then which it is important to understand at least in outline.

Japanese history is much shorter than Chinese, and also quite different in most ways. Chinese records dating from A.D. 57 onward give a picture of Japan as a country whose inhabitants were eager to obtain the cultural benefits evolved in China. Chinese travellers from the third century paint a picture of a Japan made up of highly organized kingdoms engaged in warfare with each other. We might well note several prominent features described in these early records: the keen interest shown by the Japanese in taking from China whatever seemed useful to them; the high degree of social organization in Japanese society both before and during the period of borrowing from China; the existence of a nucleus of beliefs, attitudes, and ceremonies that were later to develop into the Shinto religious cult. All three aspects of those times in Japan have shown themselves to be important in later events and reactions.

The worship of spirits of the dead, and of nature—whether in the form of some curious tree, some mountain, or a strange rock formation—developed in Japan into the Shinto (Way of the Gods) cult. The chief deity is Amaterasu-Omikami (Great-Heaven-Shining-Goddess) at the head of a numberless pantheon, the 'eight million gods'. Amaterasu was the Sun-Goddess who sent her grandson in human form to rule as the first emperor of Japan in the seventh century before Christ. Like all future emperors, he was both human and divine—and it was not until January, 1946, that emperor Hirohito renounced the divine aspect.

Easily the most important series of events in early Japanese history was the taking over from China of much of her culture and of the Buddhist religion. Starting in the early sixth century, Shinto practices were virtually absorbed into the newly arrived Buddhist religion that had entered Japan via Korea. The leading figure in the establishment of Buddhism was the regent (for the empress-regnant of the time) Prince Shotoku (573–621) who made it the court religion.

It was fortunate that Japan happened to take Buddhism and the culture of China at a time when the brilliant T'ang dynasty ruled from the capital at Ch'angan near the middle Yellow River. At this time Chinese civilization had reached one of its peaks of achievement. China was also in one of its not very frequent liberal and outward-looking phases during which foreign ideas were accepted and quickly made Chinese. The civilization taken over by the Japanese from T'ang China was, however, far from being a newly absorbed collection of foreign ideas, although it included some of these. It represented one culmination of the lengthy history of the Chinese people and their particular genius—quite foreign to the Japanese who shared nothing of that history.

The Japanese constructed for themselves what was in most essentials a miniature replica of Chinese court and religious life on their own soil. And for two hundred years Japanese officials were sent to China to gain further insight into all aspects, many of them spending several years there before returning.

Among the important borrowings from China were: the Chinese script (Japanese had not achieved a written language of its own), the principles of Chinese art and architecture, and the manner of depicting Buddhist subjects as did the Chinese on silk and in sculpture. Also taken over were such mundane and useful things as a standard of weights and measures, the elaborate and very practical Chinese calendar that was eminently suited to the regulation of an agricultural society, and silk technology both in the cultivation and in the spinning and weaving aspects.

bust of a woman
haniwa
30.5 cm.

A bust of a woman in pottery. This belongs to the Haniwa period when rulers in Japan were buried under huge mounds which were surrounded by cylindrical pottery objects topped by representations of human faces and often whole bodies. This period is indefinite in date but the idea doubtless came from the Han and Six Dynasties periods of China

The poet and former minister at court, Sugawara Michizane (A.D. 845–903), almost concealed behind the sleeve of his white robe (left) as he looks at a robe (in the box) which was given to him when he composed a poem to the emperor. Unjust charges were laid against him, and the house of his exile is overgrown and in poor repair

Another part of the Chinese world came to Japan in the shape of the teachings of Confucius. The Japanese emperor was himself divine, so it was impossible to transfer the Chinese imperial concept of the Mandate of Heaven to him, but the Confucian insistence on hierarchical principles by which each member of society had and knew his place and was obedient to the code of conduct laid down, seems to have fitted well with Japanese ideas on social organization, obedience, and discipline.

By about A.D. 800, Japan had absorbed most of what she wanted from the now weakening T'ang dynasty in China. The following four centuries were largely a period in which the borrowed culture was 'japanized', that is, made to conform with purely Japanese concepts, and transformed into a way of life that was not just a slavish copy of a superior but alien culture, but a Japanese culture in its own right.

The fact that so many of the fundamentals of Japanese culture were taken whole from the venerable civilization of China should not be allowed to disguise the fact that quite soon the process of using them—as if they were bricks—to build a perfectly Japanese structure had begun. Beneath the Chinese surface, Japanese ways, Japanese style, were at work.

Japanese civilization showed an early appreciation of the qualities of natural wood which continues to this day. This figure of the Maitreya Buddha in Koryuji Temple, Kyoto, dates from the seventh century

Buddhism, in this way, became peculiarly Japanese and quite different in many aspects from the form of the religion in China. The difference was in part one of emphasis. The Chinese Ch'an sect, which was not a very important one, became in Japan the Zen sect with its profound intellectual and mystical outlook. The new capital built at Nara was complete in 710, and resembled in its general lines and layout the T'ang capital at Ch'angan near the middle Yellow River. Its population, however, was probably not more than 200,000, and that of all Japan about six million. At first the Buddhism that flourished at Nara was Chinese in style—we have only to look at the early religious sculpture, Chinese in its appearance and inspiration, to realize this. But with the construction of Kyoto at the end of the same century as yet another capital, the story was somewhat different. While Kyoto still followed the general grid pattern of Ch'angan town planning, Buddhism produced two distinguished and very Japanese priests—Saicho who founded the Tendai sect, and Kobo Daishi the founder of the Shingon sect. Both of these sects incorporated a great deal of Shinto, many of whose deities were transformed into aspects of the Buddha. To some extent, it was this recognition of the fundamentally Japanese nature of Shinto forms of worship that permitted Japanese Buddhism to grow strong.

Himeji castle, first constructed in 1356, and later rebuilt in 1601 and 1956

There are many other examples of this process of 'japanization', of making what was new comfortable for Japanese and conformable to their own particular ways. Chinese written characters taken over for purposes of Buddhism and literature denoted monosyllables and did not fit the polysyllables of Japanese words. Thus, in the early times after Chinese culture came to Japan, the literature composed was almost wholly Chinese in concept and inspiration and consists mostly of anthologies of poetry and prose, historical chronicles, and works on Buddhism. But by the tenth century cursive signs called *kana*, derived by simplification from Chinese characters, were being evolved. With these in their eventual role of a phonetic syllabary, it was possible to write the Japanese language with more accuracy. Chinese characters, however, by no means went out of currency, as a glance at any modern Japanese newspaper will confirm. The Japanese once more had simply converted something they took over to a purely Japanese form and use.

Similarly, by the year 1000, the witty Sei Shonagon in her *Marura-no-Soshi* (Pillow-book) became the originator of a peculiarly Japanese literary form dealing with impressions and moods, called *zuihitsu*. The crisp, rather ironic style is excellent for what she has to tell of current court life. Another woman writer, Murasaki Shikibu (978–1031?) produced one of the masterpieces of Japanese literature, the tale of the life and loves of a prince, called *Genji Monogatari*. It is obvious, therefore, that with its new-found means of writing, literature had already become definitely Japanese.

The further development of Japan, both social and political, took a course that was entirely different from that of China. The power of the emperor of Japan was

Samurai of the Edo shogunate in varieties of formal dress

若年寄支配の諸役

御小人目付　御小人目付組頭　御徒目付の勤務姿

Mounted *samurai* warriors of the eleventh century

not for long a reality. Real power was usurped first by the Fujiwara family after the death of the reforming Prince Shotoku, and the jealousy of rival leaders brought a period of civil war lasting all but four decades. From this conflict the Minamoto family emerged the victors over their rivals the Taira clan in 1185, and Minamoto Yoritomo established his capital at Kamakura in eastern Japan, setting up his *bakufu*, or army headquarters, there. The *bakufu* of this and later shoguns became the organ and the seat of government, and so remained until 1867 when the last shogun surrendered his authority to the emperor.

Yoritomo was named *Seii-Tai-Shogun* (Barbarian-quelling Generalissimo) by the emperor in 1192, the title and position from then onward indicating the real ruler of Japan. The strong military dictatorship under Yoritomo was a period of comparative peace in Japan. Had his successors been endowed with Yoritomo's good qualities of dispensing feudal justice and sensible treatment to former enemies, the history of Japan might well have been different. On his death in 1199, his sons proved to be incapable of ruling and the country was governed by a series of regents between 1205 and 1333.

The rule of the shoguns was strengthened by the emergence of the *samurai* ('those who serve'), whose loyalty to their lord was unswerving and as absolute as was his command over them. The development of a military class as the result of a long succession of feudal wars was hardly surprising. Its code of behaviour was at first called 'the way of the horse and the bow' and its adherents bore a general resemblance to the knights of medieval European chivalry. Later this code of honour became *bushido*—'the warrior's way'.

In the year 1260, during this confused period, the Mongols set up their Yüan dynasty (1260–1368) in Peking. A mere fourteen years later, the emperor Kublai Khan, having made Korea a vassal state, sent an invasion fleet against Japan. The threat of a severe storm drove the fleet away, but in 1281 another and even bigger armada succeeded in landing Chinese troops on Kyushu, the southernmost of the four large islands of Japan, lying only a little over a hundred miles from southern Korea. The '*kamikaze*'—divine wind—of a strong typhoon destroyed this second Mongol fleet, and Japan was saved.

But the invasion, and the various Japanese lords who supported the forces of the shogun when engaged with Chinese troops and now demanded compensation, were factors in weakening the shogun's power. In 1333, the capital at Kamakura was destroyed by the forces of the Ashikaga family whose general, Takauji, was made shogun in 1338. The rule of the Ashikaga shogunate lasted in theory at least until the late sixteenth century.

A Japanese warrior of about 1600. His armour is made of lengths of bamboo, and the two swords indicate his *samurai* status

There was little peace in Japan but, contrary to what might be expected, the arts flourished, and there arose a new phenomenon—a strong and continually expanding merchant class. Both internal and external trade grew rapidly—the former to supply the growing needs of increasing urban populations, and the latter to deal with export and import business with China and with Southeast Asia. The position of merchants was a low one in the social stratification—the soldier being rated first, then the farmer, the artisan, and the trader—and merchants were at first regarded rather with surprise at the riches they could amass, than with the disdain that merchants in China encountered.

During this time the power of the *daimyo* also increased. *Daimyo* were feudal lords, the holders of large untaxed estates, rulers of large numbers of people, and commanders of local armies and *samurai*. Savage conflicts between them had reduced their numbers and strengthened the hands of the victors. Their power was such that Japan was in peril of being partitioned into several separate states.

A section of a scroll painting dating from the thirteenth century. It shows events during the Heiji wars of 1159. The careful grouping of figures, the delicacy of line, and the richness of colour make this one of the best paintings of the period

This was avoided by the emergence from an obscure feudal family of a man named Oda Nobunaga (1534-1582). Partly because of the strategic importance of his eastern territories, partly by war and matrimonial alliances, Nobunaga improved his position and was appointed deputy shogun. With the aid of his general, Hideyoshi, a man of very humble origins, and of Ieyasu, a small landowner of a family named Tokugawa, Nobunaga succeeded in destroying or subduing rivals, including the armed forces of the big monasteries. Nobunaga was killed in 1582 before he had quite completed his tasks, but his companions carried on. Hideyoshi was made regent in 1584, and by 1590 was virtual master of all Japan. Despite his ambition to conquer Korea, which led to invasions there in 1592 and 1597 (the first failed, and the second was called off on the death of Hideyoshi), the power he had accumulated in Japan passed undiminished to the third of the original trio, Ieyasu. And by the year 1615, Ieyasu and the Tokugawa family were undisputed rulers of Japan. The Tokugawa shogunate was to last for 250 years.

Japan under the Tokugawa rule was made into an even more closely controlled and disciplined state, its inhabitants were allotted their exact places and roles in the social pattern. The degree of fluidity in Chinese society, although slight, found no reflection in Japan. With the establishment of the shogun capital at Edo (now Tokyo), the *daimyo* and their *samurai* were forced to spend alternate years there, thereby reducing their influence in their native estates and forcing them to keep two large establishments. To some extent this system impoverished them, just as it neutralized their power.

From the need of the *daimyo* and their retinues to maintain in Edo a standard of life far above the simplicities of their native places, came the further rise of the mercantile class, and the beginnings of a credit system as the *daimyo* contracted loans. The foundation of several of the most important banking families' businesses dates from these times—an example being that of the Mitsui family.

Early European arrivals at the shores of Japan found themselves in this context of all-powerful shogun and *bakufu* ruling from Edo, and a puppet court pursuing its intellectual and artistic way powerlessly at Kyoto.

Part of a pair of six-fold screens by the artist Hasegawa Tohaku. His subject is pine trees. He had studied the techniques of the even more famous Zen painter-priest named Sesshu. This work was painted in the late sixteenth century

A bowl with handle. This piece of Mino ware of the Oribe type could only be Japanese. Whatever the Japanese learned from Chinese ceramic techniques they quickly absorbed, producing pieces distinctively their own. Seventeenth century

3 China and the West

CHINESE ports had been accustomed to the foreign faces of many traders for centuries before any Western face appeared in the orient. Arabs, among others, are known to have traded with China by sea since at least the T'ang dynasty. These

The Manchu Dynasty, 1644–1912

RUSSIAN EMPIRE

Amur
1689–1858 to China
1858 to Russia

Aigun

MANCHURIA
Russian Occupation 1900
under Japanese influence
1905
1905

Harbin

Vladivostok

Dzungaria
1757 under Chinese suzerainty
1847 to Russia

Urga

OUTER MONGOLIA
1697 under Chinese suzerainty

Urumchi

INNER MONGOLIA
1635 under Chinese suzerainty

Mukden

Jehol

Antung

Pyongyang

SINKIANG
1724–1866, 1878
under Chinese suzerainty

ALASHAN

Peking
Paoting

Dairen
Pt. Arthur

Taku

Seoul

KANSU

Taiyuan
Tientsin

CHIHLI
SHANSI Tsinan
Tsingtao

Chefoo

KOREA
1627–1895
under Chinese suzerainty
to Japan 1895

TSINGHAI
1724 under Chinese suzerainty

Sining

SHENSI

Kaifeng KIANGSU

TIBET
1720 under Chinese suzerainty

Sian

HONAN

ANHWEI Chinkiang
Nanking
Wuhu

Shanghai

Lhasa

SZECHUAN

Chengtu Wanhsien

Chungking

HUPEH
Hankow Anking

Ichang

Hangchow
CHEKIANG

NEPAL
1792–1908 under
Chinese suzerainty

SIKKIM

BHUTAN

Changsha

KWEICHOW
Kweiyang

HUNAN

KIANGSI

Foochow

INDIA

Myitkyina

YUNNAN Yunnan

Tengyueh

Kweilin

FUKIEN
Amoy

Taipei

Taiwan
(Formosa)
to China 1683–1895
to Japan 1895

Szemao

KWANGSI

KWANGTUNG

Canton
Swatow

Mengtz

BURMA
1769–1886 under
Chinese suzerainty

TONKING
Fr. Protectorate 1884

Hanoi Haiphong

Macao
Hong Kong

LAOS
Fr. Protectorate 1893

Kiungchow

BRITISH EMPIRE

SIAM

ANNAM
Fr. Protectorate 1885

China in 1912	Leased Territories (and surrounding neutral areas)	• Treaty Ports
Japanese Empire, 1912	Area affected by Boxer Rising, 1900–01	⚬ Province Capitals
Occupied by Japan, 1912		—— Railways, 1912

were simple sailors carrying to China whatever they knew would find a market there, and taking away from China whatever they knew would sell elsewhere. It was they, incidentally, who brought the knowledge of that Chinese invention the compass to the West, and thus unwittingly helped Westerners on their way to the East and to China. They had no feelings of personal, or national, or racial pride, and if the Chinese regarded them as inferiors they were not worried on that account. At the time of the Mongols, Western travellers to China such as Marco Polo and Friar Odoric recorded the existence of large foreign communities in ports and inland cities, apparently living in harmony with the Chinese.

We have already noticed that representatives of peoples bordering China and from further afield came to Peking with their 'tribute' goods (and with merchants who did normal trade), and returned to their homelands in peace.

The problem, from the Chinese point of view, came when traders and others began arriving from Europe. The Europeans had several attributes that made them quite separate in Chinese eyes from the simple traders of non-Western origin. The first of these was the Europeans' assumption that to trade was their right. The lowly position of all merchants in Chinese society did not concede to any merchant (Chinese or otherwise) any right to trade. And when Europeans attempted to trade at gunpoint, the Chinese reaction was even more furious because of the insult they felt at such unheard-of arrogance.

The second aspect of the Europeans was that some of them came with the intention of converting ordinary Chinese to a religion which the Chinese distrusted. Christianity was soon seen by the Chinese as a threat to the established order of their own way of life. Western missionaries could hardly have been expected to understand how this could be, but in fact (as we shall see when we consider Christianity in China at a later date) acceptance of the religion by Chinese undoubtedly ran contrary to many of the fundamental beliefs and principles of government and social conduct in China.

The third attribute of Europeans as seen by the Chinese was their aggressive nature. This arose from the common belief among Europeans who went to China (most of the early traders were uneducated or at least had little schooling, and were hardly worthy representatives of Western civilization in its wider aspects) that they were superior to the Chinese. They felt much the same toward all non-Western peoples. Their ignorance and their rudeness hardly fitted them for the contacts they wished to make with Chinese officials who were, for the most part, highly educated men in terms of Chinese learning and, moreover, men whose conduct was strictly regulated by a code of behaviour that tended to conciliate and to resolve disputes by discussion and compromise. The Chinese therefore saw no reason at all to treat Western merchants with honour and every reason to try to get rid of them because there was no ready-made way of dealing effectively with their demands.

Before we follow the outline of Western contacts by sea, it is worth noticing that the Nestorian form of Christianity was established in China and enjoyed great repute for some considerable time during the T'ang dynasty. It was eventually suppressed in the same dynasty along with the excesses of Buddhist activities. Both Buddhism and Nestorianism were described as 'foreign religions' and declared to be dangerous to Chinese society.

A T'ang dynasty glazed pottery figure of a Western (possibly Armenian) wine-seller with his skin of liquor

The Nestorian Stone found near Sian (formerly the T'ang capital named Ch'angan). It details the arrival of the Syrian Nestorian monk Alopen, and the progress of the religion in China. Nestorian Christianity had virtually disappeared from China by the end of the T'ang dynasty

In another period of easy communication across the Asian continent from the West, the Yüan or Mongol dynasty, we find Christian travellers and Christian communities in Peking and in at least one coastal city in China. There was even a Christian Archbishop, John of Montecorvino, in the capital, where he had two churches.

But on the fall of the Yüan, when the new and deeply Chinese dynasty of the Ming (1368–1644) had driven the hated Mongols from the land, the Christians vanished too. Ming decrees forbade the introduction of any foreigner into China.

The Portuguese

A new and ominous era in the orient was ushered in by Portuguese success in rounding the Cape of Good Hope, and by the achievement of Vasco da Gama in reaching India in 1497. By 1511 the Portuguese were in Malacca, and in 1517 they arrived in Canton. A year earlier, a relative of Columbus, a man named Perestrello, seems to have reached south China and to have returned to Malacca. Reports from him or others in his ship (which apparently traded peacefully and to some profit with the Chinese) caused a comment from a responsible Italian on the Chinese: they were *de nostra qualita*—people like ourselves—he wrote.

In 1517, a flotilla of Portuguese ships bringing an 'ambassador' from the Portuguese king to the emperor of China sailed up the Pearl River in defiance of orders to remain downstream. The Chinese were justifiably annoyed to find a foreign fleet flying Portuguese flags and discharging a salvo of cannon just offshore from one of the principal ports of the country. But they finally allowed the 'ambassador,' Tomaso Pirès, to land. The flotilla was forced to sail away because of death and disease among the crew, leaving Pirès in Canton.

This was the first messenger bearing a letter from a Western king to the Chinese emperor whom the Chinese had ever received. There were no regulations on the subject of ambassadors, only on how to deal with foreign tribute-bearers. The matter was referred to Peking, and it took two years before Pirès was forwarded there. He was unfortunate in that just as he arrived in late 1520 news reached the capital of Portuguese violence in Malacca, where the ruler regarded himself as under Chinese protection. Pirès was sent in chains back to Canton.

The Portuguese flotilla had traded profitably, and soon another arrived, this time seizing an island at the mouth of the Pearl River, and assaulting the local people. The attitude that underlay such acts cannot be passed off simply as piracy. It stemmed from Western opinion about the right to trade. The Chinese did not agree.

> '...the Portuguese had chiefly themselves to thank. Truculent and lawless, regarding all Eastern peoples as legitimate prey, they were little if any better than the contemporary Japanese pirates.... The Ming authorities can scarcely be censured for treating them as free-booters.'
>
> Latourette: *The Chinese*

Persistent attempts by the Chinese in the Ming and later the Ch'ing dynasty to restrict contact with Europeans to Canton were in part a response to provocation.

'...it is only too plain from the records, both Chinese and European, that the unfavourable treatment of the Europeans was the consequence of their own violent and barbarous behaviour.'

Fitzgerald: *The Chinese View*

The Portuguese, however, eventually managed to establish themselves on the small peninsula of Macau at the mouth of the Pearl River, and a flourishing trade developed there as they acted in the capacity of carriers of Chinese goods to Japan— the chief commodity being silk. This trade ceased, and the importance of Macau declined, when the Portuguese were prevented from entering Japan in 1639. Macau continued, however, to be a missionary training centre.

Missionaries

The saintly priest Francis Xavier, first missionary to work in Japan, died in 1552 on an island off the south China coast, having failed to gain entry to China. Another priest, a Jesuit named Matteo Ricci, managed to enter China from Macau, and after eighteen years of arduous work in China finally reached Peking in 1601. He remained there for the remainder of his life, and died in 1610. Ricci was one of the most brilliant Western men ever to live in China, a worthy representative of all that was best in the Europe of his time. In order to achieve what he did he had, in his own words, to become one half Chinese. His success was much less in making converts to Christianity than in becoming the first European to learn Chinese so well that he was regarded as an equal by the most eminent Chinese scholars of the era. The respect in which this almost incredible man, deeply learned in Western and Chinese culture, was held by the Chinese has probably never again been accorded to any single Westerner.

Matteo Ricci, probably the most distinguished of all the Christian priests to come to China. His extraordinary memory and his amazing grasp of Chinese language and literature brought him honour from the most scholarly and most influential Chinese of his time

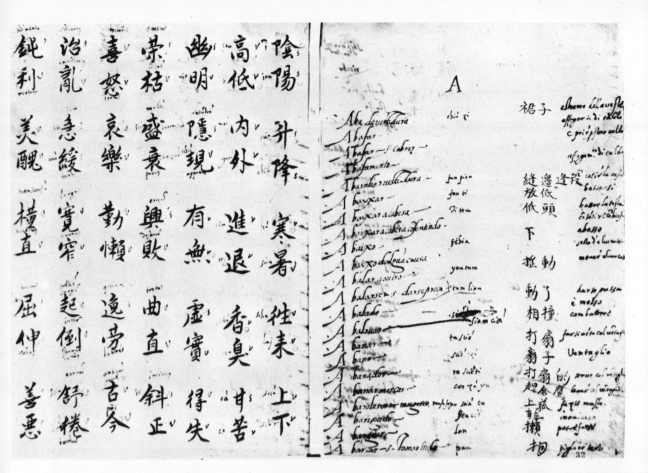

Above, the first pages of Matteo Ricci's Chinese dictionary.
The left hand page consists of pairs of characters of opposite
meaning—'blunt' and 'sharp', 'beautiful' and 'ugly', etc.
The right hand page is the first of the dictionary proper.
The first column has Portuguese words written by Ricci.
There are some attempts at phonetic pronunciation of the
Chinese in column two. Then come Chinese characters and
the Italian translation by Ricci's colleague Ruggieri

Right, the first telescope made in Peking, presented to the
Wan-li Emperor by Matteo Ricci in the first years of the
seventeenth century

Ricci's founding of a Jesuit mission in Peking led to a succession of learned and
less learned European priests who in many cases spent the better part of their lives
there. The most remarkable and influential were perhaps Adam Schall and
Ferdinand Verbiest. Both were mathematicians and astronomers, both were used
by the emperor and high officials in various scientific positions, notably in correcting
the complex and not altogether accurate Chinese calendar. Verbiest became a close
friend of the greatest of the Manchu emperors, K'ang-hsi (1654–1722), and taught
him a great deal about the civilization and learning of the West.

Right, Ferdinand Verbiest in the robes of a Chinese official. He is shown in this Japanese print with his sextant and celestial globe. Verbiest succeeded Ricci in Peking and became a close friend of the Emperor K'ang-hsi

Below, Verbiest's observatory on the east wall of Peking. Reading counter-clockwise from the top centre the instruments are: sextant, quadrant, horizontal circle, ecliptic armillary sphere, celestial globe, and equatorial armillary sphere. The observatory is still on the Peking wall, although it now sits on almost the sole remaining portion since most of the wall has been removed recently

Specula astroptica Pekinensis iuxta exemplar ex China missum.

R·P·IOANNES ADAMVS SCHALL, GERMANVS.
è Societate IESV: Pequini Supremi ac Regij Mathema
tum Tribunalis Præses; indefessus pro Conuersione
gentium in Chinis Operarius ab annis 50. ætat: suæ 77
Johann Steger delin.   *Maurit Lang sculp. Vien*

Adam Schall, a Jesuit priest whose stay in
Peking extended from the end of the Ming to
beginning of the Ch'ing. He was a brilliant
astronomer

Oddly enough, the main influence of the great Jesuits in China was felt in Europe rather than in the Middle Kingdom where they made very few converts and where in the end they failed to maintain their position. Europe, in the decades of the Enlightenment during the eighteenth century, was to be struck with what amounted to adulation of the alleged perfection of Chinese government, which was viewed as altogether more rational than any in the West. This curious view, held at one time and another by such eminent men as Voltaire in France and Samuel Johnson in England, was based on the glowing reports of later Jesuits to their superiors in Rome and elsewhere—reports coloured in part by Jesuit desire to make worthwhile in Western eyes their efforts in the East.

The unfavourable reaction among intelligent Westerners, when it was later discovered that China did not really have a perfect Confucian government any more than Europe, was as strong as had been the first delight. And it was during the time of this reaction that Westerners first went in numbers to China to trade. They were therefore to some extent influenced by the ideas about China prevailing in their own countries at the time.

Despite some successes in China, the Jesuit and other missionaries in the Ch'ing dynasty failed because Chinese officials recognized that fundamental aspects of Christianity were incompatible with traditional Chinese authority and the Confucian teachings on which it was based. They could not accept that Chinese persons should regard themselves responsible first to God and only after that to those in authority.

The first Protestant missionary to reach China was a late arrival on the scene. Robert Morrison of the London Missionary Society arrived in Canton in 1807.

The first Chinese terrestrial globe, made in Peking in 1623 by two Jesuits. The surface with its seas and continents, its European-type ships, its place names and long description in Chinese, is made of Chinese lacquer. The description is placed under the area of China, which is coloured imperial yellow

A Russian ambassador and his suite, 1627. This ambassador was not in China, but doubtless Spathary and his men appeared very like those in this picture when they came to Peking in 1675. The ambassador wears a wide fur hat and is surrounded by his three principal aides. His secretary carries a dispatch case, while others carry sable-skins as gifts

Russians and Dutch

By 1651, news of the Manchu effort to conquer Siberia reached Tsar Alexis of Russia who sent a force of three thousand men toward the Amur River to occupy the territory. The force reached the Amur in August, 1653, but encountered severe Manchu opposition and retired. Further Russian armies reached the Amur in 1657 and were defeated by the Manchu. Ambassadors such as Baikoff were despatched to Peking by the tsar with letters to the emperor. Baikoff, like others before and after him, was given orders he could not carry out—such as that which forbade him to give the tsar's letter to anyone but the emperor of China in person. This was contrary to all precedent and the Chinese could not allow it. Baikoff was sent back to Russia. The Chinese refusal to entertain him was also hardened by the Amur River incidents, and doubtless by the fact that the tsar—who claimed equality with the emperor, which also could not be admitted—sent an illiterate man such as Baikoff to deal on his behalf with the highly cultured and urbane senior officials of China.

Just before Baikoff was sent away, there arrived in Peking a party of Dutch merchants sent by the governor of Batavia. In charge of the party were Peter de Goyer and Jacob de Keyser, and they brought a man named John Nieuhoff whose sketches were as inaccurate as his later book but were the first by a Westerner to show Peking. The Jesuit Adam Schall was employed by the Chinese to deal with the Dutch, who performed the *kowtow* in the correct manner at audience in the imperial palace, but who were sent away with a letter from the emperor stating that a company of traders might be sent to China only once every eight years.

Later Russian embassies had little more success, not even that of the princely Spathary that arrived in 1675, a brilliant retinue loaded with expensive gifts.

It was not until the Treaty of Nerchinsk (1689), negotiated with the help of another Jesuit priest named Gerbillon, that Sino-Russian relations were put on a reasonably safe footing at last.

The Treaty of Nerchinsk was the first signed by China with a Western power. It defined the border between them (in China's favour), regulated caravan trade in Russian furs and gold which were exchanged for Chinese silks and the tea that Russians were beginning to drink in quantity. Certain Russians were permitted to live in Peking in order to deal with this trade, and priests of the Russian Orthodox Church were allowed to minister to Russians in their own place of worship, but not to make Chinese converts.

These provisions embodied what the Chinese regarded as huge concessions. First, they had admitted for the first time to some sort of political equality between China and another country. Second, they had been forced by the power and proximity of a Western nation to establish something like diplomatic relations in the accepted Western manner, and not to treat the Russians as bearers of tribute like all other neighbouring and more distant countries. The reason for such fundamental concessions was the desire to settle a border dispute that could have turned into a dangerous war which, with her long land frontiers and numerous troublesome tribal neighbours, the Chinese did not wish to risk at that time. The Treaty of Nerchinsk remained, with only minor alterations, the basis of relations until 1858.

British and others

The British made a fiery entry on the Chinese scene in 1637 with a flotilla of four trading ships, partly financed by Charles I of England, under the command of Captain Weddell, which shot their way up to Canton in the face of determined Chinese opposition and discouragement from the jealous Portuguese at Macau.

The type of ship in which Captain Weddell probably sailed to south China in 1637

Drawing of a Chinese eating with chopsticks, by Peter Mundy who went to China with Weddell and was doubtless interested at this (to him) unusual mode of eating. Westerners thought the use of chopsticks a poor substitute for knife and fork

Even then, the Chinese allowed them to do a limited trade, but Weddell was forced to sign a document humbly apologizing for burning Chinese junks and setting fire to a small town, and promising never to return. Like most of the early Portuguese, his approach was aggressive. He was certain of his right to trade, and (correctly) of the superior power of his guns over those of the Chinese. The expedition was commercially a complete failure.

The letter of James I of England to 'The High and Mightie Monarch, The Great Emperor of China', dated 1613. This document probably had some effect on the establishment of the first commercial relations between Britain and China in 1616

This unhappy beginning, however, did not deter the British in their desire to trade with China. From the year 1600, British trade with the East had been exclusively in the hands of the British East India Company—often called simply John Company, in the same manner as the British later referred to the Chinese as John Chinaman—and Weddell's flotilla had been allowed to reach China only because King Charles had a hand in its financing.

The K'ang-hsi Emperor of China—one of the most brilliant emperors, although a Manchu and the representative of an alien race that had conquered China in 1644—decided in 1685 to open all the ports of China to foreign trade. Some years later, in 1715, the East India Company decided to attempt to put the China trade on a more satisfactory footing. At least one reason for this was the delay experienced when ships entered Chinese ports, and the different charges made in, what seemed to them an arbitrary way by the Chinese. An example makes the point clear. On the arrival of an English ship in Canton:

'...two weeks elapsed before the Hoppo's [an English attempt at *Hoi Po*, Cantonese pronunciation of part of the title—*Yüeh-hai Kuan-pu*—of the Administrator of the South Sea Customs] agents would consent to measure her, as a preliminary step before she could be permitted to enter port; and then began...the old...battle to decide how much must be paid outside the official scale of charges. The official measurer began by measuring the ship from stem to stern but, on getting a bribe, consented to measure her from before the mizzen-mast to the after-side of the fore-mast...the only legal...rule for measuring any ship, native or foreign. The sum of Taels 2,484 was demanded; this the supercargoes [British agents dealing with sale or purchase of goods] refused to pay.... A week later it was reduced to Taels 1,500, of which Taels 1,200 were declared...measurement fee, and Taels 300 a gratuity to the Hoppo.'

Morse: *The International Relations of the Chinese Empire*

In 1715 the Company set up a factory at Canton—not what we nowadays mean by that word but a building in which goods could be stored, and where its officials might stay and work. The word is derived from 'factor', meaning an agent. Arrange-

The aged Emperor K'ang-hsi

The line of European 'factories' at Canton in the 1840s. The river is crowded with Western and Chinese ships. The central one of the three flags is the British. Note the paddle steamer

ments with the Chinese included the conducting of all trade and business through a group of Chinese merchants called by various names but eventually known as the Co-hong (*hong*=company, in Cantonese). Regulations were laid down to control the activities of the foreigners and these altered from time to time, eventually numbering eight when, in 1757, the Ch'ien-lung Emperor (1711–1799) issued his decree confining all foreign trade strictly to Canton. They stated:

> Warships must remain outside the Pearl River.
> Women must not be brought to the factories, and no firearms were permitted.
> The Hong merchants must not be in debt to the foreigners (they often were).
> Foreigners must not engage Chinese servants (this was not usually enforced).
> All petitions must be sent to the Co-hong (which meant that complaints about trade conditions had to be presented to those who made the conditions complained of).
> All trading must be done in the season from November to March, after which the merchants must leave for home or for Macau.
> Foreigners must not leave the factories except on three days per month when, under the supervision of a Chinese interpreter who was responsible for their good conduct, they might walk in a public garden near by.
> Foreigners must not learn the Chinese language.

It is obvious that, had the Chinese government wished merely to exploit the foreigners' desire for trade in order to make money from them, many of these regulations need not have been applied. The purpose of the regulations was to control people whom the Chinese authorities felt they could not trust, and who might, if uncontrolled, do damage to the Chinese way of life and economy, and disturb the peace. The Chinese merchants of the Co-hong had to pay large sums to the Peking government, to the viceroy of the province, and to others for the privilege of trading with the foreigners.

A knowledge of the general climate in which trade was conducted between the foreigners and the Chinese at Canton, is important in understanding the events which certain aspects of that trade later caused. The Chinese were perfectly within their rights in making whatever conditions they wished in relation to foreign trade and traders. If the trade at Canton had not been so profitable for the Westerners, doubtless they would have stopped going there and ceased to bother trading with the Chinese. But it was obviously very profitable, so they stayed on, grumbling, protesting, and meanwhile making money.

There were various very real problems for both Chinese and Europeans in their contact at Canton. Since similar fundamental differences were to underlie Chinese-Western relations throughout the next many decades, we should take a look at the major ones and try to gain some understanding of what brought about the serious and tragic consequences that attended the contacts between the West and China.

We have already noted the Chinese opinion that the right to trade granted to the *fan kwei* (a common expression for Westerner meaning 'foreign ghost' or 'devil') was regarded as a favour granted, and that it could be revoked when the Chinese did not wish to continue with the trade. The low place occupied by merchants in Chinese society prejudiced the Chinese against foreign traders. Yet in their own home lands these traders enjoyed considerable prestige. They belonged to the rapidly expanding middle class in England—a class that sprang from success in industrial, wholesale and retail, and trading opportunities that opened out on all sides as the country turned more and more from cottage industry and agriculture

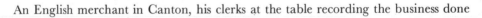

An English merchant in Canton, his clerks at the table recording the business done

to intensified and mechanized industry in factories. Respected and powerful at home—or at least concerned and connected with enterprises that brought big money to the pockets of leading manufacturers and traders—it was all the more unacceptable for the merchants of the East India Company with its monopoly of oriental trade to find themselves the target of official Chinese disdain, and of extortion by local officials.

The prevailing climate of the industrial revolution in England was none too scrupulous, and the seafarers and merchants who went to China in search of quick profits were certainly no different in outlook from the more ruthless of their contemporaries at home. The arbitrary levies on their cargoes, and other unpredictable acts by the Chinese authorities at Canton, made the merchants angry, and at times their anger spilled over. But it was generally to no avail. The Chinese merchants of the Co-hong with whom and through whom all dealings had to be made were mostly co-operative with the foreigners, but they had their own problems. All of them had to pay large sums of money for permission to trade, and they were also 'squeezed' by officials who extracted as much of their profits as possible.

The Hoppo, for example, was a low-ranking official, far below the Kwangchou Fu (Governor of Canton), and very far below the top-ranking Viceroy of the two Kwang (Kwangtung and Kwangsi) provinces. The Hoppo was appointed to extract as much customs revenue as possible from trade at Canton. His appointment (which he had to pay for in money) was for three years during which he had to remit official revenue to Peking in large quantities, and also to sweeten his superiors with more cash in case he was suspended in favour of some rival. He also expected to amass a fortune of his own and see that his family were in fine financial circumstances before his lucrative office terminated. He had no interest in any alteration for the better in the trading or other administrative aspects of the port of Canton.

This approach to the foreign traders was a gross error on the part of Manchu authorities. Instead of curbing the operations of the traders, it served only to make them more insistent on getting their own way later.

In fact, to extort or otherwise gather money as the Hoppo did was not thought to be dishonest on the part of an official, provided that his acts did not outstrip the bounds of moderation. Official salaries were very poor in China, and opportunity to increase them not lacking. The Hoppo, in charge of customs collection, levied on the cargoes whatever charges he felt he could get. Since he knew the profits of the foreigners were quite large, he saw no special reason not to get as much as possible.

This form of corruption was of course not unknown in the West during these times. Most officials of the East India Company were very rich after serving a few years. The outlook of both Chinese and Westerners was in this respect fairly similar. Foreigners at Canton in their factories were usually well treated by the Chinese, and relationships between them and the members of the Co-hong were often those of individual friendship. The Chinese merchants were in a much more insecure position than the foreign merchants since they were responsible for the good conduct of the foreigners, and could be held responsible for any problems that arose.

Nevertheless, trading conditions at Canton were not regarded as good, and finally the complaints made to the British government in London were met with action.

The Macartney Embassy

By the second half of the eighteenth century, the British were by far the biggest traders at Canton. Such was the importance of the trade that, to attempt to clear up outstanding difficulties encountered there by the merchants, Lord Macartney was sent to China in 1793 at the head of a group of talented men. Macartney himself was an excellent choice. A good diplomat, an aristocrat, a highly educated and intelligent man, he was at least the equal in Western terms of the scholar-officials he encountered in Peking at the court of the Emperor Ch'ien-lung toward the end of his long reign (1736–1796).

The party was accompanied by several hundreds of cases of gifts ranging from scientific products such as the latest telescope and other astronomical instruments, to various clocks that played music. Macartney also carried a letter from King George III of England to the emperor. The Chinese relaxed several of their rules of court procedure and permitted Macartney to kneel before Ch'ien-lung instead of performing the *kowtow*, and also to hand over the king's letter in person to the emperor, instead of giving it to officials.

The visit of the British party to China was at all times made pleasant for them. A bland and friendly atmosphere prevailed. But the ambassador found he could make no progress at all in his attempts to establish a better basis for trade, and that the British desire to have an official stationed in Peking to represent them and to attend to matters of mutual importance was absolutely not to be considered.

The results of the Macartney embassy were few. The British learned a great deal more about China, and something more about the Chinese outlook on foreigners. The members of the embassy saw how in Peking the great mandarins (the word is probably derived from the Portuguese 'mandar', to command) pretended not to be surprised at the scientific and other presents when these were shown.

A portrait statuette of George III of England by a contemporary artist. The English king makes a striking contrast to the elegant Ch'ien-lung Emperor of China who addressed a letter to him

御製紅毛嘆咭唎國王差使臣嘆嘆
嘆咭唎本英吉利詩叭說事
博都雅昔游貢嘆咭唎今效藎誠
覽爾械軍輸近步
祖功
宗德遠邁現如常卻心嘉篤不貴
其脫怡訓精眼達傳來而厚注衷深
保奏以持盈

A tapestry now in the Museum of the Royal
Observatory, Greenwich, showing the
presents brought by Macartney to Peking
being carried through the gardens of the
Summer Palace. The artist was undoubtedly Chinese, as can be seen by his awkward
attempts to show Westerners, and the way
he composes his picture as if it were a
normal Chinese scroll painting

Lord Macartney's official interpreter,
Dominus Nean, whom he brought from
a seminary in Naples. The seminary was
set up by a former Catholic missionary who
lived long in Peking before retiring to his
native land of Italy

Lord Macartney was himself an
elegant figure in his court robes
as he was sketched by the artist
Alexander before having an
audience with Ch'ien-lung

Macartney even brought a balloon which could be flown by means of hot air,
but while all the Western world was marvelling at such balloons rising with ease
into the clouds, and with men taking their first aerial view of the earth—the Chinese
would not allow a demonstration. Chinese scientific and technical achievements by
the end of the eighteenth century had fallen far behind those of the West—as any
Chinese might see from the type of manufactures presented by Macartney—but they
did not want to learn. The deeply conservative and literary quality of Chinese
intellectual life still ran strong, preventing an interest in technical matters and thus
at the same time preventing the growth of knowledge in China from keeping pace
with that in the West. Even on military matters, which Macartney thought might
be of interest, no interest was shown.

'On this occasion I proposed to amuse them with...our small brass field-pieces....
Though they were remarkably well cast and of a most elegant form, fixed on light
carriages...and fired from twenty to thirty times in a minute, yet our conductor
pretended to think lightly of them, and spoke to us as if such things were no novelties
in China.'

Macartney: *Journal*

In fact, as Macartney suspected, the Chinese had no modern guns. They were still using cannon of a type cast in the seventeenth century by Jesuits for the last Ming and early Ch'ing emperors.

All the strength of fire-power that they had seen in Western ships at Canton, all the ingenious inventions and scientific instruments they now saw in Peking, made no impression on the officials. An army commander even refused an invitation to watch the British soldiers brought along by Macartney perform arms drill—yet the most modern weapon of Chinese soldiers was the outmoded matchlock, and there were very few of these.

Macartney made several important observations in his journal about what he saw and what he thought of China just before the beginning of the fateful nineteenth century.

'In fact the volume of the empire is now grown too ponderous...to be easily grasped by a single hand.... It is possible, notwithstanding, that the momentum impressed on the machine by the vigour and wisdom of the present Emperor may keep it steady... for a considerable time, but I should not be surprised if its dislocation or dismemberment were to take place before my own dissolution.'

And in another passage, Macartney wrote:

'[The] political system seems to...endeavour to persuade the people that they are themselves already perfect and can therefore learn nothing from others.... A nation that does not advance must retrograde and finally fall back to barbarism and misery.'

In a famous paragraph, Macartney calls China an

'old, crazy, first rate man-of-war, which a...succession of vigilant officers have contrived to keep afloat for these one hundred and fifty years past, and to overawe their neighbours merely by her bulk and appearance, but whenever an insufficient man happens to have the command on deck, adieu to the discipline and safety of the ship. She may perhaps not sink outright; she may drift some time as a wreck, and will then be dashed to pieces on the shore; but she can never be rebuilt on the old bottom.'

This is perhaps the best summing up of the state of China on the eve of the nineteenth century, when her basic political and other main systems were about two thousand years old and entirely inconsistent with the facts of life in the world outside. And it is also a remarkably accurate prediction of what the future held for China as a sovereign state—a succession of mostly 'insufficient' emperors, the country drifting like a wreck, finally to be broken up by internal and external troubles. Only a little more than a hundred years after Macartney wrote these words, China sank into almost total chaos, just as he said she would. His reasons were, however, only one part of the cause of China's final predicament.

The letter which Ch'ien-lung sent with Macartney in reply to that of George III of England—a country that was then easily the greatest sea-power and industrial producer the world had ever known—is a masterpiece of misconceptions and ignorance of what was going on in the outside world. The emperor refers to the king's letter as a 'memorial', as if it was a message from one of his officials or from the king of some petty tributary state. 'The humble terms in which it is couched reveal a respectful humility on your part, which is highly praiseworthy', he continues. Even if these words are a mere formula used in all replies, they at once reveal an attitude completely unsuitable when communicating with the head of a powerful country.

'As to your entreaty to send one of your nationals to be accredited to my Celestial Court and to be in control of your country's trade with China, this request is contrary to all usage of my dynasty and cannot possibly be entertained.'

As to Britain's request for a Chinese ambassador to Europe to be sent:

'How could you possibly make for him the requisite arrangements? Europe consists of many nations besides your own; if each and all demanded to be represented at our court, how could we possibly consent? The thing is utterly impracticable.... We possess all things. I set no value on objects strange and ingenious, and have no use for your country's manufactures.'

When Macartney and, later, British government officials read the letter, they were astonished at the assumption of a power to command, and at the idea that China ruled the world, which were both completely unsupported by facts. The only correct statement in Ch'ien-lung's letter was that about China's not needing Western goods. It did not. China was still dreaming its own dream, but the reality of the outside world was quite different.

Foreign Mud and Foreign Power

While Macartney was in Peking, Ch'ien-lung, emperor of China, was not entirely in control of his country. The real power behind the Throne was his prime minister, an unscrupulous and able man named Ho Shen. Both Lord Macartney and Ho Shen were perfectly well aware that the trade done at Canton consisted of the Chinese exporting tea, porcelain, silks, lacquerware, and (strangely enough) rhubarb which was much used by physicians in England at the time; and the payment by the British for these goods in silver—the sole acceptable currency in China. There was very little that could be brought to China from England that had any chance of sale. The Chinese, as Ch'ien-lung had written, had no use for Western products, except, it had been discovered, for opium.

Not a word was said on either side in Peking on the subject. Probably Ch'ien-lung had not heard of the increasingly large quantities of opium being imported. Ho Shen certainly had, but it is probable that his pockets were suitably lined with presents from the officials in Canton. So he would not be likely to bring the matter up.

Opium has been the subject of a great deal of bitter statement and reproach from those days when the foreigners began to bring it to China and ever since. To see what really happened we have to look at the subject from both sides—the Chinese and the British—for very soon the British were the most deeply involved of all those at Canton in the opium trade.

The first Chinese mention of opium seems to be in the T'ang dynasty, in 618, and its use in medicine dates from 973 when it is mentioned in the *Herbalist's Treasury*. Later a medicament called 'fish-cake paste' from the shape of the portions, containing opium, was in regular use for intestinal symptoms.

Opium smoking was introduced with tobacco-smoking via Taiwan and is reported in Fukien province in 1620. Like King James I of England, the Chinese emperor of that time thought tobacco-smoking obnoxious. There are edicts against smoking tobacco in the middle and latter part of the seventeenth century. Opium was probably little smoked by itself before 1800.

The first edict against opium dates from the Yung-chêng reign in 1729, and prohibited its sale for smoking, and also the keeping of opium divans. It did not penalize the smoker. In that same year, 1729, foreign opium was first introduced by the Portuguese, and the import rose to about 1,000 chests a year by 1773. A chest generally contained about 100 catties ($133\frac{1}{3}$ lbs).

In 1773, the East India Company took over the monopoly of opium growing and sale in the three huge areas of Bengal, Bihar, and Orissa in India, where thousands of acres were forcibly put under cultivation of the opium poppy. In that year, 1773, the first English merchant imported opium into Canton. By 1790, the import stood at 4,054 chests a year.

In 1796, two years after Macartney left China at the conclusion of his unsuccessful mission, former edicts prohibiting the use of opium were renewed. The definitive edict prohibiting the import of foreign opium and also the growing of opium in China itself was made by the Chia-ch'ing Emperor in 1800.

We should note particularly that until 1800 it was not illegal to import opium into China. Opium, up to that time, 'formed part of a ship's inward cargo as much as English broadcloth or Indian cotton, and was handled as openly, and sold in the same way through...a member of the Co-hong.' The historian H.B. Morse, whose book *The International Relations of the Chinese Empire* is the source of this quotation, goes on to remark that the increasing sale of opium was welcomed by the

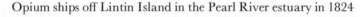

Opium ships off Lintin Island in the Pearl River estuary in 1824

A drawing of a man smoking opium, dating from 1843

foreign merchants just as would the sale of any other commodity have been, as a means of counteracting the huge drain of silver into China to pay for the purchase of the tea and other goods the English bought.

After the 1800 edict prohibiting the import, this open trade stopped. The East India Company ceased to import, the Co-hong ceased to handle opium. The East India Company, however, discovered that rather than lose its huge revenues in India derived from the sale of opium, the substance could be sold to independent merchants who were free to ship it where they wished. The Co-hong were required to give bonds for ships trading at Canton, stating they contained no opium, but this was a mere fiction in many cases. The opium was sold for cash over the sides of the ships and smuggled into China. For the first twenty years after the prohibition, little notice other than formal was taken of the edict.

At this point we come to an unavoidable question. Why did the demand for opium grow so rapidly in China at this time when, for hundreds of years, it had been available in China? No one has come up with any very convincing answer. There is a kind of parallel in the sudden growth of the habit of drinking cheap Dutch gin in England in the eighteenth century when a populace no more addicted to excessive alcohol intake than any other, seems to have abandoned itself to the effects of it. It would seem that the drinking was worst among the miserably paid and badly housed sections of the people. Possibly there were in south China in the late eighteenth and early nineteenth centuries social conditions that in some ways paralleled the miseries of urban and industrial England, and led to similar addiction.

There is, however, no excuse for the British, the principal importers, for continuing after 1800 what was a completely illegal commerce by smuggling opium into China. An incident in 1821 forced the viceroy at Canton to take public notice of the illegal import trade, and after that it was carried on more secretly. The effects of this trade were seen not only in the increasing use of the drug in China, and the increasing drain of silver out of China to pay for it (which caused considerable financial disruption there), but also the growth of a class of Chinese and British dealers in opium whose daily acts were of a criminal nature. The huge sums of money involved encouraged bribery and corruption on a large scale, with demoralizing effects. The quantities imported rose to 9,708 chests in 1828, and after that time the trade spread increasingly up the China coast where the goods were smuggled in after the local officials had been bribed to turn a blind eye. By 1835, the number of chests sold was nearly 19,000, and by 1839 this had become 30,000 chests (about 4,000,000 lbs).

The foreign merchants had discovered the most profitable trade that had ever been found in the East. Their determination to pursue it led to the corruption of almost every single official in the southern Chinese provinces—from the viceroy down to the smallest clerk.

Commissioner Lin burns the opium

In 1834, in response to growing free-trade ideas in England, the monopoly of the East India Company was ended. The British merchants at Canton (increased in numbers from 88 in 1832, to 158 in 1836) were represented by a British official, Lord Napier, called the Chief Superintendant of Trade. Like other foreigners before him, he was saddled by the British Foreign Secretary, Lord Palmerston, with impossible instructions—to announce his arrival at Canton 'by letter to the viceroy.' No viceroy would accept a letter from a British or any other foreign official unless it was in the form of a petition and forwarded by the Co-hong. No British Foreign Secretary could admit the inferior status implied in this procedure.

Lord Napier's eventual successor, when he had failed in his mission and died of a fever, was Captain Charles Elliot. Elliot was a great optimist and a man of quick temper. The concern of the Chinese court at the opium trade was known to have caused a series of investigations and reports within the Chinese governmental system in Peking and Canton. While the results were awaited, Elliot was confident the emperor would legalize the trade. But instead, in 1836, orders were given by the viceroy for the expulsion of several foreigners connected with opium trading, and later for the abolition of the 'passage boats' that smuggled it in coastal waters.

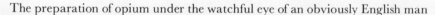

The preparation of opium under the watchful eye of an obviously English man

Commissioner Lin. Despite the general hatred the foreign community had for him, (because of his activities in suppressing the opium trade) he was a highly intelligent man. He was also a patient of Dr. Peter Parker, the first medical missionary to China, who had set up a hospital in Canton

Then all foreign vessels were forbidden to remain inside the port of Canton and orders given to Elliot to stop the opium traffic up and down the coast.

Here we see the Chinese placing responsibility for the illegal trade on the shoulders of one man. This was a normal procedure in China where if the actual criminal could not be punished his relative or some other person connected with him was punished instead. This approach to law-enforcement was intensely disliked and always opposed by the British and other Europeans in China.

The confused situation continued with an embargo on trade, riots in Canton, protestations by Britain on the impossibility of the British stopping altogether the import of opium since half of it was not grown in British territory, and even that which was so grown could be imported by non-British ships. The insincerity of the arguments was quite open for all to see. The situation became more and more dangerous as time went by. The British and others were unwilling to sacrifice what they viewed as their right to trade in opium and, with even greater vehemence, to sacrifice their astronomical profits from the trade; the Chinese officials of all ranks, deeply involved in the opium trade, were fattening on the profits as the population progressively impoverished its health and its purse for the sake of opium.

By the end of 1838, the emperor in Peking took action. Tao-kwang (1782–1850) was doubtless more concerned at the deteriorating economy of his realm than with the health of the population. But he now acted decisively. There was only one way to cut through the tangle of British and Chinese hypocrisy—to send a man empowered to stamp out the trade, while placing the blame for wrongdoing on the foreigners who were responsible for continuing it against Chinese law. The man was Commissioner Lin Tse-hsü, a man of known integrity, former Governor of Hupeh and Hunan provinces where he had gained a reputation for stopping the use of opium.

Despite the fact that Lin knew almost nothing of foreigners (in common with most Chinese at that time) he emerges from his task at Canton with credit as one of the few level-headed and fair minds involved. His first acts were to write letters to various sections of the people in and around Canton—to school teachers requiring them to report any pupils who smoked or sold opium, to captains of patrol ships to surrender all, not part, of the opium they captured, to the Co-hong threatening that if they persisted in giving certificates to ships they knew contained opium he would 'select for execution one or two of the most unworthy'.

Finally he wrote to Queen Victoria a letter of sage and, as we read it now, reasonable advice:

'The Way of Heaven is Fairness to all; it does not suffer us to harm others in order to benefit ourselves.... I am told that in your own country opium smoking is forbidden under severe penalties. [He was misinformed. It was not.] This means that you are aware of how harmful it is...better than to forbid the smoking of it would be to forbid the sale of it and, better still, to forbid the production of it...So long as you do not take it yourselves but...continue to tempt the people of China to buy it, you will be showing yourselves careful of your own lives, but careless of the lives of other people, indifferent in your greed for gain to the harm you do to others; such conduct is repugnant to human feeling....'

It is doubtful if the queen received the letter, and highly unlikely that it would have been acted upon if she had. But its reasonable tone makes it one of the few sensible documents of the age connected with the opium problem.

Lin reminded the foreign merchants it was only by the favour of the emperor that they were enabled to trade at all, and that they must surrender all opium stocks within three days and never import the drug again. The merchants failed to comprehend that Lin meant what he said. On March 19, 1839 he confined all foreigners to the factories at Canton. Captain Elliot, who was not there, managed to reach Canton on the evening of the 24th, only to discover that a drunken English sea captain had fired nine shots at a Chinese frigate near his own ship, an action that did not improve the situation. In the end, Elliot had to agree to surrender all the opium stocks, and Commissioner Lin, sitting in great state on an island at the mouth of the Pearl River, supervised the burning of 2,613,879 lbs of it in the presence of a representative of the only foreign company (American) that did not deal in opium at Canton.

Macau showing the Praya Grande as seen from Penha Hill. The picture probably dates from the early nineteenth century

Elliot forbade all British merchants to sign the bond stating that they would not import opium again, and in May he removed the entire British community to Macau. Later, the British had to flee once more, this time to whatever ships were in the neighbourhood, as Commissioner Lin paid a visit to Macau in state.

Already Elliot had called for armed assistance. In Britain, most importantly in Parliament, opinions on the morality of exporting opium legally or illegally to China, and even more forcibly, on backing opium merchants in their trade with the force of British arms, was sharply divided. Such influential publications as *The Edinburgh Review* expressed dismay:

'The importation of Indian opium into China has increased in an extraordinary manner.... We cannot make this statement without some feelings of regret, since a contraband trade in this drug, carried on with great obstinacy, is naturally calculated to increase the dislike of the Chinese Government towards the strangers engaged in it.'

But the equally important *Quarterly Review*, with the problems of gin-drinking and general alcoholism at home in mind, doubted that 'the evils of opium were worse than those of gin and whisky'.

Lord Palmerston, the Foreign Secretary in London, was a man peculiarly susceptible to anger when he heard of Chinese actions to prevent the import of opium into their realm, and he followed the conclusion of a Parliamentary Committee of 1852 which thought that it was 'inadvisable to abandon so important a revenue' as the income derived from opium export. He listened to the views of the newly returned opium merchant James Jardine (now a member of Parliament), and to those of his partner James Matheson, who had written that the Chinese were 'truculent, vainglorious people'.

Fearing that Parliament would not agree to do so, Palmerston confidentially ordered the dispatch of troops and warships from India. When news of this eventually leaked out in London, the ensuing debate was a battle between Palmerston and Gladstone, who said:

'A war more unjust in its origins...more calculated to cover this country with permanent disgrace, I do not know....'

and he accused the Government of not wanting to suppress the opium trade. Did the Foreign Secretary not know

'that the opium smuggled into China comes exclusively from British ports [Bengal and Bombay]?...Then we require no preventive service to put down this illegal traffic. We have only to stop the sailings of the smuggling vessels....'

This, we may note, was substantially what Commissioner Lin had written to Queen Victoria. The young historian, later to achieve such great fame, Thomas Babington Macaulay, then Secretary of State for War, in his speech called the whole affair a 'most rightful quarrel', and went on to paint a vivid and untrue picture of the plight of merchants imprisoned by Lin in Canton and looking for protection from their countrymen.

CHINA AND THE WEST 49

A mere two months after he had spoken, (in June, 1840) 15 men-of-war, 5 armed steamers of the East India Company, and 4,000 troops were assembling off Macau to carry out Macaulay's determination to see Britain vindicated at all costs.

The pathetic unpreparedness of the Chinese is well summed up in the words of Ch'i-shan, Governor-General of Chihli, in August 1840:

'Our military affairs are in the hands of civil officials, who are very likely admirable calligraphists but know nothing of war.'

The First Anglo-Chinese War, 1839–1842

The more common name, the Opium War, is often used and is justifiable since the basic cause of the hostilities was British insistence on illegally importing opium. The events that triggered off the shooting were trivial in themselves.

In July, 1839, some drunken British and American sailors who were ashore at Kowloon Point were involved in a riot 'occasioned by their attempt to obtain spirits to drink; a shameful riot attended with unmanly outrage upon men, women, and children, and the loss of innocent life.' But the court that judged the affair could not decide which sailor struck the blow that killed a Chinese named Lin Wei-hsi. Commissioner Lin in Canton demanded the culprit be handed over, and Captain Elliot refused, saying he was unable to find out which man was guilty. To the Chinese, this was no excuse as, by their own customs, one of the party involved should be punished, even if he was not technically guilty.

The British (who were still at Macau) were then deprived of food by order of the Commissioner, and eventually had to leave in boats and take shelter in Hong Kong harbour. On August 31, a proclamation was issued to the villagers of Hong Kong forbidding the supply of food and water to the ships. On the same day the warship H.M.S. Volage arrived in their midst. By September 4, there was severe shortage of food and water aboard all ships, and Captain Elliot, attempting to make sure some Chinese boats bringing provisions were not stopped by Chinese war-junks gave the order to open fire on them.

After a month of arguments on both sides, there came a Chinese demand that all ships should sign the bond stating they did not carry opium, and that all ships should proceed to trade at Canton or else the Chinese would 'send our war-vessels to Hong Kong to surround the ships and apprehend all the offenders, those connected with murder [of Lin Wei-hsi], those connected with opium. . . .' Elliot then told the captain of the Volage to prevent any British ships entering the river mouth for Canton.

On November 3, twenty-nine war-junks approached H.M.S. Volage near Chuenpi Island and the surrender of the murderer of Lin was again demanded, and again refused on the same grounds as before. The captain then opened fire on the Chinese junks, sinking four and damaging the rest. The war had begun.

The 'battle' of Chuenpi lasted less than an hour and the British suffered only slight damage. Reported to England, pressures mounted in Parliament for a show force against China. The young Mr. Gladstone was against this, speaking of the evils of the opium trade and the injustice of supporting it with a war against the

A battle during the Opium War. Bombardment by Western guns shatters a Chinese vessel

Chinese. Most members of Parliament, however, supported Palmerston who claimed he was protecting British life and property and not supporting the opium trade. By this stage in the events, he could hardly have done one without doing the other. The real issue was the refusal of Britain to condemn and stop the opium trade.

A force of British occupied Chusan Island up the coast, and it became apparent to the Chinese that Commissioner Lin's opinion that the British would not make trouble was incorrect. Having won praise for his burning of the opium, Lin now encountered the reverse for his failure to stop the trade and to tame the British. It is obvious that he was taken completely by surprise at the strength of British guns and the deadly accuracy of their aim. The emperor eventually dismissed him, writing: 'You are no better than a wooden image.' He appointed Ch'i-shan (called Kishan by the British), a Manchu with an even more distinguished career than Lin. His persuasive manner made Elliot think that he would agree to the demand for the cession of the island and harbour of Hong Kong to the British Crown.

Ch'i-shan could not do so. Elliot decided to force the issue and on January 7, 1841, captured the forts protecting the channel to Canton. The Chinese fought bravely, losing five hundred dead. A few days later Ch'i-shan signed the Convention of Chuenpi. Its terms were:

> An indemnity of six million dollars to be paid by China.
> The cession of Hong Kong.
> The re-establishment of the British merchants at Canton.
> Direct official contact between China and Britain on a footing of equality.
> A British promise to evacuate Chusan Island.

The Convention was promptly repudiated by the emperor who dismissed Ch'i-shan and deported him to the Amur River. Elliot was also dismissed and his place taken by Sir Henry Pottinger.

Part of the British force, now arrived at Hong Kong, proceeded to blockade Canton, and another part sailed up the Chinese coast to reach the Peiho, the river entry to the port of Tientsin, only ninety miles from the capital. In the end, various military actions having been taken up and down the coast and the city of Nanking being threatened, the emperor sent two high-ranking Manchu officials to negotiate.

There was nothing else the Chinese could do. Nanking was defended by a garrison of 1,600 Manchu troops and less than 1,000 Chinese soldiers. Their arms were pathetic—ancient matchlocks, bows and arrows. So the Chinese eventually signed the second treaty with a Western power—the Treaty of Nanking. The date was August 29, 1842. It marked the beginning, all unknown to the Chinese, of what was to be the most terrible century in their long and turbulent history.

The terms of the Treaty of Nanking were:

> Perpetual peace and amity. The ports of Amoy, Canton, Foochow, Ningpo, and Shanghai were to be opened for foreign trade and residence.
> Consuls could be appointed to these ports, and were to be enabled to communicate directly and in conditions of respect with the Chinese authorities.
> Hong Kong Island was to be ceded to Britain.
> China would pay $6 million in compensation for opium 'surrendered as ransom for the lives of British subjects. . . .' (It was not originally surrendered for that reason).
> The Co-hong monopoly was to be abolished, allowing foreigners to trade with anyone they wished to trade with. $3 million was to be paid to settle Co-hong debts with the British.
> $12 million was to be paid for the costs of the war.

The signing of the Treaty of Nanking. Lord Palmerston in London was carefully guided by William Jardine, the man who had probably sold more opium in China than any other. Palmerston remarked of the treaty that 'it will form an epoch in the progress of the civilization of the human races. . . .' In a sense this was true—but the eventual results were hardly what Palmerston or Jardine had expected

A supplementary treaty (Treaty of the Bogue) contained important additions:

> A tariff of 5% of the value of goods, unalterable except by mutual agreement.
> Extraterritorial rights—British subjects who committed criminal offences on Chinese territory were to be tried by the principles of British, not Chinese, law.
> The 'most-favoured-nation' clause: all privileges granted to other nations were automatically to be enjoyed by Britain too.

The treaty and its supplement included most of the demands of the merchants, enabling them to trade where and when and in almost whatever way they wished. It spelled out to China that she was powerless to stop Britain (or any other Western power, in effect) from doing more or less what she wanted on Chinese soil. The Chinese have always called it the first of the 'unequal treaties,' signed as it was at gunpoint.

'The Chinese, except for frontier regulations made with the Russians, had never been subjected to the give-and-take requirements of a treaty; they knew nothing of international law or the rights of nations; these treaties had been imposed upon them without their consent, and every one of their stipulations was deeply resented....'

Morse: *International Relations*

Other nations were not slow to seize their opportunity. In 1844, the Americans concluded the Treaty of Wanghsia, and the French the Treaty of Whampoa, their contents similar to the Treaty of Nanking. The French forced the Chinese to accept Catholic missionaries and to allow them to live and preach and build churches in the treaty ports. Belgium, Norway and Sweden (then a single country), and other nations also, soon concluded similar treaties with China which was in no position to resist. British, American, and French treaties were due for revision in twelve years.

The most obvious omission in the Treaty of Nanking was the problem of opium. It is not mentioned except in the compensation clause. Perhaps that fact indicates more than any other the nature of the treaty. It was an imposed settlement. The Chinese never regarded it as anything but a temporary nuisance, the result of a setback, something to be torn up as soon as they were in a position to do so. Over a hundred years were to pass before China regained complete sovereignty over her own land. The original Chinese opinion of Western traders—that they were determined to trade by force—proved perfectly correct. Where China completely misjudged them was to scorn their technical attainments, their fast ships equipped with powerful guns, their modern small arms, and their military expertise.

Hong Kong

Ratifications of the Treaty of Nanking were exchanged by British and Chinese governments on June 26, 1843, at Hong Kong. On that day also, Hong Kong was proclaimed a Crown Colony, with Sir Henry Pottinger as the first Governor. The island had been ceded originally by the terms of the Chuenpi Convention in January, 1841, and at once merchants and others recognized it as holding out opportunities for settlement and for trade from a stable base in place of the uncertainties of Canton and Macau. Although the cession was rejected by the British government, Elliot had already promised the local people government by Chinese law, and others by British Law. Land sales were held and with remarkable speed both permanent and temporary buildings sprang up. Elliot appointed officials, set up a rudimentary form of administration, and declared Hong Kong a free port. Within months, not only Westerners but also Chinese from the mainland had seen the possibilities of employment and trade in the new settlement, and the original 5,000 Chinese inhabitants were soon joined by many others. Ten years later, in 1851, there were 1,520 non-Chinese and 31,463 Chinese in the Colony.

When it became known that the British government did not wish to take over the island, the fate of Hong Kong should have been sealed. But it was not. Pottinger's new instructions from London arrived in May, 1842, and were to the effect that

The geographical setting of the Anglo-Chinese Wars

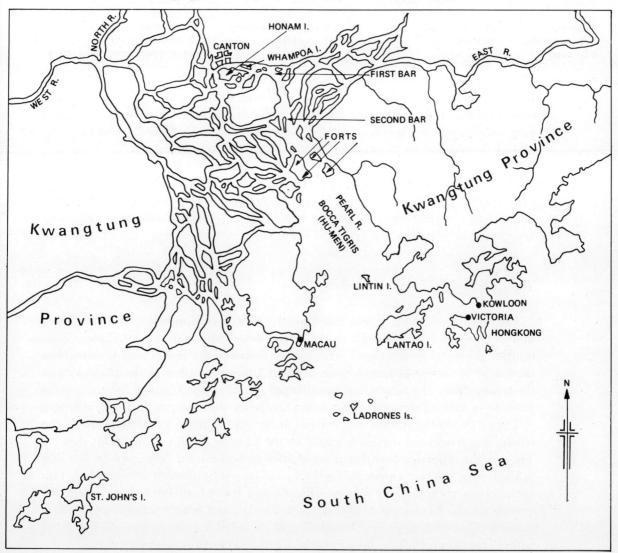

The rapid development of Hong Kong, and early reclamations to accommodate it

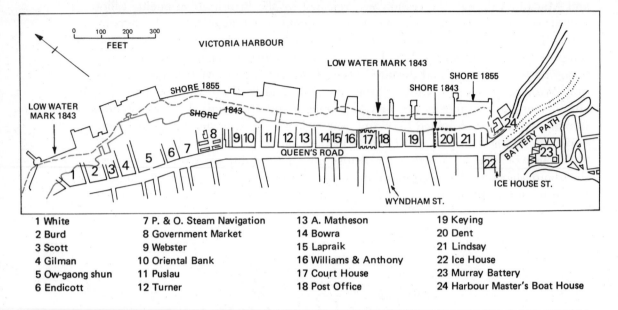

1 White	7 P. & O. Steam Navigation	13 A. Matheson	19 Keying
2 Burd	8 Government Market	14 Bowra	20 Dent
3 Scott	9 Webster	15 Lapraik	21 Lindsay
4 Gilman	10 Oriental Bank	16 Williams & Anthony	22 Ice House
5 Ow-gaong shun	11 Puslau	17 Court House	23 Murray Battery
6 Endicott	12 Turner	18 Post Office	24 Harbour Master's Boat House

Britain wanted not territory but facilities at various Chinese ports. But, so favourably impressed was Pottinger at the development that had taken place in little over a year since Elliot's marines had planted the British flag on the island, he had already moved the office of the Superintendent of Trade to Hong Kong.

The Foreign Secretary, Lord Aberdeen, who succeeded Palmerston, found that Pottinger's ideas were different from his own. 'This settlement has already advanced too far,' Pottinger wrote to Lord Aberdeen, 'to admit of its ever being restored to the authority of the Emperor'. Britain finally came round to Pottinger's opinion by accepting the island in the Treaty of Nanking.

The Effects of the Treaty of Nanking

The Treaty of Nanking was, like most treaties, a compromise. In a very short time it was seen by the British to be unsatisfactory although it gave them opportunities never before obtained. The friction between foreigners and Chinese was caused by a variety of factors, one of them Chinese evasion of the provisions of the treaty. Since the treaty had been forced on them, the Chinese felt themselves justified in making things as difficult as possible for the Western traders and others.

The settlement of traders and consuls at the treaty ports went smoothly on the whole, and residential sites were leased by the Chinese to the various treaty powers. These areas of foreign settlement were later to become the 'concessions' familiar in the future, the best known being the International Settlement at Shanghai. This enclave was controlled by foreign officials and housed all foreigners, except the French who had a concession of their own. The law and order eventually prevailing in the foreign settlements in Shanghai, and the relative immunity of all who lived within them from Chinese law, induced Chinese to acquire property there.

Shanghai developed more rapidly than Hong Kong. Its accessibility to the sea, its geographical position at the mouth of the great Yangtze River—one of the main arteries of trade throughout the huge area of central China with its vast population —and its nearness to the great tea-producing and silk-growing lands, were the main factors underlying its growth. By 1846, Shanghai's share in the tea export trade of China was one seventh, and five years later, in 1851, the port was handling one third of the trade.

Hong Kong did not do so well initially. The opium trade was at the root of both its prosperity and its troubles. Opium was still an illegal import, yet officials in China connived with foreign merchants to get it into the country by one means and another. Peking had no satisfactory force to suppress the trade. ·

Other problems arose out of Chinese unwillingness to fulfil their treaty obligations to allow foreigners to reside and trade in Canton itself. This meant they were still virtually confined to the old factories.

On the other hand, the British and others engaged in doubtful ways of making quick money. The system whereby fishing and trading fleets of Chinese vessels sought protection in being convoyed by armed foreign ships was at first apparently a fine safeguard against the piracy that was so common up and down the coast. Chinese naval vessels were too poorly armed to deal effectively with pirates, while the escort ships hired by the Chinese merchants were most effective. Gradually, however, the charges demanded by the foreigners from the Chinese ship-masters became so high that it was hard for the Chinese to pay them. Yet without escort, the risk of losing all to pirates was very high. The business was sheer extortion.

Foreign evasion of Chinese law was common. One example was the conduct of the coolie emigrant trade. Chinese law banned all emigration. In the fifteen or twenty years following the Treaty of Nanking, developing areas such as Peru, the Malaysian Peninsula, Indonesia, Hawaii, and the West Indian Islands were all eager for cheap labour not to be found on the spot. Conditions in China's coastal provinces had deteriorated, partly as a result of economic disruption caused by Western trading, and partly due to the weakening powers of the Ch'ing dynasty. So there was no lack of Chinese from Macau and the coast of Fukien province willing to accept contracts guaranteeing them a small wage and food. But what often happened when—after a nightmare voyage, crammed like cattle into some foreign vessel, many of them dying on the way—they arrived at their destination, was that contract conditions were not honoured. News of the tragic fate of many thousands of Chinese eventually reached China itself and the supply of willing men dwindled. The foreigners and their agents then began kidnapping. It is hardly surprising that this inhuman and dishonourable trade caused deep resentment among Chinese. 'Buying men', as it was called by them, did not make Westerners any better liked.

One more factor making for friction was the Westerners' omission to provide magistrates and courts to enforce law according to British, French, or other Western procedure in their concessions. Foreign offenders—when their offence was against a Chinese—very often went free. And foreigners also thwarted Chinese law by protecting Chinese offenders under the umbrella of extraterritorial privilege.

Less than ten years after the Treaty of Nanking was signed, relations between the British and the Chinese were reaching what the British felt to be an unbearable state of frustration and deadlock. The year 1852 brought the appointment of the anti-foreign Yeh Ming-ch'en in August as Viceroy and High Commissioner for Foreign Affairs at Canton. It came two years after the accession to the throne in Peking of the Emperor Hsien-fêng, who was also anti-foreign. The Hong Kong governor from 1854 was Sir John Bowring, at first well disposed toward the Chinese but later—finding it impossible to deal with Yeh—taking a harder line. The French and American representatives at Canton found it impossible, as did Bowring, to make any personal contact with Yeh, despite his position as Commissioner for Foreign Affairs.

In China itself the situation was deteriorating. Rebellion threatened in the Yangtze area, and the problems posed by payment of the indemnity called for in the Treaty of Nanking made worse an already poor economic situation. The power of the central boards of government in Peking was decreased by corruption, one aspect of which was the ever-increasing practice of buying jobs in the government service. As if to underline the ills of China, the Yellow River changed its course in 1852. With incalculable loss of life from drowning and famine, the river deserted its channel south of the Shantung Peninsula, and cut northward to reach the sea at the Gulf of Chihli instead. The beginnings of the T'aip'ing rebellion had already caused a ferment in South China, and the whole of Kwangtung Province was in a state of uproar—so much so that in 1855, in an effort to quell rebellion, 80,000 people were said to have been put to death.

As the anti-foreign outlook of the Chinese, both of officials and of the ordinary man in the street, grew in South China, matters were obviously reaching a head. In the summer of 1856 placards were put up in Canton warning foreigners that if they entered the city or went into the country they would be exterminated. These could have been interpreted as a warning of the popular distrust of foreigners, but in fact were interpreted by the British and others as an insult. Two Englishmen, riding near Canton in July of that year, were shouted at and stoned by the country people. An American at Foochow (one of the treaty ports) was severely injured in disturbances that almost turned into a riot, and died soon after. An English missionary who had travelled overland from Shanghai dressed as a Chinese was arrested, but in accordance with the treaty and its extraterritoriality clause was delivered to the British consul at Canton. There was no doubt of the violence of Chinese feelings about the foreigners.

Already, in 1855, Palmerston had written:

'The Time is fast coming when we shall be obliged to strike another blow in China. . . .
These half-civilized governments such as those of China, Portugal and Spanish America
all require a Dressing every eight or ten years to keep them in order. . . .'

But this was not the only opinion on the subject. Lord Derby organized the opposition to Palmerston, condemning Governor Bowring's 'utmost arrogance', his 'perfect monomania about getting into Canton', his 'menacing, disrespectful and arrogant language' to the Chinese. And he hoped that Britain would not 'on any consideration give the sanction. . . to shedding of blood of unwarlike and innocent people without warrant of law and without moral justification'. So, there were doves as well as hawks, peacemakers as well as warmakers in high places in England.

The excuse for war, however, was not hard to find in and around South China in these lawless times. And the huge sums of money involved in the opium trade made it likely that war would come to make it easier to sell more.

The Second Anglo-Chinese War

The Hong Kong government permitted registration of ships owned by traders resident in the colony, whether they were British subjects or Chinese, in order to offer some protection from piracy.

On October 8, 1856, the Hong Kong registered *lorcha* named Arrow (a *lorcha* was a boat with a Western-style hull and Chinese sails) lay off Canton flying the British flag. She was boarded by Chinese officers who hauled down the flag and took the Chinese crew away. The consul, Sir Harry Parkes, protested to Commissioner Yeh and asked for their release for investigation. Yeh replied that he had acted to arrest a notorious pirate aboard, that the *lorcha* was owned by a Chinese and not entitled to use the British flag.

What he did not know was that even her certificate of registration had expired eleven days previously. There were other irregularities as well, and it was certainly illegal to presume the boat still registered, as the British did, when it was not. The British finally demanded an apology and the return of the crew, adding that they wanted these within 48 hours. When full satisfaction was not obtained (although Yeh handed over nine of the twelve detained and gave an assurance of non-interference with British-owned boats), the British took the forts four miles south of Canton and destroyed them, took an island in the river opposite Canton, and occupied the Canton foreign factories. The forces then retired since they were not adequate to hold their positions.

War did not immediately follow these first engagements. The British were waiting for reinforcements from India. There were many incidents, in one of which a Chinese mob in Canton burned the factories. It was plain that popular Chinese feeling was strongly anti-foreign.

About this time the French received news of the murder of a missionary, Father Chapdelaine, and on protesting to Yeh were informed that he had no right to be preaching in the interior in what was a rebel-controlled district. Yeh pointed out that several previous wandering French missionaries had been sent back unharmed to treaty ports. When Napoleon III heard of the incident he allied himself with the British once more (they had been allied in the newly ended Crimean War of 1854–1856). The Americans, like the French, were pressing for revision of their treaties at this time and were therefore also disposed to take the British part.

Napoleon sent his plenipotentiary Baron Gros, and the British government sent Lord Elgin as their representative, each with instructions to achieve several objectives:

> Compensation for loss of life and injury to British and French subjects.
> Assurances that the Chinese would observe the terms of the treaties.
> Enlargement of trade facilities and revision of the treaties.
> Permission to appoint ambassadors to the court at Peking.

The bombardment of Canton in the Second Anglo-Chinese War, 1857. The suburbs are ablaze. The sketch was made by an English officer

The two envoys arrived in Hong Kong in mid-1857, but due to insufficient forces and the fact that the Peiho, by which they would have to approach Peking, freezes over in winter, they remained in the Colony and wrote to Commissioner Yeh for assurances on the first two points of their instructions. No satisfactory reply was forthcoming.

On December 28, bombardment of Canton began and on the following day the city wall was attacked from the north. The northern part of the city was occupied by the afternoon, while the rest of it lay at the mercy of the ships' guns in the river. Canton was taken. Yeh was captured and sent to Calcutta in case he became the focus of popular rebellion. He died there a year later. He had not managed his country's affairs well. His resolute denial of all demands for interviews with Western officials, and his misjudgment of Western determination and strength, ended in China's speedy defeat at Canton, and the continuing war of the following year, 1858. But owing to military and governmental weakness, probably he could not have delayed these events much, even had he been more efficient. The Western powers were determined to trade and to establish equality in their relations with China. Commissioner Yeh had no means to stop them.

Canton was occupied by an allied force until 1861, with comparatively little trouble. Trade soon began again.

Lord Elgin and his French counterpart were of the opinion that, since no headway with their demands could be made in the south, they must attempt to capture the attention of the court at Peking itself. When reinforcements of troops arrived and the expedition had formed up in Hong Kong, they set off north accompanied by American and Russian representatives.

America and Russia were not at war with China, but the United States had nationals and trading interests at Canton and other treaty ports, while Russia intended to alter the Treaty of Nerchinsk signed long ago (1689). According to that treaty she could trade with China only at the frontier town of Kiakhta. She intended to press for revision of the Sino-Russian border, and also for rights at the treaty ports.

Troops from the allied ships landed at the mouth of the Peiho and captured its forts which guarded the way to Tientsin and to Peking upriver. After unsatisfactory exchanges on the subject of the various demands of the Allies, the force pushed on up to Tientsin where the four envoys arrived by the end of May, 1858. A few days after, two high-ranking plenipotentiaries from the court at Peking arrived with powers from the emperor and at once conducted interviews with all four Western envoys. It was quite obvious that the Chinese at last understood how grave the situation was, and how the armed might of this quite small force could conquer all Chinese forces sent against it. They decided to come to terms with the Westerners.

The Russians completed their treaty negotiations first, acquiring, by the Treaty of Aigun, a considerable tract of Chinese land up to the left bank of the Amur river, permission to trade at the treaty ports, and other minor concessions including that of the 'most-favoured-nation' treatment.

Lord Elgin and Chinese plenipotentiaries signing the Treaty of Tientsin on June 24, 1858

The texts of the treaties signed by the four powers differed somewhat, but on account of the operation of the 'most-favoured-nation' clause, anything granted to one nation was automatically granted to the others. The main provisions of the Treaty of Tientsin, signed in June, 1858, were:

> The four powers had the right to send their ambassadors to reside in Peking or to visit the court at Peking from time to time. They would not be asked to perform the *kowtow*.

> Eleven ports were to be opened to foreign trade, including ten ports more than those opened by the Treaty of Nanking. These included Chingkiang, Kiukiang, Nanking, and Hangkow on the Yangtze river, which was thereby opened to foreigners and their ships for a distance of 600 miles.

> Foreigners were allowed to travel in China on their own country's passport countersigned by local Chinese authorities.

> Warships were permitted to call for repairs and supplies at any Chinese port.

> Missionaries were permitted to live anywhere in China and to preach Christianity to the Chinese, under protection of the Chinese government itself.

> Widening of the concept and practical details of extraterritoriality. Foreigners accused of illegal acts in parts of the country under purely Chinese jurisdiction were to be conveyed safely to the nearest consul of their nationality, and were to be tried by officials, and under the laws, of their own country. In disputes involving foreigners and Chinese, the foreign consul should attempt to settle the problem; but, failing that, a joint court consisting of the consul and a Chinese magistrate would deal with the matter. In criminal cases, the accused was to be tried under the laws of his own country.

> Provision for extradition of criminals.

> A prohibition on the use of the character 夷—*yi*—used by the Chinese to signify foreigners and meaning 'barbarian'—in all official documents.

> Payment of 4 million taels each to Britain and France as reparations.

> Provision for the revision of tariffs. (When the new tariff was set, it provided for a duty on opium whose import was then legalized.)

It was agreed that ratifications of the treaty would be exchanged in Peking in June the following year, 1859. The Chinese, forced by the West to concede piece by piece the integrity of their territory and their sovereignty over it, had again signed a treaty as a last resort only. The next act in the drama came when the time for its ratification approached.

4 The T'aip'ing Rebellion, 1850–1864

SEVERAL factors were at work in China during the first half of the nineteenth century which must be considered important in the development of the T'aip'ing movement.

One was the decay of traditional Buddhism and Taoism, and the identification of the alien and increasingly hated Manchu rule with Confucianism, thus bringing the latter into disrepute. Another was the increasing restlessness of the Chinese under Manchu rule, a rule whose corruption and parasitical nature affected every aspect of life for the worse. And yet another factor was the increasing disparity between the growing wealth of the silk- and tea-producing areas south of the Yangtze river and the comparatively poor northern sections of China. Such matters as these, taken in combination with the economic changes largely caused by Western trade, and the demoralizing influence of Western dominance in treaty ports, led to deep disillusion about the Manchu dynasty and encouraged rebellion and separatist ideas.

It is necessary to take a closer look at each of these factors so as to understand the extraordinary events of the period which shook the Manchu dynasty to its already unsteady foundations. A process began at this time which was to lead a century later to the Communist revolution in China.

Decay of the Old Beliefs

The Chinese never believed in anything like the jealous Christian God. Buddhism accepted many aspects of Confucian teachings that were already five or more centuries old in China when the religion arrived from India. Taoism accepted much from Buddhism, and in turn some of its deities were incorporated into the Buddhist pantheon. Educated Chinese found no difficulty in being Confucian in thought, but in attending Buddhist ceremonies of various kinds.

A Chinese scholar has said that by the nineteenth century the educated classes believed in nothing, while the uneducated majority believed in everything. And it was true that by the mid-nineteenth century the great religions had degenerated for the most part into superstitions attended by corrupt priests. Their precepts no longer influenced the morality and behaviour of most people. The sole survivor was the ancient Chinese belief in the necessity of worshipping one's ancestors. This at least was a universal practice that served as a unifying force, a focus of true Chineseness. Confucian filial piety, respect for parents, elders, those in authority, which lay at the foundation of the Chinese state and society—still had firm hold on the populace in general.

Manchu Decadence

The warlike and highly organized conquerors who overthrew the last of the Ming in 1644, and whose great emperors K'ang-hsi and Ch'ien-lung had presided over a China for the most part firmly and successfully ruled—the proud Manchu were now a decadent race. Glutted with the riches extorted from China, their last few ineffective rulers were typical symptoms of the running down of the dynastic machine. The Mandate of Heaven, as the Chinese said, was being withdrawn from the dynasty. Everyone could see that. Social and economic distress in many parts of the country led to various small uprisings that were suppressed by the government. But there was a mood of restlessness and despair in the country at large, a disbelief in the power of a dynasty that extorted more and more each year from the people at large, and one that had failed to prevent the Westerners from gaining sovereignty over various parts of China.

The population was growing fast, increasing three times in the century 1740–1840, to reach 400 million. Pressure on the never abundant supply of food increased, as did starvation, banditry, the incidence of epidemics such as plague, and a general lawlessness.

Economic Factors

The seaborne trade in the south, particularly at Canton, had brought enormous and very unevenly distributed wealth. This in its turn caused great changes in the economy of the country. Its effects were strengthened by another process.

> '. . . the rise of the south and the decay of the northwest. From the reign of Ch'ien-lung onwards the south, and in particular the Yangtze delta and the tea-producing districts . . . became by far the wealthiest and most populous part of the empire . . . the focus of economic life.'
>
> C.P. Fitzgerald: *China*

It was exactly in these areas of the south that opposition to Manchu rule had always been strongest, and where in the first half of the nineteenth century Western influence had the most effect on both the economy and the current of ideas and reactions of people. The economic changes in this area formed part of the underlying causes of the rebellion.

T'ien-wang—The Heavenly King—and his Ideas

Into this scene of increasing unrest and uncertainty of life, came the son of a Hakka farmer who was a village headman. His name was Hung Hsiu-ch'üan (1813–1864), and he was destined to have an effect on his native land that was more radical and led to greater changes in the Chinese way of life than perhaps even he suspected. Despite the eventual failure of the rebellion which he started, he had begun a process that led finally to the destruction of the ancient system of dynastic rule and to the search for something entirely new.

Hung Hsiu-ch'üan, the Heavenly King of
the T'aip'ing rebels

Hung worked as a village schoolteacher, meanwhile studying for the imperial
examinations which he sat in Canton in 1837 for the second time. For the second
time he failed, but while in the city he happened to hear a foreign missionary
preaching in the street. Hung was not greatly impressed, but carried away with him
several religious pamphlets consisting of extracts from the Bible, and sermons. This
literature had been translated by the first Protestant missionary in China, Robert
Morrison.

Returning to his village he fell ill with a high fever and was unconscious for many
days. When he recovered he recounted a dream or vision he had had, evidently
believing that he had seen God and had been commanded by Him to cleanse
China of its evils. He seemed from then onward to believe that he was the mouth-
piece of the son of God, and also destined to be emperor of China, for he began to
use the vermillion ink used only by the emperor. He turned to the translations of
the Bible in the religious pamphlets, and it seemed to him undoubtedly that the
old man of his vision was God, and that the other man in the dream must be Christ.
He assumed that Christ was his elder brother.

Hung once more sat the examination at Canton and once more failed. This
embittered him, since he believed that he had (as a southerner) been discriminated
against by the Manchu government which preferred the less rebellious northerners.
He was thus, even before he became an active rebel, anti-Manchu in sentiments.

It was not until years later, in 1847, that he studied for two months in Canton
with an American Baptist missionary, Issachar J. Roberts, from whom he received
a complete translation of the Bible by Karl Gutzlaff, another Protestant missionary.
Roberts described Hung as:

'The most earnest and deeply interested student of Christianity he had ever found in
China; but...strongly tinctured with fanaticism....'

Charles Taylor: *Five Years in China*

Hung had meanwhile managed to persuade some relatives to join him in smashing the gods in village temples, incurring the wrath of the local authorities. By the late 1840s he was the leader of a growing band of God-Worshippers. His remarkable success indicated a natural aptitude for persuasion that perhaps came from his extremely strong conviction that he was chosen to lead the world of China as head of the new religion. His knowledge of Christianity was patchy and slight (partly due to the imperfections of the translations he had read), and after some initial interest on the part of foreign missionaries at the apparent spread of Christianity from a Chinese source, he was discredited in their eyes as a heretic.

The activities of Hung and his followers, denouncing Buddhism and causing disturbances, eventually led the Manchu authorities to attempt to suppress them. At this point the God-Worshippers armed themselves, and the rebellion began. There were other groups of rebels in the south at this time, but the excellent organization of Hung and his men was superior to theirs, and in fact at once brought startling victories over the poorly organized, demoralized, and often unpaid Manchu troops against whom they fought. The first official mention of them said:

> 'The head-brigands Wei Chêng and Hung Hsiu-ch'üan and others, relying on their growing numbers, are opposing our troops everywhere. As soon as first-class troops have been collected, they should attack and disperse them, capture the ringleaders and frighten off the rest....'
>
> *Tung-hua-lu,* February 5, 1851
> (*Tung-hua-lu* is an official record of events in the Manchu empire)

It proved to be infinitely harder to do this than any Manchu at that early stage in the rebellion could have imagined. Meanwhile, Hung had proclaimed himself in 1851 as follows:

> 'Our Heavenly Prince has received the Divine Commission to exterminate the Manchu —to exterminate all idolaters generally, and to possess the Empire as its True Sovereign. It and everything in it is his...you and all you have, your family...your property.... We command the services of all and we take everything...but whoever acknowledges our Heavenly Prince...shall have full reward...due honour in the...armies and Court of the Heavenly Dynasty.'
>
> Thomas Meadows: *The Chinese and their Relations*

The rebels soon captured the town of Yung-an in Kwangsi province and there set up a headquarters. Here Hung and his associates developed a programme of social and political aims.

Some beliefs of Hung Hsiu-ch'üan coincided with Christian beliefs. These were: belief in one God, father of all human beings and opposed to evil; belief that Jesus Christ died to save the world from sin. Hung did not, however, believe that Christ was divine, but that Christ and also himself, Hung Hsiu-ch'üan, were selected by God to teach humanity. Hung had apparently no idea of the Christian doctrine of the mercy of God held out to repenting sinners, and this proved a serious defect.

The social and political programme of Hung was based on the eradication of Manchu rule, and its replacement by a theocratic state to be called *T'aip'ing T'ien-kuo,* The Heavenly Kingdom of Great Peace. Hung himself was to be the Heavenly

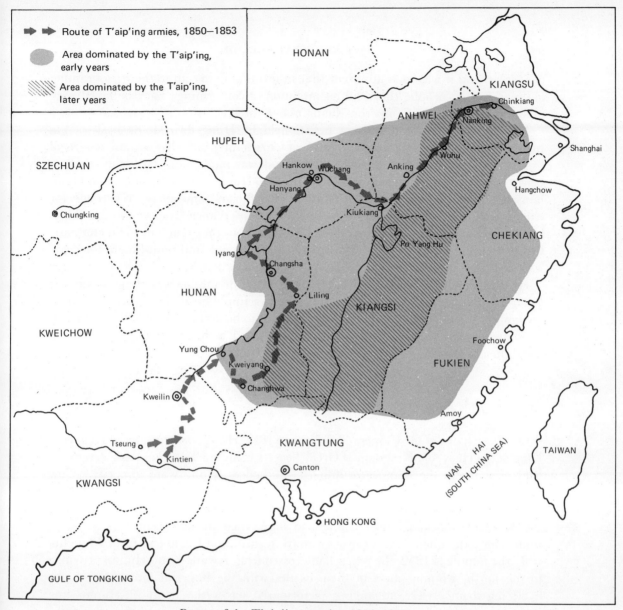

Route of the T'aip'ing armies, 1850–1853

King (T'ien-wang), and he was to have five other 'kings' forming a state council. It was laid down that a civil and also a military administration would be set up; but in fact the T'aip'ing rebels relied on the military aspect first to conquer the country, and later to defend the territory taken.

Reflecting the desires and the grievances of the country people as a whole, land was to be redistributed, as also was wealth. In trade, the T'aip'ing wished to prohibit importation of opium and forbade its smoking, but they encouraged the export of tea and silk. Such new ideas as the promotion of industry by the institution of a banking system and the construction of railways were envisaged.

On the social side of the programme, the old Chinese customs of footbinding and the keeping of concubines were to be eradicated. Monogamy and equality of men and women were advocated. The written language was to be simplified, and hospitals and other institutions for the sick and needy were to be set up. The T'aip'ing leaders themselves soon disregarded the prohibition on concubinage, among other new rules, and it was soon apparent that in terms of living up to their programme outlined for the people, they had no intention of conforming. They behaved very much in the manner of emperors, being above the law.

The peculiar form of Christian beliefs held by Hung formed the basis of the religious part of the programme. T'aip'ing Christianity included certain aspects of Confucian, Buddhist, and Taoist beliefs. God was named the Heavenly Father, Christ, the Heavenly Elder Brother (according to Hung's original vision), and Hung himself was Heavenly Younger Brother. Confucian filial piety, reverence for elders, were incorporated, along with Sunday observance, respect for the Bible, and a fanatical desire to destroy images and idols of other religions. The emphasis was very much on discipline and obedience to the creed, and punishment for those who indulged in gambling and opium smoking was harsh.

Hung Hsiu-ch'üan did not himself claim to be divine, merely that he was the *hsiung-ti* (younger brother) of Jesus. This did not imply his divinity any more than the emperor's title Son of Heaven made him out to be divine. In the official portrait circulated among his followers, Hung is described as T'ien-tê, Celestial Virtue, which he chose as his reign title.

Progress of the Rebellion

On the first day of the Chinese New Year in 1851, Hung was proclaimed Heavenly King of the Heavenly Kingdom of Great Peace (T'aip'ing T'ien-kuo) at a ceremony held at dawn in the manner of imperial audiences. Hung wore imperial yellow robes with the imperial five-clawed dragon on them. The generals and five 'kings' had grown their hair long in the old Chinese style that had been abruptly ended by the Manchu who had forced Chinese to shave their heads except for the crown from which the queue was grown—a mark to distinguish Chinese from Manchu.

By the middle of 1852, the rebels had crossed from Kwangsi into Hunan province to the north, winning most of their battles with the imperial forces. When the T'aip'ing armies were advancing victoriously across the heart of Hunan, the *Tung-hua-lu* was still recording their advance as a retreat from Kwangsi, but admitting that: 'they have captured one town after another as if the country was undefended.... If the rebellion is allowed to spread in this way, how can it ever be suppressed?'

How indeed? Later still, in the *Tung-hua-lu* entry for October 12, 1852, we find:

'The total number of bandits outside Ch'ang-sha is no more than three or four thousand men, while our soldiers...number several times as many.... Why do the troops... attack in separate bodies, thus allowing the rebels to repulse their sorties with superior numbers?... There has never been found an occasion to wage real war against the brigands. After the brigands run far away our troops begin to notice it....'

The answer was partly that the imperial forces were unwilling troops, but more importantly that the T'aip'ing generals had understood the basic principles of guerrilla warfare. The essential was not to stand up to frontal attack, but to hit and run, to attack only when the enemy was at a disadvantage.

There are many parallels between the tactics of the early years of the T'aip'ing advance that swept all before it in a great arc across China to Nanking in Anhwei province, and the tactics of the Red Army of almost a century later as it tackled Japanese and later Nationalist armies. The present regime in China has called the T'aip'ing rebellion a revolution. And in some ways, in its social programmes and in the successful use of its ill-armed fighting units, this is true. But the social programmes were never put into widespread practice.

In January, 1853, Wuchang and Hangkow on the Yangtze were taken. The T'aip'ing forces crossed the great river, following its northern bank to Kiukiang and reaching Nanking, which fell to them on March 20. The Manchu garrison of the city—about 5,000 men—was slaughtered almost to a man. The rebels renamed the city T'ien-ching, Heavenly Capital. And there they stayed for the next eleven years.

Nanking, the T'aip'ing Capital

From the comparative security of the walled city, the T'aip'ing administration organized the populace into units consisting of groups of families. Each unit was under the supervision of a controller who had complete power over his charges. There was a common treasury for each unit, and a meeting place for worship. Food was shared, and the surplus food and money was sent to the central treasury of the Heavenly Kingdom. It has been said that the Nanking social organization was a kind of communism. But it resembles more a kind of Christian-based paternalism in that all power was really in the hands of the leaders and the populace as a whole had no say. Its real riches came fundamentally not so much from work as from plunder. And the leaders were not responsible to the people but (presumably) only to God.

The T'aip'ing programme of social and economic measures as written down, however, was basically an early form of socialism. It was undoubtedly the result in this respect not of any foreign political doctrine, but of a common-sense approach to righting the social injustice of the times which everyone in China could see all around—landless peasants subject to extortionate landlords who took the greater part of their produce in rent and interest, ancient customs such as the subjection of women, and ingrained habits like opium smoking and gambling. These were to be swept away in a reform movement that aimed to right such gross social evils in one huge programme of reform. The organ of government was to be a State Council headed by the Heavenly King and by his five assistants taking their moral and ethical powers from the more or less Protestant form of Christianity that Hung Hsiu-ch'üan had learned.

We can see that T'aip'ing ideas as shown in this programme were far in advance of anything known in China at that time. A whole new order in which ordinary people were the chief and most numerous benefactors was what they mapped out. Despite the strange insistence on a foreign religious backing, and despite the fact that the Heavenly King and his assistant 'kings' had insufficient administrative experience to make it work, and that they never had the peace and quiet in the country to do so—there was no precedent in all Chinese history for such ideas, sweeping away the two-thousand-year-old order of dynastic power backed by Confucianism and a scholar-bureaucracy.

In the countryside the T'aip'ing forces were harried by imperial and provincial armies, and it proved impossible to establish a kingdom in the proper sense of that word. Thus the land reform programme and other articles of the reforms laid down were never put into practice.

In the capital, the Heavenly King took less and less direct interest in the military situation, and his advisers complained of his decreasing capacity to make essential decisions. Like many an emperor of China, with the enormous riches of the city at his command, and complete power over its people, he turned into a pleasure-loving and rather remote figure, very far from the energetic and sincerely Christian man he had been at the start of the great movement that he inspired. When Nanking was eventually recaptured, he committed suicide and his body, exhumed by the victors from a sewer under the palace, was found wrapped in imperial yellow silk.

Lack of Foreign Recognition

Hung and other leaders had imagined that when they established the Heavenly Kingdom at Nanking they would be recognized by various foreign governments, and also that the religious communities among the foreigners would lend their support to a Chinese Christian state. They were mistaken in both ideas. French representatives, both priestly and lay, visited Nanking, as did the Governor of Hong Kong, Sir Samuel George Bonham, the British representative in China. Protestant missionaries paid visits also. While all these visitors to the T'aip'ing came away with the knowledge that there were aspects of Christianity in T'aip'ing beliefs, the Christian visitors could find no room for a form of Christianity that was different from their own varieties. Christianity, each of them argued, took this or that established form and unless Hung would submit to instruction from properly qualified Christian teachers, his Heavenly Kingdom could not be acceptable, and must be judged to be heretical.

On the political side, the opposition to the T'aip'ing movement and government at Nanking and elsewhere was inspired more by expediency. By the time that the Treaty of Tientsin was eventually ratified in 1860 (after the capture of Peking and the sacking of the imperial Summer Palaces), the foreign powers had achieved what they wanted in China. The Manchu government was virtually in their hands—especially from the financial point of view. This came about because of the vast indemnity it had to pay the British and French, for which it had to raise money. When forces friendly to the T'aip'ing armies, injudiciously attempting to capture that stronghold of foreign trade and power—Shanghai—overran the customs house, its Chinese head fled. Later, the foreign powers arranged with the Manchu government to take over the running and control of the Chinese Maritime Customs service in order to extract the greatest possible revenue. This suited both the foreigners and the Manchu government. It was therefore to the advantage of the foreign powers in China to keep the Manchu on the throne. The T'aip'ing movement was a threat and could not be recognized without danger to foreign interests.

There is an interesting comment, not untinged with national jealousy, in the diary of a French naval officer, de Marolles, on action taken against the rebels.

'Today the French and British admirals have decided to undertake a series of expeditions against the T'aip'ings, whose destructive deeds keep increasing as a result of the Chinese authorities' incapacity and cowardice. It was of great importance to the British that the silk- and tea-growing areas continue to ship their products to Shanghai, and that the opium grown in Bengal further poison the Chinese....'

Brouillion: Memoire....

The Defeat of the T'aip'ing

After 1853, the energy and success of the T'aip'ing greatly diminished. They lost numbers of their best military men, and their leadership was progressively poorer. They also encountered the opposition of the scholar-gentry class whose strongly Confucian outlook made them enemies not only of rebellion as such but most especially a rebellion that aimed to dispossess them and change the structure of state power. Nonetheless, the T'aip'ing were probably over a million strong. A brief revival of energy in the early 1860s under the leadership of the Loyal King, Li Hsiu-ch'eng, threw the coastal provinces into panic, and Soochow fell to his armies.

The Viceroy Li Hung-chang photographed some years after the T'aip'ing rebellion was suppressed. He is wearing his string of beads, official hat, and robes with the embroidered square on the chest denoting his rank

But meanwhile, in 1860, a British and French force had driven the rebels away from a nervous Shanghai and its community, and provincial armies led by the three great Chinese of the period were slowly gaining strength in the country. Li Hung-chang, who first fought them in his native Anhwei province in 1853, later joined Tsêng Kuo-fan to fight them again in 1859. And although he disagreed with Tsêng and left, when the latter recaptured Anking, he was invited to rejoin this force. The third commander, Tso Tsung-t'ang, fought in Chekiang and was later governor of that province and very active against the rebel armies. The organization of these provincial armed forces came very much as a reaction of the scholar-gentry classes against the threat to their own established position in the hierarchy of the Chinese power system. The T'aip'ing attempt to take Shanghai lost them any sympathy they might have gained from foreign interests. One more source of potential support was the anti-Manchu secret societies, but these found the Christian element in T'aip'ing life abhorrent, and they did not assist.

A Chinese painting showing the destruction of an army of 'Yüeh bandits'. (Yüeh is an old name for Kwangtung and Kwangsi provinces, and the T'aip'ing rebels were originally called this.) The rebels are destroying a temple on Chin Shan (centre). To the right, the governor of Chingkiang sits on top of the city wall, having ordered his troops out to destroy the rebels. Similarly, the governor of Yangchou (left) has his troops attacking the rebels, some of whom are being led into the town as prisoners. This is an extremely interesting compression into one picture of an actual event, in a most expressive and graphic manner

Left, a painting of General Gordon wearing his mandarin robes with one of the banners given by the emperor (on the table, left)—each of which empowered him to conscript a certain number of men to his army. Right, General Gordon's mandarin cap with its plumes of distinction given by the emperor, and its false queue of black silk threads. Gordon's Christian prayer book, given him by his mother, a large dark seal and its impression of the characters for his name lie beside it, while some of the banners are in the stand behind. These objects are in the museum of Gordon's regiment, the Royal Engineers, Chatham, England

In the early 1860s rebel-held cities began to fall one by one to armies loyal to the Manchu—the Hsiang Braves of Tsêng Kuo-fan, the Huai Army of the brilliant statesman Li Hung-chang, and the Chekiang armies of Tso Tsung-t'ang. In 1860 an American 'soldier of fortune' named Frederick Townsend Ward backed by money from Shanghai merchants (at first Chinese, and later also foreign) organized an army to protect the city, and as we have seen, drove off the T'aip'ing. This force under Ward, who was later killed in action, was an effective one especially in defence, and it was the same force that Captain (later General) Charles Gordon, known as 'Chinese Gordon', took over with such success. But the real contribution of Gordon to the suppression of the T'aip'ing rebellion was in his effective training of Chinese troops and the brilliant manner in which he deployed them—always surprising the by now inefficient command of the enemy. The T'aip'ing armies were eventually beaten in 1864 by the provincial armies and by the imperial army with the aid of Gordon's force. Despite the somewhat grudging tributes to him paid by Li Hung-chang, it is historically certain that Gordon's recapture of the cities of Chekiang province permitted troops under the direct command of Tsêng Kuo-fan's brother to take the long-held rebel capital of Nanking. Thus ended the most serious threat to its survival that the Manchu dynasty had so far experienced.

The Effects of the T'aip'ing Rebellion

The loss of at least ten million lives in the fifteen years of the rebellion (some sources put the number at twenty million) was a disaster, even in populous China. The ravages of both T'aip'ing and loyal armies threw the affairs of a dozen of the richest provinces into utter confusion. With the breakdown of administration and of traditional morality, poverty, famine, and banditry spread. The consequent loss of revenue from uncollectable taxes meant that the government found it harder to restore order because of impoverishment. And it was during this time, late in the rebellion, that large armies thrown against the rebels had to be supplied and paid; and a further burden on the state resources—the huge indemnity demanded in the Treaty of Tientsin by the foreign powers—had also to be paid. Manchu reaction, far from instituting reasonable economies, was to increase taxation on a populace already heavily taxed and also heavily 'squeezed' by corrupt officials.

The recruiting and arming of the provincial armies which eventually overcame the forces of the rebels, was the beginning of a process in which the Peking government after 1860 began to appoint greater numbers of Chinese (instead of Manchu) to high positions in the provinces. The historical tendency of the huge land mass of China, in times of weak central control, to split up into several more or less self-contained parts was encouraged by these factors, and the process continued for the remainder of the Ch'ing dynasty.

The introduction of a tax on goods in transit from one place to another (the *likin* tax, first mentioned in 1853) was one of the most serious mistakes of the government. At a time when domestic trade of all kinds needed direct and strong encouragement it came under taxation that tended to deter the movement of goods from place to place, and hence encouraged illegal movement, banditry and other forms of lawlessness.

The harsh treatment by the T'aip'ing of those who would not subscribe to their form of belief, treatment quite as unchristian as that meted out to the victims of the inquisition in Europe long before, became common knowledge in China and turned Chinese away from any attractions that Christianity might otherwise have had. To the ordinary man and woman, Christianity—whether the T'aip'ing variety or those other types preached by missionaries who seemed often to quarrel about their subject and to contradict each other—was a single foreign religion. The upsurge of anti-foreign and anti-Christian feeling in China in the latter part of the nineteenth century was in part caused by this.

One strange but financially beneficial side-effect of the rebellion was, as we have noted, the formation of the Chinese Maritime Customs staffed by well-paid officials and led by Europeans. The head of this British-administered service from 1863 to 1908 was a remarkable man named Sir Robert Hart. Under his intelligent direction, the Maritime Customs expanded its activities in many ways. A postal and telegraph service was introduced, European officers were encouraged to learn Chinese, Chinese employees learned how a Western organization worked with efficiency and without corruption. Moreover, Hart's attitude to the Chinese set a good example by encouraging Europeans to regard themselves as the equals and not the superiors of their Chinese colleagues.

The early success of the T'aip'ing encouraged other rebellions: the Nien Fei in the northern provinces between 1853 and 1868, the Muslims both in Yunnan and in the northwest, where the Hui people are numerous, from 1855 to 1873, and the rebellion of the numerically strong Miao tribes in Kweichow province. All these revolts were suppressed by about 1878.

The pathetic weakness of China, which could only with difficulty suppress internal revolts and was powerless against the external world of the West, was not lost on the foreigners. Nor was it missed by the intelligent minds of such men as the three great officials whose exertions had been instrumental in suppressing the T'aip'ing— Li Hung-chang, Tsêng Kuo-fan, and Tso Tsung-t'ang. The Western powers proceeded to support the unpopular Manchu dynasty which, now financially in their power to a large extent, could be manipulated so that the maximum trade benefits were wrung from its reluctant but powerless administration.

A majority of Chinese resented foreign intervention but saw no way to stop it. But a small number of intelligent men began to think about rational means of strengthening their country and saving a way of life that had endured so long and had produced so much that was of value. We will follow both these and also other elements in the stream of events in the turbulent times ahead.

5 Japan and the West

IN 1543 a Portuguese ship was blown off course and arrived by chance at a small island south of Kyushu. The Japanese appeared to have welcomed the crew, and to have shown great interest in their muskets. In the following years other Portuguese ships did a thriving trade with Japan. Initially the Portuguese acted as carriers of Chinese goods, chiefly silk, but later they brought European manufactured goods such as telescopes and clocks. The Japanese quite soon learned how to make firearms for themselves. After Macau was settled by Portuguese (1557), the Great Ship, as it was called, made regular trading visits.

	Japan and the West
1543	The Portuguese arrive. Introduction of firearms
1549	St. Francis Xavier arrives in Kyushu. The beginning of the Jesuit missionary movement
1571	The beginning of Nagasaki as a port for trade with the West
1587	Hideyoshi's decree expelling Christian missionaries. Traders permitted to remain. Successive persecutions of Japanese Christians
1609	Dutch 'factory' established at Hirado
1613	English 'factory' established at Hirado
1622–23	The most severe Christian martyrdoms
1623	The English abandon their Hirado 'factory'
1624	Contact with the Spaniards forbidden
1639	Expulsion of Portuguese traders
1641	Dutch permitted to trade only at the islet of Deshima in the harbour of Nagasaki
1720	Lifting of the ban on import of Western books containing no mention of Christianity. *Bangaku* (barbarian learning) now more politely called *rangaku* (Dutch learning)
1804	The Russian envoy Rezanov visits Nagasaki
1808	The British ship *Phaeton* visits Nagasaki
1811	Translation bureau established to render Dutch books into Japanese
1846	Commodore Biddle of the United States visits Edo Bay and Uraga
1852	Visit of Russians to Shimoda
1853	Arrival of Commodore Matthew C. Perry at Uraga
1854	Second arrival of Commodore Perry and the signing of the Treaty of Kanagawa (March 31). Establishment of trading posts at Shimoda and Hakodate Signature of a treaty with Britain (October 14)
1855	Signature of a treaty with Russia (February 7)
1856	American Consul General Townsend Harris arrives at Shimoda
1857	Signature of a treaty with the Dutch (October)
1858	Signature of a commercial treaty with the U.S. (July 29)—the Treaty of Edo

Japanese artists struggled hard to represent the large and, to them, clumsy Portuguese in their equally surprising clothes, when they came to Japan. Their servants were often from countries already conquered by the Portuguese, like this negro holding the parasol over his master's head. Perhaps the greatest surprise, and the most difficult thing for the Japanese to draw was the wide and round European eyes

Portuguese carracks (a type of armed merchant galleon) of the kind that first came to Japan

Christianity

Christian missionaries were not slow to avail themselves of the chance to go to Japan. The name that stands out above all others is that of the Jesuit St. Francis Xavier who landed at Kagoshima on Kyushu in 1549. He began his mission with the full backing of the Lord of Satsuma—the local clan ruler—and had considerable success. By the end of the century, Jesuit missionaries in Japan were claiming (probably with some exaggeration in order to impress their Order in Europe) 300,000 converts. Certainly their immediate success tells a completely different story to that near-total failure in making converts experienced by Matteo Ricci in China at the end of the sixteenth century and the beginning of the seventeenth.

What were the reasons? We cannot be wholly certain, but the internal situation in Japan seems responsible in various ways.

During the preceding Ashikaga shogunate Japanese ships had sailed far from home in search of trade goods. After 1615, *shuinjo*—meaning vermillion-stamped permits— were issued in huge numbers by the *bakufu*, allowing mariners to visit Macau, Thailand, the Philippines, and even more distant Southeast Asian countries. Ieyasu even sent trading representatives across the Pacific to Nueva Hispania, as Mexico was then called, to open mercantile relations. The feudal lords who were mostly responsible for this maritime trade grew rich on the proceeds. But also, their outlook naturally came to include interest in the outside world and its ideas and doctrines. Moreover, the introduction of firearms and the use of superior Portuguese navigational skills had been of great assistance to the feudal lords. In fact there was competition between feudatories on the east and west coasts for the visits of Portuguese ships, and the use of firearms in civil strife became widespread. The missionaries who came with the traders, and were obviously held in deep respect by them, naturally enough, had to be accepted. The price of muskets and technological information was acceptance of Christian missions. But it must also be noted that, in Francis Xavier, Christianity had a man of extreme dedication to the task of setting Asia on fire for Christ, as he put it.

Both Nobunaga and, at first, his successor Hideyoshi were cordial in their approach to Christianity, but in 1587 came Hideyoshi's edict banning all missionaries from Japan, although permitting traders to remain. His reasons for this step seemed to have been fear either that the Portuguese would take sides with some great feudatory, or that Christianity itself would form a focus of unity in some coalition aiming to usurp his power. Other factors were the rivalry between Jesuits and the not long arrived Spanish monks from the Philippines, the intolerance of some priests and converts which caused them to destroy Buddhist and Shinto shrines, and the knowledge of Portuguese territorial acquisitions at Goa and other places.

From 1587 onward there were other edicts and persecutions, and under the shogun Ieyasu until his death in 1616 drastic measures were taken against high-ranking Japanese Christians. Under his successor Hidetada it seems the shogunate felt sufficiently strongly entrenched to complete the process of persecution of ordinary Japanese Christians, under which they showed immense bravery and devotion to the faith. Such was the ferocity of the persecution that 37,000 Christian peasants and others staged a last stand in a castle on the Shimbara peninsula near Nagasaki.

Above left, Oda Nobunaga, the *daimyo* who ruled over three provinces which lie around the modern city of Nagoya to the east of Kyoto. By his seizure of the capital in 1568, he made himself virtual dictator in central Japan. He laid siege to the great temple-castle of the Pure Land Sect at Osaka and captured it after ten years. He was assassinated by a vassal in 1582. Right, Nobunaga's successor was his best general, Toyotomi Hideyoshi, seen here in his formal robes in this remarkable painting. Rising from the humblest ranks of Japanese society, he eventually fell victim to the desire for world conquest. His first step was to conquer Korea on the way to conquering China, but he died in 1598, and the plan was not pursued

The shogun Ieyasu. His robes are decorated with the *mon*, or crest, of the Tokugawa family. His obsession was with constructing a political system in Japan that would be strong enough to survive his own reign

They held out for some months against all that the Shogun could throw against them, but eventually were slaughtered wholesale. Christianity then died out in Japan.

Isolation

Japan entered on a period of isolation (*sakoku-seisaku*, the closed country) enforced by shogun decree. The English, established at Hirado, abandoned their factory there in 1623, and the Spaniards were forbidden entry in 1624. Twelve years later, Japanese were forbidden to leave the country, and the size of ships built was limited in order to make overseas voyages impossible. Portuguese traders were expelled in 1638. By 1640 Japan was effectively isolated from the outside world. Portuguese envoys who arrived in that year were beheaded, although they came simply to seek a renewal of the trade relations of the past years. Only a limited number of Chinese, Koreans, and Dutch were permitted to trade at the islet of Deshima in Nagasaki harbour.

There is a contemporary European report on the enforcement of the closed country policy:

'[The shogun Iemitsu] having ordered for three successive years, maps, globes, and an explanation of the way to Europe, after investigating the size of the world, the multitude of its countries, and the smallness of Japan [which had not before been realized]—he was greatly surprised, and heartily wished that his land had never been visited by any Christian.'

Francois Caron: *Dagh-Register Batavia in voce* 21. iv. 1641

The period between 1600 and 1868 has been characterized as one of mature feudalism—Ieyasu being the shogun who put the finishing touches on the process begun by his two predecessors in office, Nobunaga and Hideyoshi. We have already noted the outline of the social structure in Japan at this time which (from 1615) is known also as the Edo Period. Ieyasu finally established his *bakufu* at Edo (now Tokyo) in that year after two decisive battles against rivals. The social structure then established was a strict and authoritarian one. The *kuge*, or nobles of the Court, had little power or influence. The *buke*, or warrior class, was the ruling class under which the farmers and the *chonin*, or townspeople, worked—a very different state of affairs from that in China where the order of importance was scholar (ruling class), farmer, artisan, merchant, with the warrior relegated almost outside the pale of society altogether. The accent in society in Tokugawa Japan was on strict obedience. In each class the bond of duty of each man to his master was clearly spelled out and enforced.

The warrior *daimyo*, formerly active in military positions, now in time of internal peace lived a curious form of life forced upon them by the shoguns for fear of uprisings against their rule. We have noticed how the *daimyo* were required to reside at Edo every alternate year, (*sankin-kotai*, attendance by turn) leaving wives and families there during the years they spent on their own estates. They were also forbidden to build new castles, or to enlarge the fortifications of those they had. The Edo government formed what was probably the first secret police force—the *metsuke*—to check on *daimyo* activities.

Edo, a mere village before 1600, had a population of 500,000 by 1723, and reached the million mark by 1800. Naturally this phenomenal growth meant the rapid growth of facilities for the *daimyo* and their families, and for the growing and wealthy merchant class that in its turn expanded to deal with the business generated by the expansion of population. Rice, previously the chief medium of exchange, was gradually replaced by metal currency, and a money economy developed. The needs of the *daimyo*—to upkeep a large town house for their families and their numerous retainers in Edo,—and the strain put on their resources by having to pay for this as well as their country establishments, were such that they were often forced to borrow large sums of money from the merchants of Edo. The merchants therefore became bankers as well, and the wealth of their class grew rapidly in comparison to, and at the expense of, the *daimyo*.

Decline of the Shogunate

The *daimyo* became increasingly a demoralized class—resembling in this respect the Manchu in China who, having conquered the country, found no further need for their military prowess, and often no other outlet for their energies. A warrior in peacetime is generally under-employed, and his standard of conduct and sense of responsibility as a member of an élite, tend gradually to diminish.

Meanwhile, as the morale of the military class decreased, that of the mercantile class rose. A comfortable, well-dressed, pleasure-loving society of merchants constituting a bourgeoisie grew up in Edo, and at the turn of the seventeenth century the city had one of the liveliest societies anywhere in the world. The *bakufu*, shocked and not a little perturbed at this emergence of a new society unforeseen in

The retinue of a *daimyo* on the road. The cost of transporting the *daimyo* and his retinue to and from his domains and Edo every alternate year slowly weakened the economic strength of the *daimyo* class. It was intended, however, merely to prevent rebellion against the shogunate

their scheme of things, took repressive measures in the form of new taxation hitting at the wealthy. Between 1786 and 1837, the sternest laws were announced by the shogun Ienari. These included the decree that anyone with an income of less than 50,000 bushels of rice was forbidden to buy anything new, and others forbidding women to employ barbers to dress their hair, and turning all barbers into washermen.

The alarm of the ruling Japanese can be seen in the detailed sternness of such edicts. At the same time the military cult of *bushido* was officially fostered, emphasizing the principle of loyalty to leaders that had been the code of the warriors of the past in times of strife. The teachings of a Chinese Confucian philosopher, Chu Hsi of the Sung dynasty, were also promoted as a replacement for Buddhism which had little or no influence in the Edo period since its eclipse under the disapproval of Nobunaga. The philosophy of Chu Hsi was a ready-made instrument for the shoguns at this time, since it emphasized loyalty in an atmosphere of moderation, and underlined the need to keep things as they were. During the seventeenth and eighteenth centuries Chu Hsi's brand of ethics reigned supreme in Japan.

Beginnings of Nationalism

The very supremacy of a Chinese philosophy aroused the enmity of increasing sections of the Japanese, and a revival of the Shinto cult and Japanese literature came about as a direct result. Scholars such as Mabuchi (1697-1769) and Motoori (1730-1801) promoted these studies and began to support the claims of the imperial dynasty.

The eighteenth century was a time of numerous rice riots caused by the distress which increased as the *bakufu's* policies led to impoverishment of the *daimyo* and enrichment of the merchant class. Rice riots were invariably suppressed with savage retaliatory force, but this only fed the fires of unrest and resentment. Conditions were sometimes so bad as to necessitate infanticide.

> 'One boy only is kept, the rest destroyed. If two or three be preserved, the parents are ridiculed for cowardice.'
>
> Chikusan Nikai (an economic historian)

And while the *bakufu* continued to rule Japan, real power slid into the hands of the merchants, to whom the *daimyo* sold their rice allocations, their estates, and from whom they were forced to borrow at huge interest rates. To rescue the *daimyo* from their sad state, now and then their debts to the merchants were officially cancelled. But the interest rates on new loans soon overtook this measure. The currency was debased by the government in order to curb the merchants, but this merely encouraged more business in the new currency. Eventually the *bakufu* threw the richest merchants into jail, but it was not long before others took their place.

This process by which the merchant class rose steadily to power as feudalism slowly and on the whole peacefully declined was broadly similar to what had happened in England some three centuries earlier. There were peasant and other uprisings in increasing numbers as the eighteenth century gave way to the nineteenth.

A Japanese painting of a Dutchman.
There is a strong element of caricature
in the work—the clumsy shoes,
the feminine attitude,
the immensely long pipe

But there was no uprising in any way comparable to that of the T'aip'ing rebellion in China.

The rising tide of nationalism among scholars and a small group of intellectuals could not be stopped. These men, and also a growing number of penniless *daimyo*, came to the conclusion that Japan needed a change of rule. Their study of ancient written records led them to the opinion that the emperor was the rightful ruler of Japan, and that he should rule, and not just reign in Kyoto as a figurehead.

This factor and another, the rise of Shinto at the expense of Buddhism, reinforced each other. Shinto emphasized the worth of traditional Japanese beliefs, tending to confirm opinions that shogun and *bakufu* were a form of government resulting from usurpation of the imperial power.

The Outside World

Although Japan had been a closed country since 1640, the Japanese had prudently left opportunities for learning about what was going on in the rest of the world. At Deshima where a handful of Dutch had all along been allowed to trade, knowledge of foreign countries filtered in. The shogun Yoshimune who came to power in 1716 was by chance a man interested in scientific subjects. It was he who issued an edict permitting the import of foreign books so long as there was no mention in them of Christianity. Japanese scholars were thereby able to study not only Western science and technological subjects, but also to learn of various political and military events which were later to affect them. These studies that, under the term *bàngaku*, or barbarian learning, had been going on ever since 1640, were now called politely *rangaku*, or Dutch learning. In the shogun capital of Edo a school of languages was started as one of the results of the 1716 edict. Not only Dutch, but also Russian, English, and French languages were taught there.

A Dutch East Indiaman of the Edo period. The artist has made an attempt (perhaps from memory) to write its name on the stern

Opposition to the closed Japan policies grew as Japanese discovered the facts about Russian opening up of the great Siberian lands, and also of the Kamchatka Peninsula, the Kuril Islands, and the Island of Sakhalin which form the borders of the Sea of Okhotsk to the north of the northernmost Japanese island called Hokkaido. These events were very near home, it seemed.

From the outer world Japanese also learned of the eclipse of other Western powers in the orient by the British. The establishment of British India, the settlement of Singapore, and finally the capitulation of the Chinese government to British demands in the Treaty of Nanking, and the colonization of Hong Kong—all these things must have seemed signs of danger.

It was obvious to numbers of intelligent Japanese in the first part of the nineteenth century that Western powers were far ahead in military power, and in technology. They noticed that, broadly, Western systems of government were well suited to dealing with the advances made in industrial expansion. It was obvious also that the means of government in Japan which had remained largely the same for a long time somehow had to be changed.

Official policy toward foreign countries, however, remained largely unchanged, and many attempts in the nineteenth century by British, Americans, and Russians to persuade Japan to open her ports were repulsed.

Commodore Perry Arrives

The Americans were the most urgent of Japan's suitors. Their whaling vessels had for long been fishing the North Pacific and the seas around Japan, and American cargo vessels bound for China in the 1840s passed quite close to the Japanese islands. They wanted facilities ashore to take on water and stores.

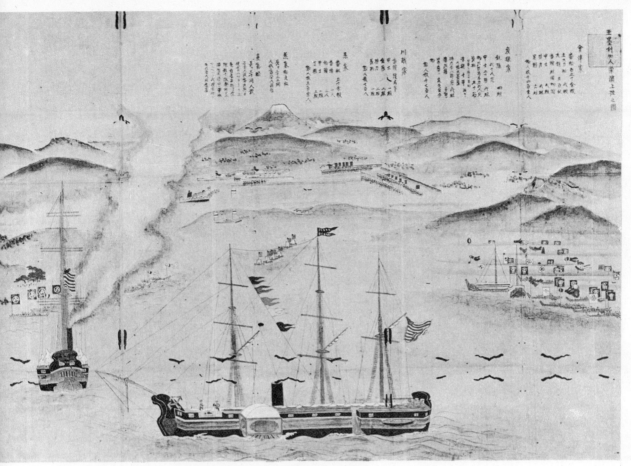

A Japanese painting of the squadron of Commodore Perry as it arrived in Japan on his first visit in 1853

The American government decided eventually to force open Japan's doors. A sizeable naval force under the command of Commodore Matthew C. Perry steamed into Edo (Tokyo) Bay on July 8, 1853. A letter from the President of the United States addressed to the emperor was presented. In fact, Perry's force was not the first to be sent. In 1846, two years after Caleb Cushing signed for America the Treaty of Wanghsia with the Chinese, a force under Commodore Biddle had arrived in Edo Bay but was soon warned to depart. Commodore Perry's force was the result of American opinion that another attempt should be made.

The American President's letter requested trading rights, coal for American steamships, protection for shipwrecked American seamen, and the beginning of friendly relations between the two states. The force of what the Japanese called the four 'black ships' then sailed off to the Ryukyu Islands, leaving notice they would return early the following year.

Matthew Calbraith Perry was an excellent choice for the task of effecting American entry to Japan. He had in fact many qualities similar to those of General Douglas MacArthur who played an even more important role in Japanese history after World War II. Perry was a careful planner, had a strict sense of discipline, and his natural dignity and perhaps pomposity, combined with a dramatic approach, made him an acceptable negotiator to the Japanese. His approach matched their own formal one in several particulars.

The somewhat pompous Commodore Matthew Perry. He was nearly sixty years of age when he went to Japan, an astute and autocratic man. With the knowledge that his predecessor Commodore Biddle had been warned to act extremely cautiously in Japan, and that this had seemed mere weakness to the Japanese, Perry wrote his own instructions. These gave him a very free hand. Only perhaps General MacArthur at the end of World War II had such sweeping powers to make decisions, and he was quite conscious of the parallel between himself and Perry a century before

The reaction to the American ships with their large and evidently powerful guns anchored at Uraga, the narrow entry to Edo Bay, was at first one of great confusion. The capital Edo lay, as the Japanese realistically noted, at the mercy of Commodore Perry's guns, as did much of its food supply that came by ship and would have to run an American blockade if the foreigners so decided.

The government split into two factions: those who simply wanted the expulsion of the foreign force; and the rest who saw plainly that in the face of the American force, the realistic thing to do was to accept American demands. The shogun and his *bakufu* at Edo then took the most unusual step of asking (for the first time in six hundred years) the advice of the emperor in Kyoto. They also asked advice of the *daimyo*. The answer from both of these sources was the conservative one: expel the foreigners and keep Japan intact.

The *bakufu*, however, knew this advice was impossible to carry out. The shogun (whose title, it will be recalled, signified Barbarian-quelling Generalissimo) was ironically quite unable to fulfil that task, and in fact died a few days after Perry sailed away. The *bakufu* strengthened coastal defenses, abolished the restrictions on repairing feudal castles, and permitted large ships once more to be built. But it was increasingly obvious that the shogunate was in its last decline. The period between Perry's first visit in 1853, and 1868 is known as the *bakumatsu*—the end (*matsu*) of the shogunate (*bakufu*).

The Signing of Treaties

Perry returned to Japan with a force of eight ships in February 1854. Three of the ships were steam frigates (actually one quarter of the American navy at that time). The Japanese tried to negotiate with Perry at Uraga (at the entry to Edo Bay where he had anchored before) but Perry insisted on steaming further up to Kanagawa—now part of Yokohama, which at that time was a mere village.

With a great show of ceremony, Perry was given the 'emperor's' negative answer to his demands. (It should be noted that Perry still did not know he was dealing with the shogun and not the emperor). The Japanese cleverly and secretly used a Japanese who knew English, and were therefore able to judge what was said between the Americans, unknown to them. Several days of negotiation followed and the Japanese saw they could do nothing but accept American demands.

The Treaty of Kanagawa was signed on March 31, 1854. By its terms, the Americans were allowed to provision their ships and to do a small amount of trading at two ports. One was Shimoda, a small harbour rather isolated from the main mass of Japan at the far end of the mountainous Izu Peninsula; the other was Hakodate far away from Edo on the northern island of Hokkaido. There was a provision for shipwrecked Americans to receive good treatment, and one American consular agent was permitted to reside at Shimoda. The Americans, learning from the Chinese treaties, included the 'most-favoured-nation' clause whereby privileges granted to other nations would automatically be theirs too.

Before the signing ceremony an exchange of presents took place. The American gifts included a small locomotive set up on a circular track, a complete telegraph set by which to send messages, various farm implements, and a hundred gallons of whisky. After witnessing a display of *sumo* wrestling by the Japanese, the Americans put on an impromptu minstrel show. Perry then sailed up and past Edo, and departed—having succeeded in opening the closed door of Japan by an inch or two.

Perry had returned to Japan earlier than he intended, for in his absence he had heard of the arrival of a Russian mission under Vice-admiral Putiatin. Putiatin, however, failed to negotiate either a commercial treaty or a boundary settlement concerning the Kuril islands north of Hokkaido. But when the Americans concluded the Treaty of Kanagawa, the *bakufu* soon signed treaties with Britain (October 14, 1854), with Russia (February 7, 1855), and with the Dutch (October, 1857).

The treaty with Britain opened the Japanese door somewhat further. Admiral Sir James Stirling managed to obtain permission for British ships to use the remote Hakodate, as had the Americans, but he also obtained the use of Nagasaki with its fine harbour.

The Russian treaty gave them permission to use all three ports, and settled the boundary between Japan and Russia in the Kuril islands. The boundary on Sakhalin Island was, however, not settled. The Russians were granted extraterritorial rights.

Among the presents brought to Japan by Perry was this set of machines for transmitting telegraphs which the Japanese found fascinating

A conference between Commodore Perry and his staff (their names below at the left) at Yokohama in March, 1854. The representatives of the shogun (whom Perry still thought were emissaries of the emperor) are seated right and named below. In the centre, identified by the letter C, is the Japanese Moriyami who interpreted in Dutch

Commodore M. Perry
Commander H. A. Adams
A. L. C. Portman · Interpreter
D. H. Perry Secretary
S. W. Williams · Chinese Interpreter.

Conference room at
Yokohama Kanagawa
Japan.
March 1854.

B Hayashi Daigaku no kami
Ido Tsusima · no · kami
Isawa Mimasaka no kami
Udono Minbu Shiogu
Matsusaki Michitaro

C Moriyama Dutch Interpreter

The peaceful signing of this series of treaties with the Western powers was in sharp contrast to the wars and intimidating acts which resulted in the signing of treaties with China. Several factors contributed to the ease with which these first settlements between Japan and the West were made. First, the treaties were obtained without violence because the Japanese State Council, against the expressed opinion of the majority of Japanese, took a realistic attitude to the military weakness of Japan in relation to America and her fleet. Second, the Americans and others knew that in obtaining agreements with Japan less was at stake commercially than in China. Japan, they considered, was a small country and had not the great trade potential of vast China. Third, although it revealed the extreme weakness of the shogunate, its leading members had little to lose in signing, since it must have been obvious to them that the *bakufu* was a dying institution.

PART TWO

THE WEST IMPOSES ITS WILL

6 Two More Treaties

T HE Treaty of Tientsin, signed in 1858, was due for ratification in Peking in June, 1859. As arranged, the British and French ministers (The Honourable Frederick Bruce, brother of Lord Elgin, and Count Bourboulon of France) proceeded to Tientsin on their way to Peking, but were diverted by the Chinese to Peitang—a port used for the reception of envoys from tributary states. An attempt to take the Taku Forts failed because the Chinese had strengthened them since the events of the year before. The ministers returned to Shanghai, their mission unfulfilled.

Realizing that China either did not intend to ratify the treaty, or would try to delay doing so for as long as possible, the Western powers sent for troop reinforcements. In March, 1860 they dispatched an ultimatum demanding immediate apology for the treatment of the ministers, ratification of the treaty, strict adherence to its terms, and a further indemnity.

The Chinese rejected these demands. They felt strong enough to do so, now that the barbarians were not actually at the gates of Peking. Britain and France declared war on China on June 24, 1860. Lord Elgin and Baron Gros, accompanied by a force of British, French, and Indian troops 16,000 strong arrived at the Peiho once more. The Taku Forts were now easily enough taken by August 21, and the allied forces proceeded by land toward Tientsin, which was also occupied with little resistance. Negotiations were conducted with Chinese envoys sent from Peking at several stages in the campaign, notably with Prince Kung. When a negotiating party under a white flag was taken prisoner by the Chinese and sent to Peking, Lord Elgin and Baron Gros informed Prince Kung that unless they were released the armies would attack Peking itself.

At this point the Emperor Hsien-fêng left the capital for his summer retreat at Jehol, taking with him among a numerous court his secondary wife Tz'u-hsi, the mother of his only son. The emperor died at Jehol the following year, 1861. He was succeeded by this five-year-old son who became the T'ung-chih Emperor. To negotiate with the foreigners, Hsien-fêng left Prince Kung, his brother. Twenty-one

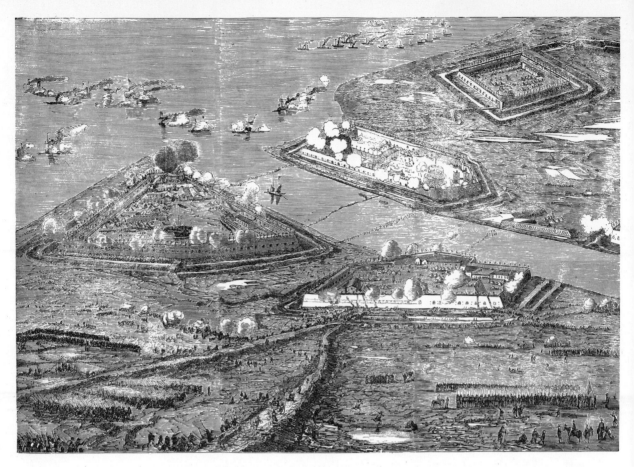

Above, a general view of the attack on the forts at the mouth of the Pei River, forts whose primary importance was to guard the river entry to Peking. This sketch was made in 1860

Below, the Anting Gate taken by the British and French forces. Through this gate they entered Peking. The artist was a special correspondent of the *Illustrated London News*. Note the British and French flags flying to the right of the gate-tower

The Emperor Hsien-fêng, a
contemporary Chinese painting

of the Western prisoners were already dead when the prince released the rest. The
allies entered Peking and occupied it. But it was thought that some further action
was needed to avenge the death of the British prisoners, and at the same time teach
the Chinese a lesson they would not forget. Lord Elgin ordered the destruction of
the old Summer Palace, the Yuan-ming-yuan, parts of which had been designed and
built by Jesuits long ago. This treasury of Chinese art was looted by uncontrolled
mobs of British and French officers and men, and burned to the ground. Prince
Kung then accepted the allied demands.

The Convention of Peking Signed

Ratifications of the Treaty of Tientsin were exchanged on October 24, 1860,
and a supplementary Convention of Peking was also signed. This provided that:

> Tientsin would be open to trade.
> The costs of the 1860 expedition to Peking, a total of 16 million taels of silver,
> should be paid by the Chinese to Britain and France.
> Canton would remain under foreign occupation until this indemnity was paid.
> Kowloon Point across the harbour from Hong Kong Island, and also Stone-
> cutter's Island, would be ceded to Britain.
> Church property confiscated since 1724 would be handed back to the Roman
> Catholic Church. Catholic missionaries would be allowed to rent or buy
> land anywhere in China and to construct buildings thereon.
> It was permitted to recruit Chinese labour for work abroad. (This was a
> straightforward legalization of the coolie trade.)

Russia seized the opportunity of expanding her existing treaty by negotiating a
Peking treaty of her own. By the 'most-favoured-nation' clause she gained all the
privileges of the other Western nations, and also obtained control of the whole
region between the Ussuri River and the sea.

Above, Lord Elgin, in a closed palanquin borne by numerous bearers, preceded by troops and cavalry, passes down a Peking avenue lined by allied soldiers standing shoulder to shoulder. The general view of Peking sketched at this time in 1860 remained quite similar to the view of the city until about fifteen years ago

Below, under the watchful and arrogant gaze of British and French soldiers, the first install-ment of the huge indemnity extracted from China under the Treaty of Tientsin, arrives at the port of Tientsin for shipment out of China

The Treaty of Edo Signed

After Commodore Perry had left Japan, the first American consul to Japan, a wealthy businessman named Townsend Harris, reached Shimoda in August 1856. His job was to work for a comprehensive commercial agreement with the Japanese, and he was successful. Soon after the 1858 Treaties of Tientsin were signed in China, the Japanese agreed to the terms of the Treaty of Edo. Agreement was reached in a climate of verbal threat. Harris implied that there was some danger of Japan's being attacked by France and Britain, which was not the case, and he stressed the contrasting friendly intentions of the United States. The Japanese attempted by every means in their power to delay the agreement. This was partly due to the fact that the *bakufu* was so weak that it had to make a show of obstructing the Americans in order to satisfy its opponents. The second Anglo-Chinese War and the signature of the Treaty of Tientsin with its harsh terms was probably more convincing to the Japanese than any argument of Harris that it would be better to sign with America than be forced to sign with Britain and France. On July 29, 1858 the treaty was signed. Its provisions were:

> Four more ports besides Shimoda and Hakodate should be opened. Edo, the capital, was one of these.
> Both Edo and Osaka should be open to the residence of foreigners.
> There should be an exchange of ministers and consuls.
> Import duties were to be imposed at low rates by a convention. The import of opium was forbidden.
> Americans were guaranteed extraterritorial rights and freedom of worship.
> America was granted 'most-favoured-nation' treatment.
> Revision of the treaty at the request of either nation could be demanded after four years.

Townsend Harris, the first American Consul in Japan. Harris was a wealthy man representing his country; in the case of diplomatic appointments, this is common practice even today

The Edo Treaty and the Second Treaty Settlement compared

Analysis of the contents of the treaties signed with China and Japan reveals large similarities.

> Both countries were *forced* to sign the treaties, China as the result of losing a war waged against her, Japan under threat of aggression.
> Both countries had their ports opened to foreign trade, China being perhaps more thoroughly opened by the permission extracted from her for use of the Yangtze river ports.
> Both countries were forced to accept resident representatives of Western governments in their capitals. In China the old office in charge of foreign relations (*Li-fan-yuan*) was replaced by the *Tsung-li ko-kuo shih-wu ya-men,* the Office in Charge of Affairs Concerning Foreign Nations (usually called the *Tsungli yamen*).
> Both countries were forced to fix tariffs dictated by the West.
> Both countries were made to accept Christianity, in the form of missionaries given freedom to convert their people.
> Both countries promised to observe the right of Westerners to extraterritoriality —that is, Westerners' immunity from Chinese or Japanese law.
> Both countries were forced to concede 'most-favoured-nation' treatment.

For China, the Second Treaty Settlement (as the Treaty of Tientsin together with the Convention of Peking were collectively named) went further than the treaties signed with Japan. Japan was not requested to surrender any territory, whereas China (which had already lost Hong Kong Island) had to cede the Kowloon Peninsula to Britain, and a huge tract of territory to Russia. Russia, by the Treaty of Aigun and the Convention of Peking, gained 350,000 sq. miles of Chinese land.

Whereas opium was made a legal import in China, the Japanese treaties forbade it. China had also to pay huge indemnities to the British and French, and to see its major port in the south, Canton, occupied until the money was paid. Not only were tariffs fixed, but the Chinese Customs Service was run by foreigners. By comparison, Japan was more lightly treated, retaining control of her own institutions and not being required to pay indemnities.

Yet the results in both China and Japan struck very deeply into the heart of each nation, with effects we will now see.

7 China, 1860–1894

FOR China, the signing of the Second Treaty Settlement in 1860 ushered in a long period of doubt and bewilderment in the minds of both the government and the intellectual section of the population. It also put relations between China and foreign powers on a footing which the foreigners called equality, but which was seen correctly by the Chinese as one of great inequality. China was internally weak, ruled by a faltering dynasty; the West was strong and in a period of expansionist activity in all fields.

The events of the period may best be considered under the two headings of internal affairs, and matters involving China and the Western powers and her near neighbours.

INTERNAL AFFAIRS

Opinion and Action—The T'ung-chih 'Restoration'

The former concubine Tz'u-hsi, who had risen to high rank since she had given the emperor his only son, masterminded a *coup d'état* on his death. When this child became emperor (T'ung-chih 1862–1875) she managed to take the reins of power as one of two regents (the other being Tz'u-an, the empress-consort, who took little interest in affairs of state). Prince Kung was appointed to a newly created position as Prince Adviser. The violently anti-foreign opinions of Tz'u-hsi had to be modified in the light of the 1860 treaty, and Prince Kung, the only one of the Manchu ruling

Prince Kung, uncle of Emperor T'ung-chih. Perhaps the wisest of Tz'u-hsi's councillors, he was unusually intelligent among the dull ruling Manchu family. It has been suggested that had he not died in 1898 the Boxer troubles would not have arisen, and Sino-Western relations might have taken a very different course

Tz'u-hsi, the empress dowager, surrounded by ladies of the court. This photograph was taken in 1903. Tz'u-hsi wears the famous pearl cape which formed part of the treasure amassed by the corrupt 'prime minister' Ho Shen at the court of the Emperor Ch'ien-lung. Her feet are encased in jewelled shoes fitted with square platforms several inches high

family who showed statesmanlike qualities, became the main agent in forming new policies.

In a revealing memorial to the Throne in January 1861, he wrote:

> 'Now the Nien rebellion is ablaze in the north and the T'aip'ing in the south...the barbarians take advantage of our weak position and try to control us. If we do not restrain our rage but continue the hostilities, we are liable to sudden catastrophe.... If we overlook the way they have harmed us and do not make any preparations against them, then we shall be bequeathing a source of grief to our sons and grandsons....'

He advocated acting strictly according to the treaties for the present, and the creation of new organs of administration to assist in this. Giving details of the new office of foreign affairs required to deal with the Western powers and their ministers in Peking (the Tsungli Yamen) he continued:

> 'As soon as the military campaigns are concluded and the affairs of the various countries are simplified, the new office will be abolished and its functions will again revert to the Grand Council...so as to accord with the old system.'

It was not in his mind to take any final new step in the area of Chinese dealings with foreigners, but rather to get back to the old ways as soon as possible.

Prince Kung also suggested the appointment of High Commissioners to 'facilitate the handling of affairs at the northern and southern ports'—the treaty ports. He also wanted two men each from Canton and Shanghai with a knowledge of written and spoken foreign languages to be stationed in Peking to advise and consult with the Tsungli Yamen. This proved to be the beginning of the *T'ung-wen Kuan*, or interpreters' college. Finally he wanted the conditions in each of the treaty ports and the contents of foreign newspapers reported to the Tsungli Yamen once a month.

The Tsungli Yamen, once created, did not in fact give way to the old methods of dealing with foreigners but remained much as Prince Kung outlined its functions until 1901, when it became a ministry of foreign affairs on the Western pattern.

The aims of Prince Kung seem to have been to keep the peace with the Western powers while internal problems such as the T'aip'ing rebellion were cleared up. His handling of the provincial administrators to whom he gave great freedom of action was in part responsible for the T'aip'ing defeat. The prince was not a man of outstanding ability, but he was wise enough to take advice. His main assistant in the Tsungli Yamen was Wen-hsiang (1818-1876), an able Manchu who had been brought up in poverty far from the luxuries of Peking, and whose outlook was more realistic than that of most Manchu.

The functioning of the Tsungli Yamen was only one aspect of the process of dynastic renewal which for a time breathed new life into the flagging Manchu regime in the 1860s. The defeat of the T'aip'ing and the pacification of the ravaged provinces, the restoration of law and order in the country, and the reduction in land tax together with other help to the agricultural economy, had an invigorating effect. The civil service examinations (suspended for some years because of troubled conditions) were begun again and the principles of Confucian morality were underlined. The Confucian philosophy that had formed and guided life and government in China for over two thousand years, had been a great unifying and strengthening factor. But its conservative nature was now to prove the stumbling-block in China's response to new and deeply disturbing conditions. Whatever new institutions and new methods were invented and applied to make the country more vigorous, these were always conceived within the orthodox framework of Confucianism. The leading roles were still played by Confucian scholar-statesmen. Once more, China sought the old goal of the 'Golden Age'. Whatever new things had to be introduced, they were there solely to promote a return to former and better times. Not only was there no revolution in thought, but there was not even an *evolution* of any real kind.

The Self-Strengthening Movement

Not only the T'ung-chih 'restoration' but also the wider self-strengthening movement must be seen against this unchanging backdrop of opinion.

Feng Kuei-fen (1809-1874) was probably the first to use the phrase *tzu-ch'iang* (to make ourselves strong) in relation to China's way out of her problems. He was a scholar-official with a wide experience of government who had served with Lin Tse-hsü and with Li Hung-chang. His learning embraced not only the Chinese classics but also mathematics, astronomy, geography, and agriculture—a fairly unusual catalogue of interests in a high official. It was at his suggestion that a school of Western languages was set up in Shanghai in 1863.

His forty essays written around 1860 were presented to Tsêng Kuo-fan who thought highly of them and wanted to have them published. The author declined the honour, but in fact they were eventually copied and, on the orders of the Kuang-hsü Emperor much later, in 1898, were the subject of discussion in all government offices.

The basis of Feng Kuei-fen's thinking is similar to that of a fellow reformer of a later date, Chang Chih-tung, whose famous phrase *Chung-hsueh wei-t'i, hsi-hsueh wei-yung* means: take Chinese studies (culture and values) for the base (basis of thought), and take Western studies for use (for practical matters). With this outlook, we can see how impossible it was for even the most intelligent and open-minded of Chinese at this time to break out of the cage of Confucian thinking and Confucian ideas.

Feng Kuei-fen was appalled that so few Western books on scientific subjects had been translated into Chinese, and that these were so little known in China.

> 'According to...the maps by the Westerners, there are not less than one hundred countries. From these...only the books of Italy, at the end of the Ming dynasty, and now those of England have been translated into Chinese, altogether several tens of books.... Western books on mathematics, mechanics, optics, light, chemistry, and other subjects contain the best principles of the natural sciences. In the books on geography, the mountains, rivers, strategic points, customs, and native products...are fully listed. Most of this information is beyond the reach of our people.'

Feng has nothing but contempt for the so-called linguists who serve as interpreters, calling them 'frivolous rascals and loafers' whose abilities reach to no more than a superficial knowledge 'of the barbarian language and occasional recognition of barbarian characters...limited to the names of commodities, numerical figures, and some slang expressions.... How can we expect them to pay attention to scholarly studies?' He recommends putting translation services on a sound footing by inviting Westerners to teach their languages. He also felt that mathematics was the basis of Western science. And he suggests that the libraries of the American Presbyterian and the London Missionary Society's presses, and the thousand volumes presented in 1847 by the 'Russian barbarians', be sent to the translators' schools.

Noting that many foreigners have learned Chinese and can read Chinese books, he says:

> '...our officers from generals down, in regard to foreign countries are completely uninformed. In comparison, should we not feel ashamed?'

As he sees it, the main problem is to control the foreigners, yet the 'pivotal function' is entrusted to the stupid 'interpreters'.

The gravity of his doubts and fears for China are underlined by his appreciation of the fact of China's great size in comparison with small Britain and France. 'Why are they small yet strong?' he asks. 'Why are we large yet weak?'

His answers are that China makes poor use of her manpower and natural resources, and her words do not always accord with her deeds. He ridicules the policy of sowing dissention among the foreigners, saying that China cannot do this without knowledge of foreign languages and diplomatic usages. He recommends ship and armament industries under foreign supervision, and the unheard-of step of making proficient students in these fields equal in status to the scholars who compete in the imperial examinations.

And, significantly, Feng noted that Japan 'knows how to exert her energy to become strong'. But for China in its present weakness, he recommended straight dealing with the foreigners, who 'always appeal to reason'. Looking at China with its huge resources in natural and human material, 'naturally the mouths of all nations are watering with desire'. How true that statement was, can be seen in the sorry story of China and the Western powers in the years to come.

The ideas of Feng Kuei-fen had in fact been anticipated by the proposals of Hung Jen-kan, the prime minister and minister of foreign affairs of the T'aip'ing Heavenly Kingdom in 1859. His catalogue of Westernization in all manner of institutions was to be one of the two main political ideology texts of the T'aip'ing movement. But he had great difficulty explaining his proposals because he used classical Chinese expressions unadapted to such work. The literary civilization of China had produced a literary language not adaptable to scientific ideas.

Tsêng Kuo-fan (1811–1872)

We have already seen Tsêng Kuo-fan in his military role against the T'aip'ing rebels. Now, along with two others met in the same circumstances, Li Hung-chang and Tso Tsung-t'ang, we should take account of his great influence in China during the twelve years that remained of his life after the 1860 treaties. Tsêng is a man whose stature commands attention now, as it did in the China of a century ago. There are parallels between those times in which China sought to control the actions of foreigners and hoped to cast them out, and desperately sought a means of doing so; and between modern times when at last the dead hand of Confucian thought is coming under heavy fire in modern China in the effort, it seems, toward another self-strengthening movement.

Tsêng Kuo-fan has been called "the chief architect of victory over the T'aiping rebels". He was outstanding as a leader of men and as a Confucian administrator. He kept a very full diary, and in it we can trace the gradual growth of his opinion that Western science was necessary to build up China's strength

Tsêng Kuo-fan, like Mao Tse-tung, was born into a farmer's family in Hunan province. He passed the civil service examinations and spent the years between the age of twenty-eight and forty-two in Peking in high office. The next twenty years were largely spent in military affairs suppressing the Nien and T'aip'ing rebels. By this time he had acquired enormous experience in several fields (both military and civil), and great prestige as a man of unswerving loyalty to the dynasty and to Confucian principles.

In his letters to Li Hung-chang and in his diary, his main ideas, principles, and policies are clearly expressed, and we may follow the gradual growth of his opinions on self-strengthening.

His first ideas on Westernisation came in 1853 with a memorial on the need to improve China's defences by constructing an efficient naval force. In 1855 he set up small arsenals in Kiangsi province, convinced that to possess foreign guns was not enough and that China must make them herself.

In his diary of June 3, 1862, he wrote:

'If we could possess all their [Western] techniques, then we would have the means to return their favours when they are obedient, and we would also have the means to avenge our grievances when they are disloyal.'

But he was unsure as to the best method of gaining the use of the techniques, unsure too about their fundamental value. While noting in his diary the new Chinese terms for such concepts as light, chemistry, botany, electricity, and magnetics, he remained very conservative about Western medicine and suffered agonies of toothache rather than seek relief from non-Chinese remedies. Yet he received many Westerners and developed his interest in Western science. But his statement in a letter of 1862, addressed to Li Hung-chang, remains perhaps the most fundamental part of his outlook:

'The barbarian affairs are fundamentally difficult to manage, but the basic principles are no more than the four words of Confucius: *chung, hsin, tu,* and *ching*' [faithfulness, sincerity, earnestness, and respectfulness].

He made, however, great efforts to build up armaments and to construct modern ships.

'It has been learned that in building steamships the boiler, the engine, and the hull are the three most important parts.'

The memorial in which Tsêng sums up the work of the Kiangnan Arsenal at Shanghai recounts how only the hulls of ships were formerly built there, the boiler and engine being purchased from Westerners. But at last, in August, 1868, the design, the hull, and the boilers were all executed in the Arsenal, only the engine being bought secondhand from Shanghai. He goes on to tell how he has commissioned three Westerners to translate technical books.

Asked for his views on revision of the treaties with foreigners in 1867, Tsêng expressed his basic Confucian moral attitude with deep conviction and sincerity:

'We should absolutely never half spit and half swallow [meaning waver between two courses of action].... The foreigners in Europe have been annexing each other's territories for several hundred years, to seize the profits of the...people of one country so that ambitions of the attacking country may be satisfied....If we allow the foreigners to transport salt then the livelihood of the salt merchants...will be ended....'

And it would be the same with allowing steamboats on the rivers, the building of railways and telegraph lines. The sole matter proposed by foreigners in the treaty revision that might be 'worth trying is the matter of coal mining in which we shall borrow foreign tools for the operation of the mines to produce permanent benefit for China.'

He points out that the faith of the Westerners has split 'in divisions and that its missionaries are mostly poor. Therefore such faiths vary in their effectiveness from time to time.' Whereas the Confucian ethic 'has never been worn out through all the ages'. It should therefore be strengthened in every way.

In a nutshell, Tsêng Kuo-fan's opinions, which became a sort of blueprint for the treatment of foreigners for a decade, advocated fair dealing, strict adherence to the ancient Confucian Chinese ways, and the use of foreign expertise whenever possible.

Li Hung-chang (1823–1901)

The life and work of Li Hung-chang even more than that of his friend and colleague Tsêng Kuo-fan, were dedicated to the survival of the China he knew and loved. They were also dedicated to the aggrandisement of his own family, but that was normal in China at the time. Like Tsêng, he was a man of high scholastic

Li Hung-chang. He was a man so powerful and so sure of his own opinions (many of which were correct) that he wrote to the empress dowager after the catastrophe of the Chinese defeat in the Boxer affair that he could not 'help recalling to mind the folly which has now suddenly destroyed that structure of reformed administration which, during my twenty years...as Viceroy of Chihli, I was able to build up....' This was a direct criticism of her conduct in laying siege to the foreign legations in 1900

attainments, and also of great military experience as we have noted in his part in the suppression of the T'aip'ing rebels and his use of foreigners such as General Gordon. On the death of Tsêng, Li Hung-chang was to become the most influential of Chinese leaders in the latter part of the nineteenth century, holding such posts as Grand Secretary, Viceroy of Chihli (for 24 years), and being a member of the Tsungli Yamen. In nearly all treaty negotiations from the 1870s onward he played a prominent part. The essence of his policies toward strengthening China and dealing with the foreigners was to push forward with industrialization, improvement in transport and communication facilities, and to make and obtain supplies of Western armaments and machines. To him, in fact, China owed the beginning of many industrial ventures such as mines, cotton and paper mills, and the construction of Western-style shipping, and telegraphs and railways.

But, reading some of his writings, we can see how his dependence on Western industrial products and Western methods of warfare was the only part of the outside world's achievements he thought it necessary to borrow.

'They [Chinese officials in peacetime] sneer at the sharp weapons of foreign countries as things produced by strange techniques and tricky craft, which they consider it unnecessary to learn. In wartime...they are alarmed that the effective weapons of foreign countries are so strange and marvellous and regard them as something the Chinese cannot learn about. They do not know that for several hundred years the foreigners have considered the study of firearms as important to their bodies and lives....
'Everything in China's civil and military systems is far superior to the West. Only in firearms is it...impossible to catch up with them. What is the reason?'

Li goes on to point out that in foreign countries the artisan who actually makes the firearms is in close contact with the researcher and designer and is not regarded as a mere workman. 'He who can make a machine that can be used by the nation can become a prominent official....'

In a clear-thinking and far-sighted passage, Li states his certainty that Japanese progress in being able to stand up to the West is due to their understanding of such matters. 'They also bought the machines for making the machines.... Now they can navigate steamships and make use of canon.' And in a prophetic sentence or two he goes on:

'If we have some weapons with which to stand on our own feet, they [the Japanese] will attach themselves to us, and watch the shortcoming or strength of the Westerners. If we have nothing with which to make ourselves strong, then the Japanese will imitate the Westerners and will share the Westerners' sources of profits [in China].'

Summing up the situation as regards China and the rest of the world, he wrote in another memorial:

'The friendliness or opposition of foreigners always depends on the strength or weakness of China. Certainly Japan is not the only one to consider us in this way. If we can strengthen ourselves then we can live peacefully with others....'

But with his rooted conservatism and lack of an overall fundamental plan, the wise words and dedicated life of Li, and that of Tsêng also, were destined not to be really effective.

Tso Tsung-t'ang (1812-1885)

The twelve years between 1811 and 1823 produced a third great Chinese, Tso Tsung-t'ang, whom we have already seen quelling the T'aip'ing rebels. Another man from Hunan province, as was Tsêng, but of a poor family, he became a school-teacher (like Mao Tse-tung). He failed in the imperial examinations three times and abandoned the attempt to become an orthodox scholar. The T'aip'ing rebellion gave him the chance to show his talents and he was soon made governor-general of the coastal provinces of Fukien and Chekiang. Later he served the Ch'ing dynasty well in suppressing Muslim revolts in the northwest.

He was greatly influenced by conversations with Lin Tse-hsü with whom he stayed up all of one night talking. A frank and self-assured man, he felt it was dangerous to rely on foreigners and that China should try soon to make things herself without foreign aid. His shipyard near Foochow was built with the aid of two French engineers, and he must be considered as the first proponent of a modern Chinese navy. His school attached to the shipyard turned out such students as Yen Fu (1852-1921) whom we will later discover as a brilliant reformer.

The Hunanese general, Tso Tsung-t'ang, seen by Chinese as the equal of Tsêng Kuo-fan. The Chinese regarded Tsêng as the conqueror of the T'aip'ing rebels, and Tso of the Muslim rebels. He despised wealth for himself. When Tz'u-hsi presented him with 10,000 taels of silver, he divided it among his soldiers and the poor

The other, perhaps greater achievement of Tso was in the far northwest where he spent twelve years (1868–1880). There, in the face of shortage of money, food, ammunition, and transport, he formulated a five-year plan which he sent to the emperor before it was put into effect. Much in the manner of today's People's Liberation Army, he made his army into military colonists, raising their own food, working on irrigation, planting avenues of trees still there today. He also encouraged cotton planting and the mechanization of the spinning and weaving industries. Reorganizing the tax structure, he negotiated through Shanghai foreign loans of about one hundred million taels, opened free schools, tried to form a banking system, together with many other often successful experiments. He was constantly up against conservative Manchu officials. He was a man with a firm grasp of detail and a vigorous imagination. His views, like those of Tsêng and Li, were Confucian at base. His firm intention was always to make China strong enough to expel the Westerners.

Chang Chih-tung (1837–1909)

Chang Chih-tung is better known for his role as a reformer in the last few years of the century. His efforts toward self-strengthening in China, stimulated by the ineffectiveness of Western arms in the hands of ill-trained Chinese soldiers in the Sino-French war of 1884–1885, were in the academic field. He founded various schools on self-strengthening lines. His governorship of the two Kwang provinces and of Hunan-Hupei showed him an able administrator with ideas. Basically his opinions were similar to those of the trio—Tsêng, Li, and Tso.

Chang Chih-tung was a better scholar than reformer or administrator. He once received a pair of scrolls from an anonymous donor, one of which said of him—'As an administrator a bungler, but remarkable for originating magnificent schemes'

China's First Industrial Ventures

1863	Foreign language school set up in Shanghai
1865	Kiangnan Arsenal established at Shanghai, a translation bureau attached
1867	Nanking Arsenal built
1870	Tientsin machine factory, established 1867 by Ch'ung-hou, was enlarged
1871	Planning of a Western-style fort at Taku
1872	Students go to America for study, officers to Germany to take military courses
	China Merchants Steam Navigation Company set up
1875	Plans to build steel warships
1876	Request made for the opening of a bureau to study Western science in each province, and to add sciences to the imperial examination syllabus
	Men from the Foochow shipyard sent to study in England and France
1878	Kaiping coal-mine opened
1879	Taku-Tientsin telegraph line opened
1880	Plan for a modern navy, and to purchase foreign warships
	Naval school established at Tientsin. Plan for more telegraph lines approved
1881	Li supports plans to build railways
	One line of six miles north of Tientsin completed
	Shanghai-Tientsin telegraph opened, and merchants invited to develop telegraph services in all parts of China
1882	Dockyard begun at Port Arthur, completed 1891
	Cotton mill planned for Shanghai
1885	Army school set up at Tientsin. Naval office established
1887	Mints opened at Tientsin and Paoting
1888	The Peiyang army organized
1889	Moho goldmine in Kirin planned
1891	Lung-chang paper-mill in Shanghai founded. Review of the navy held at Port Arthur

---

The Internal Situation

Quite apart from the efforts of the great men of the era, other factors were involved in the struggle to build up China's strength. One was the social and economic climate of the decades after 1860. Another was the clash of opinion between those who held views such as we have just examined, and others whose opinions were wholly or partly opposed to them.

By the 1850s, the population of China had risen to about 300 million. Although this growth was sharply checked by the long years of the T'aip'ing rebellion and the devastation it caused in many Chinese provinces, it was not matched by any great rise in farm productivity. There were many reasons for this, among them the system of inheritance that divided land into ever smaller parcels, the agricultural taxation system, the corruption of officials, and the massive debts of the peasants to unscrupulous landlords.

The great famine of the years 1876–1879 was one result of this situation, when weather conditions easily removed the precarious hold that most peasants in north China had on subsistence. In those three years it is estimated that between ten and twenty million people died—perhaps as many as perished in the T'aip'ing rebellion. An English missionary gave a first-hand account of it:

> 'As the winter drew near, the distress became more acute. Reports came in from villages where…there had been forty inhabitants reduced to ten survivors. The price of grain rose rapidly…. [Many people] were forced to pull down their houses and sell every inch of woodwork in them…and so get money to buy millet chaff to try and keep body and soul together.
> 'In order to keep warm in the depth of winter the poor wretches dug deep pits underground, where twenty…even fifty persons would live together….'
>
> T. Richard: Forty-five years in China

Prince Kung and Tz'u-hsi

Prince Kung had nothing of the brilliance of the leaders of the self-strengthening movement. But he was to some extent a realist. He knew that in order to retain the Manchu dynasty on the Dragon Throne of China some changes were necessary. Unfortunately he was outclassed in brains and cunning by the Dowager Empress Tz'u-hsi, although even she realized that it would be foolish to try to get rid of the West by offensive means at that time.

Tz'u-hsi, who was the real ruler of China for most of the time between the death of her husband the former Emperor Hsien-fêng in 1861, and her own death in 1908, was a woman of great ambition. Born in 1835 of the Yehonala clan, a noble Manchu family, she was sent to the palace as concubine at the age of seventeen. From concubine of the third class she rose dramatically to that of the first class when she gave birth to the emperor's only son. She had the benefit, unusual at the time for women, of a good education and had studied the classics and Chinese art. As the health of Hsien-fêng deteriorated, she came to have an ever deeper influence on his decisions at all levels. It is generally thought to have been her influence that made China so unyielding in the years between the first and second treaties signed with the foreigners.

Even before the death of Hsien-fêng at Jehol, her growing power had aroused jealousy, and attempts were made to turn the emperor away from her and also from Prince Kung. But as the emperor grew more feeble Tz'u-hsi sent word to Prince Kung, who was in Peking, informing him of the dangerous position they were in, and asking him to send to Jehol troops loyal to her own Yehonala clan.

On the day before the emperor died, a state council was held in his bedroom, from which she was excluded. The emperor signed a decree appointing a board of regency for his successor, the son of Tz'u-hsi. This consisted of men opposed to her and to Prince Kung. But the decree was not valid as it had not been sealed with the dynastic seal—for the simple reason that Tz'u-hsi had taken care to remove it from the emperor's care before he died.

The court took to the road, accompanying the emperor's cortège back to Peking. But before it got there, Tz'u-hsi had left it and gone ahead to the capital. By the time the cortège reached Peking, she and Prince Kung had laid their plans. She dismissed the regents—pointing out that the decree was unsealed and invalid—and with the late emperor's consort (Tz'u-an) assumed the regency. Those who protested were either relieved of their duties or permitted to commit suicide.

When her son, the T'ung-chih Emperor, died in 1874, she made sure that her sister's child took the throne as the Emperor Kuang-hsü. Thus she had a further fourteen years of regency after that until he came of age. In 1889 she retired, but again seized power in 1898. From then until she died in 1908 she was the effective ruler of China, a ruthless, brilliant, ultra-conservative woman of great talent and boundless greed.

Tz'u-hsi had throughout her life a deep hatred of foreigners and proved unwilling to do more than pay lip-service to the self-strengthening movement. She was clever enough to permit a much larger number of Chinese to attain high positions in the provinces, rather than favour her own people, the Manchu. These Chinese naturally became even more fervent supporters of the Manchu dynasty, thus to some extent strengthening its hold at a time when power was in danger of slipping from its grasp. But in other ways—in the acceptance of enormous gifts from all those in high office—she greatly added to the profound corruption that was prevalent in every walk of life.

The most notorious of the scandals surrounding her greed was that concerning the millions of taels collected to make a start on building a new Chinese navy. These were turned over at her orders and used to build a new summer palace. It is doubtful, even with the navy that China would have had in 1894 when war came with Japan (as Li Hung-chang had predicted), whether she would have won that war. But the diversion of the naval funds certainly sealed the fate of China in no uncertain manner.

The Marble Boat in the form of a rather ugly paddle-steamer that the empress dowager built for her Summer Palace. It has more curiosity value than beauty. Peking crowds on days off swarm all over it, taking photos of their children

Wo-jen and the Opposition

Entirely in line with the anti-foreignism of Tz'u-hsi and others, were the views of the Grand Secretary Wo-jen, a Mongol scholar who was tutor to the emperor and head of the Hanlin Academy. As soon as the T'ung-wen Kuan with its concentration on Western studies was formed, he rose in protest.

> 'Astronomy and mathematics are of very little use. Your slave [himself] has learned that the way to establish a nation is to lay emphasis on propriety and righteousness.... The fundamental effort lies in the minds of people, not in techniques....'

His views were at once challenged by the Tsungli Yamen (that is, by its head, Prince Kung), who reported:

> 'His [Wo-jen's] principles...are very lofty and the opinion he maintains is very orthodox. Your ministers' point of view was also like that before they began to manage foreign affairs; and yet today they do not presume to insist on such ideas, because of actual difficulties which they cannot help....'

In other words, if Wo-jen had the management of the foreigners at China's doorstep, he would be forced to alter his opinion in order to deal with them. The statement concludes with a sarcastic call for Wo-jen to reveal his master plan to deal successfully with the West. Naturally, he had none.

The Results of the Self-strengthening Movement

These can be placed under three general headings: Educational, Military, and Industrial.

Educational Results

Efforts in the educational field took two directions. One was the establishment of curriculums dealing with foreign subjects in various schools, while the second was the sending abroad of Chinese youths to study.

Schools established to teach foreign languages and scientific subjects included:

1862	The T'ung-wen Kuan at Peking
1863	Shanghai) (suggested by Li Hung-chang)
1864	Canton { foreign language schools (founded by Chang Chih-tung)
1866	Foochow)
1865	Kiangnan Arsenal school of mechanical engineering (founded by Tsêng Kuo-fan and Li Hung-chang)
1893	Wuchang self-strengthening school (founded by Chang Chih-tung)

A cartoon drawn by the Mexican painter and oriental traveller Covarrubias, showing three Chinese students returned from their studies in (left to right) Britain, France, and the United States —their clothes reflecting the fashions in these countries at the time

Of these perhaps the T'ung-wen Kuan was the most influential. In 1869 an American missionary, W.A.P. Martin, was appointed head. In years to come when China sent diplomats abroad most of them had studied in this college.

It was realized that to send students abroad might be a good method of educating the best brains among the youthful population, not only in the sciences but in the customs and traditions, as well as the industrial potential and armed capabilities of foreign countries. The memorial to the Tsungli Yamen sent by Tsêng and Li in 1871 may be seen as the beginning of the process.

> 'To establish arsenals . . . and to open schools for instruction in China is just the beginning of the struggle to rise again. To go abroad for study, to gather ideas and the benefits of greater knowledge, can produce far-reaching . . . results. . . . Regardless of whether they [Westerners] are scholars, workers, or soldiers, they all go to school to study . . . the principles, to practise on the machines. . . . If we wish to adopt their superior techniques and suddenly try to buy all their machines, not only is our power insufficient to do this, but also there is no way for us to master either the fundamental principles or the details of the profound ideas contained in these . . . techniques, unless we have actually seen them and practised with them for a long time.'

And he quotes a proverb: 'To hear a hundred times is not as good as to see once'.

Between 1872 and 1881, one hundred and twenty students went to study in the United States. Army officers went to Germany and naval cadets to Britain to learn the principles of naval warfare. And thirty young men from the Foochow shipyard school went to France and Britain for further technical study.

The first Chinese to graduate from an American university was Yung Wing (1828–1912).

One of Li Hung-chang's protégés, Ma Chien-chung, studied in France. He reported on an examination paper in political science:

'There were eight examination questions....The third was on the commercial proceedings of all nations, dealing with the basis of credit for commercial organizations and bank drafts....The seventh one was on the similarities and differences of administrative methods, government, and education in the three countries, England, the United States, and France.'

Ma went through the whole examination paper and told how he answered it. He got good marks, and the 'results were announced in the newspaper'. But he felt that his brilliant results were only brilliant because the Westerners despised the Chinese and were surprised that he understood half of what he had to learn. He formed a poor opinion of Western democratic processes as a whole.

The programme of studies abroad came to an end due to disputes on the subject of its administration, and because Li Hung-chang insisted that Yung Wing (the first graduate from America, who was co-chairman of the organization) was putting too heavy an emphasis on Western studies, to the exclusion of Chinese studies. It was doubtless true that in foreign lands, Chinese students neglected their Chinese studies. Even today, students from the orient find difficulties in studying abroad due largely to their different background, and they have little time to study Chinese subjects. So it is perhaps surprising that so many Chinese of the nineteenth century—who could learn almost nothing of the West until they arrived there—actually managed to do as well as they did in Western colleges.

Military Undertakings

Arsenals were constructed at:	Anking—— 1861	Nanking—— 1867	
	Shanghai——1865	Shensi———— 1871	

Shipyards were built at Foochow after 1866, and another was completed at Port Arthur (Lüshunkow). The Taku Forts were the subject of Western-style plans for strengthening, and there were projects for the purchase and building of Western naval vessels. Naval schools were set up at Foochow and Tientsin, a naval college at Nanking, and a military training school at Tientsin. Army officers went to Germany and naval officers to England for training.

New Industrial and Trade Developments

Inspectorate of Customs established, Peking	—1865
Shanghai-London-San Francisco telegraph completed	—1871
China Merchants Steam Navigation Co. founded	—1873
First trains on the Shanghai-Wusung railway	—1876
The Kaiping coal mines opened	—1878
Postage stamps first issued	—1878
Shanghai-Tientsin telegraph line opened	—1881
Tientsin-Tongshan Railway opened	—1888
Hanyang Ironworks (Hupeh) opened by Chang Chih-tung	—1889
Cotton mills opened at Wuchang	—1891, 1894

There were, besides, various factories, an iron mine in Hupeh, and such under-takings as a flour mill and a match factory, also opened as a result of industrial development.

But the scale and scope of what was done was small, and most of these and also government military projects were accompanied by corruption, leading to in-efficiency.

The scheme by which a close connection was maintained between officials and merchants (*kuan-tu shang-pan*—official-supervision, merchant-operation) did not work well. Officials untrained in business methods held authority over merchants who were of inferior social status and in no position to use their initiative. This system probably developed from the traditional way of running the government salt monopoly, where the officials were overseers and the actual work of production, distribution, and retailing was in the hands of groups of salt merchants. Corruption allowed the officials to invest money in the name of the merchants and therefore gain the profits while merely paying a salary to the merchants.

The failure of China's self-strengthening movement may be attributed to several causes. The first was that it came at a time of corrupt and inefficient government under the rule of a very corrupt throne. The second was that the age-old Confucian basis of thought and action was so deeply ingrained in life that no such movement could shift it. And to get rid of Confucian thought, which constituted both the strength of dynastic China and its weakness in modern times, was work for a revolu-tion rather than for a mere handful of officials. Even the most enlightened of them could hardly have been expected to put aside the Confucian basis of life, any more than the British cabinet could be expected to put aside the democratic process.

FOREIGN AFFAIRS

After the ratification of the treaties with Western powers in 1860, the situation between China and the West was one of comparative calm. A certain amount of progress was soon made in relations, on a footing that may have been strange to the Chinese but was reassuring to the West. The establishment of the Tsungli Yamen through which foreign ministers could deal directly with high-ranking Chinese officials on terms of equality was a forward step. So too was the sending of Chinese missions abroad. But the repeated requests of Tsêng Kuo-fan for Chinese representatives to be appointed to Western countries were refused.

With the events of 1870, however, this climate of co-operation and intention to please came to an abrupt and violent halt.

Western Co-operative Policy

The conciliatory policy adopted by the ministers of Britain, France, Russia, and America in Peking toward the Chinese in agreeing to maintain her sovereignty and to help in modernization was appreciated at the Tsungli Yamen. The Chinese were reassured somewhat and did not attempt as in the past to evade their treaty obligations. The four ministers of the Western powers—Sir Frederick Bruce for

Britain, M. Berthemy for France, General de Balluseck for Russia, and Anson Burlingame for the United States—also found the policy useful as a check on each other's activities in China. The as yet inexperienced officials of the Tsungli Yamen turned frequently to Sir Robert Hart, the British Inspector General of Customs, for friendly advice. Both he and the American minister Burlingame were seen by the Chinese as dependable friends.

The Alcock Convention

Sir Frederick Bruce was replaced in 1865 by Rutherford Alcock whose efforts in Peking were an extension of the co-operative policy. The Tientsin treaties of 1860 were due for revision in 1868, and long before that year British merchants had begun to put pressure on the government in London for more privileges to be granted them in China, including decreased customs duty and exemption from the *likin* transport tax.

Alcock's restrained and statesmanlike conduct of the whole complicated discussion that went on in China and in England was summed up in a convention which he signed with the Tsungli Yamen in 1869. It is worth noting the important points in this convention for, although it was not ratified because of merchant opposition in Britain, it contained much that would probably have put trading relations with China on a sounder footing.

> China might appoint consuls to any British port (including Hong Kong where it was hoped this might 'control the smuggling propensities of his own countrymen in league with foreign merchants'.)
> Rationalization of duty and internal tax on the movement of foreign and Chinese goods (the controversial *likin*).
> Increased duty on opium.
> Increased duty on silk.
> Rationalization of the role of Hong Kong in Chinese import and export trade.

Rutherford Alcock whose moderating policies were not followed. He once wrote: '. . .our position in China has been created by force—naked, physical force; and any intelligent policy to improve or maintain that position must still look to force in some form. . .for the results.' He was a realist, but his actions in China all tended to minimize the use of foreign force

These and a few other clauses would have removed the causes of a great deal of friction. British merchants, avid for exactly the reverse—more concessions—effectively prevented the measures coming into effect. The non-ratification renewed Chinese suspicions of the intentions of the Western powers.

Other effects of the co-operative policy were more positive. Under the wing of the Customs Service and its director Sir Robert Hart, a modern postal service was begun, and the navigational aids at various ports and harbours were improved. Hart also subsidized the T'ung-wen Kuan—Foreign Languages School—with money taken from customs payments.

Diplomatic Relations

It was unfortunate that China did not respond to the residence of Western ministers in Peking by sending envoys to foreign capitals. A low-status mission under an ageing Manchu named Pin-ch'un went to Europe in 1866, but had no apparent influence on Chinese foreign policy and was more of a gesture than anything else.

The following year, however, the Chinese government asked the retiring American minister, Anson Burlingame, to take charge of a mission to Western countries. With him he took a Manchu official, Chih-kang, and a Chinese, Sun Chiah-ku—both officials of the second grade. The mission, with two Western secretaries and about thirty Chinese participants, left Shanghai on February 25, 1868. Its sponsors had high hopes and some misgivings, but Burlingame had accepted the invitation to lead it with great pride. At a banquet for the mission in San Francisco, he was toasted by the Governor of California as 'the son of the youngest, and representative of the oldest, government'. Burlingame was an orator himself, and sometimes became carried away with his own facility in this field. At San Francisco he declared his mission meant that China was launched on the path to peace and progress. Reason must have afterward told him that this was hardly true at that time. And he hoped (in another somewhat embarrasing speech) that 'the day would soon arrive when this great people would extend its arms towards the shining banners of Western civilization'. He wanted missionaries to 'plant the shining cross on every hill and in every valley'. Americans were greatly impressed, the Chinese government quite unimpressed.

The Chinese were even less impressed by the agreement signed between America and China by Burlingame, the Seward-Burlingame Treaty, 1868. This document failed to give any concrete provision regulating the relationship between the two countries. It encouraged Chinese emigration (which pleased the Americans) and stated American intentions not to interfere in the 'development of China'. The Chinese government, which had not been consulted on the terms, ratified it reluctantly. It was an almost meaningless document.

In London the mission was received coldly, but obtained an assurance from the Foreign Office that Britain would not apply 'unfriendly pressure inconsistent with the independence and safety of China'. Burlingame died while in Moscow, and the mission returned to China.

The results of the mission were mixed. In America it led to the false impression that China was ready to accept Christianity and Westernization with open arms, which was not the case. This was noted by Burlingame's successor in Peking.

'An impression seems to have been obtained in the United States that the Government of China is peculiarly friendly to our country, and that great advantages to our commerce are about to result from this preference. . . . I need hardly say these anticipations are without foundation. The Government of China may have preferences; but it has no special regard for any foreign power.'

J. Ross Browne, American Minister at Peking

The Seward-Burlingame Treaty had little significance, and the putting of Sino-American relations on a footing of equality did little but permit more Chinese labour to enter the United States. Very soon after, there was serious trouble on the Pacific Coast on this very subject, and when the trade depression of the 1870s came, the Americans soon ceased to honour their treaty obligations on equality and the free entry of Chinese to their country.

In England the mission may have helped to delay the revision of the British Treaty of Tientsin so urgently called for by merchants.

At heart, Confucian Chinese for all their compliance in treaty regulations on terms of equality, still found it hard to admit that Western nations should be treated as equals. The old stumbling block, the performance of the *kowtow* before the emperor, came up once more when the ministers in Peking wanted an audience. Pleading the minority of the emperor, the Chinese put the matter off. But when T'ung-chih came of age in 1873 the ministers were granted audience. They bowed three times but did not *kowtow*, feeling that they had succeeded in overcoming the final barrier to Chinese superiority. But in fact they had been received not in the customary hall of audience but in that reserved for receiving tributary countries' missions.

Christianity in China, and the Tientsin Massacre, 1870

Under the Tientsin Treaties of 1858, Christianity was made legal in China. Missionaries were free to travel anywhere in the country. The agreement of 1860 between France and China also permitted Catholic missionaries to buy land and build. Although the Chinese later stated that these clauses had been inserted in the treaty without their knowledge or approval, the French ignored the claim. It was not long before Catholic priests were to be discovered in most Chinese provinces.

Protestant missionaries were also at work, their numbers always increasing. Along with their spiritual functions and the making of converts to Christianity, the schools which they ran and the medical relief they gave brought some benefits to small numbers of Chinese. But these were heavily outweighed by the wave of hostility that Christianity and Christian missions aroused throughout China. British and American officials in China claimed that most of the complaints brought to them by Chinese authorities involved the activities of the missionaries.

Chinese hostility to Christianity and its missions is a complicated matter about which a great deal of research has been carried out. But it can be reduced to several

One of a series of Chinese cartoons intended to warn the people of the evils of Christianity and its foreign promoters. The title is: The Terrible Punishment of the Pig Incarnate [Jesus]. The text on the right describes the sufferings in store for the devils [meaning foreigners] in 'dark hell's eighteen levels'. The left hand inscription reads: 'You who in this life have committed ten thousand malicious acts, castrated boys, taken the foetuses from pregnant women, removed people's eyes, and cut off women's nipples—do you think the gods will allow themselves to be deceived by your evil deeds?' The word for 'Lord' (Jesus) in Chinese sounds somewhat similar to the word for 'pig', hence both Jesus being sawn into two, and the missionary being pounded (at the lower right), are shown as pigs

elements on several levels. The officials and scholar-gentry—the real rulers of China at the local level—disliked missionaries because they assumed the right to protect their Chinese converts, thus removing them to some extent from the jurisdiction of the local authorities. A frequent cause of trouble was missionary protection of a Chinese accused of some crime. The Chinese, backed by the missionary who himself had privileged status and could not be judged by Chinese processes, often escaped either trial or conviction.

The way of life in villages and small towns where missionaries exercised control over numbers of Chinese was disturbed by the fact that Christian converts became a privileged group. This caused jealousies and recrimination.

The educated classes regarded the reincarnation of Christ and the doctrine of virgin birth as mere superstition. And the claim of Christianity to be the one true religion, thus denying the importance of ancestor worship and the various sacrifices made according to the Confucian rites—was also seen as undermining the traditional way of life and tending to civil disturbances.

The Chinese knew Christianity was the religion of the foreign powers, and that it was permitted in China because their government had been forced to sign treaties at gunpoint. The religion was therefore suspected for this reason too. And of course in the ports where Westerners could be seen by Chinese, they were often seen to violate the very principles that their missionaries declared to be fundamental to the religion.

The horrors of the T'aip'ing rebellion were still present in the countryside during the first few years after the 1860 agreements, and everyone knew that the T'aip'ing professed some form of Christianity. Even if the villagers did not know precisely what form it was, they all knew it was a foreign religion.

None of these factors worked in favour of either priests or the religion they sought to teach. The people at large showed their dislike of both by increasingly numerous attacks on missions and churches, and by their attitude to converts. There was a readiness to believe stories about missionaries using their hospitals to remove the eyes and other parts of patients for use in medicines. The large number of poster-cartoons that appeared in many parts of China during the latter part of the nineteenth century left nothing to the imagination in their depiction of what Christianity as the Chinese conceived it might mean to Chinese.

Many of the missionaries were dedicated men and women whose intentions were undoubtedly the betterment of the Chinese at large. They sought to improve the lot of Chinese people by teaching Christianity, and by giving medical aid and schooling. But what was not perhaps fully understood by them was the profound acceptance of ancient Chinese beliefs and customs, and the manner in which Chinese society was unobtrusively ruled and regulated in almost every particular by them. The missionaries hardly understood that to replace these beliefs by Christian beliefs was tantamount to a revolution not only in thinking but in the whole of living. The opposition from the Chinese was understandably fierce.

The scholar-missionary James Legge who came to Hong Kong in 1843. He was one of the early students of Chinese literature, some of which he translated into English. He trained Chinese as Christian priests

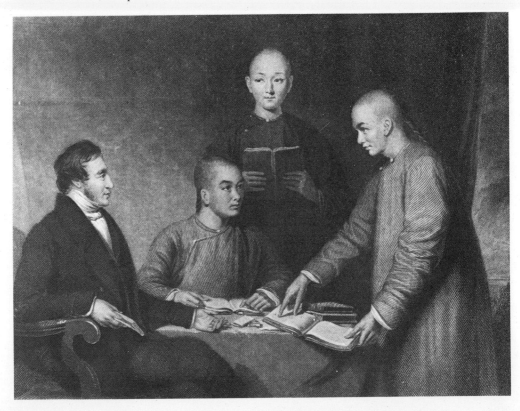

The Tientsin Massacre

In Tientsin, on June 21, 1870, the tensions generated by such factors as these boiled over, almost causing a third China war. At Tientsin the populace had experience of foreign occupation from 1860 to 1863. While British troops left a generally good impression, the French soldiers, and even more so the French officials, left what the historian H.B. Morse calls 'a legacy of bitter feelings'. Foolishly they had occupied the imperial palace there, and even more foolishly had built a Catholic cathedral on the site of the imperial temple, completing it in 1869. 'It is not too much to say', Morse sums up the situation, 'that . . . the French nation and French . . . missionaries were detested.'

The activities of the Sisterhood of Mercy in trying to save deserted and orphaned children of poor Chinese, were concentrated on a hospital and orphanage. But since few children were voluntarily brought to them for care, they offered a cash reward for each. This led to kidnapping and to dying children being brought in. When dead, the children were cremated. Local fancy built a picture of incitement to kidnapping, mystic baptismal rites, cutting out of the eyes and heart before the ritual cremation of the children.

An epidemic hit the orphanage that summer, and between thirty and forty children died. The rumours sparked off by the disappearance of these children brought a mob which destroyed the building and also burned the cathedral, and killed the French consul, two priests, ten of the Sisters, and thirty Chinese employees of the hospital. American and British chapels were also looted and ruined.

The French consul had only himself to blame for his death, having fired into a crowd of Chinese and insulted a Chinese official in his own *yamen*.

The foreign powers acted swiftly. A return to 'gunboat diplomacy', abandoned for some time, came in the shape of French, British, and American warships ordered to Tientsin, and demands that in future missionaries should be protected. There

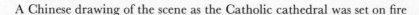
A Chinese drawing of the scene as the Catholic cathedral was set on fire

was little the Chinese could do but yield. Some of the people involved in the massacre were executed. France demanded an indemnity of 250,000 taels and an official apology.

Western thinking on the subject of spreading Christianity backed by gunboats against the evident wish of most Chinese was not changed by this unhappy event. The whole story of Christianity in China is clouded by the background presence of Western force to be used in backing up missionaries in what seemed, to official China and the mass of Chinese at large, activities contrary to Chinese tradition and life. The Manchu government and its officials lost increasingly what respect they still commanded as they were seen to protect the foreigners and their converts against the expressed wishes of most Chinese. By treaty, the Chinese authorities could do no less, however unwillingly.

The Margary Affair, 1875, and the Chefoo Convention, 1876

By the 1870s, the foreign net was beginning to tighten round China. French penetration of Indo-China, traditionally tributary to China, and the British presence in Lower Burma, meant that the two nations would soon push along the routes to China's southern provinces. The British were interested in a route from Upper Burma to the southwestern provinces of Yunnan, Szechuan, and Kweichow. The first British expedition in this direction found its way to Bhamo, a mere fifty miles from what is today the Yunnan-Burma border. A second expedition led by Colonel Horace Browne was joined by a consular official named Augustus Margary who had been sent from Peking to act as interpreter in the penetration of Yunnan territory. Leaving Bhamo, Margary went ahead with a party of Chinese to reconnoitre the route. He was attacked and, with five of his party, killed. It was presumed the murderers were Chinese. Neither the Chinese nor the Burmese desired the opening of such a trade route as was being explored.

In Peking, the British minister, Thomas Wade, on hearing the story indignantly made several demands which were out of all proportion to the importance of the incident. These were embodied in the Chefoo Convention signed for China by Li Hung-chang, and for Britain by Wade. There were three sections to the document:

> The first redressed the Margary incident. China agreed to pay 200,000 taels indemnity and to send a mission to apologize to the British government, and to permit stationing of British officers in Yunnan for five years.
> The second provided for better official communication between foreign officials and Chinese authorities both in Peking and at the ports. Administration of justice at the ports was to be reorganized.
> The third dealt with trade concessions. Four more treaty ports—Ichang, Wuhu, Wenchow, and Pakhoi—were to be opened, and six other Yangtze river ports were designated as ports of call for the British.

The Convention was at once ratified by the Chinese (1876), but British merchants' great dissatisfaction with the concessions granted was such that the British did not ratify it until 1885.

The immediate results were the opening wide of the whole Yangtze valley to trade and residence of foreigners, and the more considerate treatment and easier access granted by the Chinese to foreign diplomats.

The other importance of the Chefoo Convention was that it marked the end of the joint policy of co-operation between the Western powers and China. The French, Russians, and Germans made objections to the agreement and the powers once again began to take separate action in order to suit their individual interests in China. Britain had broken her promise to China, made in London to the Burlingame mission, to exercise forbearance.

First Chinese Legations Abroad

Among a number of memorials sent to the Throne in 1875 on the urgency of establishing Chinese representatives in Western countries, one contained the revealing opinion that the Chinese were 'like men thinking to see with their faces set against a solid wall, and to hear with covered ears.' After many delays, some on the Chinese and some on the British side, Kuo Sung-tao was sent to London as minister and Liu Hsi-hung as his associate. They arrived there in January 1877. Kuo was accredited to France as well in the following year, but was replaced by Tsêng Chi-tse, better known as Marquis Tsêng, the second son of Tsêng Kuo-fan.

The United States received its first Chinese minister Ch'en Lan-pin, in October 1878. Berlin, Vienna, and The Hague shared one minister, appointed in December 1877, while Ho Ju-chang was sent to Tokyo in 1878. A minister went to Russia in 1879.

The Chinese minister in London and all his successors for the following thirty years until the end of 1905 were advised by Dr. Halliday Macartney, a man who had been involved in the suppression of the T'aip'ing rebels, and was afterwards director of the Nanking arsenal.

Tsêng Kuo-fan died in 1872; and also Wen-hsiang—the man whom Sir Robert Hart once called 'the working man of the Tsungli Yamen', who died in 1876. In 1878 changes took place in the Tsungli Yamen, which now numbered eleven members. It now came to include all members of the Grand Council and most of the presidents of the various government ministries, and was more a cabinet than a ministry of foreign affairs.

During this period in China the resources of the state were severely strained. The devastation of the T'aip'ing period followed by the floods and droughts of the 1870s that produced widespread famine and damage to property and land, meant that there was little to spare for relief. The indemnities that had to be paid out to the West did not help the situation. China resolutely refused to contract foreign loans on an official level.

During the seventies and eighties, a sporadic and protracted rearguard action was fought by authorities in various Chinese provinces to hold up the passage of foreign goods by exacting taxes of various kinds not stipulated by treaty, or in excess of the legal amounts. Repeated orders from Peking to provincial authorities to obey the letter of the treaties in this respect produced late and reluctant obedience. The authority of the central government was gradually being undermined.

The Chinese and the United States

The effect of the Seward-Burlingame treaty was at first to increase the flow of Chinese immigrant labour to the United States. Most voluntary emigration from China was to the United States and to Australia's gold mining areas. The victims of the 'coolie trade' found themselves unhappily transplanted across the Pacific to Peru and to Cuba.

In California, by 1867, there were about 50,000 Chinese. The demand for cheap labour for railway construction seemed limitless, but the financial depression of 1873 brought racial considerations to the fore, and there were riots, discrimination, and violence against Chinese. Opposition to the treaty requirements grew rapidly. A bill that passed Congress in 1879 sought to limit to fifteen the number of Chinese any one ship could bring at one time. But the president threw out this bill on the grounds that it violated the Seward-Burlingame Treaty. The Americans then sought to revise the treaty, and eventually, in 1880, a new one was signed which allowed the United States to suspend or to limit Chinese immigration, but not to abolish it. Congress then suspended immigration for ten years.

The ill-treatment of Chinese in America, and the shamefully discriminatory local measures against them in such places as San Francisco where living conditions in the Chinatown ghetto were very poor, served to poison relations and to excite anti-American sentiment among Chinese in China.

It is interesting to note that a man named Arnold Genthe with an early camera succeeded in making a telling historical documentation of Chinatown and its inhabitants before the great earthquake and consequent fire that destroyed the area in 1906. This is perhaps the best visual record, certainly one of the very few, of a nineteenth century overseas Chinese community.

Border States

The venerable Chinese tradition of receiving deputations at yearly or longer fixed intervals from the various 'tributary' states had for many centuries proved itself a generally useful defence mechanism. These small states surrounding China were assured of Chinese help against greedy or aggressive neighbours in return for their general friendship to China. The exact state of affairs in each was checked by various means, but especially at the time of the regular tribute mission's arrival in Peking.

It was the disruption of this relationship with Burma and Burmese border tribes caused by the British advance into Upper Burma that doubtless caused the Margary affair. Burma in fact became a British protectorate in 1886, and the Chinese acknowledged it.

China had already ceded Hong Kong and Kowloon Point to Britain—no great loss by territorial standards. But at the hands of foreign powers she was to lose all her tributary states and dependent territories (except a small area on the Ili river southwest of Lake Balkhash) by 1895.

After Hong Kong, the first to be lost was the Liu-Ch'iu (Ryukyu) chain of islands stretching between Japan's southernmost island, Kyushu, and the northern tip of Taiwan. By the 1850s these islands had come under the control of the *daimyo* of

Satsuma. An incident in 1871 involving some Liu-ch'iu islanders who were shipwrecked on Taiwan and murdered by aboriginal peoples there, caused the *daimyo*
to demand action by the Chinese against the murderers. The Tsungli Yamen
refused. The Japanese sent an avenging force against Taiwan. China averted war
by paying an indemnity to the Japanese for the cost of this expedition, and by
compensating the relatives of the murdered seamen. This was tantamount to
recognition that the Liu-ch'iu chain belonged to Japan. Japan then formally took
possession in 1879, making the islands part of the Okinawa prefecture.

The encroachments made by foreign powers on territories bordering China, 1870–1895

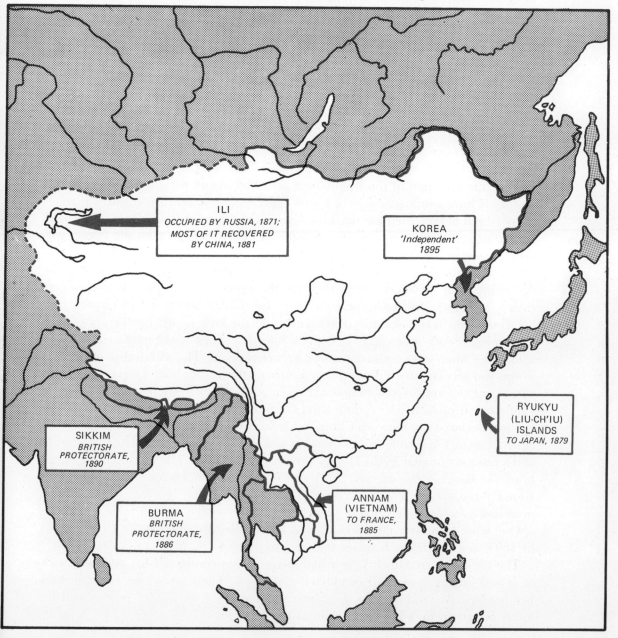

ILI
OCCUPIED BY RUSSIA, 1871;
MOST OF IT RECOVERED
BY CHINA, 1881

KOREA
'Independent'
1895

RYUKYU
(LIU-CH'IU)
ISLANDS
TO JAPAN, 1879

SIKKIM
BRITISH
PROTECTORATE,
1890

BURMA
BRITISH
PROTECTORATE,
1886

ANNAM
(VIETNAM)
TO FRANCE,
1885

Meanwhile, the Russians occupied a region on the Ili river southwest of Lake Balkhash in 1871. This area of Sinkiang (Chinese Turkestan) was claimed by them to be essential to the protection of commercial interests which were threatened by Muslim dissidents in revolt against the Manchu government. But after the suppression of the Muslims in 1878 by Tso Tsung-t'ang, Russia did not yield the territory. On the contrary, she negotiated a treaty for its cession by China with an official named Ch'ung-hou. But the central government in Peking rejected this, and the matter was not settled until the Treaty of St. Petersburg in 1881. This treaty was negotiated by Marquis Tsêng (who had been minister in Russia for a year). Charles Gordon, whom we noticed helping suppress the T'aip'ing rebels, was summoned to Peking to advise on what to do about the Russian refusal to give up the Ili. His advice was:

'If you make war, burn the suburbs of Peking, remove the archives and emperor from Peking, put them in the centre of the country, and fight [a guerrilla] war for five years. Russia will not be able to hurt you.'

It was either that or give up Ili altogether. His advice was not taken. The Russians managed to retain a part of the area by the treaty. But the treaty was a diplomatic triumph for China.

French penetration of the Indo-China area had begun early in the seventeenth century. Chinese influence was of course older by many centuries, and Annam—the northern part of Vietnam touching Yunnan and Kwangsi provinces—had been a tributary state for a very long time. A confrontation between China and France was made inevitable by the French seizure of Hanoi and the transfer by the Annamese ruler of his allegiance to France. The French then withdrew from Annam. The Annamese king, however, cared little for the French and at once sent tributary envoys to China with an appeal for help. In 1882, Chinese troops assisted him but Hanoi was taken again by the French and the king signed the Treaty of Hué confirming French sovereignty over the whole area. Tonkin, the northernmost part adjoining China, was administered by a French resident. The withdrawal of Chinese troops was secured in 1884 by the signature of the Li-Fournier Convention. This agreement also approved commercial movement between Tonkin and the adjoining Chinese territories. Border disputes and misunderstandings between the two parties led to undeclared war between China and France. One of its incidents was the French destruction of Tso Tsung-t'ang's shipyard and arsenal at Foochow. The Convention of Tientsin negotiated by Li Hung-chang and Sir Robert Hart brought hostilities to an end. Basically this agreement restated the terms of the Li-Fournier Convention. China recognized French sovereignty over Annam and Tonkin while France promised to respect the Chinese border.

One more tributary state, Sikkim, was made a British protectorate in 1890. And by 1895, as we shall see, Korea was to go too.

The old order by which China had for centuries conducted her relations with near and further states had completely crumbled. There were now no buffers on her borders. By land and by sea China was encircled by foreign powers and by forces impatient for commercial gain at her expense.

8 Japan, 1860–1894

T HERE is a Japanese saying that goes, *shussei sureba nanigoto mo tassuru*, meaning: by diligent application anything can be achieved. The response of Japanese to the opening of their country to the West resembled the spirit of this saying. Almost from the outset, response to the West was positive in a way that differed quite markedly from the confused and defensive response in China.

The pattern of Western acts in Japan resembled that in China. Demands were made on a sovereign state to surrender some parts of its sovereignty, and the demands were backed by superior armed strength. The treaties signed were signed under the shadow of that armed might, and the majority of people in the state were against the signing. But there the similarities stop.

Anti-foreign Actions

Once the Treaty of Edo had been signed, opposition, nationalism, and anti-foreign feelings grew rapidly in Japan, and positive action came swiftly. The *Sonno Jo-i* (support the emperor, expel the barbarians) movement, with the massive support of the western clans, gained strength and momentum. Its leaders were nobles and young *samurai* from the Satsuma, Choshu, Hizen, and Tosa clans forming the Satcho Hito group (from the initial syllables of their clan names). This was an anti-*bakufu* party, with its headquarters in Kyoto where the emperor resided, and its financial strength derived from the support of the great merchants of nearby Osaka.

The residence of the British mission at Edo

Above, Japanese attacking British diplomats in the corridors of the first British mission at Edo. Laurence Oliphant (left) armed only with a riding whip was seriously wounded

Below, both Japanese and Chinese found the hairiness of many Western men a subject for amusement and surprise. Here, the Japanese wife of a European has just given birth to a child with a beard, to the consternation of everyone concerned

Events moved with increasing speed. The shogun's regent, Ili, was assassinated in Edo, and Westerners, who were already in Japan in considerable numbers, came under sporadic attack. A Russian naval officer and two seamen were set upon in Yokohama in 1859. The American consul Harris's secretary was murdered in 1861, and the British legation in Edo was twice burned down. These and other incidents showed the foreign powers clearly that the *bakufu* was not really in control of affairs any longer. While assuring foreigners that it would protect them according to treaty, it also assured the anti-foreign groups of its support in expelling foreigners.

The murder of an Englishman, C.L. Richardson, while he was out riding near Yokohama, was the deed of a Satsuma clansman. When the British demanded compensation from the *bakufu* and the Lord of Satsuma, and received no satisfaction, they resorted at once to the familiar use of gunboats, and bombarded Kagoshima, the Satsuma capital. While there was little life lost in the bombardment, the city was reduced to ashes, and the Satsuma clan at once agreed to pay up. At the same time they made enquiries about buying a warship from England. Suddenly, the most conservative and anti-foreign of the clans reversed its stand and decided to acquire the means of modern power. The Satsuma in fact were later to play a leading part in the new Japanese navy. The Satsuma reaction was clearly a positive one.

In the same year, 1863, the Emperor Komei had summoned the shogun to Kyoto, feeling strong enough to do so. The shogun obeyed, feeling the weakness of his position, and was told to expel all foreigners from Japan and to close the ports to them by June 25.

Unfortunately for the shogun, he had no power to put such orders into practice. So he did nothing. On the day set for expulsion, it was the troops of Choshu, whose domains overlooked the Straits of Shimonoseki at the western entry to the Inland Sea, who fired on an American merchant ship. The straits were closed for a year after French and Dutch ships had also been attacked. The power of the Choshu lay in their use of Western firearms, and the complete break with *samurai* tradition in the use of ordinary peasants trained as soldiers.

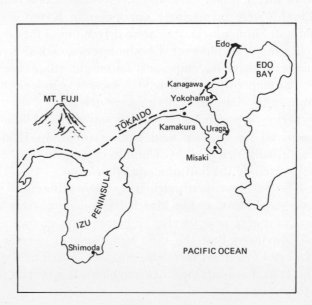

Edo at the head of the long, almost land-locked, Edo Bay at whose entry stands Uraga

Retribution naturally followed. In September 1864, a fleet of British, French, and Dutch ships, and one American vessel bombarded and captured the Choshu forts which had repeatedly fired on them. The Choshu had to pay indemnities, to promise not to reconstruct the forts, and to keep the straits open.

The effect on the clans was decisive. They decided to re-arm completely on Western lines. At the same time they saw it was essential to abandon their anti-foreign stance. Hiring foreign instructors and using Western arms, they trained themselves thoroughly, and in the coming struggle with the shogunate this strength was to prove a vital factor.

Next year, 1865, pressure was exerted on the *bakufu* to obtain approval of the treaties from the emperor. A display of foreign naval strength off Osaka persuaded the emperor and the *Sonno Jo-i* party at Kyoto to ratify the Treaty of Edo. Thus the strong anti-foreign movement realized it had to submit to the will of the foreign powers. But the reaction was positive, in that the Japanese did not waste time lamenting their lack of ability to expel foreigners. They decided to strengthen themselves by foreign methods at once.

Internal Disputes

The path to that goal was not yet clear. The shogunate was weak, but it still ruled. In 1862 the old *sankin kotai* system had been relaxed and the *daimyo* were now required to reside in Edo for only one hundred days every three years, and there was no longer a requirement to leave hostages in the capital. The exodus of *daimyo* and families at once began. What Edo lost in dissident *daimyo* Kyoto gained in *daimyo* plotting and planning against the shogun. So the balance of power began to shift to the imperial court.

At this point there was little unity in Kyoto. The Choshu still wanted to expel the foreigners, while Satsuma clansmen favoured trading with them, and also advocated some sort of union between emperor and *bakufu* (called *kobu gattai*). The extremist Choshu were increasingly unpopular in Kyoto and after the shelling of foreign ships at Shimonoseki, they were driven out of the city by Satsuma-Aizu forces. The following year, however, Choshu forces attacked Kyoto, intending, as they put the matter, to save the emperor from misguided advisers.

The emperor then ordered the *bakufu* to suppress the Choshu rising and, with help from other clans, the Choshu were defeated.

Seeing a possibility of wiping out the rebellious Choshu, the *bakufu* in 1865 prepared for another fight against them. In 1866 they joined battle but were continually defeated by Choshu troops. In this campaign the *bakufu* was not supported by the Satsuma and other clans.

The Satsuma then patched up their differences with the Choshu, abandoning *kobu gattai* ideas, and in March 1866 made a secret alliance with them, whose aim was to restore power to the emperor. This alliance was soon joined by other clans, all convinced that the time had come to overthrow the shogunate. This very powerful force had merchant support as well as that of the imperial court and of the Tosa, Uwajima, and Echizen clans. It even had the moral support of the British government.

The reasons for the strength of Satsuma and Choshu are interesting in themselves, and important in relation to the fact that for several decades to come the leaders of the two clans dominated Japanese history.

The Satsuma, whose lands lay in south Kyushu, and the Choshu with their domains at the western end of Honshu, had several advantages over other *han*—the 265 feudal domains existing in the middle of the nineteenth century. They were the largest in area, and Satsuma ranked second in tax yield. Choshu and Satsuma had a higher ratio of fighting men to tax income than the national average, thus greater actual military potential than their economic strength suggested. The 27,000 *samurai* of Satsuma contained a high proportion of *goshi*, peasants doubling as part-time fighters, and Choshu had about 11,000.

Internally both were united, and both were located far from the main cities of Japan, and were backward economically and socially compared to the Tokugawa strongholds—thus the morale of their feudal lords was still more or less intact. Without their wealth they would not have had the possibility of buying Western arms.

Satsuma, through its vassal domain of Ryukyu (the Liu-ch'iu Islands) had trading contacts with the outside world, and was a centre of learning in Western technologies and science.

The End of the Shogunate

The large movements in Japanese internal affairs involving great numbers of people and profound changes in traditional outlook were of course not wholly inspired by anti-foreign sentiments. But Western intervention in the Japanese scene undoubtedly greatly hastened the end of shogun rule. It was the positive nature of the various responses in Japan, whose proponents then proceeded to fight it out with each other, and at the same time arm with Western equipment and make use of Western tactics, that made reaction to the West in Japan so different from that in China.

The impact of the treaties was felt in other fields also. Foreign traders often found it was more profitable to operate on the gold-silver exchange (which was in their favour) than to indulge in general trading. Silver was dumped in large quantities in Japan, and gold removed, resulting in gross fluctuation of prices and serious dislocations in the economy. Heavy demand for silk and tea for export made nonsense of the local prices. Imported goods—cotton fabrics and other cheap manufactured goods—were to make even deeper wounds in the economy, bringing ruin to the corresponding local industries. While the shogun made great efforts to limit the scope of such imports, governmental power was frustrated by the determination of Western traders and the resolute desire for quick profits shown by Japanese commercial groups.

The large sums required for defence preparations further weakened the shogun treasury. This drain on finances was coupled with payment of indemnities occasioned by the attacks on foreign ships and persons which were now beyond *bakufu* control.

In 1866, the shogun Iemochi died, and in the following year the Emperor Komei also died. Iemochi's successor, Keiki, knowing that nothing could be done to prolong

In January, 1868, opponents to the restoration of imperial rule were defeated in the battles of Fushimi and Toba in the outskirts of Kyoto

the rule of the shogunate, agreed in November of that year to the proposal of the Lord of Tosa backed by the other western *han* to surrender his powers (such as they were) to the new emperor. This was a fifteen-year-old boy named Mutsuhito (reigned 1867–1912). The new reign was called Meiji (Enlightened Government). Under this arrangement the shogun was to head a council of the foremost *daimyo* which would govern in the name of the emperor. This did not happen because Satsuma, Choshu, and other powerful *han* forces decided that they would complete the over-throw of the shogunate once and for all. On January 3, 1868 they took the imperial palace, and issued a decree that stripped Keiki of his title and of his lands. The shogunate was abolished and the rule of the emperor restored. With the Meiji Restoration, the 635 years of shogun rule came to an end.

The young *samurai* of the Western *han* who had toppled the shogun had to face a brief civil war as those forces faithful to the shogun attempted to reverse the position. But the crushing defeats they suffered at Fushimi and Toba south of Kyoto on January 27, brought Tokugawa resistance to an end. In May of that year, 1868,

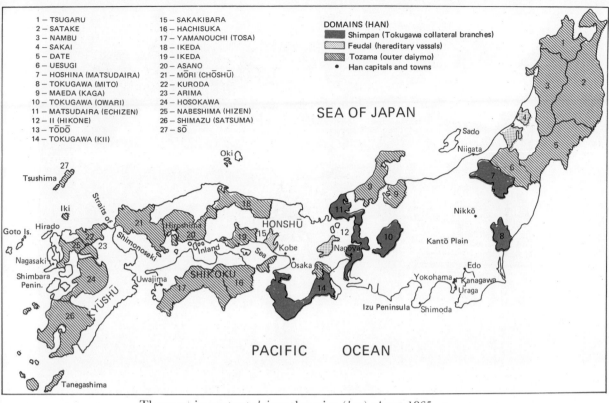

The most important *daimyo* domains (*han*) about 1865

The last shogun, Yoshinobu Tokugawa, announces that he has relinquished power in favour of restoration of imperial rule. The scene is at Nijo Castle in Kyoto on November 7, 1867

On the restoration of power to the emperors after so many centuries of shogun rule, the Emperor Meiji crosses a bridge to reach the new imperial residence at Tokyo Castle, 1868

the imperial forces occupied Edo and renamed it Tokyo (Eastern Capital). Soon after that the emperor moved his court there, and Tokyo became the seat of the Meiji government.

New Leadership

The leadership of what was in fact a revolutionary force that came to power in a *coup d'état*, suitably equipped with an undoubted hereditary and legitimate emperor, was composed of young and dynamic *samurai*. Many of them were of humble birth. Their advantage was a certain freedom from traditional constraints, and openness to rapid change. They also recognized that in order to overcome the Western military powers, to free the country from the five percent customs rate imposed by treaty that allowed foreign cheap goods to flood into Japan, they would have to create a modern central government and carry out great social reforms.

At the time of the *coup d'état* the three most important *samurai*, Kido of Choshu, Okubo and Saigo of Satsuma, were all aged between 35 and 41, Inoue and Ito of Choshu were 33 and 27, and two court nobles, Iwakura and Sanjo, were only 43 and 31 respectively. So it was a comparatively young group in command. The majority were men of great talent who on account of their mostly humble origins had no special affection for the former regime. Their rise to power had been against the rules of the feudal class system, and it was not surprising that they should advocate a more free system for the future.

The Leaders of the Meiji Restoration

Samurai

Kido Koin (1833–1877)
Inoue Kaoru (1835–1915)   } of Choshu
Ito Hirobumi (1841–1909)
Yamagata Aritomo (1838–1922)

Saigo Takamori (1827–1877)
Okubo Toshimichi (1830–1878)   } of Satsuma
Matsukata Kasayoshi (1835–1924)
Kuroda Kiyotaka (1840–1900)

Okuma Shigenobu (1839–1922)   of Hizen

Itagakai Taisuke (1837–1919)   of Tosa

Court Nobles

Iwakura Tomoni (1825–1883)
Sanjo Sanetomi (1837–1891)

Four of the leaders of the Meiji Restoration seen in later life. Saigo Takamori (a) and Okubo Toshimichi (b) belonged to the *samurai* of Satsuma; Itagaki Taisuke (c) was of Tosa, and Iwakura Tomoni (d) was a court noble

New Forms of Government

The first obvious necessity for the new rulers was to create a centralized form of government to replace the old decentralized system of the Tokugawa shogunate. This was rather easier to recognize than to carry out. There were still elements of feudal power to combat, the economy was in a shaky condition, and it was essential to build up military strength. As a result of these factors, the first attempts at administrative machinery were of an experimental kind and were replaced later, in 1890, by a more stable form of constitutional government.

Even before the overthrow of the shogunate, the youthful emperor had been made to issue a 'Five Articles Oath', more often known in the West as the 'Charter Oath', drafted by two *samurai* of Echizen and Tosa and approved by Kido of Choshu. The articles were:

> Deliberative assemblies shall be widely established and all matters decided by public discussion.
> All classes, high and low, shall unite in vigorously carrying out the administration of affairs of state.
> Among the common people, no less than the civil and military officials, each shall be allowed to pursue his own calling so that there may be no discontent.
> Evil customs of the past shall be broken off, and everything based on the just laws of nature.
> Knowledge shall be sought throughout the world so as to strengthen the foundation of imperial rule.

The first article was not a democratic pronouncement but an assurance to those elements not yet involved in affairs at Kyoto that they would not be left out. The second article was really no more than a pious hope. The third is the revolutionary statement abolishing feudalism and (in line with the aspirations of the young *samurai* revolutionaries) permitting all people to lead their own lives without frustration. This is followed by the fourth article which, though vague and general, fills out the third in a promise of positive action. The last article, again positive, is the most important because it contains the statement at the basis of the new philosophy. We may see in this frank admission that by acquiring Western knowledge the Japanese would modernize and strengthen their country and its institutions, a complete break with the 'expel the barbarians' movement. The new leaders had not forgotten their anti-foreign outlook, but they had realized that a pragmatic, more practical approach was essential. Through Western technology the ideal of *fukoku kyohei* (rich country, strong military) was to be achieved.

They also made it clear when the emperor received representatives of the foreign powers in March 1868, and when they very quickly punished by death those who attacked foreigners and at once paid indemnities, that they had taken a new view of Western presence in Japan.

There was no intention to set up a democracy, an institution whose principles were quite unknown to most people in Japan at that time. But the machinery of government that was set up differed from that of the shogunate and was eventually modelled on Western political systems. The form of the administration went through many changes as the young and inexperienced leaders experimented.

Above, in a highly stylized painting (as befits the divinity and remoteness of the emperor), the Five Articles of the Imperial Covenant are being read before an altar. The Meiji Emperor, sheltered by magnificent screen sits listening on the right. Below, the first audience ever granted by an emperor of Japan to a foreigner took place on March 23, 1868. The Emperor Meiji received the minister of the Netherlands

At first the *sanshoku* (three offices) were set up in January, 1868—the same day as the 'restoration' of the Meiji emperor. They were: the General Director (the post occupied by an imperial prince), a group of men who discussed or conferred (some court nobles and leading *daimyo*), and Councillors (*san'yo*) who included many young *samurai*. Of the three bodies this last endured for the next twenty years since it usually included the majority of the real leaders of the new Japan.

Soon after the 'three offices' were established, a deliberative assembly, as in article one of the Charter Oath, was set up. But on June 11, 1868, the governmental structure was completely revised. In imitation of the American style, a constitution was issued embodying the Charter Oath and setting up a Council of State (*Dajokan*) as the supreme government organ. This council consisted of a legislature divided into two chambers, an executive body named the Department of Administration, and six other administrative departments.

Not surprisingly this quite clumsy structure did not work. But we should notice the rapidity with which it was formulated and brought into being, and also, when it was seen not to work, the speed with which by the following spring (1869) the whole system was again revised. Two years later, in September 1871, a further revision was made. The final shape was a Council of State divided into three chambers: the Left Chamber (*Sa-in*) which theoretically determined legislation, the Right Chamber (*U-in*) which supervised the ministries, and the Central Chamber (*Sei-in*) which had all the real authority in legislation and also over the ministries.

Abolition of Feudal Society

Just as they had done in the field of government, the new rulers of Japan attempted with equal boldness to wipe out the whole feudal structure of society. Further progress in reforms could not come without a clean break with the past.

The principal step that had to be taken was to remove the political and economic power of the *daimyo*. It was fortunate that the *samurai* leaders of the most powerful clans were able to persuade their own *daimyo* to give up control of their lands. The document in which the Lords of Choshu, Satsuma, Tosa, and Hizen surrendered their lands is explicit about the reasons for doing so:

> 'There is no soil within the Empire that does not belong to the Emperor...and no inhabitant who is not a subject of the Emperor.... Now that Imperial power is restored, how can we retain possession of land that belongs to the Emperor, or govern people who are his subjects? We therefore reverently offer up all our feudal possessions ...so that a uniform rule may prevail throughout the Empire.'

This was done in 1869, and soon the remainder of the *daimyo* followed suit.

Class restrictions on professional employment were removed in the same year, and in 1870 commoners were permitted to take family names—something they never had before. The old classification of the population into court nobles, warrior class, and farmers and townspeople, was changed by the emergence of new classes. The new nobility (*kazoku*) consisted of court nobles as of old, but was now joined by former *daimyo*. The gentry (*shizoku*) were the former *samurai*. And the rest of the people were *heimin*—commoners. The rigidity of the old class system gave way to a greater mobility in the new.

By 1871, the government was strong enough to decree the end of feudalism. The feudal lands were divided into forty-three prefectures called *ken,* each of which had a governor appointed by the central administration. The civil service was recruited by examination.

The Effects on Society

Formerly the *daimyo* had great financial difficulties and were often in debt to the merchants. They had to pay their *samurai,* maintain an Edo and a country establishment. Now the government took over some of their debts, and in abolishing the feudal estates abolished the payments to *samurai.* Some *daimyo* became merchants, their capital being the payments received from the government.

But for the *samurai* the change was a severe blow. The pensions they got from the government were too small to live on and many of them went into business. With the setting up of a national army in place of many feudal armies, they no longer had the monopoly of carrying arms. There were several *samurai* rebellions after 1874. The most serious was the Satsuma Rebellion led by Saigo in 1877. Saigo, who had helped form the restoration government, became disillusioned with it and led (somewhat against his will) a *samurai* force in revolt. This was suppressed by Yamagata of Choshu who pushed back the rebel forces on Kagoshima. There Saigo and his rebellion met their end in 1877.

This was the strongest and most serious challenge to the new government. The failure of the rebellion removed the last chance of a return to feudalism in Japan. The government proved that its policies of modernization in many fields had made it strong enough to cope with any domestic problem that might arise.

The merchant class was on the whole in favour of the government's abolition of feudalism. Merchant capital was no longer lent out to impoverished *daimyo* who in the past frequently escaped repaying their debts. And, under the new regime, most of such debts to merchants were officially settled.

The peasant farmers who were the majority of Japanese were no longer controlled by feudal lords. But many of them were forced by financial problems to become tenants of their lands and to work for a new landlord class. So theirs was not so happy a life. The result was a peasant drift to the expanding towns. Peasant uprisings became more frequent after 1868 and rose to a peak in 1873 when the conscription act came into force. They diminished after the land tax was reduced in 1876.

Educational Developments

The most important document concerning the new government's attitude to education is the imperial rescript on the subject, dated October 30, 1890. Copies of this were hung in every school beside the emperor's portrait, and its contents were to form the basis for all moral and civic instruction after it was issued. It represents a less progressive aspect of governmental thinking, being strongly

136 THE WEST IMPOSES ITS WILL

traditional in tone and Confucian in principles. It was in fact largely drafted by a *samurai*, Inoue Kowashi, well known as a Confucian scholar.

> 'Our Imperial Ancestors have founded Our Empire on a basis broad and everlasting, and have deeply and firmly implanted virtue. Our subjects, ever united in loyalty and filial piety, have from generation to generation illustrated the beauty thereof. This is the glory of the fundamental character of Our Empire, and herein lies the source of Our education. . . .'

The rescript continues, exhorting everyone to respect parents, to live in peace with each other and to be modest, to 'pursue learning and cultivate arts and thereby develop intellectual faculties and perfect moral powers'. And it continues:

> '. . .always respect the Constitution and observe the laws; should emergency arise, offer yourselves courageously to the State. . . . So shall ye not only be Our good and faithful subjects, but render illustrious the best traditions of your forefathers. . . .'

Japanese education under the feudal regime had been left to the feudal lords, and was confined almost wholly to the *samurai* class. There were also some Buddhist schools for commoners. Studies were mostly confined to Chinese learning although toward the time of the Restoration some Western and Japanese subjects were introduced. In one sense, this was a good situation, because when a national education system had to be introduced there was no established system to get rid of. And in Japan there had never been much connection between education and religion—a factor that tended to hinder educational reform in many parts of the West. One other favourable aspect was that Japanese mass education was just beginning and could utilize all the most up-to-date educational ideas from any source. It was not confined by traditional ideas on the subject.

A scene in a primary school of the pre-Meiji era. The pupils sit on the floor at low tables on which they have Japanese-style books, ink-slabs, and brushes. The emphasis is evidently on traditional learning

A Ministry of Education was formed in 1871, and an Education Act was officially announced in 1872. This Act contained several features important and new to Japanese life:

> The country was divided into eight university districts, and subdivided into middle school and primary school districts.

> Sixteen months of schooling were made compulsory for all children after the age of six. (This was lengthened to three years in 1880, and to six years in 1908. Fees were abolished in public primary schools in 1900.) There was to be one primary school for every 600 children.

The Ministry of Education's proposal that no one of either sex in Japan should be illiterate was easier to put forward than to put into effect. The shortage of teachers, of school buildings, of experience in what were basically Western forms of instruction and often Western subjects, all contributed to the difficulties. The ministry began building thousands of primary schools and by 1879 there were in the region of 26,000 of them with an enrolment of 2,500,000 pupils. Many scores of secondary and technical schools were also built (often against local opposition which saw the whole venture in education as a source merely of heavy taxation).

The degree of local autonomy given to the prefectures in education was largely withdrawn in the 1880s. The government by then was firmly in the saddle of affairs, not afraid of being unseated. The trend toward lessening the emphasis on purely Western styles of organization affected the educational structure. In 1882 primary schools put greater emphasis on morality by which Western influences could be combatted. And this influence may be seen in the Imperial Rescript on Education.

The contrast between the pre-Meiji class and this drawing of a new post-Meiji class is sharp. The pupils no longer sit on the floor, some wear Western clothes, and their teacher uses various Western aids such as wall charts and maps. Western-style books are lying on the table and held by some of the pupils

But even in that document there is the concept of mass education and mass indoc-trination. This was a modern and not a traditional concept. Mori Arinori, who was a returned student from the West, became Minister of Education in 1885. He felt that education was 'not for the sake of the pupils but for the sake of the country'.

Another student from the West, Kato Hiroyuki, who was president of Tokyo University for many years, came increasingly to underline the supremacy of the state in education. In this he was under German influence.

Education as a whole tended increasingly to teach two aspects. One, nationalistic outlook with near-fanatical loyalty to the emperor and the country. Two, utilitarian skills and knowledge rather than the ability and necessity of thinking for oneself. The fifth article of the Charter Oath with its recommendation that knowledge should be sought from all over the world, became something of a dead letter. And a thoroughly Japanese approach to education was gradually adopted.

In an incredibly short time—by 1906—about ninety-five percent of Japanese children were in primary schools, and Japan became the first Asian country with a fully literate population. The first Japanese daily newspaper, Nichi-Nichi, came out in 1872, and soon many more appeared. But such was the control of the press by government that freedom of speech was hardly possible.

There is no doubt, despite the rapid and good results in literacy that educational policies produced, that education also fostered an extreme form of nationalism which had effects in the future that were not favourable to Japan as a whole.

The first page of the Nichi-Nichi newspaper's first issue, dated March 19, 1872. The news-paper is the present-day Mainichi

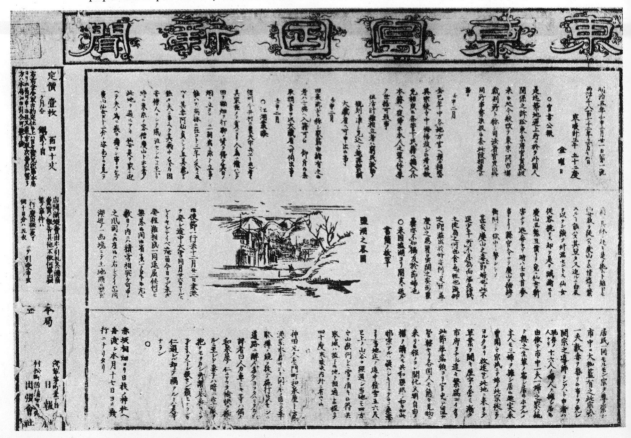

Further Political Reforms

The constitution of 1868, which had been hastily drawn up to put the terms of the Charter Oath into practice, was by no means a declaration of democratic government. What it principally ensured was that the oligarchy of ruling *samurai* might govern in a relatively free manner. In fact the only representative institutions were on a local level—the Prefectural Assemblies established in 1878 and Municipal Assemblies permitted in 1880.

By 1881 there were signs of a general agitation for some form of representative national assembly. The desire was broad-based, voiced by *samurai*, by newspapers in so far as they dared, even by government officials. But at first it was not especially the demand to share power with the all-powerful élite that forced democratic ideas into the forefront in Japan. Rather it was because, influenced by the facts of Western political life where in Britain, France, and the United States national strength seemed to be based on democracy, the Japanese felt they would have a lot to gain by adopting democratic ways too. It was also felt that some form of Japanese democracy would gain them the respect of the West, and eventual Japanese equality with Western powers.

The introduction of representative government was in fact so cautious and so slow that it has been described as a series of failures. It is possible that its slow acceptance was a big factor in its eventual success.

Various political parties were formed. The Society to Establish One's Moral Will (*Risshisha*) spread in popularity in the Tosa area among *samurai* and commoners, and its effects were carried north by the formation of another, the Public Party of Patriots (*Aikoku Koto*) which included in its ranks students returned from the West, and called for the establishment of a 'council-chamber chosen by the people'. Itagaki of Tosa was intimately connected with these movements. One explanation of why a man who was fundamentally military rather than political should involve himself in the clamour for a democratic process, is that Tosa people resented the dominance of Choshu and Satsuma men in the new government. Certainly under Itagaki and one other Tosa leader, it was Tosa men who led the country in wiping out feudal class distinction in Japan in the years between 1868 and 1871, and this led on to their leadership in demands for a parliament after 1873.

The government itself continued to experiment in various ways with more democratic institutions, Ito Hirobumi emerging as the leading government figure. The Left and Right Chambers were abolished and replaced by a Supreme Court (*Daishin-in*), and a Chamber of Elders (*Genro-in*) which was asked to prepare for a National Assembly. In 1876, it began to do so with the help of a book on parliamentary government in England. But its draft presented in 1880 was thought to be too close to the English model and was shelved by Ito and others.

The movements under Itagaki spread, and the *Aikoku Koto* party changed its name—significantly—to *Kokkai Kisei Domei*, the League for Establishing a National Assembly. The movement began to be called *jiyu minken undo*, 'movement for freedom and people's rights'. The chief supporters of the movement were the well-off peasant landowners, doubtless because they were the main group of tax-payers.

In 1881 in October, the government promised that a National Assembly would come into being in 1890. This was its response to what has been called 'the crisis of 1881' when demands for a change in governmental system came to a head. Okuma of Hizen had submitted in March of that year a scheme of far-reaching suggestions for a kind of British parliamentary democratic structure, and elections to be held in 1882. Ito was surprised by his colleague's radical thinking, and he arranged for Okuma's removal from office. Okuma joined others including Itagaki, Inukai Tsuyoshi (known as Ki; 1855–1932) , and Ozaki Yukio (1859–1954)—these last two men to become prominent democratic politicians later.

The government was now basically what was popularly called a 'Sat-Cho clique' —that is, composed mostly of men of Satsuma and Choshu.

It was during this crisis that a strong opposition to the government formed, resulting in the date for the creation of a parliament being decided.

Preparations for 1890

Itagaki and others reorganized in 1881 the League for Establishing a National Assembly, and renamed it *Jiyuto*—literally, Liberty Party. It proclaimed hopefully that 'liberty is the natural state of man' and its preservation man's 'great duty'. Its adherents were landowners and small businessmen hit by taxation.

In 1882 Okuma and others set up a less radical party called *Rikken Kaishinto*, The Constitutional Progressive Party, its support coming from intellectuals and business interests such as Iwasaki, the head of Mitsubishi.

There was dispute between the two parties about the need for democratic processes, and they challenged the right of the Sat-Cho clique to interpret the imperial will, preferring democratic means. These two parties in many different

Ito Hirobumi of Choshu. His travels in the West convinced him that democracy on the Western model should not be adopted in Japan, but that some system not unlike that of Germany might be the best. Basically his ideas on government were autocratic

forms have continued to be the important political groupings in Japan down to our own days.

Ito Hirobumi went West with a delegation to study European political institutions in 1882. He spent nine months in Germany and was in London only six weeks, in other capitals even less. Ito's views were heavily influenced by what he saw (and much approved) in Germany. His previous opinions, however, show the turn of his thoughts on ideas of democracy as applied to Japan:

'Since the Restoration it has been the aim of our government to excel the nations of the whole world. Still, the administration, following conventional and long-established customs, preserves the form of a despotic monarchy. This form may well be applicable for the present...but it must not be insisted upon for the future.... Must our government assume the form of a democracy? I say no.... Democracy must not be adopted, nor should despotic monarchy be retained. In the framing of a constitution our aims should be determined by the ideal of a government which conforms to our country's geography, customs and sentiments of the people, and the spirit of the times.'

Ito Hirobumi, 1873

On his return from abroad he became (in 1884) chairman of a commission to draft the constitution. In July of that year a new peerage was created in order to form an eventual House of Peers, most of them former *daimyo*. The following year the State Council gave way to a Cabinet made up of heads of ministries under a prime minister. This meant that the real rulers—the *samurai* oligarchy—were free from any supervision by the court aristocracy and also united against opposition

The structure of political power and governmental responsibility under the Meiji constitution

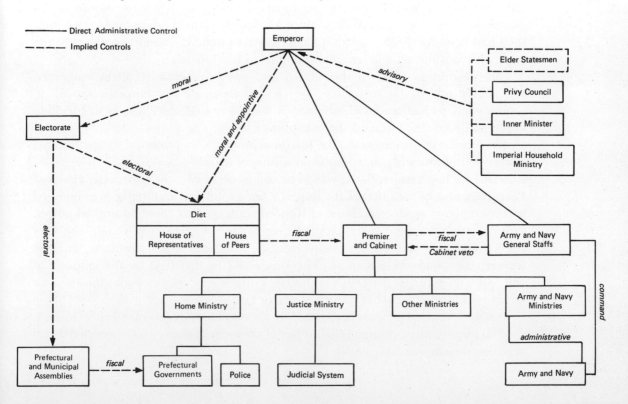

attack. In 1887 a civil service examination system on a German model was adopted. The cabinet was basically composed of Choshu and Satsuma leaders:

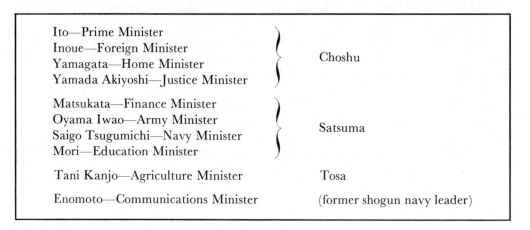

The members of the cabinet were appointed by the emperor—but actually, in the first instance, on the advice of Ito.

The Constitution, 1889

On the anniversary of the traditionally accepted date on which Japan was founded in 660 B.C., the constitution was handed by the emperor to the prime minister, an act designed to symbolize the idea that it was an imperial gift to the Japanese. This constitution formed the base of Japanese governmental structure until the end of World War II. Its principal features, therefore, require to be examined with some care. We should note that its contents remained secret until they had been finalized, and that there was no public discussion on them before that. The constitution was an imperial 'gift' to the Japanese.

The constitution affirmed the 'sacred and inviolable' quality of the emperors, who should govern Japan in line 'for ages everlasting'. The emperor should be commander-in-chief, and with him rested the power to declare war·or to conclude peace. Only he could amend the constitution.

The subjects of the emperors, the Japanese people, were promised rights: freedom of speech and assembly, freedom from arbitrary search.

A Diet, or law-making body, was to be composed of two chambers: the House of Peers consisting of members of the imperial family, nobles, and deputies nominated by the emperor; an elected House of Representatives. This Diet had limited power. Cabinet ministers were mainly responsible to the emperor, and should the Diet reject budgetary proposals, the government or cabinet might continue with the former year's budgetary scheme. The Diet could be dissolved by the emperor at will. All laws required the Diet's approval. When it was not in session, the emperor might issue ordinances that had the force of law.

Basic government policy was dictated by the emperor advised by a Privy Council.

Ministers and the commanders-in-chief of the army and navy were granted direct access to the emperor.

Meaning and Working of the Constitution

The constitution was not really a charter of democracy in Japan. The 'rights' granted to the Japanese of freedom of speech and assembly were made 'subject to law'. In practice, this being undefined, the rights were little but a mockery. If the government did not approve the purpose of an assembly or the opinions of some citizen, they could be suppressed.

The lower, elected, house of the Diet was in fact elected by less than one percent of the population for many years to come. The right to vote was not granted to all adult males until 1925. The House of Representatives had little power (it had to agree to any imperially decreed law, for example) and was really in the hands of the cabinet. The cabinet was appointed or dismissed by the emperor and was dominated by the *genro*—the leaders of the Restoration. They held most of the important posts and advised the emperor, although in fact this was unconstitutional. Until World War I, the *genro* were a sort of super-government without any check of a democratic kind. They controlled most of the ministries because through them most of the ministers were appointed.

The constitution's statement that the emperor ruled and was advised, meant that just as under the shoguns, the emperor was a figurehead and rule was in the hands of other people. The influence of the *genro* was nearly always paramount whether within the cabinet or unofficially. The last of the *genro*, a Fujiwara, Prince Saionji, did not die until 1940.

The key problem with the working of the constitution, other than this backstage manipulation, was the imperfect control that the House of Representatives had over the budget. When the house would not approve the prime minister's budget, it was apparent that he could not carry through reforms, so he dissolved the Diet. In the end, what happened in regard to this ridiculous situation was that prime ministers were forced to ally themselves closely with political parties in order to win the support they needed in the lower house. The original constitutional aim of allowing the cabinet complete freedom from the veto of the Diet was thus defeated, and in Ito Hirobumi's fourth term as prime minister, he appointed party members to the cabinet. Not, of course, in sufficient numbers to have control of the cabinet. The militarist faction, led by the *genro* Yamagata, who was the most important figure in the formation of a national army, often succeeded in pushing through its policies against the parties' opposition.

The assurance of direct access to the emperor for the military commanders meant that their policies had a disproportionately strong effect from time to time.

Prime Ministers of Japan, 1885–1894

1885–1888	Ito Hirobumi—Choshu
1888–1889	Kuroda Kiyotaka—Satsuma
1889–1891	Yamagata Aritomo—Choshu
1891–1892	Matsukata Masayoshi—Satsuma
1892–1896	Ito Hirobumi—Choshu

New Legal Procedure

Just as the beginnings of democratic processes in Japan did not come about because of popular demand but were introduced to strengthen the country in the face of Western invasions of its sovereignty, and to gain the respect of the West—so judicial reform was aimed first at eliminating extraterritoriality. The humiliation, from the Japanese point of view, of having foreign nationals in Japan judged by their own and not Japanese law, was great. The Japanese determined to end it as soon as they could.

By 1890 a penal code on French lines and a commercial code on the German model were already in operation. The civil code was at first similar to the French system but later modified to resemble the German one. Ito Hirobumi's opinion that government and justice, and the reverence for the emperor that he found in Germany, were the most suitable system for Japan, can be seen in the choice of a German-style civil code. Under this, the rights of the individual were subordinated to the authority of the state.

When Western powers saw that these changes were made, Britain (in 1894) signed a treaty promising to relinquish extraterritoriality in 1899. Other powers followed soon afterwards. In this aspect of their relationship, equality with foreigners was attained quite early by Japan.

The emperor hands the new Constitution of Japan to the prime minister as an imperial 'gift' on February 11, 1889. In this ceremony at the imperial palace in Tokyo, everyone present (in contrast to the scene as the last shogun relinquished his powers) is in Western court dress. Even the throne, its raised dais, and the decoration of the hall, are Western, a sign that a drastic change had come about in the life of Japan

Financial Reforms

After the Restoration, the government had need of large sums of money to compensate the *daimyo* and *samurai* on the abolition of the feudal domains. Money was also needed for governmental administration. The imperial and shogunal treasuries were empty. The situation was complicated by the fact that there was no standard currency, and that the government had no power to impose taxation.

A beginning in replenishing the treasury was made when the government began land sales, issuing ownership titles. In 1873 landowners were taxed on the value of the land, not on that of their crops. In 1876 the income which had been given to *daimyo* and the rice allowances given to *samurai* were stopped and replaced by government bonds. The administration did not then suffer such a huge and steady drain of cash from its reserves.

The confusion of gold, silver, and copper coins, and a further problem over notes issued after the Restoration, was resolved in 1871 by the adoption of the decimal system and of the yen as the basic currency unit. The widely used gold standard was adopted as the backing for the currency.

The comparative financial strength soon attained by Japan under the Meiji meant that Japan had little necessity to contract foreign loans. Britain made two loans during the period—one to assist in the construction of a railway, the other to cover interest payments on government bonds.

Industrialization Begins

The need to establish Western-style industry was appreciated by the new government. Despite the fact that even before 1870 a commercial class had grown quite strong and the old agrarian economy had already been modified by this growth of commercialism, there was not enough capital to finance private industry on a large scale.

One of the early heavy industry undertakings—the Shibaura Engineering Works

The government therefore decided to take a hand, and began to sponsor industrial development with state money and with money drawn from the loans of merchants. The need for industrialization was urgent for several reasons. The country needed modern communications and modern defensive weapons, and such essential processes as mining had to be developed if Japan were to attempt to turn herself into a modern state. There was also the question of employing numerous workless and discontented *samurai*—a potential focus of rebellion.

During the 1870s, the government began importing spinning machinery, selling this to manufacturers on an instalment plan. Pilot industries such as cotton and woollen mills, cement, paper, glass, and clothing factories were established as guides for private enterprise to follow. Great strides were also made in the building of ships and the making of munitions and artillery.

Foreign technologists were brought to Japan and foreign techniques diligently studied. Industrialists were given subsidies to assist them in starting new factories and eventually, in the 1880s, in buying government-established industries from the government. This proved to be a factor of central importance in the future story of Japanese industrial expansion. The financial and industrial combines that bought such industries were in very many cases owned and managed by one family. They were called *zaibatsu*, meaning financial group, or clique.

The names of the biggest and most powerful of these *zaibatsu* are interesting to note, since many of them are still in existence as major companies in Japan today: Mitsui, Mitsubishi, Sumitomo, and Yasuda. The smaller ones included Okura, Asana, Ogawa, Kawasaki, and others.

The *zaibatsu* were important not only in the massive and rapid development of modern manufacturing and other industries in Japan, but also in their role as bankers. Through their banks they lent capital to others interested in setting up businesses of all kinds. Thus the government was largely released from the necessity of incurring large foreign loans, and also from the need to apply heavy taxation. The industrial revolution, after a good hard push from the government in the right direction, then sustained its own momentum both in material growth and in financing.

The only section of industry over which the government retained its hold was the military segment. But the relationship between government and *zaibatsu* remained close and the industries essential to development of a national defence capability were carefully supervised by the government. The beginnings of Japan's drift toward militarism may be discovered at this point in her history. The need for expanded profits in a small land with very restricted mineral deposits meant in time the inevitable urge to expand. We shall soon see the course that was followed in the search for more national and industrial 'elbow-room'.

In spite of the tremendous energy spent and the mostly logical and sensible line of development taken by the Japanese in the early Meiji years, the expansion of industry was fundamentally restricted by lack of large amounts of capital. But by 1895 capital accumulation was such that rapid expansion in both heavy and light industries became possible. After the defeat of China in 1895, the accent was on mining and textile expansion. Japan, with its plentiful supply of disciplined and cheap labour, found that its exports were highly competitive in price on world markets.

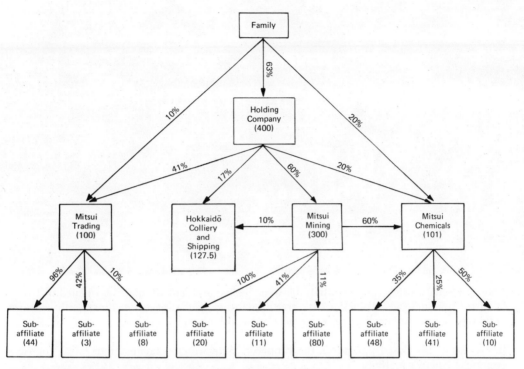

The structure of the Mitsui *zaibatsu*. The arrows show the percentage of stock held, while the numbers in parenthesis, e.g. (400), indicate paid-up capital in millions of yen

The newly built Bank of Japan, opened in 1896, surrounded by several triumphal arches resembling the Arc de Triomphe in Paris

Above, the first railway line in Japan, between Tokyo and Yokohama, was opened in 1872. With the Japanese woodblock artist's traditional means of expression, nineteenth century buildings and the unfamiliar trains are portrayed with charm

Below, inside his closed palanquin the Emperor Meiji watches farmers harvesting the rice crop near Nagoya in 1868

While industry grew, other facets of modernization were to be seen in increasing quantities as the years went past. In 1870 the first railway line was built between Tokyo and Yokohama, and later extended. A telegraph line between the two places had been in operation since the previous year, and a postal service began operation in 1873.

Whatever the Japanese did, they tended to do with energy and attention to detail, not only in Japan but in their drive for export markets abroad and their desire to participate on equal terms with the West. Tariffs set by treaties were still a limiting factor. But Japan made a start on acquiring her own fleet of merchant ships, and in the future foreign trade was to become the most important single aspect of her economy.

The increase in population from 35,200,000 in 1873 to 46,100,000 only thirty years later, meant that improved agricultural methods and better strains of rice had to be developed. The nation was for a time self-sufficient in food but the rapid population rise made Japan after 1890 an importer of food.

Military Strengthening

Imperial Precepts to Soldiers and Sailors, 1882

'When in Youth We succeeded to the Imperial Throne, the shogun returned into Our hands the administrative power, and all the feudal lords their fiefs; thus...Our entire realm was unified and the ancient regime restored. Due as this was to the meritorious services of Our loyal officers and wise councillors...yet it must also be attributed to Our subjects' true sense of loyalty.... Soldiers and Sailors, We are your supreme Commander-in-chief. Our relations with you will be most intimate when We rely on you as Our limbs and you look upon Us as your head.... The soldier and sailor should consider loyalty their essential duty.... Remember that, as the protection of the state and the maintenance of its power depend upon the strength of its arms, the growth or decline of this strength must affect the nation's destiny for good or evil.... Never be led astray by current opinions nor meddle in politics....'

Yamagata Aritomo of Choshu, the man largely responsible for the creation of the Japanese army. Here, as an old man, he is seen loaded with medals and insignia of honour. He died in 1922

The rescript continues, stressing prudence, self-control, and a disciplined loyalty.

The need for a strong military force was twofold: to strengthen the government's hold at home, and to strengthen Japan against aggression from outside. The first step was a conscription law, passed in 1873, making military service compulsory for all. The peasants now took the place of *samurai* as the core of the army, and their potential was indicated by the suppression of the Satsuma rebellion.

The man largely responsible for the creation of Japan's military strength was Yamagata Aritomo.

It was in the years following the new constitution that the beginnings of Japan's militaristic development were first seen. We have already noted the direct access by the military to the emperor stipulated in that constitution. And it was fundamentally this that allowed the commanders of the army and navy virtually to make war if and when they wanted to do so. They could by-pass the cabinet and the Diet at any time, and if the emperor was in agreement, and also the majority of the *genro*, no further problem arose in doing what the military demanded.

But this was by no means the only factor in Japanese militarism. The army and navy, as the 'limbs' of the emperor could not be morally wrong, because the emperor (being divine) could not be wrong. And as we shall soon see, territorial expansion did not have to be justified so long as it was successful and beneficial to Japan as a whole.

Another element was that Japan, like China, had no tradition of subscribing to international law. That law was found by the Japanese to be useful when dealing with Western countries, but it was not thought of as relevant to relations with oriental countries.

'One hundred volumes of International Law are not the equal of a few cannon; a handful of Treaties of Friendship are not worth a basket of gunpowder. Cannon and gunpowder are not aids for the enforcement of given moral principles; they are the implements for the creation of morality where none exists.'

Fukuzawa Yukichi

Fukuzawa's ideas found confirmation in the popularity, at the end of the nineteenth century, of post-Darwinian theories which stated that not only did the fittest societies survive, but they also conquered. These concepts were joined to ideas about Japan's own moral superiority.

By 1900 the minister of the navy in the government was chosen from the ranks of serving admirals. Such ministers wielded great power. When they did not get whatever action they desired, they could resign from the cabinet and possibly bring about the fall of the government. Thus the prime minister often had to yield to policies he and others did not agree to.

The military faction was strongly of the opinion that only by foreign conquest could the expansion of the economy and the needs of an ever-growing population be catered for. Although it would seem on the whole that business interests were not in favour of foreign conquest, it was in the end the military voice that prevailed.

Yet another reason for militarism and its growth was the at first natural one of attempting to equal foreign nations and to attract their admiration, abolishing the inferior status of Japan in the wake of the unequal treaties. We will later see

Japan joining the Western nations in their headlong scramble for concessions in helpless China.

Perhaps the final reason for growing militarism lay in the aims of the educational system itself—subservience to the emperor and state and to the ancient Japanese traditions that were being underlined partly in order to counteract the now legal Christianity.

The logical extension of this strongly felt nationalism mixed with a certain pride in Japan's achievements in such a short period since the Restoration, was the opinion that Japan should be the protector of the Asian peoples against Western powers and their steady erosion of oriental sovereignty. Coupled with this, went the idea that to protect her own territory adequately, Japan ought to control neighbouring lands. The example of England—a land of constitutional government at home and of colonial expansion—was taken as a valid model.

Achievements of Modernization

Summing up shortly before the end of the nineteenth century all this frenzy of activity in practically every department of Japanese life—what can be said?

Japan, formerly for centuries ruled by a shogun, changed from an oriental feudal state into a strong united national state with a centralized bureaucratic government. From what we would today term an underdeveloped country, Japan became in a very short time a highly industrialized state, and she managed to effect this change in less time than any Western country had taken.

In order to make such fundamental transformations in life, Japan restored the emperor to his position as the representative of ancient Japanese ancestry and traditions, and breathed new life into the ancient religion, Shinto.

The Meiji Emperor and his empress in Western dress

At the same time a new centralized government controlled by young *samurai* took charge of affairs and repudiated feudalism. Western forms of government were borrowed, but modified to suit Japan—this can be seen very clearly in the constitution of 1889 in which, although some bows are made in the direction of democracy, the real power is not even in the hands of the small number of voters but in those of the original oligarchy of *samurai* who effected the Restoration, and of the military commanders.

All the constituents of a modern state were forced and coaxed into being, including scientific and technical education, banks, and a financial system on Western lines, industries, and an efficient army drawn from the masses in place of the old warrior classes, well supplied with Japanese and foreign weapons.

Right, a sketch satirizing the manner in which Japanese of the official and wealthy classes took to wearing Western dress in the midst of a populace almost all still in traditional clothes. Below, the transition from old to new in Japan is characterized in this drawing. The man on the right is described as 'primitive' in dress, the central figure 'half civilized', while the man in Western dress on the left is labelled 'civilized'

Militarism and ideas of foreign conquest grew with military and economic strength.

Yet underneath all this obvious change and Westernization, Japan retained a great deal of what was traditionally Japanese. Despite the advent of newspapers and western-style books, scientific training, telegraphs and railways, factories and shipyards, Western-style clothes and foreign buildings, a postal service and the Western calendar in place of the old lunar one—in spite of all these it was still a formerly feudal class who ruled. The *samurai* became the *genro* who (unconstitutionally) advised the emperor and exercised real power. Government was by this oligarchy, and not one run on democratic lines.

The Japanese society that formed during the Meiji times was not a Western one. Rather it was a deeply Japanese society with Western trimmings. What was Western about it was often important to the development and the strength of the nation, but in fundamentals Japan had not greatly altered.

The constitution was not the result of activity by the people, but the gift of the emperor. Therefore only he could alter it. Education was designed to foster loyalty to state and emperor. Technical education was merely added on to this old concept. Political parties came into being but had little power, and members of the lower house in the Diet were elected by a tiny minority of the people (those who paid more than fifteen yen in tax). The old religion, Shinto, was stressed and became a state religion. Christianity was tolerated after 1873 but had little influence.

Even in industry the Japanese took a road quite different from the laissez-faire capitalism prevailing in Europe, and the government-sponsored and later government-guided *zaibatsu* industry became something peculiarly Japanese.

The opinions of Ito Hirobumi on modernization, expressed before he went to the West (page 141), were in essence still true of Japan as growing militarism led the nation into war in 1894.

Self-Strengthening—Contrasts in China and Japan

The contrast between the results of the self-strengthening movements in China and in Japan is clear and vivid. China had been forced to sign treaties that, one after the other, took away more and more of her control over her own country and people. Her efforts to acquire the strength to oppose the Western powers who forced the signing of such treaties had come to very little. In the year 1894 China was weak, entirely lacking the power to defend herself, and efforts at modernization were small and generally ineffective.

Japan, on the other hand, had changed from feudalism to a strong central government which had succeeded in pushing ahead with modernization. A strong national state had emerged in place of a traditional feudal one, and had already shown signs of its ability to meet the West on at least some terms of equality.

The contrast between the two countries is so sharp that we must look for some explanation. There is no single or simple reason—rather, there are a number of reasons that seem to have added up to weakness in China and to strength in Japan.

In China the guiding power of the Confucian idea of the state had lasted 2,000 years, allowing the Chinese to develop one of the world's great original civilizations.

The Chinese felt themselves superior to other peoples, and regarded all non-Chinese as 'barbarians' in varying degrees. For this reason they also found it hard to believe that China could be defeated by the 'barbarians', or that, after defeat, they could learn anything important from those foreigners.

Japan, however, had borrowed much of its culture from China long ago, and had made efforts to absorb Western learning long before she was forced to do so. The Japanese were much more open to accepting Western science and Western technology because they had already learned something of these subjects and saw clearly that they could be useful. The Western assault on Japan was also not so severe as that on China—for the West did not see Japan as being so valuable commercially.

When the West came in force to the shores of China and pressed its demands, the Chinese were weak, the dynasty far past its powerful prime, the country impoverished by taxation and by rebellions that continued during the times of greatest Western pressure. Under an alien Manchu dynasty, the country was far from united, and corruption deeply rooted. The response of China to Western threats was muddled. China wanted to keep the West out but, finding it could not, tried to squeeze the West out slowly by making life difficult for it. The Western powers were too strong, and this failed.

In Japan, the coming of the West brought the end of a shogun system of rule that was weakened already by internal factors. The Japanese had a time-honoured rallying point in the emperor and all that he stood for in terms of long tradition. Their response was to restore his lost authority, and destroy the shogun government. This was done by young men who, because of their youth, were perhaps more open to ideas of change and to new ways of thought.

China was led, on the whole, by old men, resistant to change. And even in Japan, we will see how, when the young *samurai* of the Restoration grew older and became the *genro* who manipulated the destinies of Japan, their ideas were largely stiff and against change. They could not give up their own power. The Chinese leaders, the scholar-officials, were of *genro* age. They could not agree to change the system that had formed their thinking and which gave them their power and authority.

For Japan, the results of Chinese weakness and rigidity of thought, provided an object lesson quickly learned. Japan saw in centralization of power the only way to initiate and control essential modernization. In China, government was highly decentralized and remained so. Therefore it was difficult to effect any country-wide change quickly.

Finally, Japan is a fairly small and compact area in which distances are not great. China is a vast country where distances are very great indeed. Communications in Japan could quite readily be improved, whereas in China this was a problem of large dimensions with no immediate solution. Communications were to prove essential to modernization—rather as free circulation of the blood in the body keeps it alive and working.

These are the main factors which seem to have caused the totally different responses of China and Japan to similar threats from the West.

9 The Sino-Japanese War, 1894–1895

W<small>E</small> have already seen how the geographical positions of Burma and of Indo-China led to European hopes of access to parts of China through their territories, and in due course to their colonization. Thailand (then known as Siam) suffered less because geographically it was not on any main access route, either by sea or by land, to what the West assumed to be the vast riches of China.

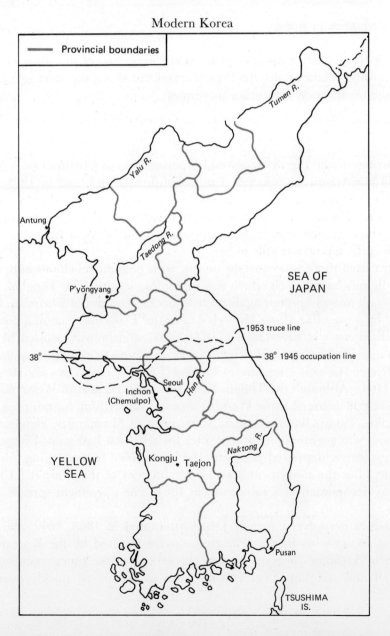

Modern Korea

Korea, however, was in the worst geographical position of all. The peninsular land with its extremely long sea-coast lay in the path of Japan if she wished to expand on to the Asian continent. It was also of interest to Russia in search of a deep-sea port that would not freeze over in winter. And it had been for centuries a Chinese tributary state. Since the Japanese invasions of the sixteenth century which ended with the death of Hideyoshi, the Korean court had also sent tribute missions to Edo. The Manchu dynasty in China conquered the country in 1636 but, following traditional practice, retained the ruling Yi dynasty (1392–1910) on the throne, and the situation reverted to the normal tributary relationship. The Confucian basis of rule in Korea was of an even more conservative kind than that of China. Possibly on this account, Korea reacted even less creatively than did China itself to influences and incursions from outside.

Foreign Intervention in Korea

1866 saw the French using the excuse of the execution of missionaries in Korea to try to establish relations. But the French attack failed and the Korean commander lectured the invaders on Confucian principles:

'How can you tell us to abandon the teaching of our forefathers and accept those of others?'

The Taewongun (the regent) renewed his persecution of Christianity.

In 1868 the Americans also failed to establish relations, and in 1871 a further American expedition, similar to that of Commodore Perry to Japan, failed too.

The Hermit Kingdom, as Korea was often called, was finally breached by the Japanese who regarded it as 'a dagger pointed at the heart of Japan' if it were to be controlled by a power hostile to her.

In Korea itself there was constant unrest, with peasant rebellions and, in 1862–1863, a religious-based revolt which was even more serious. The Tonghak (Eastern Learning) cult arose in protest against the influx of Western, or Christian, learning. It was led by a man like Hung Hsiu-ch'üan of the T'aip'ing—son of a poor village scholar. His name was Ch'oe Che-u (1824–1864), and he was inspired by news of the T'aip'ing rebellion and of foreign attacks on China to seek the mandate of the Lord of Heaven (Ch'onju—the same as Chinese T'ien-chu, which was also the Catholic name for God). Although the Tonghak cult was directed against Western influence paradoxically it assumed some Western aspects. Basically it contained a mixture of Confucian, Taoist, Buddhist, some Catholic, and Shamanistic elements. When Ch'oe Che-u was eventually captured after his rebellion had gained huge support from the extremely depressed peasantry, he maintained he was trying to eradicate Christianity. But the movement was too reminiscent of the T'aip'ing Christians, and he was decapitated as a subversive in 1864. The movement spread under his successors.

The Restoration government in Japan attempted in 1868, 1869, and 1872 to negotiate a treaty with Korea. The envoys were insulted by the Koreans. Saigo Takamori of Satsuma—a giant among Japanese of those times, standing almost six feet tall and weighing over 200 lbs—was in favour of quickly overrunning

Korea in order to forestall Russia. But he favoured first of all sending an ambassador who would almost certainly be murdered by the Koreans (asking repeatedly that he be sent in that position), thus giving an excuse for war. He was overruled by Okubo's policy of continuing internal Japanese reform before military adventures were undertaken. And the return of the Iwakura mission from its journey to the West seemed to confirm that this was the better policy.

It was not long, however, before a suitable excuse for war turned up. A Japanese warship surveying the Korean coast was fired on from the land. Japan sent a mission to Peking (which conducted Korean foreign affairs), and a naval force to Korea, to obtain satisfaction. China disclaimed responsibility and made what turned out to be a great mistake in permitting the Koreans to negotiate on their own behalf. It was hard, after that, for China to claim authority over Korea.

In 1876, Korea was forced to sign the Treaty of Kanghwa with Japan. This was rather similar to early treaties forced by Britain and other Western powers on China. In addition to Pusan, where Japanese already had permission to live, two more ports were opened. The most important clause of the treaty was that in which Japan recognized Korea's independence—thereby indicating that it was no longer a Chinese tributary.

China was powerless to do more than retaliate by assisting Western powers to gain a foothold in Korea. Li Hung-chang, who was responsible for Korean affairs, insisted all along that the tributary status of Korea be retained, but against his better judgment Britain, the United States, France, Germany, and Italy all signed treaties with Korea between 1882 and 1886. All these treaties recognized her independent status. Thus the Japanese claim (which was to their advantage) that Korea was an independent state, was confirmed by the West, and China lost instead of gaining an advantage.

The Treaty of Chemulpo, 1882

Deep-seated differences within the Korean court were at work during the penetration of the country by Westerners and Japanese. The main conservative and anti-foreign faction was led by Taewongun, the regent and father of the king (Kojong, 1864–1907) who was still a minor. When Kojong came of age he came increasingly under the influence of the other main faction led by the queen, which was in favour of opening Korea and of friendship with Japan.

In 1882 an anti-foreign riot was instigated by the Taewongun in Seoul in which the Japanese legation was burned to the ground. Japan retaliated by sending troops. But the Chinese also sent a military force. China, resuming her old role as protector of Korea, removed the Taewongun to Tientsin. She did not want war at the time since she had her hands full with the French in Vietnam.

Japan then forced the signature of a treaty with Korea—the Treaty of Chemulpo (now called Inchon). The main clauses were:

> Punishment for the attackers, and an indemnity.
> The right to post legation guards at Seoul.
> The right to travel inland in Korea.

Yüan Shih-k'ai—a man of fundamentally selfish character. His
career is a tale of efforts to gain
maximum power for himself. His
talent in training armies was
equalled only by his capacity for
betraying friends and
deceiving others

Li Hung-chang, whose role in the Korean affair had not improved his image in anyone's eyes, now ignored the independence clause in the Treaty of Kanghwa and sent a strong military force to Korea together with the young Yüan Shih-k'ai (a man of whom we will hear a great deal more later, both before and after the fall of the Manchu dynasty). Yüan was to train the Korean army into a better fighting unit. In 1885 Yüan was appointed Chinese resident in Seoul, a position he retained until the outbreak of the Sino-Japanese war. Other Chinese officials were sent to put the administration in better shape, and a German was appointed as inspector of Korean customs.

The situation as regards international affairs was confused. Korea affirmed her independence of China. China had seemed to relinquish her overlord status and then to take it up again. Japan talked directly with the Koreans on their mutual affairs.

Internally, affairs were also in confusion. The queen's faction grew more conservative and less pro-Japanese, and a progressive party took on the role of looking toward Japan for inspiration. Its leaders, Kim Ok-kyun and Pak Yong-hyo, planned and carried out a *coup* in December 1884, killing leading pro-Chinese conservatives and seizing the king. Yüan Shih-k'ai succeeded in rescuing the king, and the two leaders fled to Japan.

By this time both Japan and China realized it was time to put their relations with each other in regard to Korea on a more stable basis. Li Hung-chang and Ito Hirobumi negotiated at Tientsin the agreement known as the Li-Ito Convention (1885). In essence this was a mutual restraint document whereby both Japan and China agreed to withdraw their troops and military advisers from Korea, and in case of trouble to notify each other before they replaced them. The Japanese still felt their strength was not sufficient for war, and the Chinese felt time was on their side. But Li Hung-chang remarked:

'In about ten years, the wealth and strength of Japan will be admirable. This is China's future, not present, source of trouble.'

And he went on to urge on Korea the same sort of reforms that Britain had urged on China two decades before. Japanese influence gained ground in the following years among the younger Koreans, and the old prestige of China in the country waned.

The real problem, from the Japanese point of view, was Russia. In 1884 Russia agreed with Korea on the use of an east coast port, and offered to train the Korean army in return. The Chinese, with British assent, prevented the agreement from being carried out. Russia then made a commercial treaty with Korea (1888). Soon after, in 1891, she announced her plans to build a Trans-Siberian railway. This was the danger signal for Japan, which then knew it had to move fast, either to have Korea once and for all recognized as independent, or to get the country firmly under her own control. Only in that way could she hope to arrest Russian expansion. Since China refused to relinquish her overlord status in Korea, war had to come.

War

One of the patriot leaders of the progressives, Kim Ok-kyun, who had fled to Japan in 1884, was lured to Shanghai in early 1894 and there killed by a pro-Chinese Korean. His body was sent by Chinese warship to Seoul where it was quartered and displayed in various places in the country as a warning to those who defied the king. Japanese opinion was outraged. In March of the same year, the Tonghak rebels again rose up, and Korea asked China for 1,500 soldiers to suppress them. China sent the men, notifying Japan as the Li-Ito Convention required. Japan at once sent 7,000 men, claiming they were needed to protect her own nationals in Korea.

In fact the Korean government managed to suppress the rebels on its own. Li Hung-chang and Yüan Shih-k'ai then proposed that both countries withdraw their troops, but Japan, feeling strong enough by now, refused. After presenting the king with a programme of reforms to be carried out, which he refused to do, Japan seized the palace in July and set up a new Korean government which was forced to ask Japan to expel the Chinese troops. Two days later, on July 25, the Japanese sank the British steamer Kowshing which was carrying Chinese reinforcements.

Japan had not yet declared war, but had struck the first heavy blow (just as she was to do later against Russia, and in World War II against America at Pearl Harbour). She declared war on China on August 1, 1894.

It was the first attempt of the Meiji government to stretch its wings in the manner recommended by Yoshida Torajiro (commonly known as Shoin) before the Restoration. Shoin, who had once tried to stow away on Commodore Perry's ship, and whose spectacular career and bravery caught the imagination of a whole generation of Japanese, had said:

'We should build up our...strength, annex the weak, attack the stupid, seize Manchuria and Korea, and conquer China!'

It was a prophetic remark (one among many he made), and with the declaration of war on China the process had begun.

The destruction of Li Hung-chang's carefully built up Peiyang Fleet by the Japanese during the Battle of the Yellow Sea, September 17, 1894. In the foreground, the large Chinese vessel is no match in fire-power or speed for the smaller Japanese warship (right)

Yüan Shih-k'ai fled from Seoul. Three Japanese columns converged on P'yong-yang, winning several battles, and invaded Manchuria. But it was sea-power that decided the outcome of the war since China had no rail link with Korea by which to send troops quickly. The four Chinese fleets of sixty-five warships in all were twice the size of the Japanese fleet of thirty-two. But the real comparison lay not in numbers but in quality. In the most important naval battle off the mouth of the Yalu River (one of the first sea battles in which numbers of modern ships were engaged), each side had a dozen ships. The Japanese were equipped with faster-firing guns and could manoeuvre much more nimbly than the Chinese. They circled the warships of the Peiyang fleet (which had been built up under the direction of Li Hung-chang). After four hours' battle, four of the Chinese ships were sunk, four fled from the engagement, and four remained. The Japanese did not lose a ship.

After that they were able to dominate the seas. Port Arthur and its modern armament was captured in November and the remains of the Peiyang fleet were confined to Weihaiwei which the Japanese then surrounded from the land. They turned the guns of its own forts on the fleet, and the Chinese surrendered in February 1895.

Negotiations between Ito Hirobumi (seated at the left near end of the table) and the ageing Li Hung-chang (opposite him) which led to the Treaty of Shimonoseki

The Japanese armies appeared invincible and seemed to be advancing on Peking from Manchuria. The whole world was startled at their remarkable feats and at the total defeat of the Chinese fleet in the Battle of the Yellow Sea, as it came to be named.

Li Hung-chang, now an ageing man of seventy-two, arranged negotiations with Ito Hirobumi at Shimonoseki. Ito is recorded as having remarked to him: 'Ten years' ago at Tientsin I talked to you about reform. Why is it that up to now not a single thing has been changed or reformed?' And Li replied: 'Affairs in my country have been so confined by tradition.'

The Sino-Japanese War brought into sharp relief the success of Japanese self-strengthening and the almost complete failure of the Chinese to do the same thing.

The terms eventually arranged between the two men were somewhat less severe on China after a fanatic shot and wounded Li Hung-chang on Japanese soil. The Treaty of Shimonoseki (April 17, 1895) called on China to do the following:

> Cede to Japan: Formosa (Taiwan), the Pescadores Islands, the Liaotung (Kwantung) Peninsula.
> Recognize Korea's independence.
> Pay 200 million taels indemnity.
> Open two ports on the Yangtze and two on the Grand Canal to foreign trade.
> Negotiate a commercial treaty.

Japan followed the well-established pattern of Western powers in the imposition of this unequal treaty. The commercial treaty was signed in 1896, giving her all the privileges of the Western powers in China, and adding the right to 'carry on industries and manufactures'—using the cheap labour of China at the treaty ports. These goods were exempt from taxation.

International Reactions

The rapid and complete victory of Japan profoundly upset the balance of power inside and outside China. Events inside China will be dealt with in the following chapter.

Great Britain, previously supporting China, now began to think again. Admiration for the efficiency and grasp of modern warfare shown by the Japanese made the British react favourably toward Japan. And they were, of course, also happy with the extra privileges obtained under the 'most-favoured-nation' clause by the Treaty of Shimonoseki, which applied to them as well as to Japan. British disillusion with China's military and administrative incompetence, revealed by the course of the war, amounted to despair of ever assisting her to her feet.

Russia, the other state most concerned, was unhappy because her ambition to expand in South Manchuria and to strengthen her position in Korea was threatened.

The outcome of these attitudes was a three-power German-Russian-French diplomatic intervention on April 23, 1895, 'advising' Japan to give up the Kwantung Peninsula. Japan, now exhausted both financially and militarily after the war, agreed (for the payment of an extra thirty million taels indemnity). Naturally this caused deep resentment in Japan against Russia, with consequences that we will examine in a later chapter.

The largest single international repercussion of the war was the recognition by all Western powers that Japan had emerged as a powerful force which would have to be reckoned with in any future moves in the East. This, coupled with the obvious and hopeless weakness of China, painted a completely new picture of the political realities in East Asia.

10 China, 1895 to the Boxer Protocol of 1901

ONE immediate result of China's defeat by Japan in 1895 was the disappearance of Li Hung-chang as the main architect of China's foreign policies. He was too great a figure to be dismissed altogether, but his influence waned, and he was sent on a foreign tour.

In his place we find Chang Chih-tung, Li's rival, gaining in importance. Together with Liu K'un-i (1830–1902), a Hunanese scholar-official who fought the T'aip'ing and after that was governor at Nanking for some years, he was now the prominent man in foreign affairs. Yüan Shih-k'ai took on the training of the armies in North China, a fact that had fateful consequences later, as we will see.

The crippling indemnity to be paid to Japan (more than three times the revenues of Peking for a whole year) dealt a severe blow to thoughts of any rapid modernization on a governmental level. It also meant that China had to contract foreign loans and was then heavily indebted to foreign powers, who were thus in stronger positions to put pressure in their favour on the Chinese government. The events of the following years were to bring the ancient civilization of China as near as can be imagined to extinction, and to lead to the country's virtual partition among the foreign powers. It was only the jealousy and rivalry that existed and became ever more bitter between them that prevented China from the ultimate disgrace and humiliation of being made by the powers into a patchwork of Western colonies.

The 'Scramble for Concessions'

The weakness of China and the growing power of Japan led to what must seem to us now one of the most unprincipled series of actions ever undertaken by Western states in the orient—the rightly described 'scramble for concessions'.

Russia and Manchuria

Having succeeded in removing Japan from the Kwantung Peninsula, Russia in 1898 obtained a twenty-five-year lease on it, including the Port Arthur naval base and the port of Dairen. She then constructed with Chinese permission a railway linking these two ports and running north to connect up with the Chinese Eastern Railway. Thus Russia at last achieved ports that were ice-free, and the railway meant they were linked with Europe. Together with these concessions went mining rights in south Manchuria which became a Russian 'sphere of interest'.

The Russians and the French loaned China money to assist her in paying the indemnity called for in the Treaty of Shimonoseki, and at the end of 1895 the Russo-Chinese Bank was set up in order to deal with such matters, but also to obtain further concessions.

At this point the Chinese were arguing in high places about the ways and means open to them to quickly strengthen the country against disastrous events such as the recent Sino-Japanese war.

> 'To save the critical situation of today, nothing is better than the conclusion of a secret treaty of alliance with a strong power for assistance.... China's power today can never oppose simultaneously all the nations of East and West....
> 'Now if we wish to make a treaty, and to have a bond for mutual assistance, naturally Russia is most convenient for us, because England uses commerce to absorb the profits of China, France uses religion to entice the Chinese people, Germany has no common ...boundary with us, and the United States does not like to interfere in others' military affairs.... If China and Russia form an alliance, English influence will be considerably curbed.... By no means should we ever let Sir Robert Hart [the British head of Chinese Imperial Maritime Customs, 1863–1908] hear of it, lest he be jealous...and spoil the matter.'
>
> Chang Chih-Tung: *Memorial,* August 1895

Another voice proposed a similar course:

> '...when we negotiated peace with Japan, we made too many compromises which encouraged the...inception of a waylaying policy—glaring at us like tigers, all the various powers seek...a plump spot to bite into us.... The impending disaster from other countries is still slow in coming, but that from Japan is imminent.... But Russia does not want Japan to be strong.... Russia has had good relations with us for two hundred years....'
>
> Liu K'un-i's secret proposal, July 1895

The alliance thus proposed formed the subject of the treaty negotiated by Li Hung-chang in Russia when he went there to attend the coronation of Tsar Nicholas II in 1896. The Sino-Russian Secret Treaty (the Li-Lobanov Treaty) remained a secret until the Washington Conference of 1922 when it was briefly mentioned by the Chinese delegation.

> Article 1 provided that in the event of Japan's invasion of Russian, Chinese, or Korean territory, the treaty would be invoked. Both China and Russia would send troops and supply whatever munitions they could.
> Article 2 prohibited either Russia or China from concluding a separate peace agreement with the hostile power.
> Article 3 allowed, in emergency in such a war, Russian warships to enter Chinese ports and to be given aid.
> Article 4 permitted Russia to construct a railway through Heilungkiang to Kirin to connect with Vladivostock.
> Article 5 permitted its use in time of war for transport of troops.
> Article 6 made the treaty effective for 15 years.

The price China had paid for a military agreement was in strategic concessions in her vulnerable northeast. The results were to set a pattern for future concessions, and to result later in a complicated chain of international reactions that culminated in the Russo-Japanese war of 1904–1905.

France and South China

The French were in fact first in the scramble for concessions, obtaining railway and mining rights in mid-1895 in Yunnan, Kwangtung, and Kwangsi provinces bordering on their conquests in Indochina. The following year, France was allowed to extend her Annam railway into Kwangsi province, and China promised not to cede Hainan Island (strategically placed in regard to Indochina) to another power. In 1898 France saw other powers obtaining concessions in the north, so she demanded a long lease on Kwangchow Bay, and effectively incorporated all the southern provinces into her sphere of influence—with the exception of eastern Kwangtung which remained within the British sphere because of the nearness of the previously ceded Hong Kong and Kowloon Point.

A Chinese painting showing the French defending a fortified position in Annam against an attack by Chinese troops, armed with swords, halberds, and a primitive cannon

Germany and the Shantung Peninsula

During the summer and autumn of 1897, German ships were reported surveying the coastline from Fukien to Shantung provinces. On November 1, two German missionaries were murdered by robbers who plundered the whole village in which they were staying in southwestern Shantung. There had been several such incidents in that and the previous year, apparently motivated by local Chinese anger at the French who had rebuilt the cathedral at Tientsin following the massacre of its citizens there. Germany acted in a manner well beyond what was necessary to protect its subjects. Four days after the murder was known, a small German force threw out the garrison of Tsingtao, a port on Kiachow (Chia-chou) Bay on the southern side of Shantung Peninsula.

In Germany itself naval reinforcements were sent out under the admiral Prince Heinrich of Prussia. In his speech of farewell, the German emperor said:

'...I am conscious that it is my duty to extend and enlarge what my predecessors have bequeathed to me.... May every one in those distant regions be aware that the German Michael has firmly planted his shield with the...German eagle upon the soil of China, in order once for all to give protection to all who ask for it.... Should any one essay to detract from our just rights or to injure us, then up and at him with your mailed fist.'

The air of Europe, and indeed of Japan too, in these times of imperialist expansion, was often ringing to the sounds of such remarks—in German, English, French, Russian, and other tongues. Like some fine plump zebra on the African veldt, scented by a pack of wild dogs, soon China was surrounded by her predators and dismembered.

For China there was no way to reject German demands, and finally Germany received what she asked for:

> A ninety-nine-year lease on Kiachow Bay, the surrounding lands and all the islands, and the port of Tsingtao to be used as a naval base.
> Railway and mining concessions in Shantung.

Even among the Western ministers in Peking and Tokyo, few of them renowned for any softness of attitude, the manner and the unseemly haste with which Germany carried through her gunboat-backed demands caused extremely unfavourable comment. It was

'...the general opinion that a prolonged or possibly permanent occupation of such an important and strategical point by a Western power would imperil the peace of the Far East.'

Sir E. Satow, British Minister to Japan, 1897

Shantung was thus firmly under German control. The Germans proceeded to build a great naval base at Tsingtao—and to set up such industries as the brewing of beer, for which Tsingtao to this day is famous.

Britain and the Yangtze Valley

Britain was already the dominant Western power in China. But she feared her economic control would slowly be eaten away if China continued to grant concessions to others. She therefore appealed to the United States for support in a policy of free trade in China. Such support was not forthcoming because America had her hands full with the quarrel with Spain about Cuba which was soon to lead to the Spainish-American War of 1898.

Britain saw to the north the Russian and German spheres of influence and interest, and in the south French economic dominance. She therefore felt compelled to join the scramble for concessions. In 1898 she obtained:

> A ninety-nine-year-lease on the New Territories, regarded as necessary for the defence of Hong Kong and the tip of Kowloon Peninsula already ceded.

> The lease of Weihaiwei as a naval base 'for as long as Russia should occupy Port Arthur'. (This was suggested by the Chinese who wished to curb Russian power.)

> An agreement that so long as British trade with China was greater than that of any other power, Britain should provide the Inspector-General of Maritime Customs.

> An agreement that China would not allow other powers any concessions in the Yangtze River provinces. (This meant in practice that Britain had the entry to some of the richest markets and richest sources in China—and of course in the event of the partition of China, which many powers thought would come, these heavily populated and vast lands would be Britain's slice of the 'China melon', as it was called.)

The year before (1897), Britain had obtained additional land on the borders of Burma.

Today, with the exception of the Portuguese on the tiny peninsula of Macau, the British at Hong Kong are the sole survivors of all those Western powers who gained leases and concessions of Chinese territories in the nineteenth and twentieth centuries.

By the time of the New Territories lease in 1898, Hong Kong was already a large and thriving port. The island that was described as 'barren' with 'hardly a house upon it' at the time when Captain Elliot exceeded his instructions and annexed it in 1841, now supported a large Chinese and an ever-growing foreign business community. The town of Victoria kept spreading up the hill toward the Peak and to east and west along much newly-reclaimed foreshore. The harbour, whose capacious and comparatively safe anchorage attracted shipping from all over the world, was increasingly busy. In 1842, there had been only 381 vessels with a tonnage of 136,336 entering and leaving, but by the turn of the century Hong Kong handled forty-one percent of China's foreign trade, apart from much other business. The tonnage clearing Hong Kong harbour in 1900 was 14 million, carried in 11,000 ships. The annual value of Hong Kong trade was about £50 million.

In 1889, Sir William Des Voeux, the governor, wrote:

'There must be some still living who saw the island before the British occupation. If one of them were now to return, even the...features of the natural landscape would scarcely enable him to identify...what he would remember as bare rock, with a fisherman's hut here and there.... For now he would see a city of closely built houses stretching for some four miles along the island shore, and rising, tier upon tier, up the slopes of the mountain....'

And on the Kowloon Peninsula he would see docks, great warehouses and 'other evidences of a large and thriving population'. That population which, in 1841, had consisted of less than six thousand Chinese, had now risen to over a quarter of a million Chinese and over twenty thousand non-Chinese.

The United States and the 'Open Door'

The American stance on the unseemly scramble for concessions was for some time simply that of disapproval. She avowed her intention of attempting to preserve China's political and territorial integrity, despite the plain fact that this had largely disappeared already. But after the Spanish-American war, and when the United States had added Hawaii, Guam, part of Samoa, and the Philippines to her territories, the rather passive policy toward affairs in China turned to more active participation. John Hay, Secretary of State, sent his first Open Door note to the foreign powers in China in 1899. This requested them:

> Not to interfere in the administration of treaty ports in their spheres of interest, and not to obstruct the collection of duties by the Chinese government there.
> To levy the same port dues and railway charges on all foreign traders operating in their spheres of interest.

Britain accepted the terms of the note, as did the other powers, provided that all of them would accept. Russia did not. Even if it had come into effect, although the note would possibly have made for fairer trading for the powers, it could have done nothing to preserve Chinese territorial or political integrity.

Hay's second note on the subject in July, 1901, with the chances of partition of China even greater after the Boxer rising, was an equally futile document. It stated America desired a 'solution' leading to 'permanent safety and peace in China', preserving its territorial and administrative entity, at the same time protecting the rights of 'friendly powers' under treaties and international law, and safeguarding 'for the world, the principle of equal...trade with all parts of the Chinese Empire'.

Everyone, of course, agreed, since this was a lost cause. And no one did anything about it. America itself, busily acquiring a colony in the Philippines, was doubtless more serious about the policy of Open Door than others. But it was a policy doomed by its naiveté to be still-born.

Even Secretary of State Hay must have come to this conclusion, for in 1900 he was trying, unsuccessfully, to acquire a naval station on the Fukien coast. The Japanese, with that brand of high cynicism that characterized most of the pronouncements of the foreign powers in this discreditable decade, opposed the American attempt and quoted Secretary Hay's Open Door notes.

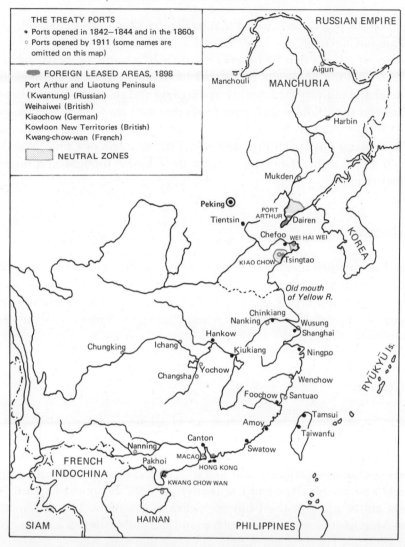

THE TREATY PORTS
● Ports opened in 1842–1844 and in the 1860s
○ Ports opened by 1911 (some names are omitted on this map)

⬤ FOREIGN LEASED AREAS, 1898
Port Arthur and Liaotung Peninsula (Kwantung) (Russian)
Weihaiwei (British)
Kiaochow (German)
Kowloon New Territories (British)
Kwang-chow-wan (French)

▨ NEUTRAL ZONES

Foreign power penetration of China under the unequal treaties, at the year 1911

A cartoon from *Punch* in 1898 showing graphically the way in which China was being torn apart by the Western powers. From left to right: Britain, France, Germany, and Russia. Britain, holding firmly to the body of China, has the lion's share

The end of this phase came with the rejection by China of a demand by Italy for a naval base in Chekiang.

It was merest chance that China was not divided up among the Western powers and Japan. It did not become a patchwork of colonies largely because of the trade and financial and military rivalries always existing and shifting between the powers, and because on the whole it was more profitable to them to have concessions than colonies. Colonies had to be administered and that was both troublesome and costly. The concessions were in the last resort the problem of China. The Western powers had treaty rights. China, and what the Chinese thought and might want, did not matter at all.

Chinese Reaction

This may be summed up in two phrases: the rise of anti-foreign and anti-Christian feeling; the reform movement and the Boxer rebellion. But these simple statements contain a complex and highly significant series of events which gradually unfolded. The drama of Chinese history was reaching one of its climaxes and no one quite knew what might happen.

Chinese Grievances

There is an excellent brief summing up of Chinese-foreign differences dating from about 1892 and applicable with even greater force to the days of the scramble for concessions. It was written by a remarkable man, Cheng Kuan-ying. He was a scholarly compradore, employed at one time and another by several foreign firms (Butterfield and Swire, Dent and Company). In 1882 he joined Li Hung-chang's enterprises and worked in the Chinese telegraph company, Li's cotton mill, and the China Merchant Company, of which from 1892 to 1902 he was associate director, and later director. He travelled widely in China and East Asia.

He was an enthusiastic reader of a journal sponsored by foreign missionaries devoted to scientific and social problems. His own book, *Warnings to a Seemingly Prosperous Age*, was much sought after in 1898 and the emperor Kuang-hsü ordered its publication and distribution to officials by the Tsungli-yamen. According to one communist writer, this was a book that Mao Tse-tung was fond of reading in his young days, although Mao himself mentions only the more influential K'ang Yu-wei and Yen Fu as authors of this type.

Cheng Kuan-ying argued, among other matters, that if greater freedom and importance were given to China's merchant class, this would be the best defence against foreign exploitation of the Chinese. One other aspect of his writings that is of great interest is his humanitarian outlook. His thesis is that government is for the people. And he has moving descriptions of the inhumanity of various aspects of life in China—the unjust penal sentences, the suffering of women, the misery of the country people. His suggestions include relief for the poor, new agricultural policies, and the revolutionary idea that China should use an alphabetic script so that 'all the people could read and write'.

On the subject of Chinese discontent at Western commercial occupation and exploitation, he gives this summary:

'The Westerners frequently take advantage of the differences in language and law to profit themselves at the cost of others, and do as they please without regard for reason.... When a foreign ship collides with and destroys a Chinese boat, the latter.... is blamed for being slow in avoiding the collision.... When a foreign stage-coach hurts a Chinese, the latter...is charged with not knowing how to yield the right of way.... Chinese employed by foreign companies or as sailors...frequently have their wages cut on some pretext or are beaten to death. Cunning Westerners ally themselves with local rascals to kidnap and sell foolish country fellows.... When a Chinese merchant owes money to a foreign merchant, as soon as he is accused, his property is confiscated....

'Where is justice and where is humanity?...their stage-coaches rush along our thoroughfares, they carry weapons in time of peace, they reduce the wages of their employees, they speculate and go bankrupt, they protect Christian converts...control the customs...kidnap and sell our people...all the various kinds of wrongdoing that should be forbidden by Western law....'

All of which, as history relates, was perfectly true. Cheng made a list of specific grievances relating to Shanghai.

The Shanghai foreign settlement was enlarging its area without permission. Chinese passenger coaches are differently taxed from foreign ones and not allowed to pass them. Chinese are fined for hunting out of season while Westerners go hunting without penalty at any time. Western horsemen destroy the fields without compensation. The Mixed Court at Shanghai issues warrants that are used by the municipal police to prey on the people, while no Chinese are allowed as representatives on the Shanghai Council. Although they pay 60 or 70 percent of the taxes, Chinese are excluded from public parks in Shanghai, and from the racecourse—in particular they are excluded from the park along the river. Land for roads is taken from farmers without proper compensation.

It is easy to see the extent, and the justice, of Chinese anger in the face of the arrogance of Western dealing in China. The list could be supplemented a dozen times by similar grievances of villagers against missionaries and their converts who were often above normal justice because of Western protection, and of the sweated labour and inhuman conditions imposed on factory workers who, when protests were raised, could simply be dismissed and an unending supply of new human material found at the old rates.

But underlying all the specific causes was the humiliating presence and authority of Westerners apparently largely in control of the destinies of China and the Chinese. The deep-seated anger that this aroused in most Chinese, other than the rich, many of whom were happy to collaborate with the foreigners, can be felt behind each statement of dissatisfaction.

The Reformers

After the shattering defeat in the war with Japan, the thoughts, and writing-brushes, of many intelligent Chinese turned with emphasis to the question of reform in every branch of government and life. The name best known in this movement is that of K'ang Yu-wei (1858–1927), whose most important writings were a book on political theory in which he developed a utopian scheme for a new society akin to socialism, and another book called *Confucius as a Reformer*. In this book he attempted to show that Confucius favoured change in times when change was obviously required—thus making the attempt to win support from the large conservative element in society.

At the age of twenty-seven, K'ang Yu-wei was in Peking to take his civil service examinations, and he was chosen by the great body of 1,300 other students sitting the examinations to be their spokesman. In a protest against the terms of the Treaty of Shimonoseki, K'ang sent no fewer than seven memorials to the Throne, with the signatures of the students. Although at first he was regarded as being insane and the memorials were rejected, eventually his *Letter of Ten Thousand Words* was read by the emperor. Its contents were of a truly revolutionary kind, going further toward a new attitude to government and society than anything that ever before gained an emperor's attention.

The suggestions in the memorial included: rejection of the treaty of Shimonoseki, relaxation of strict traditional qualifications for high office in favour of men of real ability, a rise in salaries to diminish corruption, an end to sales of official rank, reform of the civil service examinations, promotion of more schools and the translation of more Western books, rewards for inventions, setting up of agricultural and commercial schools, revision of laws of local government. And there was also some discussion of public health, relief for the poor, road repair, bank notes, shipping lines, movements of population, mining, insurance, and other modern topics.

The best known of the reformers of 1898, K'ang Yu-wei. His most important work on political theory was a treatise on 'the cosmopolitan society' called *Ta-t'ung shu* (A Book on the Universal Commonwealth), which is a development from the utopia described in the ancient Book of Rites (*Li chi*). He proposed a world government, a universal language, and other similar ideas

Few of these measures had any precedent in the minds of officials or government. They constituted a sweeping attack on the antique traditions of Confucian thought and the ordained means of running the Chinese state. As such, the contents of the letter were profoundly alarming to the majority of intellectual Chinese in the upper ranks.

Supporters of the reform movement included such men as Huang Tsun-hsien (1848–1905), a poet who went to Hong Kong in 1870 and recorded favourable impressions of its municipal government. Later he was in the Chinese legation in Tokyo and in San Francisco for three years. His *History of Japan* urges China to take the modernization he saw there as a model. His ideas were both advanced and conservative. He found Western family relationships distasteful, preferring the more rigid Chinese ones.

In 1896, after a trip to London, he made the acquaintance of Liang Ch'i-ch'ao, and had an audience with the emperor in which he said, in answer to Kuang-hsü's question, that 'the strength of Europe is entirely due to reforms'. Huang was a nationalist, a poet who wrote in emotional style to inspire patriotism. He was possibly the first Chinese poet to use slang expressions in his work. He said of his poetry: 'I use my hand to describe my mouth [meaning, I write the way I speak] without being restricted by traditional style.'

Liang Ch'i-ch'ao (1873–1929), was one of K'ang Yu-wei's associates, and one of the most widely learned and best known writers of modern China. His ideas on reform were that China must take her stand on her own past and yet confront the modern age in a spirit of reason.

In 1922, a Shanghai newspaper asked Liang Ch'i-ch'ao to review the last fifty years in China. He wrote an optimistic report, although his former faith in the West had already been deeply shaken. Among some interesting statements is the one that nowadays 'Ma-ko-ssu (Karl Marx) is almost competing for the seat of honour with Confucius.... Whether this kind of psychology is correct or not is another question, but in general the radical change of thought of the last forty-odd years was...never dreamed of during the preceding four thousand....'

Yet another name prominent in reform is that of Yen Fu (1853–1921), formerly a student at Foochow Naval School and later sent to London for further studies. He was to become president of Peking University. He was a voluminous writer, editor of a progressive magazine, translator of Huxley, John Stuart Mill, and other nineteenth century philosophers. He criticized the reform leaders for not understanding the West deeply enough. 'The Westerners are struggling in the present in order to supersede the past. The Chinese consider a period of order and a period of disorder, a period of prosperity and a period of decline, as the natural course of heavenly conduct of human affairs.' He also criticized Chang Chih-tung's 'Chinese studies for the base, Western studies for use', (which he in turn took from Feng Kuei-fen), saying that the base (*t'i*) and the use (*yung*) are the same thing in essence. 'The body of an ox should have the use of carrying heavy things; the body of a horse should have the use of carrying something to a distance. I have never heard that the ox is the body or the foundation [base] while the horse is for use.' And moreover, in a striking phrase: 'I have never heard that the left and right hands can be considered, respectively, as the foundation and the superstructure.'

The Hundred Days

Despite their differing ideas on reform, the bond uniting the progressives was that reform must come, the sooner the better. Their influence on the emperor, still a young man and perhaps therefore more inclined to change than older men, became apparent when, on June 11, 1898, he issued the first of a long series of reform decrees. On that day too, K'ang Yu-wei, Liang Ch'i-ch'ao, and Huang Tsun-hsien were recommended as advisers to the emperor in the official announcement of the proposed reforms. K'ang was later appointed secretary of the Tsungli-yamen with direct access to the emperor.

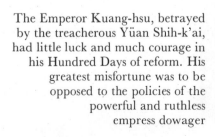

The Emperor Kuang-hsu, betrayed by the treacherous Yüan Shih-k'ai, had little luck and much courage in his Hundred Days of reform. His greatest misfortune was to be opposed to the policies of the powerful and ruthless empress dowager

Thus began what was later to be called the Hundred Days Reform. The contents of the reform decrees covered all aspects and went much further than anything in the self-strengthening movement. They were in fact quite similar to the recommendations in the letter of K'ang Yu-wei and the 1,300 students, which may be taken as a sort of blueprint for the actual decrees and their subjects.

Unfortunately, circumstances worked against the emperor and his associates in this first radical new approach to life and government in China for two thousand years. The reformers were young and inexperienced in political life—that is to say, in the cautious approach and slow advance needed to put such proposals into practice in a hostile official environment.

The real power in China lay in the hands of the Empress Dowager Tz'u-hsi, and her favourites—eunuchs and others. Even as K'ang Yu-wei was in the anteroom to Kuang-hsü's audience chamber he encountered Jung-lu, the supreme Manchu military commander and a close friend of Tz'u-hsi, who asked him about his reform programme. Jung-lu and others, together with the malevolent chief eunuch and confidant of the empress dowager, banded together to frustrate all attempts at reform. Tz'u-hsi herself was set against any such movement which could only result in lessening her power and the fortunes of her family—which were the two major considerations of her whole life.

Few of Kuang-hsü's reform edicts were carried out when the documents ordering them reached the provinces. Most of the viceroys waited to see how the empress dowager, who had been in official retirement since 1889, would react to the radical programme.

A very funny cartoon showing Tz'u-hsi under a 'dragon parasol' (whose dragon looks more like a stray dog), refusing to listen to reformers with their petitions and memorials

Reforms Decreed by Emperor Kuang-hsü

'Change is necessary. Does not the same man who wears grass-cloth in summer change into fur garments in the cold of winter?'

Kuang-hsü Emperor, 1898

Education: The establishment of new schools teaching both Chinese and Western knowledge. At Peking, a university was to be established. (It was, and remained one of the few reform projects that survived the end of the Hundred Days.) The old civil service examinations were to be modified, and the so-called 'eight-legged' essay (on the Classics) abolished. New essays to be based on current affairs. Translations of Western books on such subjects as politics and science were to be made by a new translation bureau. Foreign study tours were to be encouraged. Less attention to be paid to trivial things such as calligraphy and more to European languages.

Military: The army was to be reorganized and modernized, and a militia called up to serve. Naval training colleges were to be set up.

Economy: A modern banking system to be set up. Chambers of commerce, agricultural and other commercial bureaux to be established to promote changes in the old economy and advances in technical aspects. Similar bureaux for mining and to assist the building of railways were to be instituted, and a modern postal system to be introduced.

Government: Sinecures (appointments that carried salaries but no work) to be abolished. Moves toward the abolition of the hated extraterritoriality agreements with foreign governments were to be set afoot. The periodical, *Chinese Progress*, edited by K'ang Yu-wei, was the official government publication. Newspapers to inform the public should be printed and widely distributed.

In a final edict, Kuang-hsü wrote: 'Our statesmen and scholars think Europe has no civilization. They are ignorant of the many branches of Western knowledge which enlighten the minds and increase the material well-being of the people. My duty as a sovereign will not be fulfilled until I have raised my people to a state of peaceful prosperity.'

Only in Hunan did the reform decrees find a receptive official who began to put them into effect.

All the reformers with the exception of the emperor were Chinese and this fact, too, raised opposition from the ruling Manchu who saw their positions of authority threatened. The attack on holders of imperial examination degrees threatened all in high office, while the attack on corruption affected almost everyone in office of any kind. The emperor found he was at war with the whole 'Establishment', including the vigorous sixty-three-year-old empress dowager.

Chang Chih-tung's book, *Exhortation to Study*, appeared during the Hundred Days, putting the moderate and anti-radical view—really a continuation of the ineffectual self-strengthening movement. And as the Hundred Days went by, he became more and more aligned with the conservative opposition to the reforms. The empress dowager, the 'twin pillars of her regime' (classical learning and organized corruption) deeply threatened, awaited the right moment.

On September 21, 1898, with the help of Jung-lu she seized Kuang-hsü. The reform leaders had been informed of a plot to seize Kuang-hsü at Tientsin during an inspection of the garrison there, where he would be accompanied by Tz'u-hsi. They enlisted the aid of Yüan Shih-k'ai, in charge of the northern armies, to go to Tientsin with a strong force loyal to the emperor, and to seize the empress dowager first, together with Jung-lu, and to assassinate both. Yüan, not sure of the power of the reformers, betrayed them to Jung-lu. Jung-lu then went at once to Peking by special train, informed the empress dowager, and arrested the emperor, who was placed in the four-room pavilion on an island in one of the lakes in the palace grounds. K'ang Yu-wei and Liang Ch'i-ch'ao fled to Japan.

Tz'u-hsi resumed the regency (for the third time) on the grounds of the emperor's 'ill-health'. Almost all the reforms were then repealed. Only a few, such as the abolition of certain sinecure positions and the establishment of modern educational establishments, were allowed to go forward.

A photograph taken in the studio of a Manchu noble whose hobby was photography. The empress dowager is accompanied by two court ladies, and by Li Lien-ying, her close eunuch confidant (right). The bamboo grove in the background is painted on cloth, while in the foreground auspicious lotus blossoms bloom

Results of the Hundred Days' Reform

The main result of the brave attempt at a brave new Chinese world was clear. The attempt at a revolution from the top—resembling that of the Meiji Restoration in Japan—was a complete failure. At that time in China it was perhaps not clear, but it is quite clear now, that after the collapse of the reform, the virtual imprisonment of Kuang-hsü and the escape or decapitation of the main reformers, major and fundamental change in China would have to come from the bottom up, and probably by violent means.

Tz'u-hsi did not dare to assassinate Kuang-hsü for fear of foreign reaction, and on ceremonial occasions he reappeared to perform his part, a puppet on the empress dowager's strings. He died in 1908, one day before she did—some say finally disposed of, in case he outlived her. From late September, 1898, Tz'u-hsi ruled China. Jung-lu went from high position to higher position, as did Yüan Shih-k'ai.

The commercial encroachments of the foreigners proceeded more or less unchecked, for although the empress dowager might rule, her power was strictly limited in the execution of her orders. The rising capitalist class in the treaty ports, all the thousands of Chinese who saw their chance in every kind of co-operation with foreign business, made it hard for any administrator to enforce what laws and regulations still existed. A whole vast army of what were later to be called the 'running dogs of the imperialists' sold China and their fellow Chinese to the foreigners for whatever they could make. The law that new foreign business enterprises were required to have fifty percent Chinese capital, and that they had to be controlled by Chinese, was totally unenforceable. The Chinese capitalist class easily bribed and swindled their way out of that and any other inconvenient regulation—amply rewarded by the profits that accrued from association with foreign companies.

But among the majority—the dispossessed, the starving, and the nameless and faceless millions—anti-foreign feeling rose like a tide. Initially this was coupled with anti-Manchu sentiment, but this later was dropped when the Manchu sensed that their dynasty had little chance of survival unless it joined forces with the popular revolt that came to be called the Boxers.

Origins of the Boxer Uprising

The origins of anti-foreign feeling in China are probably as old as the presence of foreigners there. We noted earlier how the first foreigners who came by sea to south China tended to use violence if they did not get exactly what they wanted, and indeed long before when the Jesuit Matteo Ricci and other early missionaries were in China they reported the hostility of the local people almost everywhere they went.

The two Anglo-Chinese wars that resulted in the unequal treaties which gave foreigners ever-increasing rights in China were deeply resented by Chinese. We need hardly be surprised at this. If the example of the German occupation of France in World War II is taken, we find the French people deeply humiliated and resentful of the presence of foreigners in their country, and forming resistance groups dedicated to getting rid of them.

As foreign penetration of China grew in the late nineteenth century, giving the

A European correspondent's impression of how the Boxers made use of the traditional Chinese glove-puppet show as a means of anti-foreign propaganda. The pig represents either Christ or a Christian missionary. More serious recruitment of men for the Boxer forces took place in the villages and small towns, but the threat from foreigners and from Christianity was dramatized by simple, accustomed means such as the puppets

West great control of trade and industry, and as the Chinese saw their country becoming poorer instead of richer, anti-foreign feeling mounted. Superstition among a largely illiterate populace, resentment at the foreign carelessness of old Chinese customs, made people denounce the building of railways which desecrated ancestral graves and upset the *feng-shui*.

Missionaries and their Chinese converts were the prime target of anti-foreign feeling, perhaps in part because they were obvious and easily identifiable. Again, superstition credited Christian rites with all sorts of barbarous practices such as disembowelling babies to use their internal organs for medicines.

But the reality of what many Christian missions did in villages was no superstition. The local converts became a privileged group, better fed for their prayers, protected against other villagers when there was any dispute, unwilling to take part in, or contribute cash for, traditional festivals. Not only were the ordinary villagers angered, but also the local magistrates and others in positions of authority. For they saw in all this missionary activity part of their own powers being taken away.

It should, however, be noted that missionaries had no intention of causing the troubles that occurred. Much of their work was beneficial to the Chinese populace— medical treatment where none existed before, some elementary schooling for people who could certainly never have afforded it, relief for at least a tiny proportion of the populace in times of hardship. But the beliefs they taught were entirely different from traditional Chinese beliefs and customs. The two ways of life were bound to collide.

In the year of the Hundred Days' Reform, natural disasters in north China increased the hardships of an already hard peasant life, and the collapse of the re-form movement meant that anti-foreign elements were again taking the upper hand.

The Uprising

It is against this background that the Boxer Uprising must be seen. Little is known of the origins of the Boxers—the nickname given by foreigners—but it is probable that their society, known as *I-ho chüan*, was an offshoot of the Eight Trigrams Society (*Ba-kua chiao*) of the late eighteenth century. Imperial decrees attempted to suppress it in the early nineteenth century, but it survived in Shantung. The name *I-ho chüan* was improperly translated by Westerners as Righteous and Harmonious Fists. The correct meaning is that the name of the society was Righteousness and Harmony (*I-ho*) and that it practised its own kind of *ch'uan*, or physical exercises related to the ancient 'military art' (*wu-su*).

The movement had at first an anti-dynastic aim—to get rid of the Manchu. Only later did it acquire an anti-foreign outlook as well. It is hardly surprising that Shantung produced this uprising since it was in that province more than in any other in the later nineteenth century that foreign intervention in the people's life had been most serious. To the widespread famine in Shantung in 1898 caused by flooding of the Yellow River, were added the German seizure in 1897 of Kiachow Bay, the British lease of Weihaiwei, the increasing activities of missionaries, and foreigners surveying for railways and disturbing the traditionally agreed forces of good omen in the countryside.

Foreign protests about Boxer activities were answered by the sending of Yüan Shih-k'ai whose armies drove them out of Shantung into neighbouring Chihli.

'At the end of the ninth moon of last year there were Boxers openly displaying huge banners in Chihli, on which was written: "The Gods assist us to destroy all foreigners; we invite you to join the patriotic militia." At one place a Buddhist abbot...led on the mob, burning a Christian chapel. Subsequently, while they were burning converts' houses at Liupa, the magistrate came out and attacked them with his troops....

'You will no doubt agree with me...that the motive which inspires these Boxers is a patriotic one. So great is the ill-feeling that exists between the mass of our people and the converts to Christianity that we have been unavoidably dragged to the very edge of hostilities....

'These Boxers are not trained troops, but they are ready to fight, and to face death....'
                                    Letter of Jung-lu to the Viceroy of Fukien

By 1899, when the Boxers had been recruited as militia for the provincial government of Shantung to control the activities of the Germans, they altered their name to *I-ho t'uan*, Righteous and Harmonious Militia. They dropped their anti-Manchu

A Western correspondent sent back to Europe this romanticized portrait of a Boxer soldier

attitude, taking as their slogan: Protect the Ch'ing [Manchu regime] and destroy the foreigners. It was after this, when murders of converts and destruction of Christian churches were reported, that Yüan Shih-k'ai drove them from Shantung.

In Chihli, Shansi, and in south Manchuria the fury of the Boxers increased. The recruitment of peasants was not a difficult task, partly because the sentiments of the people were with them, and partly because of famine conditions resulting from the flooding of the Yellow River.

'Attention: all people in markets and villages of all provinces in China—now, owing to the fact that Catholics and Protestants have abused our gods and sages, have deceived our emperors and ministers above, and oppressed the Chinese people below, both our gods and our people are angry at them, yet we have to keep silent. This forces us. . . to protect our country, to expel the foreign bandits and kill Christian converts. . . . No matter what village you are living in, if there are Christian converts, you ought to get rid of them quickly. The churches. . .should be unreservedly burned down. . . .'

A Boxer notice

Official reaction to the rising tide of Boxer activity and its popularity among the people was divided. Many Chinese ministers urged Tz'u-hsi to suppress them. The writers of three memorials to the Throne who urged the suppression of the uprising were beheaded after their third memorial reached the empress dowager.

On June 13, 1900, the Boxers entered Peking, massacred Chinese Christians and burned foreign buildings outside the legation quarter where all foreign envoys and their families lived. The Western ministers had already sent for and received a force of 400 troops to strengthen the legation guards, and on June 10 an international force of over 2,000 more began to move from Tientsin toward Peking. On June 14, a Boxer force entered Tientsin and besieged the foreign quarter there. The relief force that had left Tientsin was attacked by imperial troops and had to return there. The Western powers then took the Taku Forts. On June 20, the Manchu regime declared war on the foreign powers. On the same day the legation quarter in Peking was surrounded and the siege began.

At the same time another less well-known siege was in progress in Peking—the Boxer siege of Pei T'ang, the Catholic Cathedral. Since their main fury was directed at Christians, and also because of the moderating influence of ministers such as Jung-lu in regard to the legations, the siege of the Cathedral was far more severe. The heroism of its defenders was much greater. In the siege of the legations rather little hardship was suffered in the fifty-five days it lasted, and at one point food and arms were brought across the barricades. But because the legations contained official representatives of Western powers, they were able to gain much more attention for themselves. In fact, after the legation siege had been lifted, it was three days before anyone there thought to investigate whether the Cathedral and its besieged Christians, both Western and Chinese, were still alive. Few of them were, and they were starving.

In July, a force of British, French, American, Russian, German, Japanese, Austrian, and Italian troops fought their way to Peking from Tientsin. They reached Peking on August 14, and released the legation inhabitants. Organized Boxer and imperial army resistance came to an end on that day. Two hundred and fifty missionaries and other foreign persons, and an uncounted number of Chinese converts had lost their lives in the provinces affected by Boxer activities.

Results of the Boxer Uprising

As the allied force began to occupy and also to loot the city of Peking, the empress dowager and the emperor left in disguise, travelling by covered cart and eventually reaching Sian, the old capital, in late October. Negotiations between the Western powers and the Manchu government centred round the acceptance by both sides of the fiction that there had not been a war but a rebellion by Boxers which had been suppressed by both sides. This piece of skilful political manoeuvering was the work of Jung-lu and Li Hung-chang (then an old man of seventy-seven). The Westerners were happy enough to accept this idea since it permitted them to continue the treaty system of relations with China, and also ensured the continuation of China's foreign debt payments.

Under the supervision of Indian and British soldiers, the contents of the Lama Temple at Peking being packed up for shipment as a gift to Queen Victoria. The Western correspondent who drew the scene inscribed this information on his picture

A group of the Western diplomats in Peking after the Boxer Rebellion: left, E. Conger (U.S.A.); next to him the Russian minister; front centre, Sir Ernest Satow (Britain); Baron Nissi (Japan) behind his left shoulder; Dr. A. Mumm von Schwartzenstein (Germany), extreme right

By the last months of 1900, there were about 45,000 foreign troops in North China. Russia had already occupied the Manchurian area. The principal clauses of a settlement between China and the Western powers were accepted in December, but the Boxer Protocol was not signed until September 7, 1901. Li Hung-chang died two months later, his successor being Yüan Shih-k'ai. The Protocol was yet one more humiliating document for the Chinese. The stipulations were severe, almost savage, and China emerged from the affair more helpless than ever in the face of the future.

The Protocol required:

> The execution of 10 high officials and the punishment of 100 others for involvement in the Boxer uprising.
> Formal apologies to be taken to Germany and Japan for the murder of the German minister and Japanese chancellor in Peking.
> Suspension of the civil service examinations for 5 years in 45 cities, one half of them in Shansi, as punishment to the scholar-official class.
> The destruction of 25 Chinese forts, and other measures to ensure direct access of Western powers to Peking from the sea.
> Expansion and fortification of the Peking foreign legation quarter.
> The effective raising of import duties to 5 percent, and an indemnity of 450 million taels to be paid in gold over a forty-year period at interest rates that would result in doubling that sum.
> The creation of a Ministry of Foreign Affairs in place of the Tsungli-yamen. (This was done in 1901, and the ministry was called Wai-wu Pu.)
> The prohibition of arms and ammunition imports for two or more years as the Western powers saw fit.

Above, beheading Boxer leaders in the presence of Chinese and Western officials. Below, the empress dowager and the emperor receiving the wives of the foreign ministers at Peking after the Boxer incident

After her return to Peking in January, 1902, the empress dowager received the foreign envoys at court with every sign of cordiality. She even received their wives, many of whom were deceived by her well-known charm into regarding her as a person of the best intentions.

In January, 1901, while still in Sian, Tz'u-hsi, at last realizing that resistance to all change was not only futile but dangerous to her dynasty, had issued an edict:

> 'All human rules must be subject to alteration. It is not foolish to put new strings in a musical instrument; nor is it unwise to change the laws of men. When necessary, our ancestors introduced change. Most laws in time become out of date. The entire system of government must be reorganized so that China will again be rich and strong.'

She went on to urge the adoption of 'good methods' from other lands, and was of the opinion that 'we must no longer distinguish between Chinese ways and foreign ways'. So far, the edict continues:

> 'We have copied only the outer clothes of the West. We must revise ancient methods, stamp out abuses in our system of government, and reform completely....'

Needless to say, Manchu reforms on the lines of the Hundred Days were almost completely ineffective. The old privileges of the ruling classes, together with the medieval backwardness of the outlook on life among all sectors of the Chinese, made reform of any kind difficult enough to achieve. And when the last dregs of the corrupt Manchu and Chinese ruling classes administered them, there was no hope of success.

To many it seemed that the partition of China was inevitable. To the makers of Western foreign policies such a solution was unacceptable. Not only were jealousies between this and that Western power strong, making it hard to define what territory each would take, but in fact it suited everyone better to hold the reins of the Chinese horse and guide its last feeble strides in a direction suitable to the West. And this was what happened. China remained in the grip of its own great past—a past whose institutions were so well constructed that they had even outlasted the facts of the last several hundred years.

11 Japan, 1895 to the Treaty of Portsmouth, 1905

THE huge success of Japan in pulling herself out of feudalism and entering the modern age had been heavily underlined by her victory in the Sino-Japanese war of 1894–1895. The reform of laws and the administration of justice inside the country succeeded in persuading the Western powers to give up their extraterritorial rights in Japan. The participation of Japanese forces in the allied capture of Peking in the Boxer uprising, the exemplary behaviour of the Japanese soldiers and the careful control of the Japanese sector in Peking, made a further good impression on the West.

The only cloud in the sky was Japanese resentment against Russia for ousting her from the Kwantung Peninsula and then herself taking a lease on the territory; and Russian determination to expand into Manchuria at the expense of possible Japanese intentions.

Prime Ministers of Japan, 1894–1905	
1892–1896	Ito Hirobumi—Choshu
1896–1898	Matsukata Masayoshi—Satsuma
January–June, 1898	Ito Hirobumi—Choshu
June–November, 1898	Okuma Shigenobu—Hizen
1898–1900	Yamagata Aritomo—Choshu
1900–1901	Ito Hirobumi—Choshu
1901–1906	Katsura Taro—Choshu

Russian and Japanese Rivalry in Manchuria

The picture of power in the East had long been one of a vaguely modernizing China whose foreign trade was dominated by Britain under what was originally a British innovation in the East—the system of treaties obtained under threat of force. For a time this lent a certain stability to the scene. But with the expansionist tendencies later shown by Japan, Russia, Germany, France, and even the United States, stability was lost and great-power rivalry took over as the principal motivation of action in East Asia. Gradually, Russia emerged as the principal threat to British and Japanese interests in China—a territorial threat to China and to Japanese ambitions in Manchuria and Korea, and a commercial threat to Britain and, to a lesser extent, to the United States.

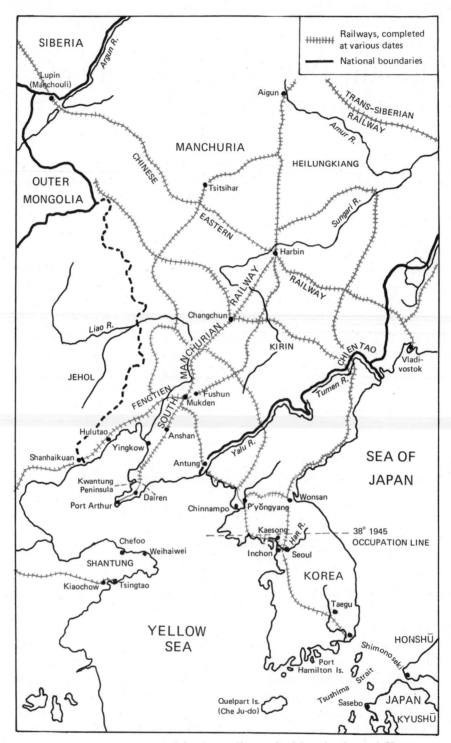

The confused pattern of foreign railways in Manchuria and Korea

Russia had quietly but steadily nudged her way against China since she acquired the Amur River frontier in 1858, and two years later the Maritime Province. Establishing a naval base at Vladivostock, Russia then began building the Trans-Siberian Railway in 1891. Even as early as 1861 there had been a Russian attempt at seizing an island (Tsushima) situated between southern Japan and Korea. Japan, with her own ambitions, was naturally apprehensive of further Russian exploits in Manchuria and Korea.

Reasons for Russian Expansionism

Russian reaction to the Boxer crisis had been to retain her troops in Manchuria. Later, after the signing of an agreement with China (the Alexeiev-Tsêng agreement) which in the opinion of the other Western powers seemed to imply Russian absorption of Manchuria, the Chinese were supported in not ratifying this document. And after the Anglo-Japanese alliance of January 1902, Russia had to withdraw from Manchuria—the process was to be completed in three stages over eighteen months. Thus Russian attempts to use the Boxer crisis to absorb Manchuria ended in nothing but diplomatic frustration.

The reasons for Russian interest in Manchuria were basically two. One was the fact that it would be much cheaper to complete the Trans-Siberian Railway by taking it across Manchuria to the sea, and also the natural resources of this territory were attractive to her. Another reason was that in gaining Manchuria she could prevent any other power from stopping Russian ships sailing between the leased peninsula of Kwantung and the port of Vladivostock. But for this to be realized, she had also to gain control of Korea.

Russian sentiments on the subject of eastward expansion at this time were briefly and forcibly expressed by a Russian minister:

'Given our enormous frontier with China and our exceptionably favourable situation, the absorption by Russia of a considerable portion of the Chinese Empire is only a question of time, unless China succeeds in protecting itself. But our chief aim is to see that this absorption shall take place naturally...in order to avoid a premature division of China by the Powers concerned, which would deprive Russia of China's most desirable province [Manchuria].'

Count Sergei I. Witte, Finance Minister, July 1903

The Anglo-Japanese Alliance

Meanwhile, Japanese leadership was divided on what action was best to take. One faction led by Ito Hirobumi drafted an idea whereby Japan and Russia would have recognized each other's special interests in Manchuria and Korea. But another faction, which eventually prevailed, drafted the Anglo-Japanese Alliance signed in 1902. This aimed at isolating Russia. Under the terms of the alliance Japan and Britain promised to fight any third power alone and to call for the other's forces only on intervention of a fourth power. Therefore Japan would fight Russia alone. Britain would come in if France (for example) assisted Russia. It was thus hoped to keep France and Germany out of a possible conflict between Russia and Japan.

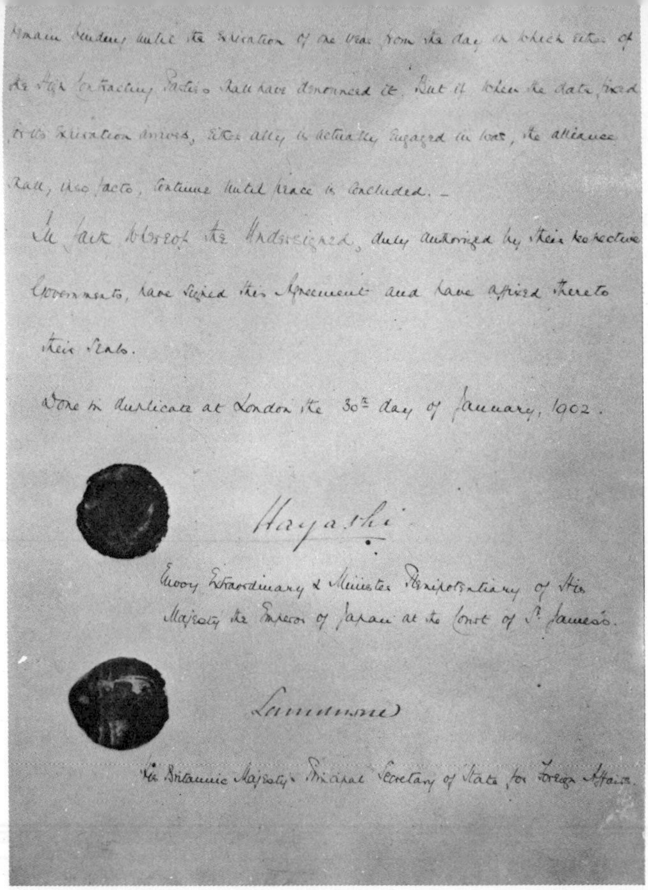

[Handwritten manuscript text, partially legible:]

remain binding until the expiration of one year from the day on which either of the High Contracting Parties shall have denounced it. But if, when the date fixed for its expiration arrives, either ally is actually engaged in war, the alliance shall, ipso facto, continue until peace is concluded. —

In faith whereof the Undersigned, duly authorized by their respective Governments, have signed this Agreement and have affixed thereto their Seals.

Done in duplicate at London the 30th day of January, 1902.

Hayashi

Envoy Extraordinary & Minister Plenipotentiary of His Majesty the Emperor of Japan at the Court of St. James's.

Lansdowne

His Britannic Majesty's Principal Secretary of State for Foreign Affairs.

Left, the last part of the Anglo-Japanese Alliance document, signed by the Japanese Minister in Britain and the Foreign Secretary. Dated 'the 30th day of January, 1902'

Below, Japanese Prime Minister Katsura making the announcement to the House of Peers of the text of the Anglo-Japanese Alliance

The terms of the Anglo-Japanese Alliance were:

> While both powers respected the integrity of China and Korea, Britain's special interests in China and Japan's special interests in Korea were recognized.
> In case of disturbances in China or Korea, each nation would protect its own interests.
> Japan and Britain would maintain strict neutrality when either country was at war and come to each other's aid only when a fourth party joined the conflict.
> The alliance would remain in force for an initial five years.

Britain cleverly gained Japanese support in maintaining the existing treaty system by this alliance, and forestalled a joint Japanese-Russian agreement to divide up Manchuria. Japan received a free hand in Korea.

Reasons for Japanese Expansionism

By the Anglo-Japanese Alliance of 1902, Japan took virtual control of Korea which, the agreement stated, was 'in a peculiar degree politically as well as commercially and industrially' her special interest.

Japan by now viewed Korea and Manchuria as vital to her security, and also as desirable additions to her territories for economic reasons. It was also thought in Japan that successful colonial expansion would give a lift to the Japanese image in Western eyes. And the militaristic aspect of Japanese government favoured expansion abroad.

Events Leading to War

When the Japanese occupied Seoul, the Korean capital, in 1894, they restored the Taewongun to power and attempted to introduce drastic reform in Korea on the model of their own self-strengthening process of the recent past. The Taewongun proved interested solely in his own power, and the conservative element backed by the queen blocked all efforts at change. The Japanese minister in Korea, General Miuru Goro, entered into a conspiracy with the Taewongun in the autumn of 1895, and succeeded in assassinating the queen and kidnapping the king.

The king managed to escape in February of the following year, 1896, and took refuge in the Russian Legation in the capital. Asking Russia for advice about how to cope with the Japanese, he granted Russia mining and timber extraction concessions. The Japanese were temporarily pushed into the background of events and influence in Korea—which considerably angered them.

Both Japan and Russia made efforts to resolve their conflicting interests without resorting to war. In June, 1896, both agreed in the Yamagata-Lobanov Protocol that they would have equal rights in Korea, would urge the government there to make reforms, and would withdraw their troops. No sooner was it signed than Russia sent advisers to assist the Korean army and managed to get an undertaking from Korea that a Russian should be in charge of Korean financial affairs.

Korea, however, did not care for the idea that Russia would manage its affairs and resisted Russian advances. Faced with Korean and Japanese opposition, Russia tried to negotiate a further settlement. In April, 1898, she signed with Japan the Nishi-Rosen Convention recognizing Korea's independence and promising not to meddle in Korean army and financial matters, as well as to permit Japanese commercial and manufacturing development in Korea.

These agreements were no more than temporary by nature, and both sides soon broke their word. Between August 1903 and February 1904, long negotiations again took place between the two powers. But the Japanese, becoming suspicious of the Russian actions, broke off the talks on February 6. Two days later, on the 8th, they launched a night torpedo attack against the Russian fleet at Port Arthur and managed to bottle it up in the port. Then, on February 10, 1904, they declared war.

The Russo-Japanese War

Russia had thought, until two days before her fleet was torpedoed by the Japanese warships of Admiral Togo Heihachiro on February 8, that she had the initiative. But on the 6th, when the talks were broken off, her troops were sent across the Yalu River into Korea.

Admiral Togo's initial surprise attack had crippled two battleships and one cruiser of the Russian fleet. The next day the guns of his ships destroyed four more Russian warships.

Admiral Togo whose masterly use of naval tactics sealed Russia's fate in the Russo-Japanese war

As the Japanese navy was torpedoing the Russian Pacific Squadron at Port Arthur, Japanese troops landed in Korea and took Seoul. With devastating precision, the following day the Japanese fleet destroyed the two Russian ships in Chemulpo harbour.

With the declaration of war on February 10, the Anglo-Japanese Alliance came into force and Britain at once gave a loan to Japan to help her in the war. China, whose treaty with Russia of 1896 ought to have brought her into the war, ignored the agreement, and the other powers also remained neutral.

As in the Sino-Russian war, the world tended to think that the war would be won by Russia against what was still considered as a tiny Japan. While Russia certainly had the forces and the material necessary for a victory, it was a question whether she could mobilize and deploy these quickly enough. Japan, with typical shrewdness, saw this point and acted as quickly as she could. Her naval superiority, after the Russian fleet was locked up in harbour and badly.damaged by them, was considerable and she could therefore land troops more or less wherever she wished. Her troop strength at the beginning of hostilities was about 330,000 compared to Russia's 100,000.

The Russians, well aware of their weaknesses, tried to avoid any engagement with the enemy until they could strengthen their numbers. The problem involved in increasing the army's strength was the single-track Trans-Siberian railway along which only about 30,000 men could be conveyed each month. And when they came, these reserves were poorly trained and certainly no match for the well trained and very well disciplined Japanese troops.

Russian and Japanese forces clashed at the Yalu River, and General Kuroki's army was victorious. The battle gave Japan control over Korea. Quite as important to Japan was that for the first time an Asian army had defeated a Western one. With soaring morale among his troops, General Kuroki pressed onward into Manchuria.

Four days after victory at the Yalu River, General Oku's army landed on the northeast coast of the Kwantung Peninsula. It was then split up into two sections. One part under General Nogi went south to besiege Port Arthur while the other part proceeded north to join General Kuroki's army. This combined force, under the command of Field-Marshal Oyama, sustained heavy losses but captured the Russian position at Liaoyang by September 4. The Russian army retreated northward to Mukden, regrouped, and made an attempt under the command of Kuropatkin to retake Liaoyang. But in the battle of Shaho they were again defeated by the Japanese.

The siege of Port Arthur to the south began on May 30, and continued relentlessly until the city fell on January 2, 1905. Its fall freed large numbers of Japanese troops to be sent up to Mukden where, between February 23 and March 10, 1905, a battle in which 750,000 soldiers were involved was fought with ferocity outside the city. Superior in numbers to the Russians, the Japanese were victorious. They occupied Mukden, the Manchurian capital.

The Russian Baltic Fleet under Admiral Rodjestvenski had meanwhile (on October 15, 1904) sailed from its base at Libau for the East. Denied access to British ports en route and also the use of the Suez Canal, the fleet had to sail round the Cape of Good Hope and, after an arduous and remarkable voyage of 18,000 miles, ap-

Left, General Nogi, the Japanese commander at Port Arthur during the long siege of the city

Below, Japanese imperial troops disembarking from boats at Port Arthur during the Russo-Japanese war. The fleet lies in the background

The Japanese army enters one of the gates of Mukden, the capital of Manchuria

proached close to its goal, Vladivostock. Admiral Togo with a repaired and wholly ready Japanese fleet was waiting for it, patrolling the Straits of Korea (the Tsushima Straits). At dawn on May 27, the Russian fleet was sighted. Off the island of Tsushima it was met by the Japanese fleet. In the battle that followed only two of the forty-two ships in the Russian fleet managed to escape and reach Vladivostock. The remainder were put out of action or sunk. Japan had proved herself superior to Russia both by land and by sea. The Japanese call the battle of Tsushima, the Battle of the Sea of Japan because the control of this sea seemed to them not only vital for their protection, but essential to their expansion on the Asian continent.

Russian defeat has been attributed to the obsolete quality of many of her ships and to their inferior communications and armament. But it was doubtless also to some extent the result of the long sea dash the ships had been forced to make from the Baltic Sea to the East. Certainly the description of the sea battle as the greatest since Trafalgar is a fair one.

A Japanese painting of the scene aboard a Russian naval vessel when one of the great guns was fired. "A Japanese?" the Russians were inclined to snort, "Pooh! He's a mosquito. Why, I'll stick a pin through him and send him home in a letter."

With Japan victorious on land and sea, Russia found the strain of continued war considerable. Her lines of communication were far extended, and although the vast bulk of her forces remained uncommitted, the financial and the domestic political position were growing less favourable as weeks and months passed. The general discontent in Russia was accentuated by defeat in the East and revolution was an ever-growing threat. Japan, too, was feeling the strain.

The state of affairs in Russia threw the other European powers into a flurry of diplomatic activity aimed at ending the war. Germany tended to feel that if revolution in Russia were further provoked and the Tsar Nicholas II unseated from his throne, the revolution might well spread to Germany and topple Kaiser Wilhelm too. Britain and France had their own reasons for not wishing the war to be prolonged, and the United States inclined to the view that a continuing Russian presence in East Asia would maintain the precarious balance of power there.

By the end of May 1905, even the warring countries had come to the decision that the war should stop. Japan requested American mediation and President Theodore Roosevelt agreed to act. Peace talks began at Portsmouth, New Hampshire, in the United States on August 10, 1905. On September 5, the Treaty of Portsmouth was signed.

The Results of the War

Terms of the Treaty of Portsmouth:

> Russia agreed to Japan's domination of Korea which was phrased as her 'paramount political, military, and economic interest'.
> Both powers agreed to evacuate Manchuria which was to be restored to China, except for the Kwantung Peninsula on which the Japanese were given a lease.

> The sovereignty of China in Manchuria was recognized.

> Japan acquired the rights of Russia in the South Manchurian Railway and in some coal mines there. Since Manchuria was Chinese territory, this was subject to Chinese consent. Both parties agreed not to interfere in Chinese development of Manchuria, and that railways other than those in the Kwantung Peninsula should be used for commercial and industrial purposes and not for military reasons.

> Russia ceded the southern part of Sakhalin (below the 50th parallel) to Japan which had, in 1875, given up her claims there in favour of control of the Kuril Islands.

Before the conference began at Portsmouth, China had sent a note to America, Japan, and Russia reminding them that Manchuria was Chinese territory. But China, unfortunately, was in no position to do more than agree to the terms of the subsequent treaty, whatever she thought or wished.

Japan got much less than she had hoped for from the treaty. She obtained a lease on the Kwantung Peninsula giving her Port Arthur and Dairen, and the area was henceforward referred to as the Kwantung Leased Territory, and the Japanese army there as the Kwantung Army. But the Russians refused to pay any indemnity, nor would they agree to reduce the size of their Pacific Fleet. Japan had to agree to these matters since both financially and militarily she had not the strength to continue the war. Russia had that strength, despite the troubled internal political situation.

Japan gained China's consent to the transfer of Russian rights in Manchuria by the Treaty of Peking, signed on December 22, 1905. By another agreement signed on the same day with the Chinese, Japan wrested further rights there, and the Japanese said there were secret agreements also in which China promised not to permit the building of any railway in Manchuria that would be in competition with the Japan-controlled South Manchurian Railway.

In the long term, the Treaty of Portsmouth put the brake on Russia's advance into Manchuria and on her influence in Korea. Japan's sphere of interest now included Korea and south Manchuria.

The Repercussions of the Russo-Japanese War

One of the most important results of the treaty, other than the implementation of its terms, was the apprehension on the part of other powers about the role of an increasingly powerful Japan in East Asia. Britain and Japan revised and renewed the Anglo-Japanese Alliance of 1902, first in 1905 and again in 1911. In 1907, France and Japan agreed to mutual support in preserving their spheres of interest in China, and Japan concluded a similar agreement with Russia in respect of Manchuria. The drawing together of Russia and Japan in this matter eroded Chinese sovereignty in Manchuria, which they had pledged to maintain.

The United States found itself worried about Japanese influence in the Pacific and East Asia as a whole. Her Open Door policy had been ignored in Japan's acquisition of exclusive privileges in Manchuria and Korea. Formerly friendly relations between the two countries grew less friendly with Japanese protests at racial discrimination against their nationals in America, and with American fear that Japan had expansionist eyes focussed on the Philippines.

Two attempts were made to alleviate the growing American-Japanese tensions. The first was the Taft-Katsura Agreement of 1905 by which America promised not to interfere with Japan in Korea provided Japan left the Philippines to America. The second was the Root-Takahira Agreement signed in 1908, by which both countries agreed to maintain the *status quo* in the Pacific—more or less a reaffirmation of the previous agreement.

In Manchuria, the story revolved basically around who should build, own, and run the railways there. The proposal of a British company, approved by China, to extend an existing railway joining Mukden to North China, ran into Japanese protests that this would be in violation of one of the secret agreements with China, signed in 1905. Although China did not agree to this interpretation, Britain persuaded the company to give up the project since the Anglo-Japanese Alliance seemed more important than another British-owned railway. One more railway plan was put forward by the Americans in 1909. This was to build a railway across Manchuria from Chinchow to Aigun. The Knox Neutralization Plan for Manchuria, envisaging a neutralized railway system, was not favoured by other foreign powers and was dropped. But its effect was to bring Japan and Russia closer toward each other in virtually dividing Manchuria between them. The treaties signed by the two countries in 1909, 1911, and 1916 aimed to make secure their interests in Manchuria against the interests of others.

The plight of Korea as a result of the Japanese victory was one of the more tragic results of the war. Even during the hostilities she had become to all intents and purposes a protectorate of Japan, signing a protocol on February 23, 1904, by which she accepted Japan's advice on government administration. And a few months later she further agreed to accept a Japanese financial adviser and to consult Japan before making any agreement with another power. Later, after the Treaty of Portsmouth was signed, Ito Hirobumi made an agreement with the king of Korea that effectively made Korea a Japanese protectorate, allowing Japan to direct foreign affairs and placing Ito himself as Resident-General at Seoul.

An appeal two years later by the Korean king to an international conference at The Hague to end Japanese control simply caused the Japanese to force the king's abdication. His son, Crown Prince Yi, became king and Japan assumed total administrative control in the land.

Political assassinations are almost always acts that do infinitely more harm than good. The murder of Ito Hirobumi at Harbin in Manchuria by a Korean patriot was no exception. Japanese opinion was inflamed by the event, and Japan formally annexed Korea on August 22, 1910. The name given to Korea by Japan was one full of irony—Chosen, Land of Morning Calm. Korea was to suffer cruelly under the Japanese for many a year to come, and Korean literature of the ensuing period describes the agony of a people oppressed.

The Anglo-Japanese Alliance stood Japan in good stead, for so long as Britain did not protest against Japanese actions, then there was less likelihood of other powers doing so. Korea and the Kwantung Peninsula served in years to come as the ideal springboard for Japan's gigantic leaps into Asia. Japanese militarism gained strong popular support at home by victory over the great Western power, Russia. The Japanese home economy entered a boom period as a result of the war and its aftermath in the shape of virtual colonies. Now Japan had Taiwan, Korea, and southern Manchuria, and had become an imperialist power on the lines of Western nations. Her prestige in Western eyes rose sharply, and even those Westerners who felt that Caucasian (or, as they were termed then, Nordic) peoples were the supreme human stock, had to admit that perhaps the Japanese were the exception.

In Russia the picture was one of deep unrest and revolt against the oppressive régime of the tsars. Russian influence in East Asia declined sharply. Some political reforms such as the calling of the first National Assembly (Duma) were precipitated by the defeat in the East. Her position in Manchuria no longer dominant, Russia concentrated on Mongolia where she attempted to build up her strength.

As for China—apart from Korea, she came off worst of all. It was once more demonstrated forcibly to the world at large that China could not breathe the word no, and dared only say yes, in the face of threats, extortion, and territorial designs of the great powers—of whom Japan was now definitely one. The movement for political reform gained some momentum, and constitutional reform was included in the belated Manchu reform programme.

It was apparent now in China that Japanese efforts at making their country strong had indeed given it not only a powerful offensive and defensive potential, but a loud and forceful voice in international affairs. Chinese students began to flow from China to the colleges of Japan in order to learn how this had been accomplished. There they met not only fairly modern ideas in various technical studies, but also encountered Dr. Sun Yat-sen's republican movement. Dr. Sun's revolutionary organization, named *T'ung-meng hui* (The United League) already counted among its members a military cadet by the name of Chiang Kai-shek (born 1887). These two names were to mean a great deal in China in the near future.

At this time also, we can see the beginnings of Asian nationalism in Southeast Asian countries. The example of Japan's (to Asia, quite incredible) victory was not lost on other peoples, who began to agitate against British and other colonial yokes. It was another irony of history in the region that at this time and later, these smaller countries should think of Japan as the champion of Asian liberty and a strong bastion against Western colonial rule. Their aspirations to self-government were not to become a reality until after the horror of the Japanese occupation during World War II, when all of them realized Japan was, if anything, a worse and certainly a more inefficient master than the West.

PART THREE

THE ORIENT IN TURMOIL

12 China, 1901–1916: Reform and Revolution

'Reformers, not revolutionaries, mainly prepared the ground for revolution. Great changes were at last under way in Chinese life, and the alien Ch'ing dynasty, trying to guide these changes, could not avoid nurturing anti-Ch'ing... forces that would eventually destroy it. Students the government trained abroad, new armies in training at home, merchants it encouraged in domestic enterprise, political assemblies it convoked in the provinces, all sooner or later turned against the dynasty. In political quicksand, the more the dynasty struggled to save itself, the deeper it sank. For modernization now meant Chinese nationalism... and the fact that modernization was strongest in the coastal and Yangtze provinces boded ill for the central power at Peking.'

Fairbank, Reischauer, and Craig: *East Asia, The Modern Transformation*

T z'u-hsi's abrupt change of heart over reform, embodied in her decree from Sian in 1901, began a period of change in Chinese life and government that was in fact much more far-reaching than any that had been projected in the decrees of the Hundred Days of 1898. The fiasco of her support of the Boxers, the deep humiliation of the Boxer Protocol, were doubtless the main causes of her new policy. It was not simply a need to adopt the 'strong points of foreign countries' that animated the new look of opinion at court. It was the need to begin and carry through real reform of China's outmoded institutions, and to find new but suitable ways of governing a country by now extremely restless and seething with rebellion.

The reform decree of 1901 (issued in the name of the emperor) remarked that the languages and machines of foreign countries were merely 'the skin and the hair of Western technology but not the fundamental source of Western government.' On April 21, 1901, an 'office in charge of Government affairs' was set up to examine memorials submitted on reform. One of its heads was Jung-lu. With a few other conservatives he had managed to remain in favour both with the court and with foreign governments and their ministers in Peking. Liu K'un-i and Chang Chih-tung, the Yangtze governors-general of Kiangsi-Anhwei-Kiangsu and Hunan-Hupei respectively, were appointed associates. In 1901 Chang and Liu submitted three memorials on reform. The first of these stated:

'We presume to say that China is poor not in natural resources but in men of ability; she is not weak in troops but in morale. The scarcity of men of ability is due to our limited knowledge and unsubstantial learning.'

The memorial outlined remedies:

The establishment of civil and military schools, primary schools in all districts, abolition of the old Eight-legged Essay on classical subjects, and means to employ the scholars who would thus be displaced. Reform of the civil service examination in order to include 'useful knowledge while never neglecting classical works.' The new studies were to include Chinese politics and history (one examination), politics and geography, military systems, agriculture, industry, mathematics of other countries (the second examination), and classical studies (the third examination).

This memorial was extremely cautious in attempting not to offend the old school of scholar-bureaucrats, but advancing at the same time far-reaching proposals for reform in education. Its chief author was Chang Chih-tung, and he also put down a few unpalatable facts:

'Popular feelings are not the same as thirty years ago. The people admire the wealth of foreign countries and despise the poverty of the Middle Kingdom.'

They admire also the 'fair play', he wrote, that they see in the conduct of the Maritime Customs Service, and the order and regularity of the foreign concessions in comparison to the disorder in China. Education to bring out 'human talent' for governing was the basic aim.

The second memorial dealt with reform in the political system. It called for frugality, cutting out of red tape (called 'customary formalities'), stopping the purchase of office and rank, raising salaries, getting rid of useless staff, regularizing punishment and imprisonment, simplifying the antique relics of Manchu military organizations. These items were called 'the hooks on which foreign countries hang their criticisms and abuse of us'.

The third memorial dealt with sending students to study abroad, reorganization of the army command on foreign lines, increases in military supplies, promotion of agriculture and industries, the drawing up of laws on mining, transport, and commerce; and new penal codes, the establishment of a uniform currency, translations from foreign books, reform of taxation, and other matters. Curiously enough, having advocated such things in detail and outlined a programme that went much further than anything in the reforms of 1898, Chang Chih-tung aimed a sharp blow at the reformer K'ang Yu-wei who, he said in effect, was a traitor. The position of even such an eminent reformer of the conservative type as Chang was still insecure. Tz'u-hsi and others might easily change their minds again and the reformers find themselves in gaol without the benefits of their own prison and penal reforms.

Political Reform

The Manchu dynasty had inherited from the Ming an administrative method and structure by which the country was managed comparatively well until about 1800. At that time the facts of life began to alter, and by the beginning of the century this extremely complicated and carefully interlocking machine with all its marvellous but outdated parts was no longer working properly. The problem was to construct a centralized governmental organ and put it in the place of the old decentralized one. The business of the country in all its forms could not now be permitted to move with the slowness of medieval times.

The old system by which provincial administrations reported direct to the emperor and were merely supervised by the Six Boards in the capital (the Boards of Civil Appointments, Rites, War, Revenue, Punishment, and Works) was altogether too slow and cumbersome for quick decision-taking. But due to the growth of treaty port industry and administration, to large revenues coming from the south and centre and to the not so large ones from the north, and the rise of regional armies (as we saw during the T'aip'ing campaigns), provincial governments were stronger at the beginning of the twentieth century than they had been for a very long time. They were unwilling to surrender any of their power to a central Peking government. Reforms in this area had to move with extreme slowness in order not to cause a revolt of the organizations concerned. It was only in 1906 that the Six Boards were finally reorganized into eleven ministries. And then, too, reductions were made in the powers of provincial governors and others. In order to regulate the imposition, collection, and transmission of revenues to Peking, financial advisers were appointed to each province.

Typical of the very real problems encountered by the reformers were instances such as the following. Legal reform, very much desired in order to persuade foreign powers to drop extraterritoriality, was hard to achieve. A 1907 draft criminal code based on Japanese and German models would have made a distinction between law and morality, thus making Confucian rules of filial piety legally unenforceable. And the equality of all (other than the imperial family) under the law would have cut out the traditional distinctions of status, age, and sex. This perfectly sensible draft was quickly rejected as unworkable in China, although it would have been quite acceptable in Europe.

Another example was the old Board of War (headed by civil officials) which was made into the Army Ministry with a new Japanese-style military administration headed by Manchu generals. But not all their efforts to diminish the power and influence of Yüan Shih-k'ai and his faction succeeded in so doing.

The institution of a constitutional monarchy like those seen in the West and in Japan seemed to many Chinese a desirable change. It seemed an effective means of uniting rulers and ruled in national affairs such as war. Efforts were made continuously between 1906 and 1911 to strengthen the central administration and reorganize government, and to give the provinces a share in government. But what actually resulted was a struggle for power on various levels. Peking was a pro-Manchu, anti-Chinese city, and the Manchu princes tightened their hold on most of the key positions in order to obstruct any fundamental reform which might tend to unseat them.

But there was an upsurge of nationalism in China, stemming from anti-Manchu sentiment all over the country. In 1905 the first boycott occurred. Students, merchants, and others in most of the treaty ports joined in mass meetings, and the press took up the cause, which was American discrimination against Chinese and the excluding of labourers from immigration to the States. Goods from the United States were boycotted and American trade suffered a severe setback in China for many months. The Peking government, although pressed by America, dared not interfere in case the movement turned against it and became anti-Manchu.

In 1905, the empress dowager sent two official missions abroad, one to the United States and one to Europe, to investigate foreign constitutional governments. The reports submitted on their return in 1906 are highly interesting. The two commissioners explain first that by adopting constitutional government the Throne would be strengthened. They stress that when the people as a whole are involved in the running of their country it is usual to expect an upsurge in their interest in the nation and its needs, leading to great development of resources and greater revenues to the government. Their interest in foreign constitutional governments was largely in practical benefits and not much in theoretical ones. The document was really meant to support the traditional scholar's case against the carrying out of drastic reform.

In August 1908, an imperial decree laid down principles to guide a nine-year programme that was to result in constitutional self-government. Consultative provincial assemblies were to take shape in 1909 and a consultative national assembly in 1910. This was in imitation of Japan where in 1881 the Diet had been promised for nine years later. The convocation of a parliament, originally planned for 1917, was put forward to 1913 on pressure from reformists, and in 1911 a cabinet was formed to be in control of the eleven new ministries.

Educational Reform

In 1901, the Peking government issued orders to all the provincial authorities to set up primary and middle schools on the lines of Japanese and Western examples. These schools were to have a Westernized curriculum but were to teach the old Confucian classics as well. Little time elapsed before it was seen that these plans, heralded in the memorials of Liu and Chang Chih-tung, catered for the ideas and aspirations of no one. The advocates of reform thought it useless to continue with classical studies, and conservative elements disliked the modern subjects.

The result, in 1905, was the drastic step of abolishing the civil service examinations. Their abolition took place at the urging of Chang Chih-tung and Yüan Shih-k'ai, and terminated the means of choosing the members of the ruling élite that had been in operation (in one form and another) since the first setting up of a kind of Imperial University as far back as 124 B.C. In 1906, a Ministry of Education took supervisory control of the new schools.

In fact new schools of all types were for long to face strong competition from Christian institutions. By 1905 Protestant missions had 2,200 kindergartens and primary schools with 42,000 pupils, and 389 'intermediate' and high schools and colleges with 15,000 students. These schools encouraged not only Christianity (without great success) but Western-style individualism and the education of women, refusing to allow students to pay homage to Confucius or the emperor, which was required in the government schools. Not surprisingly, the government prevented mission school graduates from obtaining official employment.

Government schools followed a Japanese model: elementary classes of four years, middle school of five years, and higher school of three, leading to the Imperial University for a three-year course.

The changes began at the top. The Imperial University had been set up in the short weeks of the Hundred Days reform of 1898 with an American, W.A.P. Martin (who was formerly head of the Interpreters' College) serving as first dean of Western studies. It eventually became the National Peking University (shortened from *Pei-ching ta-hsüeh* to *Peita*). The strength of the school system was largely in the provinces, but there were insufficient primary and middle schools to serve as a strong base for advance to higher studies.

One way of producing large numbers of educated youths in quick time was to send them to Japan. This had begun in 1896. But by 1898 there were only a score of students there. After the suppression of the 1898 reform movement, the student population in Japan rose to 200 in 1899, and by the end of 1905 there were about 8,000. But the number who actually graduated, was never more than about 700 per annum. We will see later the other results of this education abroad on Chinese youth when we come to follow the career of Dr. Sun Yat-sen.

The old system of education for the few quietly gave way to daily school life in China in the years 1901–1906.

Military Reform

Military academies were set up in 1901, and cadets were sent to Japanese military training places. The officer corps of the Manchu 'Banner' armies (a feeble force existing on pensions from the state since the establishment of the Ch'ing dynasty), and the Chinese constabulary (called the Army of the Green Standard), were to be disbanded. But this did not actually occur. The officers were still chosen by ancient military examinations (similar in essence to the civil examinations, but calling mainly for physical strength, mounted and dismounted archery, sword-wielding techniques, and the like). This by now comical ritual was poor training for modern war, and was abolished in 1901.

Another aspect of military organization in China consisted of the provincial armies, of which we have already seen something during the anti-T'aip'ing campaigns. These started with the Hunan Braves formed by Tsêng Kuo-fan in and after 1850, and at first consisted of battalions of 500 soldiers each, with one coolie for each three soldiers to do the work of carrying equipment, etc. This army, and Li Hung-chang's Anhwei Army created in 1862, and other forces belonging to Tso Tsung-t'ang, had all continued to exist in spite of being officially disbanded. Composed of professional fighting men (*yung*—meaning 'Braves'), they formed a kind of physical assurance supporting their powerful organizers. They were equipped for the most part with modern artillery and rifles. But they were only half-modernized. Their equipment was not completely standardized, and they had no engineer force, no proper modern communications methods, and no adequate transport or medical services.

A third type of armed force in China was the product of military academies set up in the 1880s by Chang and Li under German instructors. One of these was Chang's Self-strengthening Army organized in Nanking in 1895, which had 35 German officers and about 3,000 men. But this was eventually placed under Liu K'un-i's own Hunan army.

The most important among this third category of armies was the one trained under Yüan Shih-k'ai. Appointed in 1895 to train an imperial army on German lines with German instructors, he soon had near Tientsin 7,000 men from several provinces, all well-paid. This force, afterward called the Peiyang Army, was Yüan's backing later as head of the 'Peiyang clique'. Later still, it made Yüan the 'father of the warlords'. Ten men from the officer corps of this army were later to be military governors of provinces, and six (including Yüan) presidents or premiers of the Peking government during the republic.

Yüan had the right ideas on the establishment of a modern Chinese army. He understood both what was wrong with the old forces and what to do to remedy these defects. The Boxer defeat brought his skills out into the open.

'The military system of the various provinces is not the same. The discipline is not uniform, and rations and weapons differ. The drills are so disparate that...in peace there is no communication between provincial army units, and in time of war... neither co-operation nor co-ordination. It is therefore very difficult to achieve military unification.'

Yüan Shih-k'ai: *Memorial, 1903*

But the reorganization that took place in 1904 did not attempt to centralize the armies, which remained controlled basically at provincial level. Too many powerful personal and provincial interests were involved which were not going to be easily surrendered. The balance of power previously existing between Peking and provincial areas was therefore still much the same, and plans for a new army in any case lacked the foundations both of central control and adequate finance.

After the Russo-Japanese War of 1904–1905, Japanese replaced German instructors at new military schools such as that at Paoting near Peking. And a corps of officers who were also scholar-patriots took shape. One of the young men at Paoting was Chiang Kai-shek. At eighteen (in 1906) he went to Paoting, and he attended the Japanese Military Cadets Academy in the following year.

Death of Tz'u-hsi

The death blow to the movement toward a constitutional monarchy (whose setting up might have greatly altered the future picture of reform) was dealt by that autocratic wielder of supreme power in China for the past fifty years—the Old Buddha (*Lao Fo-yeh*), as the empress dowager was half affectionately and half sarcastically called. By a coincidence that leaves much to the imagination, the Emperor Kuang-hsü whose health was normally excellent, was announced as having died on November 14, and the announcement came with that of the death of Tz'u-hsi herself on November 15, 1908. There is little room for doubt that at her orders he was murdered, for she had already decided that the heir should be one more hapless person—this time the three-year-old Pu-i (Pu-yi), her grand-nephew. He reigned from 1909 to 1912 when he abdicated. The Regent was his father Prince Ch'un who, along with other ignorant and arrogant Manchu princes, did everything in his power to halt reform and restore the now virtually dead Manchu dynasty.

The real role of Tz'u-hsi in Chinese history remains still to be studied in depth, but there can be little doubt that it was a disastrous one. She lacked the greatness of her ancestor K'ang-hsi with his firm grasp of government and interest in other matters such as Western science. And she lacked also the real understanding of art she claimed—being hardly even a dilettante as was her other distinguished ancestor the Ch'ien-lung Emperor. Oddly enough, in death she suffered a fate not meted out to other emperors. Her tomb was plundered, and when the fact was discovered her embalmed body was found face down in a pool of dirty water, stripped of most of its sumptuous clothes, but with its stubborn face still expressing that imperial wilfulness for which in life it was well known.

With her death an age—an immense span of over 2,000 years since Ch'in Shih-huang-ti's first Chinese empire in 221 B.C.—passed from the scene of history. The Ch'ing, the last of that great procession of dynasties, was all but at an end. The great men of the latter part of its rule—Li Hung-chang, Chang Chih-tung, for example—had died in 1901 and 1909 respectively, Li soon after signing the most humiliating document he had ever been required to sign, the Boxer Protocol of 1901. Jung-lu, the empress dowager's favourite, died in 1903.

Tz'u-hsi's effect on the history of the half century of her real power was immense. She was a woman more interested in power and money and in the advancement of her own family, than in China. The extent of corruption under her rule was probably greater than at any other time in China largely because, being deeply corrupt herself, she made no attempt to stamp it out in others. The story of how she appropriated huge sums set aside for the modernization of China's navy to beautify her own Summer Palace is well known. The result was to destroy any chance China had of forming a strong naval force at a time when Japan was about to pounce with a new and very strong navy. The defeats of the Sino-Japanese War of 1894–1895 were one direct result.

While she probably held the dynasty together for a time against the unstoppable tide of change that might earlier have terminated it, she did so at the expense of progress in China. Her favourites such as the eunuch Li Lien-ying, an evil force, exerted great influence on affairs. And her action in reversing the movement of the Hundred Days Reform was probably the single most disastrous event of her days in power. When, in 1901, she was forced to accept reforms, it is doubtful if she really intended wholeheartedly to assist their being carried into effect. Her blind support of the Boxers came near to ending the Manchu dynasty in 1900. Her change of attitude to foreigners after their defeat was the result of necessity and not of a reasoned change in thought. The final probable murder of Kuang-hsü brought to an end in typical fashion the rule of one of history's most malevolent and backward-looking women.

At the end of her life, the Empress Dowager was called Tz'u-hsi Tuan-yu K'ang-yi Chao-yin Chuang-ch'eng Shou-kung Ch'in-hsian Ch'ung-hsi Huang Tai-hou: Motherly, auspicious, orthodox, heaven-blessed, prosperous, all-nourishing, brightly-manifest, calm, sedate, perfect, long-lived, respectful, revered, worshipful, illustrious, exalted Empress Dowager

Chang Chien and the Rise of a New Class

The shift in values from the formerly admired Confucian scholar to modern businessman was a phenomenon of the days after 1905 and the abolition of the old examinations. One good example is Chang Chien (1835–1926), a Kiangsu man who attained the supreme honour of being top scholar in the palace examination (*chuang-yüan*) at the age of forty-one. His success came at the time of Japanese defeat of China, and Chang became a pioneer industrialist. He started off by expanding the existing long-staple cotton grown in his native place to produce yarn that was competitive in quality and price with that of Japan and India.

His connection with other scholars such as Liu K'un-i and Chang Chih-tung permitted him to receive tax benefits and even some of the necessary capital for machinery to launch his cotton-spinning mill in 1899. He has been described as a Confucian Robert Owen—well known for his paternalistic attitude toward his employees, concerned in their living standards and their 'joys and sorrows alike'. He built several spinning mills, launched out into water transport by steamship, and into oil, salt, and flour production. Nantung, his home place, became a model district—something of a marvel in a China where it was a unique development—with schools and technical colleges, parks, paved roads, homes for orphans and the aged.

Prince Ch'un with two of his sons. The boy standing on the right is Pu-i who, at the age of three, became the last emperor of China, with his father as regent

Chang Chien, basically of the scholar-gentry, succeeded in altering his outlook and in turning into a highly successful and quite progressive entrepreneur. He later pressed for constitutional government when he was head of the Kiangsu Provincial Assembly. Later still, he was Minister of Agriculture and Commerce in Yüan Shih-k'ai's cabinet of 1913. It was to men such as Chang that the central government still had to look, for they tended to take over the duties in the provinces of the old scholar-gentry class.

Revolution Approaches

Revolution is never the simple result of a single cause. Its roots are always complex. Although there is generally one man or a small group of men who become its leaders, it is misleading to view events as the result of their activities alone. The man or the men who lead come to prominence, first of all, because of the real impulse to change that already exists within the society. They focus and direct that impulse, acting as human catalysts in a process of change already going on around them.

The revolution in China of 1911 was no exception to this pattern. But the factors in the making of that revolution were, if anything, even more numerous and diverse than those in many other revolutions elsewhere. It was hard to abolish the effects, the deep-seated way of life and thought, engendered by two thousand years of dynastic rule and Confucian outlook. The revolution of 1911 did not succeed completely in doing so, and must now be seen in its context of the later Communist revolution of 1949. Even that latter radical change can now be looked at in the light of the still later Cultural Revolution of the 1960s.

The principal factors underlying the revolution fall naturally into background causes and more immediate causes.

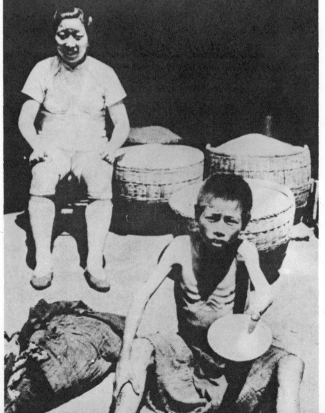

Above, a narrow shopping street in Peking in 1900. The state of the city in those days was one of such municipal neglect that, it was said, only roads leading to the houses of officials were paved. Descriptions of Peking in the early Ming give a picture of a city infinitely better cared for

Left, the contrast between the well-nourished woman selling rice and the starved beggar boy in rags tells without words the story of China for many a decade

Background Causes

We have already seen many of these in some detail, but they may be listed.

> The general misery of the population partly caused by an increase in the incidence of floods, droughts, and famines. Population increase without increase in food supply. Incidence of plague.

> Increasing taxation due to official corruption, to payment for the suppression of such uprisings as the T'aip'ing, the Nien, and the Boxer, and to payment of huge indemnities to foreign powers. Expenditure on Manchu reform programmes. China's inability to increase customs tax because of international agreements fixing it.

> Foreign trade as a factor in upsetting the traditional pattern of China's economy —foreign goods were generally cheaper than Chinese manufactured products, leading to decline in Chinese industry and depreciation in the value of the currency.

> The 'scramble for concessions' and the foreigners' success in having their own way with the Manchu government led to deep discontent and humiliation.

> The Boxer Protocol led to even greater Manchu compliance in foreign demands, which in turn produced an intensification of anti-Manchu and anti-foreign feeling, and discredited the dynasty. Manchu inability to intervene in the Russo-Japanese war fought on Chinese territory.

> The slow penetration of Western ideas on democracy stemming from students who had studied abroad.

> The rule of Tz'u-hsi that led to extensive corruption at lower governmental levels. The increasingly parasitic role of the Manchu upper classes and their monopoly of top governmental posts.

> Rising nationalism which tended to revive the cry that the Manchu were aliens and it was time they went.

> The transformation of the old scholar-gentry-landlord class into a scholar-businessman (or merchant) gentry class, leading to village neglect and absentee-landlordism.

> The growth of large urban populations in treaty ports, whose ideas were quickly, although superficially, Westernized and who regarded change in the old form of government with favour.

> The movement for a constitutional monarchy with parliamentary elections tended to give birth to more radical ideas whereby the monarchy would be abolished altogether.

The sum of all those matters added up to a ground-swell of unrest throughout the whole country. The Manchu government, caught between the demands of foreign treaties and the grievances of its subjects, was in an increasingly precarious position. To default on the treaty obligations was to invite further foreign pressure of various kinds. And to allow popular anti-foreign sentiments to be reflected in official policy would have the same result. The growing unpopularity of the Manchu dynasty was therefore inevitable.

A cartoon from the British weekly magazine *Punch* satirizing Manchu corruption—a fat official sits doing nothing at all but receiving money

More Immediate Causes of Revolution

Until 1895, most of the Chinese press had been started and run by British and American missionary activity. During the following decade and a half until 1911, the more than sixty publications started were entirely Chinese ventures. They tended to combine reformist ideas with commercial journalism. New daily Chinese papers began in Shanghai, joining the old Shun Pao that had been publishing since 1884 and had a circulation of 15,000 by 1895. The provincial press became a forum for the airing of ideas such as constitutional monarchy, but also for the more radical ideas of students and military officers.

Influences from Japan

Japan was both the model for Ch'ing reform ideas and also the base for anti-Ch'ing revolution. In fact, although Chinese are loathe to admit it, the revolution was largely made in Japan.

'Republican China went to school in Tokyo. The Japanese stimulus to modern education, militarism, and constitutionalism in China . . . was part of a broader contribution
to the rise of Chinese nationalism in general.

Japan's influence . . . was more direct, profound, and far-reaching than that of
Britain in the nineteenth century or of the United States from 1915 to 1949, or even . . .
of the Soviet Union after 1949. One reason was Japan's closer cultural . . . propinquity.
Another . . . was the historical circumstance that, in this dawn of their modern age,
China was most eager to learn and Japan most eager to teach, as yet without serious
conflicts of national interest.'

Fairbank : *East Asia*

In 1898, Japan took in the fleeing leaders of the Hundred Days Reform — K'ang
Yu-wei and Liang Ch'i-ch'ao. The former lived for a time in the house of Shigenobu
Okuma whose 'Okuma Doctrine' put forward the idea that Japan, now modernized,
should repay her ancient cultural debt to China by guaranteeing her freedom and
assisting her to modernize too. But the radical reformers led by K'ang, and the anti-
Ch'ing revolutionaries in Japan (led by Sun Yat-sen) failed to get together in any
way, and by 1900 they formed two distinct and antagonistic Chinese exile organizations. Both reformers and revolutionaries were patriotic and were banned by the
Peking government.

Dr. Sun Yat-sen

Other influences of an immediate nature with a deep effect on the build-up
toward revolution were Dr. Sun himself and those many Chinese in Japan, elsewhere
abroad, and in China itself.

Sun Yat-sen, born in 1866 in the Hsiang-shan district of Kwangtung province,
is better known in China as Chung-shan—the romanization of the characters for
the pseudonym he adopted while in Japan. Sun Yat-sen's education took place in

The house in a
village of
Hsiang-shan
district of
Kwangtung
province
where Dr. Sun
Yat-sen was
born—a
Western, not a
Chinese,
structure

Right, Sun Yat-sen in Western dress. The Chinese, like the Japanese before them, tended to look uncomfortable in Western clothes. It was several decades before photographs appeared showing them quite accustomed to the new mode of dress

Below, a meeting of the *Hsing-chung hui* (Revive China Society) in Honolulu in 1894

Honolulu, and later in Hong Kong where he graduated from the College of Medicine (founded in 1887 and incorporated into the new University of Hong Kong in 1912). As a doctor, he practised for some time in Macau and in Canton.

As early as 1885 when he was only nineteen and when France defeated Chinese forces in the Sino-French war, Sun determined that the Manchu dynasty had to be overthrown. His early idealism was later translated by him into a programme of reconstruction that developed into one of revolution. This development is generally considered to have two periods, 1894–1900 and 1900–1911.

The first period began with a letter which he sent to Li Hung-chang outlining a plan for economic development in China by means of the full use of the people's talents to increase agricultural production, together with exploitation of natural resources and the organizing of an efficient system of transport throughout the country. Nothing came of this plan.

Sun Yat-sen then went to Honolulu and founded a secret society named *Hsing-chung hui*—the Revive China Society—whose aims were to revive China by combatting Manchu government oppression and foreign plundering. Financial support was to be sought among overseas Chinese. This was an early attempt, and Sun's political ideas were still largely unformed. He left Honolulu at the end of 1894 and set up his society's headquarters in Hong Kong. The first plot of the Revive China Society was to seize the Canton provincial government offices. This was in 1895. The plot was discovered, several of Sun's associates were captured and executed, and Sun fled to Japan where he removed his queue, grew a moustache and, dressed in Western clothes, easily passed for a Japanese called Nakayama (Chung-shan, in Chinese).

From Japan, a wanted man in China, he went to the United States and to London, where he was recognized at the Chinese legation and taken prisoner in 1896. Thus 'kidnapped', he was held while awaiting a ship to carry him back to Canton and execution. His old teacher at medical college, Sir James Cantlie (who had also taught him cricket), received a message which Sun managed to smuggle out of the legation. Cantlie mobilized public opinion in Britain, and had Sun released.

He was now thirty years old, his programme widely publicized, a leading anti-Ch'ing revolutionary. Perhaps even in his own mind he was already a man with a destiny.

By the time he reached Japan once more in 1897 he had formulated much more precise opinions. These included getting money for revolution from overseas Chinese communities who were commercially minded and had developed largely outside the framework of traditional Chinese society. Another idea dealt with the use of patriotic youth from the Canton area (many from his own district of Hsiang-shan) who were modernized, semi-Westernized, and sometimes Christian. The old-fashioned part of his programme contained the traditional aim of mobilizing local bands to seize control of local power, thus starting off a chain reaction of rebellion. We may recall the beginnings of the T'aip'ing rebellion when Hung Hsiu-ch'üan worked in a very similar way by obtaining local rebel support. But it was during this two-year period (1897–1898) that the outline of what were later to crystallize as the Three Principles of the People (*san min chu-i*) was forming in his mind.

Just before the turn of the century the struggle for the minds of overseas Chinese and for the allegiance of the secret societies in China itself, polarized around the two aspects of projected change: the *Hsing-chung hui* (Revive China Society) of Sun Yat-sen, and the *Pao-huang hui* (Emperor Protection Society) of K'ang Yu-wei and Liang Ch'i-ch'ao.

Revolutionary gatherings, schools, and publications came into being in Japan, in the treaty ports, and elsewhere in the world. In Shanghai the revolutionary *Su-pao* was suppressed and one of its founders put in prison for three years. Another widely circulated publication was *The Revolutionary Army*, published by an eighteen-year-old youth in 1903. The *Kuang-fu hui* (literally: Return of Light Society) composed of Chekiang and lower Yangtze provinces students was active. And in Hunan, the *Hua-hsing hui* (China Revival Society) attempted to weld together students, officers, and secret society men to take part in a rising in Changsha in 1904. But this was discovered and did not take place. Revolutionary acts and purposes were pursued all over, but they lacked co-ordination. They lacked, too, a definite set of principles and a long-term objective.

It was against this diversity of background that Sun Yat-sen felt impelled to develop more precisely his own ideological scheme. He had to capture the minds not only of the sceptical, commercially minded overseas Chinese attracted by the rather old-fashioned *Pao-huang hui* programme of K'ang and Liang, but also those of China, in particular Chinese youth, as well.

By 1900, Sun Yat-sen's political ideas entered a second stage of development. Republicanism was growing in importance in his mind. In 1903 he began writing newspaper articles in Japan and Honolulu. His travels took him to Brussels, Paris, Berlin, and again to Tokyo, organizing student groups in each place. The Three Principles of the People, the guidelines for a republican revolution, were defined. *Min-tsu chu-i*, or nationalism; *min-ch'üan chu-i*, or democracy; and *min-sheng chu-i*, (literally, 'people's livelihood') or socialism.

At this early stage the nationalism of Sun's ideas was anti-Manchu. Its anti-foreign aspect was not stressed. Democracy meant resistance to Confucianism, and the guarantee of a constitution. And with the programme of Liang Ch'i-ch'ao in mind, the constitution was to confer executive, legislative, and judicial powers in the manner of those of the United States. But from Chinese tradition it would take examination and censorial powers. This 'five power constitution' seems to have been Dr. Sun's own invention.

The socialism of the programme was non-Marxist (in fact Sun Yat-sen remained firmly anti-Marxist all his life). It did not involve ideas of class struggle, but simply laid down principles to check the activities of speculators and monopolies.

In 1905, in Tokyo, the various strands of Sun's activities and their results came together with Japanese encouragement. The *T'ung-meng hui* (United League) was founded with Sun as its head. In it were combined the various rival groupings of Chinese opinion. Branches were set up in all the Chinese provinces (with the exception of Kansu) and in some of the foreign cities where Sun had been active. One year later its membership was about ten thousand strong.

The manifesto of the *T'ung-meng hui* set forth its four aims:

> To end the oppressive dynastic rule of the Manchu.
> To achieve a government of China by Chinese and to restore the sovereignty of the state.

> To equalize land ownership by means of a form of socialism.
> To set up a republican form of government giving the people political rights.

These aims embodied the Three Principles of the People. They were to be attained in three stages.

> Three years of military government, local self-government being implemented district by district.
> A provisional constitution to last for six years (this became known later as the period of 'tutelage' and is probably the first statement on the subject which is now called 'guided democracy'.)
> Eventual constitutional government, an elected parliament and president.

In the light of the assaults on various forms of constitutional government round the world since that time, these assumptions must seem naive. But in China before the last dynasty had collapsed entirely, before the cataclysm of World War I when many illusions were shattered, and before the Russian Revolution, perhaps they were not so childlike in their faith as they now appear. In any case, the more rational proposals in the area of constitutional monarchy set out by Liang Ch'i-ch'ao actually ceased to have any reality with the death in 1908 of the Kuang-hsü Emperor.

But the path ahead for Sun Yat-sen was a hard one. Protests from the Manchu government in Peking led to his expulsion from Japan in 1907. He transferred to Indo-China, and between May 1907 and the following May had organized six incidents in the south China provinces. The French authorities in Hanoi then decided that perhaps Dr. Sun and his *T'ung-meng hui* were undesirable in their colony since their activities might well cause incidents of a similar nature there.

The memorial to the Seventy-two Martyrs of Canton, at Huang Hua Kang

Sun was expelled. By 1909, for lack of funds and an equal lack of success, the move-ment was brought almost to a halt. Anarchist elements came to prominence with assassination plots such as that against the Prince Regent in Peking—which failed. Although anti-Manchu feeling was on the rise, the movement was frustrated. Attempts to arouse an army revolt in 1910 and to capture government offices in Canton in 1911—the 'Canton Revolution'—also failed because of the poor co-ordination of the action in which men of the same side shot at each other, resulting in the famous 'Seventy-two Martyrs of Canton'. Their leader, Huang Hsing, decided at this point that 'in instigating revolution, dictatorship is imperative. Once a dissenting voice is permitted, the revolution is bound to fail.'

Nevertheless, all these incidents added up to further discredit the Manchu dynasty. There were also factors of importance not under *T'ung-meng hui* control, which assisted the process.

The Railway Question

One of the attempts at centralization made under the Manchu reform programme was to gather control of the railways under the government at Peking. This met with stiff opposition from provincial authorities who had invested heavily in railways. While many railways were foreign-owned (by the French in Yunnan, by Russia in Manchuria, and by Germany in Shantung), the contracts for others had been bought back from foreigners with the help of the provincial gentry. The contract to build the Hangkow-Canton railway was in local hands, but not enough money was forthcoming to begin construction.

The man put in charge of railway 'centralization' was the notoriously corrupt Sheng Hsüan-huai. In his attempts to float foreign loans to build this and other railways, a consortium of French, British, German, and American banks was formed in 1910. The consortium signed the final contract with Sheng the following year (in May 1911).

> 'To the patriots in the provinces it seemed that the Manchus and their corrupt hench-men were selling China to foreign bankers for their own profit. A "railway protection" movement sprang up, particularly in Szechuan, with mass meetings and anguished petitions to Peking, all in vain.'
>
> Fairbank: *East Asia*

The movement gathered momentum. Soon shops and schools in Szechuan closed and payment of taxes stopped. Peasants joined in, and in September of 1911 government troops fired on demostrators and seized the leaders (who were gentry, most of whom had studied in Japan and were investors in railway projects). The movement was now strongly anti-Manchu. Meanwhile many of the provincial assemblies set up under the reform programme had also become (for similar reasons) anti-Manchu.

Added to these factors was the worsening of economic conditions in general, accompanied by the peasant rice riots in Hunan in 1910.

The picture of China in late 1911 was a sad one indeed. The long story of dynastic rule, and of Confucian principles in personal and in national affairs, was clearly coming to an end. Everywhere there was a near-total breakdown of the accepted rule of law and order. Corruption engulfed official and private life like some evil and malevolent tide that could not be stopped. It was a time of hunger, disease, unemployment, of very heavy taxes, little of which reached the government, of money pouring out of China in foreign indemnities and in cheap manufactures. The time for revolution was ripe. Alas, when it came, the revolution proved incapable of solving China's problems. It was to take nearly another forty years before the country once more came under a firm government with an entirely new outlook— in 1949.

Revolution of 1911 and the End of the Ch'ing

When the time came, and the revolution broke out, Sun Yat-sen was on a lecture tour of the United States. He hurriedly went to England and France to try to ensure that there was no support forthcoming from them for the Ch'ing. The events which triggered off the revolution had nothing directly to do with any activity of the *T'ung-meng hui* or Sun Yat-sen. Yet it was undoubtedly the climate of opinion fostered by the many activities of both that was crucial in what then occurred spontaneously almost everywhere in China.

At Wuhan—the agglomeration of three cities of Wuchang, Hankow, and Hanyang, on the Yangtze River banks—plans had been made by two revolutionary groups for a military uprising there on October 6. The able Manchu governor-general Jui-ch'eng learned of the plot and took steps to thwart it. Many of the plotters were army men. The uprising was postponed, but on October 9, a bomb was accidentally set off in the Russian Concession at Hankow. The authorities discovered there a list of the revolutionaries, including officers of the garrison of Wuchang.

The following day, October 10, 1911 (the Double Tenth) some of these soldiers revolted in order to save themselves from arrest. Despite the fact that less than 3,000 men revolted, their commander and also Jui-ch'eng fled the city. Wuchang fell to the rebels. A brigade commander named Li Yüan-hung was forced into taking charge in the absence of any revolutionary leader at the scene of this very peaceful and untypical revolutionary beginning.

> 'After the revolutionary army drove Governor-general Jui-ch'eng away from the city, soldiers surrounded my camp. . . . I was quickly arrested and asked to become the commander of this revolutionary army. I was surrounded by guns at the time, and I might have been killed instantly if I had not complied with their request.'
>
> A letter from Li Yüan-hung written later in October, 1911.

Li quickly occupied the other two cities, Hankow and Hanyang, and a military government was soon set up at Wuchang in the name of the Republic of China. In fact the success of the revolt was due to the flight of the military commander and the governor-general who could probably have suppressed the revolt if they had not taken fright so easily.

'At that time most of those in the new army at Wuchang who supported the revolutionary cause had been sent away to Szechuan. The few who remained made up
only a very small part of the artillery and engineering battalions, while the other
soldiers in the new Wuchang army had little appetite for the new cause. It was that
small group which was prompted, by the police discovery of the revolutionary headquarters, to make the attempt without much thought for its chances of success.'

Dr. Sun Yat-sen

The revolt spread like fire. In a few weeks anti-Manchu declarations had been
made in over 20 other centres—with the backing of the *T'ung-meng hui*, provincial
assemblies, and the New Army. There was little fighting, and by early December
most provinces were under military governors who held power jointly with the
leaders of provincial assemblies.

Yüan Shih-k'ai (who had been dismissed by Prince Ch'un) was now recalled,
and was begged in so many words to save the empire. He made his own terms, setting
himself up as head of a cabinet government and commander of all the armed
forces. The revolutionary forces set up their own government at Nanking.

Sun Yat-sen read about the Wuchang incident in a newspaper in Denver,
Colorado. He eventually reached Shanghai in time to be elected as provisional
president of the Chinese Republic. When installed at Nanking in January, 1912,
he immediately offered to stand down in favour of the premier, Yüan Shih-k'ai.

It has been rightly said that the 1911 revolution was an inconclusive one because
its aims were largely negative instead of positive. Its initial and principle aim was
to get rid of Manchu rule. But there were a few more positive subjects that found

Dr. Sun Yat-sen and members of his cabinet following his election as Provisional President
of the Chinese Republic on January 1, 1912

wide agreement among those taking part. One was that the provinces should be represented in any parliament, and that real Chinese unity was a first necessity. Another was that the best man to head a government was Yüan Shih-k'ai, on account of his known political experience and considerable abilities.

Negotiations both in public and in secret were carried on by Yüan with all interested parties, including the court. By February 12, 1912 the emperor, later to be known as Henry Pu-yi, and whose hapless life story we will touch on in part later, in a decree signed by his mother, abdicated.

'I have...induced the Emperor to yield the country...determining that there should be a constitutional republic. Yüan Shih-k'ai has full powers to organize a provisional republican government to treat with the people's forces on the methods of achieving unity, so that the five races—Manchu, Mongol, Chinese, Muslim, and Tibetan may continue together in one Chinese Republic....'

Empress Dowager Lung Yü, 12 February, 1912

Sun Yat-sen then resigned from his post of provisional president. Yüan Shih-k'ai was elected to replace him. The reasons for Sun's resignation were his lack of military power with which to back up the revolutionary republic, whereas Yüan had his own army. Sun also feared, and probably rightly, that Yüan and the northern provinces would not accept him as head of a government because he was a southerner. The strong division between north and south in China thus once more in history played a decisive and divisive part. Sun had managed to gain very little foreign support for his republican ideas, a fact which made him very bitter, whereas Yüan was assured of support from the foreign powers (doubtless because of the armed force he had at his disposal). Long before it was said, every one recognized the truth of Mao Tsu-tung's statement that power grows out of the barrel of a gun.

The First Years of the Republic, 1912–1916

Yüan Shih-k'ai had been responsible for stage-managing the abdication of the emperor and the end of the dynasty that had given him his power. He succeeded by organizing Chinese diplomats abroad and also numerous officials and military commanders at home to send messages advising the abdication and the end of the monarchy. His future acts between his election to the presidency in 1912 and his death four years later were of an even more questionable nature. Having betrayed his sovereign he proceeded to betray the revolution and the republic.

He refused to come to Nanking, the provisional government headquarters, to be installed as president. Dr. Sun stood out against Yüan's installation at Peking because of the strong elements of corruption there and because of the tangle of relationships in which Yüan was heavily involved in the north. Yüan, while willing to abide by the principles of the constitution which were being prepared, had no intention of leaving the north where his power was nearly absolute. He pleaded that his presence there was necessary to keep order in the ranks of the army—a statement that probably had little truth in it.

'The capital, Peking, has become the hotbed of all evils. Not only has the land lost its auspicious features and the water its sweet taste, but a thousand crimes, a myriad scandals, weird carbuncles and chronic diseases of this sinful world are also concentrated there. If the political centre stays there, China will never see a single day of clean government.'

Liang Ch'i-ch'ao: *Yin-ping-shih-ho-chi*

Liang was no revolutionary, but his opinion proved correct in the years to come.

In fact Yüan appears to have instigated an army mutiny in February, 1912, in Peking, in order to back up his refusal to leave for Nanking. Such was the extent of the trouble stirred up there and at Tientsin and Paoting that some danger of foreign intervention existed.

Sun Yat-sen and the Nanking Council, alarmed by the trend of these events reluctantly gave way and permitted Yüan to be installed as president in Peking on March 10. But three conditions were imposed on Yüan before they gave way. First, the president must take an oath of loyalty to the republic. Second, the nominations to his cabinet must have the approval of the provisional senate. Third, the provisional president, Sun Yat-sen, and the Nanking provisional government would cease to perform their functions when the new government was formed at Nanking.

The constitution, when it was promulgated, proved to be so full of loopholes that it was a document quite useless in restricting the autocratic and dictatorial powers of Yüan (as Nanking had hoped it would), and Yüan shrewdly accepted it without a murmur of dissent.

Autocratic Outlook of Yüan Shih-k'ai

Sun Yat-sen had always feared that Yüan in his power-base in north China, an area that had not shown marked enthusiasm for the revolution in any case, would take the law into his own hands. And this was precisely what happened.

In 1912, Sung Chiao-jen had formed the *Kuo-min tang* (National People's Party) in collaboration with Sun Yat-sen and Huang Hsing. This was done by amalgamating the *T'ung-meng hui* with other smaller parties.

The first national elections in 1913 gave the Kuomintang (KMT) a majority in parliament, and it was natural that they should also want control in the cabinet. The KMT found itself increasingly at odds with Yüan, and when he negotiated a foreign loan without consulting parliament, members demanded his 'punishment'.

What is sometimes called 'The Second Revolution', in the form of a military expedition, was planned in order to remove Yüan from his post as president. At this point Yüan showed his true colours. Knowing he was safe behind the screen of his obedient army, he simply declared the KMT illegal. Sung Chiao-jen was murdered, probably by Yüan's supporters, the military commanders associated with the KMT were replaced by Yüan's own henchmen, and Sun Yat-sen fled once more to Japan.

Yüan then set up a body whose members were more or less hand-picked, which was entrusted with revision of the provisional constitution. The new constitution, predictably, gave much wider presidential powers. Yüan's first act under the new constitution was to appoint himself president for ten years (and later for life). His vice-president was Li Yüan-hung—the officer who had been forced to take command in the Wuchang revolt. By this time it was May, 1914. Yüan had not only dissolved parliament but also the provincial assemblies, and now, buttressed by a new constitution to his own liking, and by his army, he began to show signs of making himself emperor—perhaps a constitutional monarch.

Yüan's Bid for the Throne

It was partly on the advice of an American constitutional adviser, Dr. Frank J. Goodnow, that Yüan took the step of fostering a society which petitioned the Council of State (the central legislative body) for his enthronement. A 'national assembly' chosen by the monarchists voted for establishing a constitutional monarchy, and the State Council offered Yüan the throne. On December 12, 1915, he agreed to accept.

Another American, Paul S. Reinsch, gives a characteristic picture of Yüan:

'...I had felt the almost ruthless power of the man. Republican by title he was, but an autocrat at heart. All the old glittering trappings of the empire he had preserved....
And I found him in the showy palace of the great Empress Dowager, standing in the main throne hall to receive me. He was flanked by thirty generals of his household....
Later, at a more informal interview...I observed Yüan's character more fully. He had just expelled from Parliament the...Kuomintang; then he...dismissed the Parliament itself....
' "It was not a good parliament, for it was made up largely of inexperienced and young politicians," he began. "They wished to meddle with the Government as well as to legislate on all matters...." '

R. Pelissier: The Awakening of China, 1793–1949

In preparation for his installation as emperor, Yüan had this gold medallion struck to commemorate the event (which never in fact took place). He also had several thousand pieces of specially designed blue and white procelain made, as any new emperor would have done in the past

Yüan Shih-k'ai clad
in all the finery of
his mandarin robes

With a strong and carefully guided monarchist society in Peking, and Yüan's acceptance of the offer of the throne, the reaction in the form of anti-monarchist revolt at once sprang up in Yunnan and the southern provinces (sometimes called 'The Third Revolution'). There was also dissatisfaction in the ranks of the army generals who were not too keen on unlimited power for Yüan. Among the foreign powers (who were by then in the midst of the first World War) Japan took the lead in being anti-monarchist, and the rest followed. This was a severe blow to Yüan, but it was really the opposition from south and central China (in which Liang Ch'i-ch'ao was prominent) that nipped the aspiring emperor in the bud. A National Protection Army was formed, and even Yüan's postponement of his accession did not alter its determination. The last straw for Yüan was the threatened defection of his own top military men. Yüan finally issued a statement that China would after all remain a republic. Three months later he died of uremia on June 6, 1916. Li Yüan-hung became president. He restored the old constitution of 1912. But a new era had begun in China—the years of the warlords.

Once more the deep division of China into antagonistic north and south, and of each of these into several other sections, came about. With the collapse of central authority as the Manchu dynasty fell, the revolution made a brave attempt to prevent the usual crevasses opening up. But the weakness of Dr. Sun's position without a large army to support him, and the strength of Yüan Shih-k'ai's position in the north, made the breakdown of whatever organization might temporarily paper over the cracks inevitable. China had not achieved a national government. The inherent tendency of various parts of the great country to fly apart, seen so often at the end of dynasties in the past, proved to be stronger than the need for unity.

13 Japan between 1905 and 1914

IN Japan in the years between 1905 and the First World War, the picture was totally unlike that perplexed, perturbed, and disrupted story which we have just followed in China during the same period. Japan had already proved that she had strengthened herself, and she had begun to take her place alongside the powerful nations of the West. Emerging from semi-colonial status under unequal treaties, she was now an ally of Britain, and had acquired an empire of her own in Taiwan and Korea.

The early years of the twentieth century in Japan have been described as a golden age. The fears and the medievalism of the nineteenth century had been conquered. The Western challenge had been met and countered (Japan, we should note, was the sole non-Western country to meet successfully the Western challenge to its sovereignty), and it seemed that the road to further progress and prosperity lay plainly in view.

In fact, the underlying situation in Japan gave somewhat less cause for optimism. Great changes had taken place in the four or five decades before 1905, and now there was time for the significance of many of these to become apparent in governmental, social, industrial, and intellectual fields.

Prime Ministers of Japan, 1905–1916	
1901–1906	Katsura Taro—Choshu
1906–1908	Saionji Kimmochi—former court noble
1908–1911	Katsura Taro—Choshu
1911–1912	Saionji Kimmochi—former court noble
1912–1913	Katsura Taro—Choshu
1913–1914	Yamamoto Gombai—Satsuma
1914–1916	Okuma Shigenobu—Hizen
1916–1918	Terauchi Masatake—Choshu

Politics and Government

The Meiji leaders belonged to a closely united group with common ideals and ideas. However much they might differ on the best method to carry out their reforms, they were mostly at one on what needed to be done. Just at the time when many of these men began to leave the political scene through death or old age, the question of what were the next steps in the process of consolidating Japan's huge gains in most departments of life had to be answered. There were no certain answers forthcoming. Whether the future lay in greater military strength and an ever-enlarging empire, or whether it lay in industrial expansion at home and other measures to improve life for the majority of the people—Japan was now divided on which was the right choice. The most unfortunate fact was that whereas in most Western countries the mechanisms for settling such differences of opinion had gradually grown over the centuries, in Japan a system based on foreign models of government structure had been suddenly imposed and had no roots in popular experience. The Japanese had so far consented to be governed by this system, but now they became restless under it.

The relaxation of social constraints, the introduction of mass education, some (although not much) freedom to criticize the rulers—such things tended toward the growth of democratic ideas. But in fact any open advocacy of really democratic procedures was frowned on. Concerned people tended to take up various different political systems. Socialism of various kinds, and other Western attempts to provide solutions for social problems, fragmented the once single-minded outlook of the Japanese. Others turned to Christianity, to newly enlivened Buddhism, and to new Shinto religious teachings that had been stirred into activity by the nationalism of the nineteenth century.

The voice of Japan had been one voice. Now in the years before the First World War it became many different voices.

The position of the emperor altered too. On the death of the Meiji Emperor, the young and sickly Taisho Emperor (1912–1926), who became mentally deranged, succeeded him. This led to the divorce of the emperor from decision-making to the point where he became merely a symbol. By 1912 the *genro*, as the leaders of the Meiji Restoration were called in their old age, had dwindled in numbers, and were less influential. Gradually they passed from the scene and younger men came in. A Japanese remarked that the early Meiji government was 'a strange creature with one body and many heads [the samurai leaders]'. But what happened in the early twentieth century was a transformation into one head in the form of a cabinet, and a number of bodies—élites in the form of political parties, civil service groups, military organizations, and a few others. All these struggled for political power. The story of politics in Japan up to World War II is that of the relations between them.

The Economy

Large and sustained industrial growth in Japan really began after the Russo-Japanese War, and the rate of growth continued with remarkable consistency until the beginning of World War II. Between 1900 and 1930, output of manufactured goods multiplied twelvefold and production of raw materials rose almost three times. Population grew from just below 44 million in 1900 to over 73 million in 1940. But despite this colossal rise Japan managed to improve living standards at all levels of society. Of course the distance between the income levels of the rich and the poor increased.

The economic boom between 1905 and 1913 was caused by three factors. First, wages were rising and much of the consequent new demand was for traditional items which could be made with little capital outlay. Fulfilling such a demand kept the economy running at a high level. The second part of the demand was

The industrial revolution that took place in Japan with increasing speed from early Meiji times brought changes to the countryside as hideous as those which had occurred in England much earlier. The ancient beauty of the landscape was rudely interrupted by structures entirely unconnected with it, and clean skies polluted by industrial smoke. The upper picture shows the Nakatsu Paper Mill in Gifu Prefecture. It would be interesting to know what its effluent did to the fish in the river beside it. The lower picture shows the Fukugawa factory of the Asano Cement Company. Like many another industrial complex, it altered not only the economy of formerly agrarian Japan, but brought into the Japanese scene new and often ugly forms. Just as London, Paris, and Hong Kong people have seen high-rise blocks in hundreds suddenly springing up amid the older city buildings since World War II, so the Japanese farmers were faced with factory chimneys and other strange structures of Western industry in the last two decades of the nineteenth century

for new things such as bicycles, cottons, and light industrial products. This demand was both internal and foreign. The third demand was governmental—mostly military. This increased sixfold in the twenty years up to 1913.

The old *zaibatsu* companies were joined by new giants such as Hitachi, founded in 1910. (See table on p.147: Structure of Mitsui Combine.)

The rise in population meant that Japan, once an exporter of rice, was no longer able to feed her population. Massive imports meant the need for equally massive exports to pay for them. This naturally spurred on the booming economy. Ship-building increased more than five times from 1900 to 1914, and the length of the railways in Japan more than tripled in the ten years before World War I (it was to double again before 1935). In 1906, and during the next three years, the government bought all the privately-owned main trunk railway lines.

In the period before and during World War I, it can be said that Japan laid the ample foundations of her future successful industrial economy. One interesting and unusual feature of industry in those days was what is called its *bimodal* aspect, meaning that total production was carried out by a relatively small number of giant combines and thousands upon thousands of very small workshops that employed up to five or six workers in each. In the 1930s more than half the total workforce was employed in such small businesses. There were relatively few medium-sized factories or industries.

Changing Social Structure and Outlook

Not surprisingly, change was more rapid in cities than in the rural areas. The urban population that had come into the growing towns in the nineteenth century from the still medieval and largely feudal countryside, had altered deeply by 1905. The workers found themselves vulnerable to fluctuating markets that were quite as unkind and despotic as unpredictable weather on the farms had ever been. The new proletariat became increasingly discontented, its outlook diverging sharply from that of the country dwellers. Hence there arose yet another divisive element in Japanese life.

In the country the amount of tenancy, as opposed to land ownership, was growing. At the time of the Meiji Restoration between 25 and 30 percent of the land was worked by tenants, but this proportion rose sharply to 45 percent by 1908, then levelled off. There were always more potential farm labourers than there was demand for such labour. The landlords therefore had the upper hand and could decide the rewards they offered for work. To be a landlord was highly profitable. But production declined as farmers (who constituted over 44 percent of Japan's total population as late as the mid-1930s) received an ever-shrinking share of the national wealth.

Education was almost universal at the primary level by 1901. The growth of the school age population from 4.3 million in 1873, to 11.3 million in 1935, makes the record of education in Japan a commendable one. The 90 percent of school age boys and the 70 percent of school age girls attending school in 1900 became, by 1915, 98 and 95 percent respectively. The 3,240 university students of 1900 had become almost 22,000 by 1920.

The peasants, for a variety of reasons, became a depressed class. Although free from their age-old bondage to feudal masters, they were dragged down by economic difficulties. The modernization of agriculture in Japan did not really take place until very much later; meanwhile, the farmers were at the mercy of economic forces outside their control

At the same time the closely-knit character of the expanded Japanese traditional family and the unassailable position of its head were being heavily challenged. But change was very slow in this fundamental area of social structure and loyalties. There was a shift in opinion from simple nationalism in the Meiji period, toward a family-state later. Two primary school texts quoted by Fairbank in *East Asia* illustrate this aptly. The first dates from 1904.

'Those who are peasants, merchants, and artisans increase the wealth of the nation by diligently performing their jobs; those who are concerned with scholarship and the arts strive to advance the nation's civilization by perfecting their work. In comparing the conditions of our country with America and other powers, there are still many areas in which we do not measure up. Keeping this in mind, we must plan to fulfil the nation's strength.'

By 1911, revised texts put much more emphasis on the family as base, and on national self-confidence and the picture of a conservative society:

'The feeling of respect and love of the child for his parents comes from nature. The great virtue of loyalty-filial piety emerges from the highest form of such feelings. . . . Our country takes as its base the family system: the nation is but a single great family, the Imperial family is our main house. We the people worship the unbroken Imperial line with the same feeling of respect and love that a child feels toward his parents. Thus loyalty and filial piety are one and indivisible. . . . The union of loyalty and filial piety is truly the special character of our national policy.'

Natsume Sōseki, one of the founders of the
new literary movement at the end of the
Meiji reign. While an oligarchy in effect
still ruled Japan, many of the intellectual
class were beginning to free themselves from
an inherited feudal mentality

But people began to wonder—writers, artists, and intellectuals—about the validity of these and other 'national' outlooks on life. We find the greatest novelist of twentieth century Japan, Natsume Sōseki, praising the American poet Walt Whitman whose poetry revealed, he said, the free man who, 'bound only by his own conscience, could calmly live and act amidst the evil of the world'. Natsume also held that individual morality was higher than state morality. In a passage of deep sarcasm, he wrote:

'When the bean-curd man peddles his wares he is not doing it for the state. His basic purpose is to gain the means by which to live...though indirectly this may benefit the state....But wouldn't it be awful if he always had to keep that in mind and eat his meals for the state, wash his face for the state, and go to the toilet for the state.'

Japan began in the years before World War I to examine Western philosophies of the past and the present. All shades of opinion about almost everything of importance were to be heard, and were influencing the writers and thinkers of the country. A student song of the time (quoted by Fairbank) humorously makes the point:

'Dekansho [meaning the philosophies of Descartes, Kant, and Schopenhauer]
Dekansho
Half the year we live with them
The other half we sleep.'

Besides the German philosophers, both Christianity and Marxism had some influence, the latter after the Russian revolution of 1917.

The period between 1905 and the outbreak of World War I in Japan may therefore be characterized broadly as one of industrial and economic expansion—of a boom; but at the same time it was a decade of increasing sophistication, and of the penetration of Western and other ideas that brought in question not only the traditional beliefs and thought of Japan, but also the values of the Meiji Restoration. The unity that the Restoration brought to Japan in the shape of a clear knowledge of what had to be done, now gave way to disunity of aims and diversity of opinion.

14 Japan, China, and World War I

THE causes of World War I had nothing to do with East Asia, but since all the Western countries involved had important interests in the area, East Asia was affected.

Yüan Shih-k'ai ruled China when war broke out in 1914, his position powerful and assured. As Liang Ch'i-ch'ao said, he ruled because human beings 'feared weapons and loved gold'. His was the cynical rule of a man who was able through his own cleverness to manipulate old and new methods of bribery and coercion to the full. He came to be known as 'father of the warlords' not only because he was the man under whom many of them gained their army training, but because he set the example of how to keep order in China through terrorism and corruption. His personal collapse as a leader was swift, coming as soon as it became apparent that almost no one wanted him to be emperor. And he died soon after that had been made clear.

China succumbed to an era of warlords, as it had done to similar power struggles on several occasions before in its history—at the end of a dynasty when the Mandate of Heaven was not clearly given to one force. Yüan's successor, Li Yüan-hung, was more acceptable as a man, but had little authority. The real power was wielded by those military governors whom Yüan had placed in various strategic areas of China.

To follow in detail the shifting power, the duplicity, the horrors in human terms, and the various rivalries of the warlord era between about 1917 and ten years later, would require a book in itself. It will suffice to outline the events and personalities of the wartime period here, and deal with the post-war period later.

In the south, Sun Yat-sen established a military government in Canton to oppose the northern warlords. With Kuomintang colleagues and most of the Chinese navy, he set up an administration with himself as generalissimo despite the fact that it was the southern warlords who were in effective command.

In Peking a similar figure was Liang Ch'i-ch'ao, also more or less powerless and attempting to provide a civil part to the warlord-dominated government of premier Tuan Ch'i-jui. Both Sun and Liang were prevented from exerting an important influence. Sun Yat-sen's Canton parliament was split, and a militaristic clique dominated south China just as a similar one held sway over the north. At the end of World War I, for reasons of national interest that we will see shortly, there was pressure on both north and south factions to come together, but their negotiations in Shanghai in 1919 ended in a conference that solved and settled nothing.

Liang Ch'i-ch'ao wrote, in despair: 'In China today only cunning, crooked, vile, and ruthless people can flourish.' This was his own and Sun Yat-sen's problem—neither was ruthless and both were straight in a crooked world.

World War I and East Asia

When the war broke out in 1914, Yüan Shih-k'ai proclaimed the neutrality of China in the conflict. Since Japan was allied to Britain, he probably feared Japanese influences rather than any problem with the Germans in their Shantung base. But he let it be known that he would not be averse to taking over the German-held territories at Kiachow if the Allies wished. Britain and France were far too busy fighting the Germans in Europe to pay much attention to the problems of China, so they made no move. The Japanese did not favour Chinese recovery of Kiachow, for they had it in mind to take the place themselves. Peking's timid approach to the German question was fundamentally dictated by her financial troubles and the fact that it was the Allies who, by various loans, kept the government more or less solvent.

A complicated situation evolved by 1915. Britain and France desired China to come into the war on their side, partly because they planned to seize the German shipping in Chinese ports. But from the British point of view it was essential first for Japan to agree to have China as a British ·and French ally alongside herself. The government of Okuma Shigenobu made it clear Japan did· not want China in the war. But by 1917, with a new Japanese government in power led by Terauchi Masatake, a new attitude to China had come about in official Japan, and China eventually declared war on Germany on August 14, 1917. America had come in on the Allies' side in early April of the same year.

China had neither the potential nor the intention of doing much actively to aid the Allies in their fight. In fact her main contribution to the war was the flow of Chinese labourers sent to France, an operation financed by China. There were close on 200,000 of them working behind the fighting lines in France by the end of the war.

The real intention in China was to gain recognition by the foreign powers and to edge herself toward equality of status with them and with Japan when it came to victory and the conference table. The other attraction for China in entering the war was a promise of the lifting of the Boxer indemnity for five years, and revision of the tariff scales.

As usual, China in the end got the worst of nearly all the bargains that were struck—the reason being that everyone knew she could do little but protest while the Western powers and Japan shared out the fruits of victory. She did not know that Britain, France, and Russia had secretly promised to support Japanese claims to German interests in Shantung.

Japan also had little interest in fighting a German war for the benefit of Britain, her ally. She was interested in placing herself in the best possible position to get what she wanted in China. For this reason she sent an ultimatum to Germany on August 15, 1914, demanding unconditional surrender of Kiachow. The Germans ignored this, and on August 23, Japan declared war.

Japanese troops with the help of a small number of British then attacked Kiachow and captured it. Japan also took over Tsingtao port and all other German interests, inclusive of the Tsingtao-Tsinan Railway. Finally, the German colonies of the Marshall, Caroline, and Marianas Islands in the Pacific were occupied. The German Far East interests had been absorbed.

The Twenty-one Demands

Japan was not content with what she had gained. While her Western Allies were fully occupied in Europe, she attempted to obtain secretly a number of objectives not so far reachable.

On the pretext that China had abolished the war zone round Kiachow, which Japan described as an unfriendly act, Japan (who had absolutely no right on Chinese soil at Kiachow in any case) presented what came to be called the Twenty-one Demands. This paper was handed by the Japanese minister in Peking to Yüan Shih-k'ai on January 18, 1915, with the request that the whole matter be kept secret. Japan thus hoped to achieve her aims in China without the knowledge of her allies in the West, and to make the results known only when they were obtained. The document they handed over was in five parts.

I.   Shantung
  > China would concur in any agreement reached between Japan and Germany about the German rights.
  > China would agree to the Chefoo-Weihsin railway being built by Japan if Germany agreed.
  > China would open further parts of Shantung to foreign trade and residence.
  > China would agree not to cede or lease any part of Shantung to another foreign power.
     Since Japan already had the promise of the Allies that they would not block her aspirations in Shantung after the war, this document would effectively clinch the matter if accepted.
II. Manchuria and Mongolia
  > Extension of the lease of the Kwantung Peninsula and related railway agreements from 25 to 99 years.
  > Japanese subjects to be allowed to lease or own land in south Manchuria and east Inner Mongolia for commercial, industrial, or agricultural use.
  > China would not grant any privileges to anyone else in these regions without Japanese consent.
  > China would consult Japan before she engaged foreign advisers in the regions affected.
III. Mining Rights
  > Japan requested that the Han-yeh-p'ing company be made into a Sino-Japanese company and that it should have the mining monopoly in parts of the Yangtze valley.
     This demand was aimed at easing Japan's shortage of iron and coal.
IV. Exclusion of Other Powers.
  > China would undertake not to cede or lease any harbour, bay, or island to a third power.
     By this Japan sought to confirm the non-return of Shantung to Germany and to cut out the United States after the war.
V.   General
  > China would declare Fukien province a sphere of Japanese interest, and would employ Japanese advisers. China would grant Japanese permission

to buy land in the interior of China, to set up schools and hospitals, and to preach the 'Japanese faith'. China would allow Sino-Japanese police control in disputes, and would grant further railway concessions, and buy fifty percent of her armaments from Japan, or set up joint Sino-Japanese arsenals.

For the Chinese, part V was the most serious. To accept such terms would have made China a kind of Japanese protectorate.

Yüan Shih-k'ai had no way out but to publish the supposedly secret demands in the hope of enlisting foreign support. The resulting Chinese and foreign outcry forced Japan to modify her terms.

But China had no allies. The powers who might have been friendly were preoccupied—America with the sinking of the Lusitania, Britain with the war. She had to accept a modified list. And after much negotiation, and an ultimatum from Japan, China agreed to an edited version of parts I-III. On part IV, she said she would not lease bays, harbours or islands to *any* power at all. Part V was 'postponed'. On May 25, 1915, China signed the Twenty-one Demands.

Results of the Settlement

The enforced signature of the modified Twenty-one Demands caused considerable jealousy among the Western powers who had a stake in China. But at this point in the war with Germany in Europe and on the high seas, they could not afford to grumble too loudly at Japanese acts. Japan was an ally of Britain (which therefore could not publicly protest) and in any case Japanese naval strength was an important factor at a time when Allied naval power was stretched to its limits. Britain's main interests in China were the vast Yangtze area, and provided that Japan did not upset commerce there she was prepared to close her eyes to other matters.

The sole protest came from the United States in the form of what came to be called the 'non-recognition doctrine'. This was proclaimed by the Secretary of State, William J. Bryan, in the form of a notification that America would not recognize any agreement which would infringe the United States' treaty agreements with China, or which would diminish China's sovereignty and conflict with the Open Door policy. The statement had rather small influence on the course of events since Japan did not in any way alter her demands on China.

In 1916, Japan secured recognition by Russia of the new situation between Japan and China in the wake of the Twenty-one Demands by agreeing to Russian claims to Outer Mongolia. As a further shield for herself, Japan made secret agreements with the Allies to prevent any opposition to her plans in China once the war was ended. The comparative ease with which Japan gained the agreement of Western powers in her schemes was caused by the necessity to keep Japan in the war (which in 1916 was going badly against Britain and France). Japan was thus, at little cost to herself, able to gain support for her claims to Shantung and German territories in the Pacific.

The United States resisted for a while before agreeing, in the Lansing-Ishii Agreement of November, 1917, that because of Japan's 'territorial propinquity' to China, she had 'special rights' in that country. The agreement ran contrary to the Open Door policy, and America sought assurances from Japan that she would not infringe this. China herself was forced to agree to Japan's position in Shantung since a loan of 145 million yen had just been made to her by Japan. This was the Nishihara loan.

East Asia and the Paris Peace Conference

The Peace Conference opened in Paris on January 18, 1919—a couple of months after the Armistice of November 11, 1918. The Chinese delegates representing both the Canton and Peking governments were Lu Chen-hsiang, C.T. Wang, and V.K. Wellington Koo. Their position was to urge termination of all treaties that infringed China's sovereignty. China wanted the German and Austrian rights in China restored to herself—which would necessitate the ending of the Sino-Japanese agreements of 1915 and 1918 regarding Shantung. The Chinese delegates asked for cancellation of the Twenty-one Demands signed under duress and not ratified by parliament. And finally China asked that all foreign powers give up what they had acquired under the unequal treaties signed since the Treaty of Nanking of 1842.

The Japanese, on the other hand, took the stance that everyone knew they would, from which they had every chance of gaining their demands. Led by a former premier, Prince Saionji, assisted by Baron Makino Nobuaki, Japan asked for confirmation of its claims to former German rights in Shantung; Japanese control of the former Pacific colonies of Germany (which Japan already occupied); agreement on the principle of racial equality as basic to the proposed League of Nations. This was aimed against the United States and some British colonies where Japanese were discriminated against by immigration laws.

V.K. Wellington Koo
who led the Chinese
delegation at the
Paris Peace Conference

Japanese delegates to the Paris Peace Conference. Their leader was Prince Saionji

Results of the Paris Peace Conference

The conference hinged on the Shantung question as regards the East Asian issues. Japan held the strong cards because she had agreements with China stipulating her right to the territory. This committed her ally Britain, and also France and Italy, to uphold Japan's demands for Shantung. As a compromise the Americans proposed a five-power take-over in Shantung—the powers to include Japan but to exclude China. Japan vetoed this and threatened to leave the conference altogether. Whereupon the American president, Woodrow Wilson, allowed the Japanese claim to Shantung to pass.

The Chinese request for cancellation of the Twenty-one Demands was rejected, the conference declaring that to rule on this was not within its powers. The real reason for the rejection was quite simply that none of the countries having treaties with China was willing to tear them up. To condemn the Twenty-one Demands would lead inevitably to the necessity of so doing.

The final Treaty of Versailles in June, 1919, made it clear to all that China had gained none of her demands, and that her participation in a war that was not directly her concern in order to gain favour with the West had completely failed to have any effect.

The Treaty of Versailles granted China very little: relief from the need to continue obligations to Germany under the Boxer Protocol, and the cancellation of unequal treaties with Germany and Austria. The German concessions at Tientsin and Hangkow were returned to China, and China was granted membership of the League of Nations.

Japan, however, gained all she asked for, with the exception of the racial non-discrimination clause. The Americans refused to accept this because it infringed their rights to make laws in their own country; and Australia, set on a 'White Australia' policy, also refused to accept the idea of Japanese immigrants.

Japanese rights in Shantung were secured and Japan promised to restore Chinese political (but not economic) rights in the peninsula later. The former German North Pacific Islands were handed to Japan as Mandated Territories, by which it was agreed that while the League of Nations was responsible for the islands it had delegated its administrative control to a member state. Fortification of the islands was not permitted, but otherwise Japan had a free hand.

The Paris Peace Conference decision on Shantung naturally caused great anger in China. And in the light of the decision to hand the territory to Japan, the Chinese delegates did not sign the Treaty of Versailles. They would have signed with reservations on Shantung, but this was not permitted. China and Germany ended their hostilities on September 15, 1919, and by the Sino-German Treaty of May, 1921, Germany gave up all rights in China. This treaty was the first to be signed after the war which was reciprocal and not unequal.

Reactions in China—The May Fourth Movement

When the results of the Paris Conference and the secret agreement signed by the Chinese government with Japan about Shantung became known in China, there began a period of passionate indignation against the government and a patriotic upsurge against Japan and all other infringers of Chinese rights.

The beginnings of what was later to be called the May Fourth Movement came with a decision by the students of Peking to hold a National Humiliation Day on May 7, to commemorate the acceptance of the Twenty-one Demands. A student at Peking University later recalled:

'When the news of the Paris Peace Conference finally reached us we were greatly shocked. We at once awoke to the fact that the foreign nations were still selfish and militaristic and that they were all great liars. I remember that the night of May 2, very few of us slept. A group of my friends and I talked almost the whole night. We came to the conclusion that a greater world war would be coming sooner or later, and that...it would be fought in the East. We had nothing to do with our government...and at the same time we could no longer depend on the principles of any so-called great leader like Woodrow Wilson....Looking at our people and at the pitiful ignorant masses, we couldn't help but feel that we must struggle!'

The date of the demonstration was advanced, on news of the Paris decision on Shantung, to May 4. In the afternoon of that day more than 3,000 students from some thirteen colleges gathered at the Gate of Heavenly Peace and marched on to the foreign legation quarter which was quite close. Their manifesto contained the statement:

'China's territory may be conquered, but it cannot be given away. The Chinese people may be massacred, but they will not surrender. Our country is about to be annihilated. Up, brethren!'

May 4, 1919. The crowd of demonstrators being addressed through a megaphone in front of Tien An Men in Peking. The banner reads: 'National Assembly'

Peking University students carrying banners and marching in Peking as part of the May 4 demonstration. Some wear Western dress, while others are still in traditional long gowns

Significantly the manifesto was written in clear vernacular language to underline the desire to break with the classical past.

The marchers failed to pass the legation guards, and after a peaceful start the demonstration became violent when the house of a 'traitorous' Chinese cabinet minister was burned and a pro-Japanese Chinese official beaten up.

The popularity of the movement was unquestioned. It was as if the whole people were ready for just this sort of lead. The revolt of the students and intellectuals spread quickly all over the country, bringing mass demonstrations and protests against the government's policy which was seen as a sell-out to Japan. The government attempted in June, 1919, to suppress the student movement by making the university (Peita) into a prison camp. But in the end they had to reverse their decision and the 1,150 students marched triumphantly out of their campus prison. Pro-Japanese officials were dismissed. The cabinet resigned.

The movement was joined by people in all walks of life, becoming a truly national demonstration of anger and disgust with the state of affairs in China. The press and the merchant class made common cause with the union of students. Dr. Sun Yat-sen in Canton expressed support, as did the warlords of the An-fu clique, and many others. Strikes and boycotts of Japanese goods obtained huge popular support, and in May and June, 1919, more than two hundred cities all over China closed their schools.

The importance of the May Fourth Movement can hardly be exaggerated. It involved almost all China's young intelligentsia in deep questioning of old values, in the rejection of the authority of Confucian ethics as they had traditionally been applied in state ideology. There was a vast quest for new solutions to China's problems in terms of Western scientific thought and Western democracy. Without question, the ideas and the tendencies that were thrown up during the approximately four years of the movement have had the deepest effect on subsequent Chinese history.

We will look in a later chapter in more detail at what some of the important effects were and what influence they had in China in the years between the two World Wars.

15 The Washington Conference, 1921–1922

THE Treaty of Versailles had done nothing to restore China's sovereignty to her, and everything to encourage an already militant Japan. It succeeded in putting the seal of approval on a state of affairs in East Asia that was certain to lead to further degradation for China and to Japanese expansionism at Chinese and other nations' expense.

As further background against which the Washington Conference was called by the Americans, we have to note the successful Bolshevik Revolution in 1917 in Russia, and the question of Siberia.

The collapse of the tsarist régime in the face of the Bolshevik revolution in 1917 left a power vacuum in Siberia. The battle for control of the huge area was a confused struggle with many participants. The principal ones were the Bolshevik armies and the anti-revolutionary White Russian armies under admiral Kolchak. By November, 1918, Kolchak had established a government at Omsk, which claimed to control all Siberia. This was disputed by the Bolsheviks and various other groups. The whole confused scene was made more chaotic by bandits and others whose aims were personal or group plunder. Another problem appeared when, at the collapse of Russian fighting against Germany, a group of Czech soldiers was permitted to cross Siberia toward the Pacific in order to circle the world and join Allied forces still fighting the Germans in France. But in the wake of the signature of the Treaty of Brest-Litovsk in March, 1918, between Russia and Germany, they were stopped in Siberia. When the Bolsheviks attempted to disarm the Czechs, they resisted.

It was on the feeble excuse of rescuing the Czechs that the Allies intervened in Siberia. In actual fact what the United States and Japan, with the assistance of Britain and France, desired to do was to stop the spread of Communism by preventing Bolshevik forces from taking control in Siberia.

Japan sent 70,000 troops to further her own expansionist aims there, and the United States sent under 10,000. The British and French contingents were of token strength only. Despite determined Japanese efforts within Siberia, the Allied intervention was a failure. The White Russian Government collapsed by the end of 1919. Besides, since the war in Europe was at an end, there was little point in coming to the assistance of the stranded Czechs. The Western forces left Siberia, and a Far Eastern Republic of Siberia was founded with the approval of the Soviet Union in 1920. But Japanese troops remained, occupying the area between Vladivostok and Chita. After the massacre of some Japanese troops in 1920 by Russian partisans at Nicholaevsk, they also occupied Northern Sakhalin. Japan was digging in with a view to annexing for herself the control of the Maritime

The growth of Japan's empire between 1895 and 1933

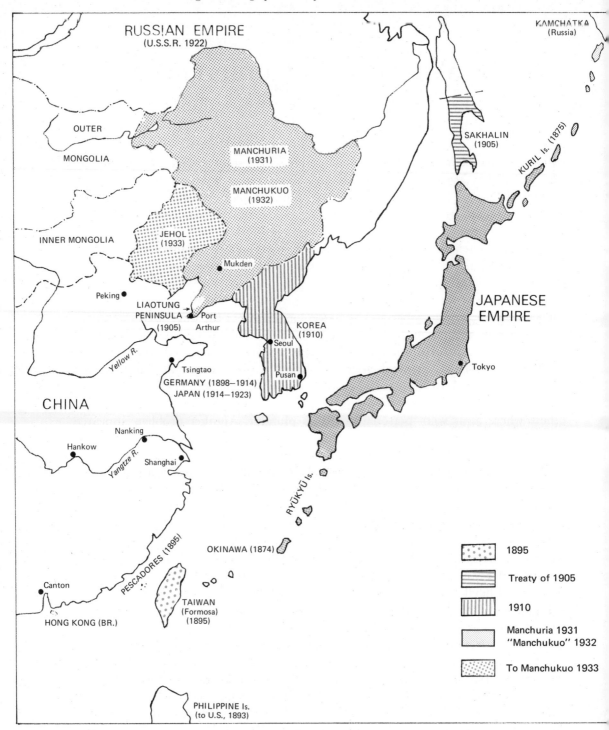

A painting of tsarist days by V.M. Vasnetsov shows three Russian knights in armour, armed with lance, sword, and bow and arrow—all heroes of the expansion into Siberia. Below, a Soviet cartoon on the same theme, designed to urge party bureaucrats into getting things done more efficiently. In this cartoon by V. Kiunnap the heroes are mounted in the same positions as those in the tsarist propagandist picture, but in workers' clothes and carrying as weapons, the tools of bureaucracy. The rider on the left wears a sports shirt and carries a large pen with a pocket-clip, and an abacus. The lance of the central figure has turned into a pen with an old-fashioned nib, while the dangling club of the figure in the old picture has become an office blotter. The right hand figure wears an undershirt, carries a record book and a ruler, and has a pencil stuck behind his ear. As the three party men look on, the women of the collective farm, on truck and tractor, are hard at work

Province and the Manchurian railways.

Japanese expansionism was seen by Britain and America to be a powerful movement, and caused them both much heart-searching. America in particular saw herself as about to be involved in a naval armaments race with Japan. President Warren Harding therefore called a conference of Britain, Japan, France, Italy, Portugal, Belgium, the Netherlands, and China to begin in Washington on August 11, 1921. The Soviet Union was not invited since she was not acceptable to the Western powers. The nine powers' discussions lasted until the following February, and the result was embodied in seven treaties, of which the most important were:

The Four-Power Treaty on Island Possessions
The Five-Power Treaty on Naval Disarmament
The Nine-Power Treaty on China

Contents of the Treaties

The Four-Power Treaty, dated December 13, 1921, and signed by the United States, Britain, Japan, and France, pledged these countries to:

> respect their several rights in the Pacific in regard to island possessions.
> hold talks if any dispute in this matter arose.
> consult together if any of their rights were threatened by another power.

The Five-Power Treaty, dated February 5, 1922, and signed by the United States, Japan, Britain, France, and Italy, stipulated:

> that the ratio of battleships and first-class cruisers held by America, Britain, and Japan should be 5:5:3. While for France and Italy it should be 1.75.
> that there would be a ten-year period in which no new battleship construction would take place.
> that limitations would be placed on tonnage, and on calibre of guns on capital ships and aircraft carriers.
> that certain ships in use or being constructed would be broken up.

For the Japanese this meant that potential threats from the United States and British navies were removed. The agreement proposed by the Japanese navy minister Kato Tomosaburo to keep the *status quo* in fortifications and bases in the Pacific area was also accepted. In return Japan did not press for renewal of the Anglo-Japanese alliance which America felt to be against her interests because it might be used against her.

Japan in fact became the strongest naval power in the Pacific because of her small size and resultant concentration of power, while the ships of the United States and Britain were required to patrol vastly larger sea areas. The treaty was to remain in effect until the end of 1936.

The other important agreement was the Nine-Power Treaty, dated February 6, 1922. All the nations taking part in the conference pledged that they would:

> respect the sovereignty of China in every possible way.

> assist China in every possible way to develop an effective and stable government and to bridge the gap between the old and the new regimes.

> attempt by all means in their power to safeguard the principle of equal trading opportunities for all nations throughout the territories of China.

> not attempt to take advantage of difficult conditions to cut into the rights of other states and curtail the rights of the inhabitants of friendly states, and to do nothing harmful to the security of such states.

The old American principle of the Open Door was thus for the first time made part of an international agreement. But the unequal treaties were not cancelled. Japan was persuaded to terminate the parts of the Twenty-one Demands relating to Shantung, which she agreed to return to China under a treaty signed between China and Japan on February 4, 1922. However, Japan kept the Tsingtao-Tsinan Railway for 15 years although she was to lend China the money to buy it back in that period. This treaty involved the cancellation of the Lansing-Ishii Agreement which was an embarrassment to the United States in any case.

Japan also agreed to withdraw from Siberia (the venture was expensive, and unpopular in Japan) and this took place in November, 1922. But she remained in North Sakhalin until 1925. Japan thus lost almost all she had gained in China and had nothing at all to show for her costly expedition into Siberia.

The Aftermath of the Washington Conference

The decisions of the conference were the main postwar settlement in East Asia. The Open Door policy with its equality of opportunity for foreigners to trade in China while preserving China's integrity as a state, was reaffirmed. Woodrow Wilson's addition of another concept came into prominence—national self-determination for China.

One of the aims of America at the conference was to check Japan's expansion, and this was largely achieved. But on the negative side it is obvious that the resolutions and good intentions of the conference and all that it decided suffered from a major snag—they could not be enforced and depended on the goodwill of the parties concerned. Although China emerged from the conference decisions with Shantung restored to her, her tariff was still fixed by foreigners; the conference projected to take place on the subject was delayed until 1925–1926. Even then, because of the differing aims of foreign powers and the absence of a firm Chinese government, it only managed to decide that China should fix her tariffs herself four years later in 1929.

The commission on extraterritoriality, also projected at the Washington Conference, did not meet until 1926 and failed to make any decision at all on the subject.

The plain fact of the matter was that all the statements by foreign powers on assisting China to get on her feet as a firmly governed nation, were proved by the deeds of those powers in the short term to be just so much talk. The treaty powers had no real intention of allowing China to regain her sovereignty just yet, and most of the unequal treaties remained substantially in force until World War II.

Possibly the fact that there was no means of enforcing the decisions of the conference was part of the reason that Japan gave up much of her gains in China—she had a shrewd idea that they could be taken back later. And she proved right in this. For China emerged after the conference just as powerless as ever against the rest of the world.

16 China between two World Wars

THE real awakening of Chinese national consciousness and popular indignation about the state of affairs in their country came, as we have seen, with the May Fourth Movement. Against the background of increasing disruption, of fragmentation of China by the warlords, and of national suffering probably unparalleled in Chinese history, the whole outlook of intelligent and educated people fundamentally altered.

Political and Social Change

The basis of the old order in China had finally collapsed but the new republican basis for rule was seen to be powerless, because it had not evolved suitable institutions through which it could govern according to republican democratic principles. The several varieties of opinion that took shape with and after the May Fourth Movement were reactions to this problem.

On the one hand there were men such as Ts'ai Yüan-p'ei (1867–1940) who advocated a synthesis of Western libertarian approach with Chinese classical tradition, and Ch'en Tu-hsiu (1880–1942) with ideas similar to those that inspired the French Revolution, putting great stress on individual freedom. Both Ch'en and

Dr. Hu Shih, whose opinion that spiritual values can grow only on a material basis was in direct conflict with the majority of intelligent opinion in China. While he was a post-graduate student at Columbia University in New York, he advocated the introduction of modern spoken Mandarin (the Peking dialect of Chinese) as the medium of Chinese literary expression. The idea had never been thought of before in China and caused deep shock in literary and official circles, implying as it did the abolition of the use of the ancient classical style

Communists and Nationalists

1920   The Russian, Gregory Voitinski, meets Li Ta-chao and Ch'en Tu-hsiu

1921   The Communist Party of China holds its first general meeting in July at Shanghai
       Chinese students in France (including Chou En-lai) form a Communist group

1922   The Chinese Communist party joins the Communist International (Comintern)

1923   The third meeting of the Communist Party in 1923 numbers its strength at 432 members
       Sun Yat-sen sends representatives to Moscow—the beginning of a Kuomintang-Communist
       alliance
       The Russian adviser Borodin sets up the Whampoa Military Academy. Chiang Kai-shek
       goes to Moscow to study Russian military techniques
       The KMT Manifesto of January 1, 1923, accepts an enlarged version of Dr. Sun's Three
       Principles

1924   First National Congress of the KMT in January. Tactical alliances with Russia and with
       Chinese Communists
       Chou En-lai in charge of Whampoa Academy's political education
       Chiang Kai-shek becomes commander of the 'party army'

1925   Dr. Sun Yat-sen dies in Peking in March
       A National Government established at Canton on July 1 by the KMT under Wang Ching-
       wei, who is soon eclipsed by Chiang Kai-shek

1926   Communist and left-wing KMT members dominate the National government
       Chiang organizes a *coup* at Whampoa, detains Communists, and sends Russian advisers
       back to Russia
       Chiang departs on the Northern Expedition, July 9
       Hankow falls, October 10. Foochow falls, December 2

1927   Central Committee of KMT moved to Hankow on New Year's Day
       Revolutionaries gain control of Shanghai, March 22
       Chiang's troops massacre the active revolutionaries in Shanghai
       Chiang stages a *coup* in Canton three days later
       Nationalist government now left with only Hupei, Hunan, and Kwangsi
       KMT-CCP co-operation ends with the expulsion of Communists on July 15
       Mao Tse-tung's Autumn Harvest Uprising

1928   Chiang takes Peking in June. The warlord era comes to an end
       Nominal unification of China under the Nanking Government
       Peking renamed Peiping
       Mao and Chu Teh join forces at Ching-kang-shan in May

1930   Unsuccessful Communist attempts to take cities
       The establishment of basic guerrilla tactics as Communist strategy
       The first of Chiang's four 'Extermination Campaigns' launched against the Communists
       in November

1931   The first Chinese Soviet Republic formed in Kiangsi in November
       Chiang's Nationalist offensives against the Communists repulsed in 1931, 1932, and 1933

1934   The Long March begins on October 16

1935   The Tsunyi Conference at Kweichow in January consolidates the leadership of Mao Tse-
       tung
       End of the Long March at Yennan in June
       The Communist party calls for a united front against the Japanese

1936   The Sian Mutiny in which Chiang Kai-shek is kidnapped
       Chiang released, agreeing that civil war should end between Nationalists and Communists

another leading intellectual figure of the period, Li Ta-chao (1888–1927), turned eventually toward Leninism.

On the other hand there was the commanding figure of Hu Shih (1891–1962) whose attitude was one of pragmatism. Against the attacks on Western materialism made by Liang Ch'i-ch'ao—who made a journey in the West after the war was over and returned condemning its civilization as leading to violence—Hu Shih made his own stance clear. He disagreed with Liang when he wrote that Europe put too much emphasis on science and too little on spiritual things. Hu Shih said that the material basis of national and individual life was fundamental, and that it was on the material basis that spiritual culture was built.

The Literary Revolution

While these learned controversies were going on, and others involving many leading figures in new directions in thought, a revolution in literature was taking place. Hu Shih, one of a group of influential men at Peita, was the pioneer in discarding the old classical style of writing in favour of the use of the vernacular style of everyday speech. 'A dead language', he remarked, 'cannot produce a living literature.' Around this idea there grew what was indeed an entirely new approach to writing and to its content and style.

The poet Kuo Mo-jo (born 1892) was one such new writer. How far from the fine phrases and restrained sentiments of classical verse he had travelled, may be appreciated from a small example. In 1919 he wrote a poem called 'The Sea of Bath'.

Kuo Mo-jo, the leader of the Creative Society formed in 1922. This was one of the two principal literary movements in the 1920s. After 1925, Kuo Mo-jo took up a revolutionary attitude in his writings. The writings of men such as Kuo Mo-jo are more related to Western literature than to any Chinese model

The sun is at its zenith!
The vast Pacific is playing its stately tunes!
What a panoramic display! What a circular dance!
I play with the waves in this enormous dancing space!
My blood and the sea's waves together rise,
My heart and the sun's fire together burn,
The dust, the dirt, the chaffs, the husks that
    I have collected since birth
Have been washed away!
Now I am transformed into a cicada that, having shed its shell,
Is screaming aloud under the fierce sun:
The power of the sun
Is going to melt the entire universe!
Oh brothers, hurry, hurry!
Hurry and come play with the waves!
While our blood's waves are still rising,
While our heart's fire is still burning,
Let us take this rotton old skin bag
And wash it completely clean!
The reconstruction of the new society
Depends completely on us!

The use of the ordinary language, *pai hua*, was substituted for the old classical one in schools by decree of the Education Ministry in 1920.

The outstanding prose writer to emerge in the new vein of *pai hua* and politically conscious literature was Lu Hsün (1881–1936). In an early satirical short story called '*Diary of a Madman*', he deals with a maniac who is convinced that people want to kill and eat him. The madman reads a history book: 'This history recorded no dates, but over every page were scrawled the words "benevolence, righteousness, truth, virtue." ' But then he also sees 'all over it in a succession of two words between the lines: "Eat men!" ' This is Lu Hsün's way of indicting traditional Chinese society. Its Confucian benevolence was a mere cloak for its ruthless nature.

The intense ferment of ideas that followed May Fourth amounted to a nationwide debate. The 'New Culture Movement' gave birth to hundreds of publications of different types dealing with all the subjects under the sun. Newspapers joined in and examined the issues of the times, and a spate of books poured from the presses, including many new translations of Western books. Foreign scholars such as John Dewey lectured in many provinces of China, often interpreted for the Chinese audience by his pupil Hu Shih. The young Bertrand Russell taught in Peking for almost a year and advocated state socialism.

A campaign to 'overthrow Confucius and Sons', as Hu Shih called it, was mounted to deny any validity to the central doctrine of Confucianism, the 'three bonds'— subordination of subject to ruler, of son to father, and of wife to husband. The three virtues of loyalty, filial piety, and female chastity were characterized as old and despicable aids to state and family despotism. Lu Hsün wrote: 'Chinese culture is a culture of serving one's masters, who are triumphant at the cost of the misery of the multitude.'

It was apparent, therefore, that profound changes were at last taking place in the traditional life and thought of China.

Warlords

By the early 1920s, various factions within China attempted in different ways to gain control of parliament. A federal system of government was suggested whereby power would be shared between the centre and the provinces. But nothing came of this.

By 1926, the north of China was in the hands of three major warlords. Feng Yü-hsiang, Chang Tso-lin, and Wu P'ei-fu.

Feng Yü-hsiang (1882–1948) was a highly colourful figure, a huge man from peasant stock who became a soldier at the tender age of eleven. He graduated from Paoting and was baptized a Christian in 1913. Foreign missionaries called him the Christian General. He was head of a highly disciplined army, even attempting to make his soldiers Protestants, and himself supporting education and social reform. It was he who eventually, in 1924, succeeded in capturing Peking and breaking the Peiyang clique of warlords and the sham of their 'parliamentary government'.

Chang Tso-lin (died 1928) was known as the 'Warlord of Manchuria'. He was an ex-bandit who had allied himself with Japan against Russia, and rose to be governor of Mukden from 1911.

Left, the 'Christian General', as the warlord Feng Yü-hsiang was often called. He once 'baptized' a large number of his troops by using a fire hose on them. More than most warlords, Feng was conscious of being part of history. He used his power and efficiency carefully in the world of warlord politics
Right, Chang Tso-lin, the 'Warlord of Manchuria'. His régime was comparatively stable and he was renowned for paying his troops well and promptly

Wu Pei-fu (at left). A correspondent of a leading London newspaper who visited the warlord at his headquarters in Loyang in 1924, said, 'Wu Pei-fu's public record scarcely prepares one for the refined Confucian scholar, connoisseur of cookery and calligraphy, apt raconteur, and meticulously courteous host whom one meets in private.' He was an able administrator and a hard worker

Wu P'ei-fu (1872–1939) was trained in the traditional classics and later under Japanese instructors at Paoting military academy. The Western nations tended to pin their hopes of peace in central China on this leader.

Just after the end of World War I, Sun Yat-sen's Canton parliament was as split as its counterpart in the north at Peking. One faction in it (the Political Study Clique) was in league with the southern warlords. But this did not stop the warlords trying to assassinate some of Dr. Sun's men, forcing him to retire to Shanghai, and leaving the south in the hands of the Kwangsi militarists. Almost every province had a militarist who was allied to one or other warlord or warlord clique.

Sun Yat-sen had failed to gain the support of the West, and equally failed to gain sufficient military backing for an expedition against the northern warlords. His ideas of making the Kuomintang function as a parliamentary party in a western-style government were altering to favour dictatorship by the Kuomintang. The success of party dictatorship in Russia after the revolution, and his own feelings about the rising nationalism associated with the May Fourth Movement, all contributed to his movement in this direction.

Meanwhile, China was torn apart by internal wars. Some idea of the ravages of the warlord era may be had from a listing of some of its battles and campaigns and treacheries:

> In 1921, militarists of Hunan and Szechuan provinces invaded Chihli province and were suppressed by Wu P'ei-fu.
> In the first five months of 1922, there was continuous war around Peking. Chang Tso-lin was defeated by Wu P'ei-fu and driven back to Manchuria.
> Two years later, militarist cliques fought the Kiangsu-Chekiang war in the general area of Shanghai and Nanking. Feng Yü-hsiang joined Chang Tso-lin against Wu P'ei-fu and seized Peking in October and Tientsin in November, 1924.

> The following year, 1925, brought the second Kiangsu-Chekiang war. The Shanghai area changed hands. There was fighting in Honan, and the Fengtien clique of warlords was forced from the lower Yangtze region by the Chihli clique.

> In 1926 came war between the Fengtien and Feng Yü-hsiang cliques, a revolt against the Fengtien, and the occupation of Chihli by Feng Yü-hsiang. Wu P'ei-fu, based in Hangkow, allied himself with Chang Tso-lin of Fengtien which, with the help of the Chihli cliques, managed to expel Feng Yü-hsiang from Peking in April, leaving Chang and Wu in power but unable to form a civil government.

In terms of human suffering, the march and counter-march of these large and mostly entirely lawless armies across the countryside of China produced profound and lasting memories of hardship, death, mutilation, starvation, ruined crops, pillaged granaries, stolen property, and all the miseries of war.

The chaos resulting from unbridled warlord activity was described in a document emanating from the First Congress of the KMT in 1924:

'...warlords have now become so...unprincipled that like knives and swords hacking cattle and fish they hack the people to pieces. No political democracy worth mentioning has yet come into existence. The warlords conspire with foreign imperialists, and the so-called republican governments, controlled by the warlords...serve the pleasure of foreign powers. In return the foreign powers, by lending the warlords money to finance unremitting civil war in China, obtain...privileges and secure their spheres of influence...'

All this was certainly true, but as yet the KMT could do little to alter the picture.

Marxism and the Founding of the Chinese Communist Party

The ideology known as Communism began to find adherents in China in 1919 when deep disillusion spread among educated people over the Paris Peace Conference, and later the Treaty of Versailles. The success of the October Revolution in Russia highlighted a subject that had hardly been considered by Chinese before. Chinese interest in Western doctrines was at almost all times until then purely practical. What assistance will such knowledge be to us, Chinese asked? They did not find Western philosophies interesting in themselves. Moreover, virtually all Western ideas had been presented to Chinese by Christian priests or Christian scholars. It was refreshing, therefore, to discover a political philosophy that was non-religious in content, just as Confucianism was agnostic in content.

One or two other factors in favour of Communism's acceptance by many scholars and thinkers should be noted. The background in Russia was in many ways similar to that in China. Both were large, backward countries, both had been defeated by Japan; and the same imperial powers who had forced on China the series of unequal treaties were seen by Chinese to be attacking the new Bolshevik state as soon as it formed. When Western intervention in Russia was defeated, the Chinese were even more enthusiastic.

Left, Li Ta-chao, who came from Peking to Shanghai in May, 1921, and was present at the meeting there which established the 'Central Chinese Communist Party'. When Chang Tso-lin's forces occupied Peking in December, 1926, Li moved into the Soviet embassy. Chang raided the embassy in April of the following year, seized truckloads of documents, and arrested Li and others. On April 28, Li and nineteen of his comrades were hung by Chang. Right, Mao Tse-tung in 1923

Later on, when Lenin made his additions to Marxism in the shape of theories on imperialism, Chinese found an explanation of what had happened to their country. By comparison, Sun Yat-sen's opinion that the Christian and liberal Western countries would be happy to welcome a Chinese republic into their ranks, seemed rather naive.

One of the first converts was Ch'en Tu-hsiu, the Dean of the Faculty of Literature at Peking University, whom we have already noticed. Another was the librarian at the university, Li Ta-chao, a man of northern peasant stock. He communicated his enthusiasm to his assistant, the twenty-five-year-old native of Hunan province named Mao Tse-tung (born 1893)—with results that we all know about today.

In these early days people took clear-cut sides. The words 'progress' and 'reaction' typified the two points of view. Hu Shih and Li Ta-chao joined forces under the progressive banner of Democracy and Science (called by the Chinese, Mr. Te and Mr. Sai.)

Soon after the revolution in Russia, the Soviet government notified China it would abandon all privileges the tsarist government had gained in China. In contrast to the actions of Japan and the Western powers, this was a gesture of what seemed real friendship. But Russia was unwilling to give up control of the Chinese Eastern Railway, its outlet to the ice-free port of Vladivostock, and in any case the area was under Chang Tso-lin's warlord control. In dealing with the warlords in Manchuria, Russia had trouble with the Peking government, and diplomatic relations were not resumed until 1924.

In 1919, the first Russian contact was made with Chinese Marxists, and in 1920 Gregory Voitinski arrived in Peking and met Li Ta-chao, and later Ch'en Tu-hsiu. The first nucleus of sympathizers met in May that year in Shanghai and another group was founded in Hunan by Mao Tse-tung. The movement rapidly gained support and in July, 1921, the Communist Party of China held its first general meeting in Shanghai. There were twelve delegates from various groups, one representing Chinese students in Japan. Voitinski was there too. Ch'en and Li could not attend. Ch'en was working in Sun Yat-sen's Canton education department, and sent a draft programme. He was made Secretary General.

Despite the secrecy surrounding the meeting, a spy scare interrupted it half-way through, and the members only just managed to escape into the French Concession. Chinese students in France formed a Communist group in 1921, among them Chou En-lai (born 1898).

Ch'en left his job and came to Shanghai. In the year 1922 over one hundred strikes were organized in the railways, the shipping industry, and in mining. One of these was the highly successful campaign of Hong Kong seamen to get increased pay.

The second general meeting took place in 1923, resolving that the Chinese Communist Party should join the Communist International. A draft manifesto stated that one funamental job of the Party was to promote a democratic revolution with workers, peasants, and petit-bourgeois, and get rid of imperialism and feudalism. It was decided on the advice of the Commintern (Communist International) representative, the Dutchman Maring, that individual members of the Party should join the Kuomintang and make use of it. The savage suppression in February, 1923 by Wu P'ei-fu of a strike on the Peking-Hangkow railway convinced the Communists that they needed an ally.

The third Party meeting in 1923 showed its strength to be 432 members.

The room in a girls' school in the French Concession in Shanghai, in which twelve Chinese and two representatives of the Comintern first gathered to form the Chinese Communist Party. The suspicions of the police were aroused by their activities, and the delegates had hurriedly to break up the meeting. They later met as if they were merely a party of friends on a boat trip on a lake in Chekiang province

The Kuomintang and Moscow

In 1923, Sun Yat-sen sent KMT representatives to attend a conference in Moscow which was aimed at opposing the Washington Conference. This move was to prove the beginning of the KMT-Commintern alliance and co-operation which strengthened when word came from Moscow that Russia did not expect China to copy the Soviet system in detail.

While Dr. Sun was against a KMT-CCP (Chinese Communist Party) alliance, he permitted individual CCP members to join the KMT. Those who did so retained CCP membership, and both KMT and CCP remained separate bodies.

Also in 1923, an adviser named Michael Borodin (1884–1953) arrived from Russia. At his direction the Whampoa Military Academy was set up in Canton, Chinese communists began to be appointed to important positions by Dr. Sun, and the young Chiang Kai-shek, Sun's Chief of Staff, was sent to Moscow to study Russian military matters.

The year 1923 also saw an attempt to reorganize the KMT and to put its aims and intentions on a surer footing. This took the form of a revised and enlarged version of the Three Principles of the People that Sun had propounded before. It was accepted as the political doctrine of the KMT in the Kuomintang Manifesto, dated January 1, 1923. The reorganization was completed at the First Congress of the KMT the following January, 1924.

The important change made in the new version of the Three Principles dealt with nationalism *(min-tsu chu-i)*. Back in 1905 this term had implied anti-Manchu sentiments, but now took an anti-imperialist stress. It was also intended to include self-determination for the Chinese (Han) and the minority groups traditionally resident in China. Dr. Sun hoped he could 'make the government the machinery, and the people the engineer'. This was to be carried out within the old framework of democracy by election, initiative, referendum, and recall. The principle of the People's Livelihood *(min-sheng)* was still undefined, largely because Sun could not bring himself to accept Marxist theories on the class struggle. He confined himself to the vague, not even truly socialist ideas of previous times—limitation of capital, equalization of land holdings, and a single-tax basis.

At the First Congress of 1924, Dr. Sun agreed to three tactical alliances—with the Soviet Union, with the mass movement of workers and peasants, and with the Chinese Communists. But throughout his life he rejected the key principles of Marxist-Leninist doctrine, although he used Communist methods in training and organization.

The Whampoa Military Academy grew rapidly. It opened with just over 400 cadets. Chiang Kai-shek was superintendant with a corps of Russian advisers. Instruction was given by Chinese who had trained in Japan or at Paoting and Yunnan under Japanese. By 1925 there were about one thousand military representatives in China to administer the Russian aid programme. Chou En-lai was head of the Academy's political education department. In May 1925 Chiang became commander of an army of two regiments of cadets—the 'party army'— which formed the beginnings of the military power Sun had all along lacked. This army had even received a shipment of 8,000 Russian rifles to boost its morale.

The result was quite dramatic. The northern warlords no longer felt they could ignore a growing military potential that was certainly opposed to their interests. They invited Sun to Peking in the hope of settling in some way the old division between the north and the south. Dr. Sun left Canton in November, 1924. By the time he reached Peking he was already extremely ill. The following March he died of cancer. Before he died he instructed the KMT to continue its co-operation with the Russians. On the very eve of the opportunity he had sought for so long—to re-unify China—the 'Father of the Chinese Republic' was cheated by untimely death.

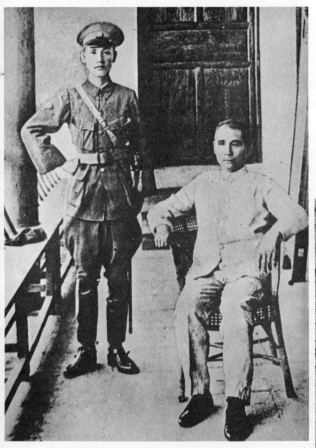

Dr. Sun Yat-sen seated beside Chiang Kai-shek in his uniform as first Commandant of the Whampoa Military Academy

Dr. Sun in Tientsin on his way to Peking in 1924 in an effort to achieve unification of the north and the south. He was already seriously ill

The National Government and Chiang Kai-shek

The immediate result of Dr. Sun's death was that no compromise between north and south came about. The KMT established a National Government on July 1, 1925, in Canton. This was led by a sixteen-member committee headed by the left-winger of the KMT, Wang Ching-wei (1883–1944). His influence was soon eclipsed by the emergence of Chiang Kai-shek, and Wang left China for France.

Within the government at this stage there were two opposed sections of opinion. One, to which Chiang belonged, was in favour of co-operation with the CCP. Addressing a meeting of the KMT Central Committee in May, 1926, Chiang said: 'For us to kill Communists would be just plain suicide.' He was right. The CCP was gaining adherents all the time.

The other section of opinion was that of the 'Western Hills Group' who wanted the expulsion of Communists from the government, and of the Russian adviser Borodin.

The strength of the CCP increased sharply after disturbances in the Shanghai concessions when demonstrators were shot by foreign-controlled police in one of the main city streets. This action triggered off a wave of strikes and anti-foreign demonstrations that came to be called the May Thirtieth Movement and spread, with incidents in Canton resulting in a strike and boycott against colonial Hong Kong.

This was the chance for the CCP to exploit the tide of nationalist and anti-foreign feeling that was sweeping the coastal and other parts of China. They had always seen collaboration with the KMT as a temporary means to an end, but by 1926 Communist and left-wing KMT members dominated the National Government. Communist policy was spelled out clearly in a document later found in the office of the Soviet Military Attaché in Peking.

'...unite with the KMT Left in a strong alliance and fight the bourgeoisie for the power to direct the national movement. Only thus can we ensure...leadership of the National Revolution by the proletarian party. Hence our policy within the KMT at this time is: to expand the Left Wing and co-operate with it...in order to deal with the Centre and openly counter-attack...the reactionary Right.'

The drift of events was obvious to Chiang and, becoming alarmed at Communist and Left infiltration, he organized a *coup d'état*, detained Communist political workers at the Whampoa Academy, surrounded the headquarters of strikers who were active at the time, put Russian military advisers under arrest and later sent them back to Moscow. It was at this point that Wang Ching-wei fled to France. But Chiang could not yet afford to break completely with the CCP and its members for he needed their help against the warlords.

There is an interesting Russian appraisal of Chiang's character made when he was in Moscow, learning Russian military techniques:

'We consider him to be an individual with outstanding characteristics, the principal one of which is an inordinate desire for glory and power, and an insatiable urge to become China's hero. He prides himself on promoting not only the Chinese National Revolution, but the World Revolution as well. His actual understanding of the problems of the revolution, however, is quite another story. He acts according to his personal views only, without the support of the masses. His ambition to be China's great hero and his desire to take advantage of the national revolutionary movement make him sway back and forth between the Right and the Communists.'

S.I. Hsiung: *The Life of Chiang Kai-shek*

The Northern Expedition

Sun Yat-sen's dream of a powerful army to back him in an expedition to wipe out the warlord regimes of the north and to unite all China had remained unrealizable in his life. But now the time had come. Despite dissenting voices, Chiang Kai-shek gained the authority of the Canton government to lead a Northern Expedition. Departing from the city on July 9, 1926, he issued a proclamation:

'The bandit Wu P'ei-fu has for his slogan "Put down the Reds!" This is the watchword of the Imperialists against the oppressed peoples of the world...aimed at destroying the united revolutionary front. What does "Red" mean? It means the Red Party... Red Army...of Soviet Russia, who use the Red Flag as a symbol of the red blood of the revolutionary masses, shed as the price of their national independence.... It means the release of mankind from misery...the abrogation of unequal treaties.... If a government is a government of the masses, and its army an army of the masses, why should it fear to be called red?'

Chiang's army consisted of over fifty thousand men. It advanced north in three columns. One column marched toward Wuhan on the Yangtze, which was the focus of Wu P'ei-fu's activities. Wu was the most formidable foe, but due to the ground-work of Mao Tse-tung among the peasants in Hunan, Chiang's armies encountered no resistance there. In fact people flocked to join him, and by strike action impeded the soldiers of Wu. Wu's headquarters at Hankow fell on October 10. Wu fled north.

The second column, marching east along the coast, did not reach Foochow until December 2. The third, led by Chiang himself, moved toward Shanghai, but slowly because of resistance and because the Nationalists mistakenly made little attempt to win the peasants to their side. The contrast between this and the effect of Mao Tse-tung's work in Hunan which brought people flocking to join the advancing army is sharp and was to be repeated many times in the following decades. Chiang decided to halt at Nanchang in November, and to winter there.

Back in Canton the Central Committee of the KMT decided to move the seat of government to Hankow (against the wishes of Chiang who wanted it with him at Nanchang). Just after this move, completed by New Year's Day, 1927, a crowd of workers in Hankow who were driving out foreign police, occupied the British concession. This exploit was led by Liu Shao-ch'i. The entirely surprising result was that Britain, realizing how hopeless it was to continue its privileges in the heart of hostile country, agreed to give up the Hankow concession and another at Kiukiang down-river toward Nanking. This caused Chinese jubilation and increased the prestige of the CCP.

Prevented from having the government with him at Nanchang, humiliated by the success of the Hankow incident, and again alarmed at the growing power of the Left in the government, Chiang determined to strike. Growing numbers of secret society leaders, representatives of banking circles, old friends from his stock exchange days, and other powerful men from Shanghai paid their homage to Chiang, and not to the Hankow government. It was in him they saw some hope of security from the unrest that was rising in the great city, encouraged by Chou En-lai. And it was they who urged him to act in Shanghai. By March 22, 1927, the revolutionaries in Shanghai had succeeded in gaining control of the Chinese city and had set up an administration, ready to welcome the Nationalist armies with whom they were still allied.

Chiang, arriving by gunboat down the river on March 26, already knew that the Central Committee of the KMT intended to end the concentration of power in his hands. He seized his chance.

On April 12, Chiang Kai-shek's troops surrounded the Shanghai Workers' General Union and shot most of those active in the movement that had taken over the Chinese city. In a few hours, and after a crowd protesting against the murder of their leaders had been gunned down, and informers had revealed the location of other activists, who were also shot, the city was in Chiang's hands. Three days later, he staged a similar coup in Canton. In April, he established a new Nationalist Government at Nanking (after purging the city of Communists). This government controlled large areas—part of Kiangsu, Chekiang, Anhwei, Fukien, and Kwangtung provinces. The Nationalist Government at Hankow controlled a much smaller terrain—Hupei, Hunan, and Kwangsi.

The Nationalist-Communist Split

The split that had all along existed now became a chasm. The left and right wings of the KMT at Hankow united with the Nanking government of Chiang after the left wing had split with the CCP. Chiang began to drive Communist elements underground in the cities, and into their country stronghold in south-central China. This was the effective beginning of Nationalist-Communist rivalry for the leadership of China in the future. It led eventually to civil war, and to the Communist revolution that ended in the 1949 victory. But that was still a long way ahead.

In the following year, 1928, Chiang marched north again with the help of militarists such as Yen Hsi-shan of Shansi, and Feng Yü-hsiang the 'Christian General'. At this point there was growing fear that Russian involvement was a prelude to military or other interference from Moscow. Wang Ching-wei, back from France, was in Peking and was gradually turning against the Communists when he understood the anti-Communist sentiments in the Nationalist Army. A raid by the warlord Chang Tso-lin on the Soviet premises in Peking was said to offer proof of Russian aggressive designs on China. Li Ta-chao who was discovered in the Soviet legation in Peking was arrested and hanged. The left wing of the KMT turned with Wang against the Communists with few exceptions. One exception was Sun Yat-sen's widow, Soong Ch'ing-ling. Borodin and Ch'en

The central figure is Chiang Kai-shek. The stout Feng Yü-hsiang in peasant dress is on the left, and Yen Hsi-shan, the warlord of Shansi province, is on the right. The picture was taken in 1928. Later, Chiang was to fight both of them for control of China

Tu-hsiu made promises of loyalty to the KMT. On July 15, 1927, the Communists were expelled from the KMT, from the Hankow government, and from the National Revolutionary Army. On July 28, the separation of KMT and CCP was proclaimed. Borodin and Soong Ch'ing-ling were already on their way to Russia.

Dr. Sun Yat-sen and Soong Ch'ing-ling after their marriage in 1914

Peking fell to Chiang's army in June of 1928, and by the end of the year the major foreign powers recognized the Nanking government. By 1931 most of the warlord strength had been liquidated, and Chiang was free to work at liquidating the Communists, and also to attempt to lessen foreign aggression and the foreign hold on China.

The Nanking Government

The name of Peking was at once changed to Peiping (Northern Peace). The capital remained at Nanking (Southern Capital). Chang Tso-lin, who had fled a few days before Peking's fall, was blown up in his train in Manchuria. His dissolute son, Chang Hsüeh-liang, having shot the rival claimants to the position, took over his father's warlordship.

Manchuria apart, Chiang Kai-shek and his army and the Nationalist government now ruled China, and began the attempt to persuade foreign powers to give up their privileges under the unequal treaties. July 1928 saw the signing of the Sino-American treaty by which the United States returned tariff control to China. She was followed by others, and by 1933 China was in complete control of her own tariff system. The *likin* (transport tax) was abolished. But the question of extraterritoriality was another matter. Most foreign powers felt China was far from having a suitable legal system, and only Germany and Russia had surrendered their rights in this respect. The Nanking proclamation of 1930 abolishing extraterritoriality did not persuade others to do so.

The Hankow and Kiukiang rights had been given up by Britain (as we saw, in the face of local hostility). Britain also relinquished the Chingkiang and Amoy concessions, together with leased territory at Weihaiwei. The International Settlement at Shanghai, with most of the other foreign concessions, however, remained in foreign hands until World War II. Britain and the United States finally surrendered their rights in 1943.

Efforts at Democracy

Sun Yat-sen's Three Principles of the People were still the avowed aim of the Nationalist Government of Nanking. Efforts to regain national sovereignty had met with some success, but efforts toward the principle of the Peoples' Livelihood were unsuccessful. A new civil code was officially announced in 1929 and 1931, and a new penal code two years later. Economic measures were taken, but their effects hardly penetrated down to the average man. Fiscal reforms were also made, annual budgets introduced, and a uniform silver coinage, central banking, and other measures lent a look of modernization but did not help real reconstruction of what was in many ways a country shattered in fact and in spirit.

There was no real profound break with the past. The power and the finance of China were still in relatively few hands. Chiang himself had prudently married into the richest Chinese banking family in 1927. His most intimate friends and colleagues were of the new industrialist wealthy classes. Many of the highest positions in the government were occupied by former warlords. The military as a whole considered themselves above the law.

Communications were expanded, railways and highways were being built—but it would appear that the intention behind this work was largely to facilitate control over the country by the Nanking authorities. Education facilities were also broadened. But the picture of Nationalist China, despite some definite improvements in various fields, is one of continuing lawlessness and widespread corruption, of a country in the hands of a few ruthless men.

The National Government established in 1928 marked the achievement of Sun Yat-sen's first stage—government by military law. The second stage, government under a provisional constitution, was instituted by the Organic Law of 1928. Under this, power was exercised by five government branches *(yüan)*. These were:

> Executive *Yüan*
> Legislative *Yüan*
> Judicial *Yüan*
> Examination *Yüan*
> Control *Yüan*

The president was head of the government and also chairman of the State Council and commander-in-chief of the armed forces, and dealt with foreign affairs. Chiang, who filled all these posts, had almost dictatorial power.

In 1931 the Organic Law was replaced by a provisional constitution which made changes in the presidential powers. The Executive *Yüan* took to itself the president's civil responsibilities, and the National Government took over his control of the armed forces. Although in theory this left the president as a figurehead, Chiang made sure that he retained both military and civil control through other positions which he kept.

To sum up, the democratic state envisaged by Dr. Sun never came into being. The KMT ruled under a one-party system, and democratic processes were thwarted. The Nationalist Government was the creation of the KMT and merely enforced party policies. The various *Yüan* were simply instruments for enforcing decisions of the leaders of the party and had no autonomy. Democracy did not emerge under such circumstances.

Signs that it might were soon suppressed by rigorous control of the press. The plain fact was that China was run by a military dictatorship. Popular support not surprisingly waned. Officially this was supposed to be the result of the need for spiritual regeneration among the Chinese people. Chiang conceived and started the New Life Movement in 1934 to counteract the ideological vacuum created by a cynical government that ran China for the benefit of a party élite. The idea was basically a return to the old Confucian virtues of *li* (propriety), *yi* (righteousness), *lien* (integrity), and *ch'ih* (conscience, or sense of shame). Chiang seemed to hope that if the old system of Confucian subordination (which had been massively rejected by the May Fourth Movement) could only be reinstated people would accept blindly the authority of his dictatorship via the KMT and its government front.

In this he totally misjudged the temper of the times—with which he was entirely out of touch. Between 1934 and 1937, 1300 branches of the New Life movement were set up. People were exhorted to practise hygiene, cleanliness, physical fitness, and orderly conduct. The methods of persuasion used were really modified from those that might be found in a military barracks. Slogans such as 'Correct your posture', or 'Kill rats and flies', or 'Be prompt', did not find much willing acceptance. The movement collapsed at the Japanese invasion of 1937.

The character of the Chiang Kai-shek regime may be perceived by examining the sort of men who ran it. Chiang himself, before his first real entry on the political scene in 1923 at the age of twenty-six, spent a great deal of time in Shanghai cultivating his friends in the stock exchange and pursuing various links with the secret societies. When he was sent by Sun Yat-sen to Moscow, it seems he was viewed with some dislike as a Shanghai adventurer, very improbable material for a revolutionary. The Nanking Government Minister of War was the 'Christian General', warlord Feng Yü-hsiang, although he was later to defect and be branded as a traitor by Chiang. The regime also had the support of the 'Blue Shirts', a secret police organization, of the so-called C.C. clique, the big bankers and wealthy industrialists of Shanghai. Chiang's vision was not solely one of political power but also of vast financial empire. In this respect he resembled the Empress Dowager Tz'u-hsi. His marriage into the Soong banking family was a good start. Certainly the 'four families'—the Soong, the Kung, the Ch'en, and the Chiang—controlled the banking system and most major industry, a fact which in the later part of the KMT rule caused great discontent among other capitalists and merchants.

It would be incorrect, however, to suppose that all freedom of speech and expression was denied under the Nationalist government. Lu Hsün, for example, who was hardly a friend of the government, lived and wrote with little difficulty in so doing, in Shanghai.

The real failure of the Nationalists was twofold. The desperate situation of the rural masses, subjected still to uncontrolled taxation and other age-old abuses, and only superficially assisted by such new things as schools, was not really tackled in a satisfactory manner. The peasants had no love for, or faith in, the Nationalist Government. Coupled with this went ruthless exploitation of the urban proletariat by the new Chinese industrialists, probably more ruthless than anything in the worst days of the Industrial Revolution in England so long before. The second aspect was the failure of the Nationalist Government to concentrate wholeheartedly on driving out the encroaching Japanese; and their preference for attempting to exterminate their rivals for power, the Communists. These two mistakes eventually cost Chiang his leadership of China.

The Communists and the Nationalists

Retracing our steps a little, we must take a look at the progress of the Communists. Their betrayal at Shanghai in the massacre instituted there in 1927 by Chiang Kai-shek was a severe blow. The only course open to the leaders was to go underground in the cities and to regroup in the country. Mao Tse-tung's 'Autumn Harvest' uprising in Hunan following on his 1927 report on the peasant movement in the province (in which he advocated such a rising in direct opposition to advice from the Comintern) was a failure. So were others in Swatow and Canton in the latter part of the same year.

Mao and Chu Teh joined forces at Ching-kang-shan in the mountainous Kiangsi-Hunan border region in May, 1928. Chu Teh, born in 1886, a graduate of the Yunnan Military Academy, and Mao Tse-tung, born in 1893, were respectively commander and political commissar. By the following year the army was ten thousand strong, and in 1930 the Communists had set up bases in no fewer than eleven provinces. While the Central Committee of the CCP worked under cover in Shanghai in an attempt to stir up workers there and in other cities, Mao was active in the country. The two points of view on future strategy, either to concentrate on taking cities or on consolidating among the mass of the peasants in the countryside, grew side by side.

The test came when the Central Committee, under Li Li-san and with Chou En-lai working on industrial action, ordered the army (the Red Army it was now called) to attack Changsha, the capital of Hunan, and Nanchang, capital of Kiangsi. These attacks failed for lack of support from the working people in the cities. Li Li-san was accused of lack of preparation among the workers and was expelled from the Central Committee. The Nationalist armies drove the Red army back to Ching-kang-shan. This defeat finally confirmed Mao in his opinion that whatever the Comintern might say about how revolution was made in Russia, the only way in China was to educate and rely on the support of the peasants. The fact should have been self-evident because the cities of China, still only minimally industrialized, held only a small proportion of what might be called proletariat. The city workers were poorly organized or not organized at all, and too few in number.

The second effect of the defeats at Changsha and Nanchang was to convince Mao and Chu Teh of the absolute necessity of using guerrilla tactics and of avoiding direct confrontation with better armed and numerically stronger Nationalist forces. Mao Tse-tung's pithy statement of this policy is a classic of its kind:

'When the enemy attacks, we retreat,
When he retreats, we pursue;
When he stops, we harrass,
When he tires, we attack.'

In the town of Juichin in Kiangsi, in November, 1931, a meeting of representatives from the various bases now numbering fifty regions with a population of about 50 million people, formed the first Chinese Soviet Republic. It also elected the Central Executive Committee of a provisional government with Mao Tse-tung at its head. The constitution guaranteed 'democratic dictatorship' of the proletariat and peasantry. Anyone over sixteen could vote and be elected, with the exception of anti-revolutionaries, landlords, and rich peasants who were to be expropriated.

Industries were encouraged, literacy drives started, trade and co-operation between the various bases, now called soviets, was encouraged.

In November, 1930, Chiang mounted the first of four offensives which were named 'extermination campaigns', against the main Kiangsi stronghold of the Communists. The policy of guerrilla war was put into operation by Chu Teh's forces against the attackers with astounding success. The Nationalists wore themselves out in attempts to come to grips with the elusive Communists. In 1931 and

1932 three more Nationalist offensives were repulsed, and by March, 1933, three of Chiang's divisions were destroyed and the Communists took prisoner two divisional commanders and captured 10,000 rifles.

Meanwhile in Shanghai the zeal of foreign authorities in the International Settlement had succeeded in dispersing Communist leaders—many being handed over by the British to be shot by the Nationalists. Chou En-lai escaped to the Kiangsi stronghold together with the remnants of the CCP Central Committee.

The fifth offensive by Chiang took place in October, 1933. He employed one million troops, 200 planes, German advisers (one of whom was later to command the Nazi occupation army in Belgium in World War II) and a carefully prepared strategic plan. The tight blockade thrown round the Communist stronghold at last forced them to break out. On July 15, it was proclaimed from Juichin, that 'the Chinese Red Army of workers and peasants would march north to resist the Japanese'. In fact, even at the formation of the Chinese Soviet Republic it had been stated that one of its objectives was to drive out the Japanese.

In October, 1934 the main body of the 100,000 set out on what was to be called the Long March, a feat of human endurance and ingenuity which has become one of the resounding legends of China. The following month the Nationalists entered former Communist areas and at once restored the land to the landlords.

The Long March

The route of the Communist forces took them on a zig-zag course calculated to have been about 8,000 miles long. During the one year of the march with all its rigours, as they crossed eighteen mountain ranges and twenty-four rivers, often

The Luting Bridge over the Tatu River, one of the obstacles overcome successfully in an heroic episode during the Long March

in freezing temperatures or in broiling sun, all but about 25,000 of the original 100,000 perished. In battles with pursuing Nationalist armies, provincial armies, hostile hill tribes, large numbers were killed.

The events of the march are too numerous to retail in this brief history, but it should be noted that in two incidents Mao emerged as the undoubted leader of the CCP at the Tsunyi Conference in Kweichow in January, 1935. One was his attack on the extreme left-wingers for their bungling of military actions by refusing to use guerrilla tactics. The other was the dispute between Mao and the powerful Chang Kuo-t'ao, commander of a Red Army from the borders of Hupei, Honan, and Anhwei, whose forces joined the Long March in June 1935. Chang wanted to deflect the march westward, but Mao refused. Chang took his forces west, but

China, 1912–1935

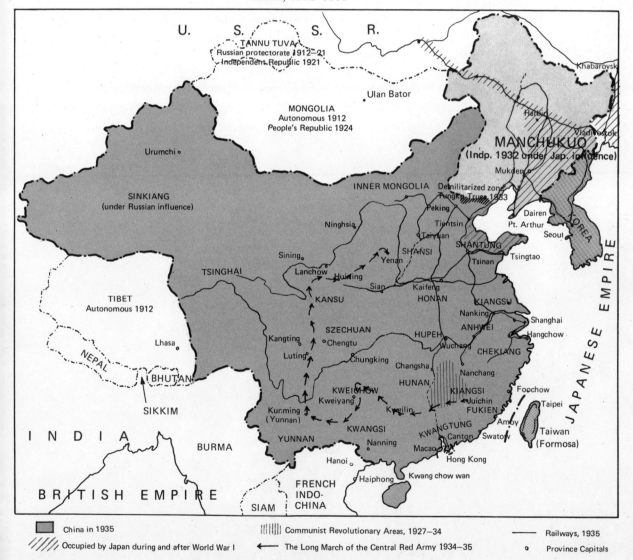

▨ China in 1935	▥ Communist Revolutionary Areas, 1927–34	—— Railways, 1935
⟋⟋⟋ Occupied by Japan during and after World War I	◄— The Long March of the Central Red Army 1934–35	∘ Province Capitals

later had to join the Mao force when it reached Shensi in October, 1935. Chang was expelled from the CCP in 1938 and went to live in Hong Kong. The Communists set about reorganizing themselves at Yenan which for long was to remain their impregnable base.

Both Communists and Nationalists took the opportunity to leave some remnant of their presence in the distant and backward areas of the country through which they had passed. The Communists left various agents to organize the peasants, and the Nationalists attempted to establish direct control.

The march also proved finally that a revolution in China had to be peasant-based. This decision resulted in Comintern disapproval of Mao and his forces. Nonetheless Russia acknowledged that Mao was the real leader of the CCP.

During the march, the policy of trying to form a united front against the invading Japanese was put forward. The most alarming part of Japanese aggression was the threat to Inner Mongolia which lay on the Communist flank in their Yenan base in Shensi. One other reason for the call for a united front may well have been to weaken the Nationalist armies in anti-Japanese fighting (of which they did as little as possible), and thus assist eventual Communist victory in China.

The Red Army working with farmers to bring in the harvest

The Tsunyi meeting hall where Mao gained the leading role in the Chinese Communist Party in 1935

Chiang Kai-shek, however, persisted in his intention to exterminate the Communists first, before tackling the Japanese.

The Sian Mutiny

Chang Hsüeh-liang, the dissolute warlord son of Chang Tso-lin, often called 'The Young Marshal', had been assigned by Chiang to fight the Communists in Shensi with his Manchurian armies which had been driven across the Great Wall by advancing Japanese. These troops had no great liking for the task, and they were influenced by Communist slogans such as those saying Chinese must not fight Chinese, and advocating a united front. Chiang Kai-shek arrived in Sian in December, 1936, hoping to put new heart into troops and commanders. What happened was that they mutinied and kidnapped Chiang. On hearing the news, Chou En-lai quickly went to Sian in order to convince the kidnappers that, however much they and the Communists might dislike Chiang, he was an essential figurehead. Chiang was released on Christmas Day when he had agreed the civil war should end and that patriotic movements should not be persecuted.

The truce was approved by the KMT. The Communists were quite willing to acknowledge the National Government, and renamed their Soviet a regional administration of 'Special Areas'. It was now inevitable that full scale war on the Japanese invaders would be undertaken by the Nationalists. The opinions of Mao had once again gained the day. Chiang's opinion that China was not strong enough to fight the Japanese depended on his orthodox strategy of direct confrontation with the enemy. His further opinion that it was essential to get rid of Communists first was a part of his attempt to get all China behind him. Mao, on the other hand, was happy to fight the Japanese first because he was convinced that his guerrilla warfare would prove effective. He had good reasons to believe this from past experience against Nationalist armies, but he needed their large force, employed in this manner, to effect his anti-Japanese strategy. Now the chance seemed to have arrived.

17 Japan between two World Wars

IN the preceding few pages the Japanese invasion of China has been mentioned without explanation. Once again, at this point, we have to retrace our steps in time in order to see what events in Japan led to this action.

Having lost at the Washington Conference of 1922 most of her wartime gains in China, Japan embarked on almost a decade of peaceful policies which are associated with Baron Shidehara Kijuro (1872–1951). Japanese policies of the 1920s are often, for this reason, called 'Shidehara diplomacy'. From 1915 to 1919, Shidehara was vice-minister of foreign affairs, and he was Japan's chief delegate to the Washington Conference. Between 1924 and 1927, and again between 1929 and 1931, he was foreign minister, held in high regard by foreign diplomats. Even after World War II, as an old man, he was Japanese prime minister in 1945–1946.

> 'One of the most urgent needs of the day is the improvement of Sino-Japanese relations and the deepening of a neighbourly friendship between the two countries. . . . In their relations each country must understand and give sympathetic consideration to the special viewpoint of the other. . . . To move troops about rashly is not the way to enhance national prestige. What this administration desires is co-existence and co-prosperity. . . . Our country is determined not only to reject an aggressive policy for any part of China but also to offer willingly our friendly co-operation in the attainment of the aspirations of the Chinese people.'
>
> Shidehara Kijuro: *Tokyo Asahi Shimbun* July 10, 1929

Baron Shidehara Kijuro, a man of peaceful policies in the period after the Washington Conference. He was to be taken out of obscurity after World War II to become Prime Minister on October 9, 1945, during the transition from war-time Japanese rule to government under Allied Occupation. At this time he headed the Progressive Party

During the period of the 1920s, Japan seemed to be moving toward a liberal constitutional government. In 1925 universal male suffrage was introduced, and we have already seen how schools were moving toward an internationalist outlook. Egalitarian ideas began to spread, and workers' and tenants' committees grew numerous. There was a remarkable unity of outlook among the various segments of the population—labour, leftist political thought, the liberal party, intellectuals in general, and others. Admittedly the description of this unanimity, by a writer of the times who said its intellectual content was 'swallowed whole without chewing', was accurate. But the mixture, while it lasted, was beneficial.

By the mid-1920s many young intellectuals were moving toward Marxism and showing distrust of parliamentary procedures. A certain disillusion set in. But Japan's policies were still basically related to expansion of trading opportunities and lower taxation.

Prime Ministers in the Party Government Era		
1918–1921	Hara Kei	Seiyukai
1921–1922	Takahashi Korekiyo	Seiyukai
1922	Kato Tomosaburo	Non-party
1923	Yamamoto Gombei	Non-party
1924	Kiyoura Keigo	Non-party
1924–1926	Kato Komei	Kenseikai
1926–1927	Wakatsuki Reijiro	Kenseikai
1927–1929	Tanaka Giichi	Seiyukai
1929–1930	Hamaguchi Osachi	Minseito
1931	Wakatsuki Reijiro	Minseito
1931–1932	Inukai Tsuyoshi	Seiyukai

(The Kenseikai party was renamed Minseito in 1927)

In 1918, Prime Minister Hara Kei became the first to have a cabinet with a majority of ministers from the same (Seiyukai) party. He was also the first person from neither the old oligarchy nor the nobility to reach the eminence of prime minister, and was known as the 'Great Commoner'. He had been a newspaper-man, a foreign office official, later ambassador to Korea, and had helped Ito Hirobumi to form the Seiyukai party in 1900. Unfortunately he was assassinated in 1921. The great earthquake of September 1, 1923 in which the city of Tokyo was largely flattened and 132,807 persons died, produced the so-called 'earthquake cabinet' of Yamamoto. It was followed by various short-lived administrations.

By 1924, Kato Komei headed a three-party coalition government and the principle of party politicians governing Japan was firmly established. Kato's party was the Kenseikai and was on the whole more liberal than the Seiyukai. Kato himself (born in 1860) graduated from Tokyo University and entered the Mitsubishi company at twenty-one. He married an Iwasaki girl (daughter of the owners of the company), spent some time in England, and became foreign minister at the age of forty. Then he became a Diet member, president of a big newspaper, foreign minister several times, and ambassador to London. He was not popular but much respected, a strong supporter of constitutional government.

Left, with Prime Minister Hara Kei in 1918, for the first time since the Meiji Restoration, Japan had a prime minister of a Diet that was the key instrument of government. He was a man neither of the old oligarchy nor from the nobility—a commoner and a professional politician

Right, Kato Komei, head of a three-party coalition government following the so-called 'earthquake cabinets', was a firm constitutionalist

Below, in the devastating Tokyo earthquake of 1923 that took over 100,000 lives, about half of the capital and almost all of its neighbouring city Yokohama were destroyed. What the actual earthquake did not wreck was destroyed by fires. The disaster not only physically cleared the ground for new buildings, but in some ways cleared the ground for what was, in part at least, a new culture

Growth of the Japanese Electorate			
Eligibility	Election Year	Number of Electors	Total Pop.
1889—Males 25 and over, paying 15 yen or more in tax	1890	453,474	40,072,000
1900—Males 25 and over, paying 10 yen and more in tax	1903	983,193	45,227,000
1919—Males 25 and over, paying 3 yen or more in tax	1920	3,069,787	55,963,000
1925—All males of 25 and over	1928	12,409,078	63,863,000
1947—All citizens of 25 and over	1949	42,105,300	78,100,000

During his term of office, the 1925 universal manhood suffrage bill was passed, increasing the electorate from 3 to above 12 million. Yet at the same time he strengthened the anti-subversive laws, and in 1928 made them even more harsh in order to suppress the Communist party. Most of his labour laws were good, as was his reform of the upper house of parliament which had been obstructive.

These and other measures of the 1920s, such as reduction in military spending and in the size of navy and army, were peaceful and progressive on the whole. Army prestige was so low in popular estimation that off-duty officers took to wearing civilian clothes. But money saved on armaments and military strength went to pay for military training in schools, often by redundant officers, and local military training was set up. General Ugaki wrote in his diary in December, 1925:

'More than 200,000 troops on active service. . . 3,000,000 in the veterans organization, 500,000 or 600,000 middle and higher school students, and more than 800,000 trainees . . . all of these will be controlled by the army. . . . The right of autonomous command over the Emperor's army is, in time of emergency, not limited to the command of the troops, but contains the authority to control the people.'

These were ominous words.

Prime Minister Tanaka took office in 1927 and party government was still strong, though assailed in its stronghold. Tanaka's 'positive foreign policies' included strengthening the Japanese position in Manchuria and taking a tougher stance on China.

Discontent with party government grew after 1931. The peasantry increasingly disliked it because they felt that it favoured the business community and the landlords, and because their taxes were proportionately higher than those paid by capitalist sections of the population. Parties were all connected in the average Japanese man's thoughts with *zaibatsu* and business manipulation of members of the Diet. But it was really the armed forces who proved the strongest opponents of party rule. Naturally they disliked the reduction in army numbers in Kato's time, and were convinced that 'Shidehara diplomacy' of improving Japan's relations with China was a mistake.

The Japanese Communist Party which had come into being in Hiroshima in 1922, had at once caused dismay in government circles. They felt it would form adherents among the growing proletariat, and it was effectively nipped almost in the bud by the Kato Peace Preservation Law of 1925. Many Communists were imprisoned and the movement virtually ended.

Other grievances were the corruption of many party politicians who were manipulated by bribes from business interests. Additionally, the effects of the Depression years after 1929 affected Japan badly and party government had no solution to offer.

Parliamentary democracy, never a very sturdy growth in Japan, died with party government in 1932, and military figures dominated the scene from that time onward. This was not surprising, given the structure of Japan's constitution. But it had disastrous consequences.

Nationalism and Militarism

By contrast to the peaceful policies of the twenties, the following decade was characterized by extreme nationalism leading to militarism. Various factors entered into the spectrum of causes of this switch in policy.

The ratio of capital ships decided by the Five-Power Naval Treaty made Japan's naval force inferior to that of the United States and of Britain. And this, with the blocking of further concessions in China under the Nine-power Treaty, was taken as a humiliation for Japan—especially since Japanese saw themselves as having more to lose and to gain in China than other nations geographically more remote.

The United States passed in 1924 the Exclusion Law by which Japanese were totally forbidden as immigrants. This was seen as racial discrimination, and resented. The Japanese, moreover, were bewildered. Only a short time before, America had been generous in her help after the great earthquake.

One more source of displeasure was the ending of the Anglo-Japanese Alliance, interpreted in Japan as British kowtowing to the United States. This was followed by the establishment of a naval base at Singapore from which Britain could police Eastern waters.

But there were other causes of rising militarism. Events in China, especially those affecting Manchuria, were noted in Japan. The advantage in Japan began to pass from political parties to the armed services and to the higher ranks of the large bureaucracy. Even more harmful to constitutional government than the Great Depression was the Mukden incident that occurred in 1931. In itself it was the result of ultranationalist tendencies typified by such men as Kita Ikki, the son of a *saké* brewer who had become interested in socialism in his youth. In a book called *An Unofficial History of the Chinese Revolution (Shina kakumei gaishi)*, he criticized Japanese activists in Japan for relying on the policies of Sun Yat-sen, a superficial user of Western ideas. He wished to curb the power of the *zaibatsu*, and do away with corrupt politicians, thus enabling Japan to lead Asia. Many of his ideas strike one now as quite normal—nationalization of industry, eight-hour working day, land reform programmes. Eventually he was involved in the several assassinations and seizure of control of central Tokyo in February, 1936. He was executed in 1937. It was such extremist ideas, and others in his other book *Plan for the Reconstruction of Japan* advocating a Fascist-type social and economic revolution led by the army, that were part of the background to militarism. His advocacy of military dictatorship and the conquest of whatever areas of Manchuria would supply Japan with needed raw materials, provided for militarists and extremists a tempting blueprint for the future.

The shift from party cabinets to the extreme militarism of the late 1930s and early 1940s can be clearly seen in tabular form.

Party Cabinet (Seiyukai)	Inukai	1931–1932
Moderate Admirals	Saito	1932–1934
	Okada	1934–1936
Increasing Militarism	Hirota	1936–1937
	Hayashi	1937
War with China	Konoe	1937–1939
	Hiranuma	1939
Diplomatic Activity	Abbe	1939–1940
	Yonai	1940
The Axis Pact	Konoe	1940–1941
World War II	Tojo	1941–1944
End of War	Koiso	1944–1945
	Suzuki	1945

The Mukden Incident

With her population increasing at the phenomenal rate of about a million a year and touching the 60 million mark in 1930, Japan's industrialization intensified to keep up with supplying it. The need for raw materials of which Japan had few in her own islands became ever more pressing. Even with the addition of Korea, Taiwan, and the Pacific Mandated Islands, the pressure of people in Japan grew every year, for Japanese had so far shown little interest in emigrating to colonial territories.

By 1931, Japan was already heavily committed in terms of industrial plant, mining, transport, and large capital investment in Manchuria. The unification by Chiang Kai-shek of most of China in 1928 was seen by Japanese as a threat to their Manchurian interests. The multi-millions of China needed industrial products quite as much as did the Japanese. A united and increasingly nationalistic China began then to take Manchuria under its own control. Japan, in Chinese eyes, was no more and no less an imperialist than Britain and other powers, and Nationalist China was determined to be rid of them all.

The way in which the Young Marshal (Chang Hsüeh-liang) took sides with the Nanking government and informed the Japanese they must negotiate with Nanking over the question of Manchuria, was also alarming to Japan.

Above, part of the Japanese expansion programme in Manchuria was the Showa Steelworks, named after the reign title of the Taisho Emperor who came to the throne in 1912 and reigned until 1926

Below, work on the Shokako dam in Manchuria, another aspect of the Japanese effort to construct heavy industry in the area

Chang Hsüeh-liang, son of the warlord Chang Tso-lin, was called the 'Young Marshal'

Chiang Kai-shek attempted to gain control of the Russian-owned Chinese Eastern Railway (which the Bolsheviks would not relinquish), and failed. He then began building competitive railways to filter off traffic from Japanese-run railways in Manchuria. Japan protested that this was in violation of the secret Sino-Japanese agreement of 1905. China, who had always disagreed with the interpretation of the pact, ignored the protest.

Another thorn in the side of the Japanese in South Manchuria was shortage of land, which had been absorbed by Chinese fleeing in the wake of warlord and other disorders in the last decades. There were almost 30 million Chinese to the 250,000 Japanese in the area in 1930. The Nationalists did a good deal of anti-Japanese propaganda among those 30 million Chinese, revealing a Japanese plan to absorb China in due course. Public opinion was hostile to Japan.

One more railway problem fed the fires smouldering in Manchuria—the news that the Russians were intending to duplicate the single-track Trans-Siberian railway. Japanese were naturally suspicious about the reasons for this.

What actually happened to trigger off the Japanese take-over of Manchuria was an explosion that blew up a small part of the track of the Japanese South Manchurian Railway. But just who blew it up—Chinese or Japanese—is a mystery that has never been solved. There had been plenty of incidents in South Manchuria in which Chinese acted against Japanese, and it would be no surprise to find that the explosion was set off by indignant and angry Chinese. On the other hand, it is equally likely, in view of other evidence that came to light many years after, that the explosion was deliberately set off by Japanese to give them an excuse for what they did next.

The promptness with which Japanese forces responded to the event led many to believe it was they who had planted the bomb. The Japanese claimed that it was Chinese sabotage. But on balance it seems more likely that the incident was an excuse manufactured by the Japanese Kwantung Army who were restless and yearning for action. A few weeks prior to the explosion two senior officers of that army, stationed on the peninsula of Liaotung (or Kwantung), were in Tokyo and told Major-General Tatekawa of the Tokyo army headquarters as well as the general commanding the Kwantung Army, General Honjo, of plans to find such an excuse.

Machine-gunning in a street after the South Manchurian Railway was blown up

Tatekawa was later sent from Tokyo to Mukden to prevent any such thing happening. When he arrived in the city he failed to deliver whatever message he was carrying but went instead to a geisha house. It was the night of September 18, and while he was thus occupied, the bomb went off.

Although there was a Japanese military faction that did not wish to interfere in Manchuria, the majority of the by now ruling military lost no time in sending the Kwantung Army into Manchuria. Mukden and strategic places were soon occupied and the conquest of Manchuria began—not to end until the puppet state of Manchukuo was set up by the Japanese.

Manchukuo, The League of Nations, Russia, and Japan

China appealed to the League of Nations, but although the League demanded Japanese withdrawal from the South Manchurian Railway, the Japanese army did not respond. The civil government in Japan no longer had complete control of its army. With the army's demonstration of contempt for its government, a wave of militaristic feeling swept Japan, and it was soon dangerous there to criticize the army in any way at all.

Chinese forces were driven south of the Great Wall and Japan had set up Manchukuo by March 1, 1932—a puppet state with Henry Pu-yi as puppet head of its government. Six months later Japan recognized its own puppet state, and in 1933 Japanese armed forces took Jehol, an Inner Mongolian province that had long been part of China. This became part of Manchukuo, now called an empire with the hapless last Ch'ing emperor, Pu-yi, as the K'ang-teh Emperor. Chiang Kai-shek still regarded Communists as his main target, and did even less than he physically could have done to stem the Japanese tide.

The United States contented itself with the Stimson doctrine of non-recognition of anything between China and Japan that was against American rights and the Open Door policy in China. That had no effect either.

The unlucky Henry Pu-yi, who had abdicated as the last emperor of China, was made emperor of 'Manchukuo' by the conquering Japanese. He was then in his twenties

The Chinese, who had more to lose, boycotted Japanese goods, which embarrassed the Japanese militarists at home because of the economic harm done to industry. The boycott caused Japanese retaliation in the shape of the capture of Shanghai in January, 1932.

Another Chinese appeal to the League of Nations brought the formation of a Consular Committee (mostly composed of the Shanghai consuls) which arranged by May for Japan to withdraw. Strong Chinese resistance and possible anger of other great powers might have threatened her hold on Manchuria had she not done so.

Japan withdrew its representatives from the League when the latter (on the advice of the Lytton Commission sent to investigate) condemned the Manchurian occupation and asked for restoration of Chinese rights. Japan resigned from the League in March, 1933. The first great test of the League had shown how completely powerless it was in the face of one determined member and a handful of apathetic great powers.

Japanese advance into north China in 1933 eventually brought a settlement between China and Japan in the Tangku truce of May, 1933, in which an area of 5,000 square miles between Peiping and Manchuria was to be a demilitarized zone with a Chinese police force to keep order. But Japan reserved the right (gained in the Boxer Protocol) to garrison the railway link between Peiping, Tientsin, and Shanhaikwan where the Great Wall runs down to the sea.

The seriousness of the breakdown of party government and the feeble growth of democratic thought in Japan may now be seen in all its militaristic consequences. The Wakatsuki cabinet was completely split over the Mukden affair, and had resigned in December, 1931, in favour of that of Inukai Ki (Tsuyoshi) who was opposed to military take-over of civil government decision-making. His attempt at negotiation with the Chinese led to his and others' assassination by a group of young army and naval officers on May 15, 1932. After which the two moderate admirals, Saito and later Okado could do little to stop the drift from the peaceful 1920s attitude to the furious militarism of the 1930s.

Assassination characterized the following years, as did the rise of 'patriotic' societies whose ultranationalist outlook was their sole unifying feature. 'Charts drawn by Japanese scholars to show the interrelationships of these groups look like the wiring diagrams for electronic computers,' as one historian has put it. Their aims were exclusion of the West from the East, elevation of the sanctity of 'Japanese virtues'. Defendants of political assassinators put forward the plea that the assassins were 'purely motivated', were getting rid of 'traitors at the side of the emperor'. The semi-Fascist confusion of thought, and the popular reaction of the times affected various successive Japanese governments.

It was dangerous to be liberal for fear of being attacked as an enemy of the emperor. The government, desperately trying to prove that it reflected popular trends, arrested liberals and radicals. In later, saner times Japanese have called the decade before 1941, *kurai tanima*—'the dark valley'. It is indeed to this decade of rampant popular aggression and militarism infecting the majority of the Japanese and giving free rein to the army, that later Japanese aggression and the dark horrors of Japanese military conquest in World War II may be traced.

Japan also had trouble with Russia in her Manchurian adventure. Border clashes, the restoration of Russian-Chinese diplomatic ties in 1932, were regarded by her as unfriendly. Japan's purchase from Russia of the Chinese Eastern Asia Railway in 1935 did little to ease matters. Russia began to deepen her influence in China's northwest and in Inner Mongolia. To counter these moves Japan signed with Germany in 1936 the Anti-Comintern Pact.

To permit a build-up of naval strength, Japan denounced the Washington and London Naval Treaties in 1934. American-Japanese relations went from bad to worse with the Amau Statement which warned the United States and the powers in the League of Nations to leave China to Japan. She withdrew from the 1935 Naval Conference, and when the treaties expired in the following year Japan was free to build as big a fleet as she could manage. The seeds of the very near future were sprouting thick and fast in the Pacific. In fact, Japanese defiance of the League proved to Germany and Italy in the West that no determined aggressor need worry about censure from this powerless organization.

In Japan there were widely differing points of view within the ultra-nationalistic movement, but there was unanimity in the face of Western opposition to Japan's imperialistic policy.

'Asia's stubborn efforts to remain faithful to spiritual values, and Europe's honest and rigorous speculative thought...have both made spectacular achievements. Yet today it is no longer possible for these two to exist apart from each other. World history shows us that these two must be united....I am afraid that a struggle between the great powers of the East and the West which will decide their existence is at present, as in the past, absolutely inevitable if a new world is to come about....It is my belief that Heaven has decided on Japan as...the champion of the East.... We must develop a strong spirit of morality in order to carry out this solemn mission....'

Okawa Shumei (an ultra-nationalist thinker)

Okawa's historic mission for Japan is complemented by the statement of a
prominent and extremist army leader, Hashimoto Kingoro:

> '...there are only three ways left to Japan to escape from the pressure of surplus
> population.... The first door, emigration, had been barred to us by the anti-Japanese
> immigration policies of other countries. The second door, advance into world markets,
> is being pushed shut by tariff barriers.'

What can Japan do, he asks? 'It may sound dangerous when we speak of territorial
expansion,' but Japan simply wants some place overseas where 'Japanese capital,
Japanese skills, and Japanese labour can have free play, free from the oppression
of the white race.' He justifies the forming of Manchukuo as being a 'splendid
new nation'. Such specious arguments were apparently widely believed in Japan,
if nowhere else.

Japan Wages Undeclared War in China

After the establishment of this 'splendid new nation', Manchukuo, Japan proceeded to enlarge its territories in China with the aim of setting up another puppet
state comprising Hopei, Shantung, and Shansi provinces, together with Chahar
and Siuyuan. One argument used by Japan was that since China could not be
united until the eradication of Communism from the country, China might as
well be liberated from the Reds by Japan.

The probability of a CCP-KMT coalition after the Sian incident was also
alarming to Japan because it seemed then that the combination would make its
objectives in north China more difficult to attain.

Japanese militarists were not in absolute control of the government, but their
influence increased steadily. Even after the Loukouchiao Incident on July 7,
1937 (this bridge some miles from Peking is commonly called Marco Polo Bridge),
Japanese Premier Konoe desired to keep the conflict localized, as did the Chinese.
But the Japanese dictated the terms of a settlement which was unacceptable to
the Chinese. The Loukouchiao incident was a simple clash between Japanese
troops on night manoeuvres and Chinese soldiers at the bridge, which is also at
a junction on the Peiping-Hankow railway. The junction was strategically valuable
to China since the railway was the only link between Peiping and central China,
which they controlled.

During negotiations, the Chinese militia under Japanese control at Tungchow,
at the end of the Grand Canal between Peiping and Tientsin, mutinied. Several
scores of Japanese and Korean (nationals of the Japanese) residents were murdered.
Japan broke off the negotiations and a full-scale invasion of China followed.

One result of this was that Chiang and Mao were thrown forcibly into each
other's arms and a united front against the Japanese was formed by KMT and
CCP—a movement already put in motion by the terms of Chiang's release after
the Sian kidnapping. So far did the agreement between the two sides go that a
National Congress was scheduled for November 1937 in order to draft a new
constitution. Chinese setbacks in the undeclared Japanese war prevented its
taking place.

Above, the Loukouchiao Bridge outside Peking was a key river-crossing. From here on July 7, 1937, Japan started its all-out war against China. The bridge itself is an ancient one. It has been considerably widened since the revolution, and the old carved lions of its decorative balusters have been retained in the new structure

Below, a scene during the 'Shanghai Incident' of August 9, 1937. Among the armoured cars and soldiers, the only familiar note is the Coca Cola sign

Foreign Powers and the Undeclared War

The League of Nations, as we have seen, proved powerless to hold back the Japanese from their Chinese prey. Shanghai was taken by Japan once more in August 1937, and what had been delicately termed the 'North China Incident', was now re-phrased the 'China Incident'. Even the United States termed the whole Japanese aggression in China an incident, for to have called it a war would, under the terms of the 1937 Neutrality Act, have prevented her sending war supplies to either side—and this would have hurt China worse than Japan.

The Japanese Premier Konoe promised Japanese that the matter 'would be cleared up in two months'. But as the fighting went on, Japanese domestic opinion hardened. The army argued that if Nanking were to fall to them the Chinese would agree to all Japanese demands. Nanking fell in December and the ruthless 'rape of Nanking' was carried out against this former centre of anti-Japanese agitation. But China did not succumb.

The fierce resistance of the Chinese pushed the Japanese into an all-out offensive beginning in January, 1938, and by October of that year Hankow and Canton had fallen. Konoe remarked that the KMT regime had been reduced to a local government in Szechuan. He then announced Japan's New Order in East Asia.

Russia signed a non-aggression pact with China in 1937 and assisted in her war effort with credit and with arms, military advisers, and supplies. This help, of course, ceased in 1941 when Russia was attacked by Germany. Germany, allied to Japan by the Anti-Comintern Pact, stopped giving military aid to China.

China was now divided into two parts—'free China' and 'occupied China'. Before Konoe could announce his New Order, the Japanese had consolidated their hold in north China. Peiping and Tientsin fell in July, 1937, and as the Japanese moved into Inner Mongolia, cutting off China's communication with Russia, they took Kalgan in August. Suiyuan was easily taken, but in Shansi the Japanese armies met the Communist Eighth Route Army. After extremely bitter fighting Taiyuan fell in November, but the Communists blocked Japanese advance toward northwest China.

The Japanese navy landed at Tsingtao and joined the forces coming down through Shantung whose capital, Tsinan, was taken in December. But the greatest Nationalist victory of the war was won by the KMT general Li Tsung-yen at Taierchuang in April, 1938. Widespread belief in China that Japanese armies were unbeatable was thus shattered.

Shanghai fell, as we have seen, but not until after a spirited three-month defence. After the fall of Nanking the Japanese spread along the Yangtze valley. Amoy fell in May, and Canton in October, 1938.

Chiang established a wartime capital in Chungking, further up the Yangtze, and a military stalemate came about with the Japanese unable to penetrate the west of China. Japan had more or less confined the Chinese forces (and had instituted a naval blockade that was effective up and down the coast). So, for the following six years she undertook no further major campaign in China. Japanese bombing harrassed Free Chinese areas, and Chinese guerrillas, largely Communists, carried on a continuous hit and run activity against their enemy. Guerrilla fighting also took place behind the Japanese lines.

The Japanese were bogged down by the vast size of China, the intense resistance of her armies, and the equally intense hatred of the people, who on the whole did not co-operate with them. The war that the Japanese had been told would be over in a couple of months dragged on, was exceedingly costly in terms of maintaining numbers of troops in a hostile environment, and became increasingly unpopular at home. Western powers were protesting at Japanese interference in

Left, the Japanese Premier Prince Konoe. Temperamentally unsuited for the task, he failed to control the army

Below, celebrating the first anniversary (in 1937) of the signing of the Anti-Comintern Pact between Japan and Germany

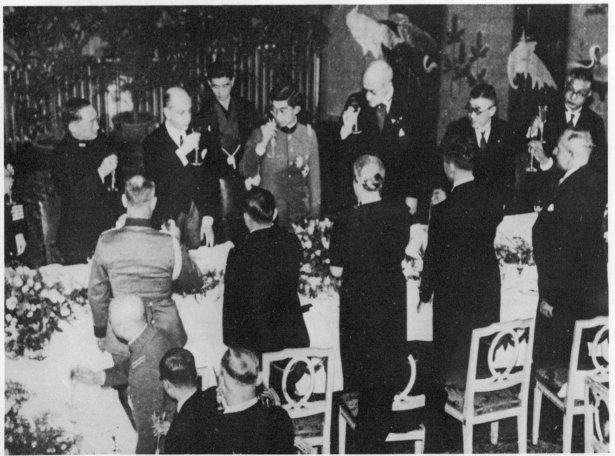

China, 1935–1949

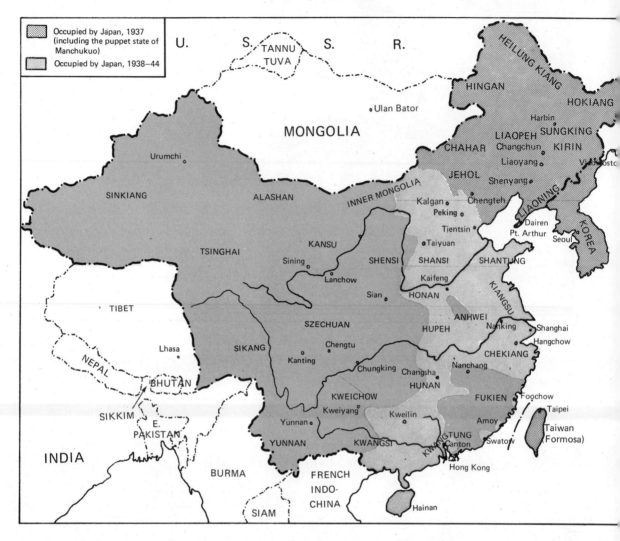

their spheres of interest in China. Premier Konoe's New Order was one attempt at stilling the unrest.

The New Order in East Asia declared that it was Japan's policy to seek Chinese co-operation and not to conquer her. Naturally no one in China believed a word of this. But a Japanese Diet member who dared to criticize the New Order was expelled from the assembly for having spoken ill of the 'holy war'. And the Social Mass Party in Japan at its meeting in November, 1937, had decided 'positively to support the holy war for the fulfilment of the historical mission of the Japanese people'. By 1940, the Diet itself had become a rubber-stamping machine for government decisions—the decisions of the cabinet and the armed services.

China was now run by three major parts of the Japanese services—the Kwantung Army controlled Manchukuo and Inner Mongolia; the North China Army controlled from Peking the surrounding terrain; and the Central China Army set up its government in Nanking to run central China under Japanese control.

Wang Ching-wei, a former associate of Sun Yat-sen. He left the Kuomintang and was eventually set up in Nanking as one of the more credible of Japan's puppet rulers

Peace offers such as that contained in the New Order were all rejected by the Chinese who hoped to keep the Japanese tied down and gradually weaken them. The Japanese then set up puppet governments in China. The first was the 'Provisional Government' at Peiping (December, 1937), and the second the 'Reformed Government of the Chinese Republic' at Nanking (March, 1938). Wang Ching-wei, whose former associations with Sun Yat-sun years before, permitted him with some credibility to take office, was made the puppet governor at Nanking in March, 1940. But the extreme brutality of the Japanese soldiers and their commanders in China prevented any sort of acceptance by the Chinese people at large.

Japan finally recognized the Wang regime and signed a treaty with it to combat Communism and co-operate in economic development. Italy, Germany, Spain, and one or two other totalitarian regimes also recognized the puppet state.

In Japan itself an Imperial Headquarters was set up in November, 1937 to co-ordinate planning between the armed services. In the same month the manifest political power they held was recognized by the formation of the Liaison Council. This body brought together for planning policy the prime minister, the ministers of the armed services, the foreign minister, the chiefs of staff of army and navy, and also when necessary the home minister and the finance minister. Meetings were held in 1937 and early 1938, but after that there appeared a sharp division between the cabinet and the military which went on until mid-1940, and no meetings were held for almost two years. In the second Konoe cabinet they were started again in summer, 1940. After this the Liaison Council became the real decision-making body in the government, its decisions being merely confirmed by Imperial Conferences.

Another institution that arose from the China war was the Planning Board of October, 1937, set up to plan economic expansion, and to administer controls that were slowly being introduced in Japan. The National Mobilization Law of 1938 was also administered by this Board, and provided for control of resources, labour, material, trade and prices and wages, besides censorship of the press and the mass media. Konoe promised not to use the provisions of this act while the war was limited to China, but in fact controls were introduced one by one, beginning in mid-1938.

18 Nationalist-Communist Relations

IN March, 1938 the CCP was represented by Chou En-lai at the national congress held in Hankow. It was decided to form a People's Political Council of 200 members, later increased to 362, half of whom would be CCP, and half KMT and other smaller parties. This council was the outcome of the military co-operation between Nationalist and Communist armies in the field, and its function was to advise the government on policy.

Co-operation did not last for long. After 1938 the Nationalists realized that despite agreements to the contrary, the Communists were unwilling to take orders from the National Government. While the Communists took very often the brunt of the responsibility in guerrilla fighting against the Japanese, they were also extremely active in the regions they occupied in promoting a new way of life among the inhabitants. What had been 'resistance bases' were now expanded. By 1939, in the north a Shansi-Chahar-Hopei Border Government was formed to administer these areas. This was Communist-dominated but at first had Chungking's blessing. There were other such areas—the Shensi-Kansu-Ninghsia Border Government, for example. By the time that the Nazi-Soviet Non-aggression Pact was signed in 1939 in the West, the Chinese Communist Party felt that it could continue to wield its already considerable political weight.

Starving children at Chungking in 1937

The Chiang Nationalist government then countered with efforts to stop the spread of Communist influence. But the 'meagre set of ideas' of the Nationalists when sweeping social reform was obviously the only way to attract the co-operation and sympathy of the demoralized Chinese peasantry, was no match for the new dynamic of the Communists. The vast and corrupt bureaucracy of the Nationalist government and its five million troops and half a million officers, could hardly help draining the country of its dwindling resources. The contrast between the strict order and organized agricultural and other production that was to be seen in Communist-held areas was sharp and painful to the Nationalists.

Making no headway against Communist ideas and their acceptance, the Nationalists sent some of their best troops to blockade the Communists in the northwest. The final split that ended CCP-KMT co-operation came with a clash in January, 1941 between the Communist New Fourth Army and Nationalist troops. This was hastened by the Nationalists who had no wish to see the territory surrounding Shanghai, Nanking, and Hankow, which was a former KMT base before the Japanese came and also one of the country's highly developed regions, fall into Communist hands.

The Chungking government proclaimed the disbandment of the Communist New Fourth Army, and the CCP no longer attended the People's Political Council. Both Communists and Nationalists were really awaiting the end of the Japanese war. Both knew the real trial of strength and the real fight for the control of China would come after that.

PART FOUR

THE END
OF WESTERN DOMINATION

19 China, Japan, and World War II

T HE long years of Japanese aggression in China and all that they entailed in social, political, and economic changes in that country, slowly merged into the conflict of World War II, and became a vital part of that war as Japan struck at the United States at Pearl Harbour, and went on to conquer Southeast Asia.

Prelude to War in the Pacific

Japanese acts in China brought American displeasure, but despite shock at indiscriminate Japanese bombing of civil population in China, the United States continued to supply oil, steel, scrap iron, and other metals needed by Japan for her war machine. The 'moral embargo' of the American government in which it 'advised' American companies not to supply aeroplanes or aerial bombs was a gesture, to which were added other articles as time went by. A total embargo was enforced in 1941.

Both America and Britain gave credits to China, and after a Japanese blockade of British and French concessions at Tientsin and the occupation of Hainan Island, which threatened Southeast Asia, the United States terminated the 1911 American-Japanese Treaty of Commerce.

Events were for some time on Japan's side. The outbreak of World War II meant that Britain, France, and America were preoccupied. And as the war at first went badly for the Allies in Europe, so the Japanese found the time opportune to exert pressure on them in the East. Britain was persuaded to close Hong Kong to imports of war materials for Free China; and the Burma Road, over which more material reached the Chinese, was closed by Winston Churchill for three months at the end of 1940. Since it was China's sole land route to the outer world, this was a severe blow.

When France fell to the Germans, and the Vichy régime was set up, the French opened the route to southern China through Indo-China, and permitted Japanese troops to move through to China and Japanese planes to use air-bases there. The Dutch continued to supply Japan with oil from Indonesia.

On the diplomatic front, Japan proclaimed an extension of the former New Order, called the Greater Asia Co-Prosperity Sphere. This scheme envisaged that all Southeast Asia, the various puppet states under Japan in China, the Pacific Mandated Islands, Australia and New Zealand, and possibly India, would become economically self-sufficient, and free from colonial domination by Britain and others under Japan's political hegemony. Each country would be a protectorate of Japan, which was characterized as the natural leader of Asia, backing truly Asian values and leading Asia away from the corrupting materialism and social disruption brought by the West.

Internationally, the Japanese position was made stronger by the change in the Anti-Comintern Pact between herself and Germany, joined by Italy in 1937, which was formed into a military alliance (the Tripartite Pact) in September, 1940. The 'Axis' partners in this alliance warned the United States not to exert herself too much in supplying assistance to Free China and Britain.

In April, 1941, Japan secured herself against possible Russian interference by signing a neutrality pact with the Soviet Union which put an end to fighting between their troops in the Nomonhan region on the border between Manchukuo and Mongolia, in which Japanese troops had taken heavy punishment.

In October, 1940, all political parties in Japan were dissolved and brought within the Imperial Rule Assistance Association. Premier Konoe evidently hoped that this would counteract the power of the military, but in this he proved mistaken. In fact Japan had now turned into a totalitarian state.

Vital moves were under way in America. Congress repealed the arms embargo of the Neutrality Act of 1937, and was legally able to supply France and Britain with war material. By the time that Nazi armies had conquered all western Europe except for Britain, and when the Tripartite Pact had been signed, America decided to mobilize manpower and resources, for her participation in the war seemed now more or less inevitable.

The following year, 1941, Congress passed the Lease-Lend act on March 11, thus permitting the United States to export goods to countries at war in her own (instead of their) ships, and on credit. This amounted to America's lending the goods and the services Britain needed. Churchill and Roosevelt met at sea in August, 1941, and drew up an eight-point declaration that came to be called the Atlantic Charter. On January 1, 1942, another declaration was signed by Churchill, Roosevelt, Litvinov (for the U.S.S.R.) and T.V. Soong (for Free China), declaring their adherence to the purposes and principles of the Atlantic Charter.

After the Lease-Lend act, Japan thought that America was about to enter the war in Europe, and that she might be in favour of settling Sino-Japanese questions peacefully. Admiral Nomura Kichisaburo, Japanese ambassador to the United States, therefore made unofficial approaches to the American Secretary of State Cordell Hull on a possible diplomatic solution. But America was determined to stop Japanese expansion in China. From the start in April, 1941, the talks were doomed to failure.

Very soon after these talks had begun, America had sent the first advisers to the Chiang Kai-shek government, and an American Volunteer Corps (later famous as the 'Flying Tigers') under Colonel Claire Chennault began to operate on behalf of Free China.

On July 26, 1941, America froze Japanese assets in the United States, and prohibited all exports to Japan. This action was followed soon by Britain and Holland. Japan lost her major sources of oil, without which she could not indefinitely continue a war. These measures were taken by the ABCD Powers (America, Britain, China, and the Dutch) in retaliation for the Japanese take-over of Indo-China, which they saw as a direct threat to their Southeast Asian territories.

Events now moved swiftly and with the inevitability of a classical tragedy. There were only three choices for Japan:

> To relinquish Indo-China—this was not possible with the militant mood of the country. National pride was involved.
> To do nothing and face economic death and the ever-decreasing ability to retain the position now held in China and elsewhere for lack of oil and war materials.
> War, which seemed to the Japanese the sole honourable way out.

Last-minute efforts were made by Japan in June, 1941, under the direction of Premier Konoe in the shape of an offer to the United States to withdraw from Indo-China in return for oil and a United States 'hands off' policy in China. He even proposed a meeting with President Roosevelt. Neither idea was accepted. The United States Secretary of State proposed that Japan should remove all armed forces from Indo-China and China, including Manchuria. His programme rested on the (as it proved) unfounded belief that Japan would not attack the United States.

In October, 1941, Konoe Fumimaro resigned the premiership, his policies of compromise having produced no results. General Tojo Hideki (1885–1948) took over with a war cabinet.

It is sometimes thought that Japan rushed headlong into war with a militaristic government dedicated to the project and without careful consideration. This is not true. Japan knew quite well how weak America, Britain, and Dutch forces were in the Pacific. And the Japanese had calculated correctly that to overrun Southeast Asia would present no great difficulty in the military sense. Once there, they could acquire many of the minerals and most of the oil they now needed, and could dispense with American and other supplies. Russia was fighting Germany and had her hands very full indeed. Britain was an embattled land in a seemingly poor position when its future was examined. America must use large amounts of its military strength in Atlantic deterrents so long as Germany was all-powerful in Europe.

All these opinions were more or less correct. But there were others held universally at this point in Japan which proved very far from the truth of world affairs. On these misjudgments, Japan was eventually to stumble fatally, as we shall see.

War

On December 1, an Imperial Conference in Tokyo decided on war. The Japanese fleet had left Japan for Hawaii in November, and diplomatic moves conducted in Washington by Saburo Kurusu ended at 2.30 p.m. on December 7, 1941, as he

The bombing of Pearl Harbour in December, 1941

conveyed in harsh terms to Secretary of State Cordell Hull that Japan could not accept the American terms.

At that exact moment it was precisely one hour after the Japanese fleet had surprised the American fleet in Pearl Harbour. (It was Sunday, December 8, at Pearl Harbour; December 7, east of the International Date Line).

The Americans, who had broken the Japanese code, realized an attack was planned, but did not know for what date. Tojo stated after the war that he did not know the full extent of the navy's preparations for the Pearl Harbour attack. Just as she had done against the Russians in 1904, Japan had attacked with devastating results *before* declaring war. The actual declaration came in the afternoon of the same day.

On that afternoon, too, came the second disaster for the Americans—the destruction of the Far Eastern Air Force by Japanese planes which attacked it in the Philippines.

The following day America and Britain declared war on Japan; China declared war on Germany, Italy, and Japan. And at long last the Japanese offensive against China had become part of the global conflagration of World War II.

The Imperial Rescript in which war was declared by Japan, was the subject of a lengthy explanatory commentary by one of the leading nationalist writers, Tokutomi Iichiro.

'Now that we have risen up in arms, we must accomplish our aim to the last. Herein lies the core of our theory. In Nippon resides a destiny to become the Light of Great East Asia and to become ultimately the Light of the World.'

The first requisite for Japan, he continues, is strength to expel the West and show East Asia that Japan is the leading nation. The second necessity is benevolence.

'Nippon must develop the...resources of East Asia and distribute them fairly to all the races within the East Asia Co-Prosperity Sphere.... The third qualification is virtue.... We must ...bring friendship among the East Asian nations and make them all live in peace with a boundlessly embracing virtue.'

This echoes with surprising fidelity the statements in the early nineteenth century of Sato Nobuhiro (1769–1850) whose writings contain a Confidential Plan for World Unification (*Kondo Hisaku*).

'In terms of world geography our Imperial Land would appear to be the axis of the other countries of the world.... Natural circumstances favour the launching of an expedition from our country to conquer others.... For Japan to attempt to open other countries, her first step must be the absorption of China.... After China is brought within our domain, the Central Asian countries, as well as Burma, India, and other lands...who yearn for our virtues and fear our power, will come to us with bowed heads and on hands and knees to serve us.'

Plan for the East Asia Co-Prosperity Sphere

From a document dated January, 1942, we have a precise and detailed picture of what Japan aimed to do at this time, a century after Sato Nobuhiro.

'*The Plan.* The Japanese empire is a manifestation of morality and its special characteristic is the propagation of the Imperial Way.... It is necessary to...cause East Asia to return to its original form of independence and co-prosperity by shaking off the yoke of Europe and America....'

'*The Form of East Asiatic Independence and Co-prosperity.* The states, their citizens, and resources, in...the Pacific, Central Asia, and the Indian Oceans...are to be established as an autonomous zone...on behalf of the peoples of the nations of East Asia. The area including Japan, Manchuria, North China, Lower Yangtze River, and the Russian Maritime Province, forms the nucleus of the East Asiatic Union. The Japanese empire possesses a duty as the leader of the East Asiatic Union....'

The document goes on to say:

'...To enable the empire actually to become the central influence in East Asia, the first necessity is the consolidation of the inner belt of East Asia.'

This meant Japan, the Lower Yangtze Area, and the Russian Maritime area; and there was to be a 'Smaller Co-Prosperity Sphere' consisting of Eastern Siberia, China, Indo-China, and the South Seas. While the Greater Co-Prosperity Sphere included the smaller one plus Australia, India, and the island groups of the Pacific.

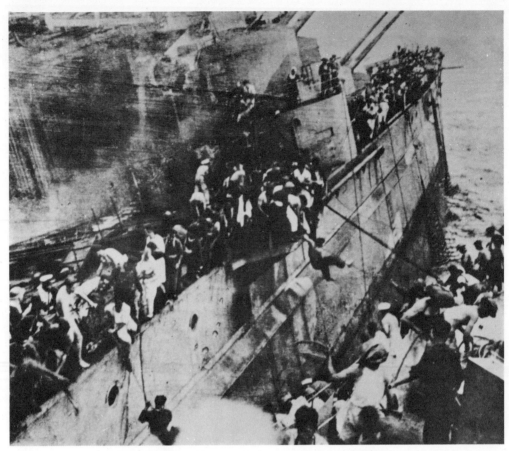

The end of the *Prince of Wales* off the coast of Malaya

The fall of Hong Kong—the first Japanese troops entering the city

'*The Building of the National Strength*. The unification of Japan, Manchukuo, and China shall be effected.... Thus a central industry will be constructed in East Asia....'

'*Political Construction*. The realization of the...Greater East Asia Co-Prosperity Sphere requires not only...the current Greater East Asia War but presupposes another great war in the future. Therefore...1) preparation for wars with the other spheres of the world; and 2) unification and construction....'

The document ends with:

'*Thought and Cultural Construction*. The ultimate aim...in East Asia is to make East Asiatic peoples revere the Imperial influence...and to establish the belief that... this influence is the one and only way to the...development of East Asia....'

Draft of Basic Plan for Establishment of
Greater East Asia Co-Prosperity Sphere

While stating that the ultimate object is 'not exploitation but co-prosperity and mutual help', it insists that there shall be but one 'world view'—that of the Japanese.

The Japanese Conquests

Late	1940		Japan establishes herself in Indo-China and Thailand
	1941	Dec.8	Attacks on Pearl Harbour, the Philippines, Hong Kong, Malaya
		Dec.10	British Far East fleet crippled—battleships *Repulse* and *Prince of Wales* sunk
		Dec.13	Fall of Guam
		Dec.20	Fall of Wake Island
		Dec.25	Fall of Hong Kong
	1942	Jan.2	Fall of Manila
		Jan.11	Landings in Dutch East Indies
		Feb.15	Fall of Singapore
Early	1942		The Solomon Islands, Gilbert and Ellice Islands, and northern New Guinea taken
		Mar.6	Fall of Batavia (Djakarta)
		Mar.8	Fall of Rangoon
		Apr.9	Fall of Bataan Peninsula (north of Manila Bay)
		Apr.30	Fall of Lashio (on the Burma Road)
		May 2	Fall of Mandalay
		May 6	Fall of Corregidor (in Manila Bay)
		Jun.4–7	The Battle of Midway (when Japanese expansion was checked)
		Jun.12	Fall of Attu (in the Aleutian Islands)
			(The only territories in the region to remain unmolested were Portuguese Timor and the tiny enclave of Macau, and French Indo-China.)

Japanese Conquest and Rape of East Asia

The destruction of the American fleet and airforce at Pearl Harbour and in the Philippines was a brilliant piece of tactical warfare; but also a disastrous psychological mistake. For America, where isolationism had had firm hold, was shocked within a few days into an unprecedented war-effort. If Japan had swallowed East Asia piecemeal, one country after another, this might not have happened. It would certainly have taken longer to happen, giving Japan more time to conquer, to

The Japanese empire at its greatest extent in 1945

consolidate, and to convert conquered peoples to something like the ideas in the plan from which we have read a little above.

The swift successes of the Japanese in East Asia may be judged from the chart (on p. 297). In a matter of six months, and almost on time according to their schedule, Japan's eleven divisions had swept through the East and gathered for the homeland an empire of around three million square miles. Its extent is easily understood from the map (p. 298). The colonial powers had been completely removed from their possessions in East Asia and the Pacific, with the exception of the French in Indo-China and the Portuguese in Macau and Timor.

Far from adhering to those high-sounding (if suspiciously generous) conditions of the Co-Prosperity Sphere, as each territory was occupied, its stocks of food and raw materials were tapped by Japan to supply herself. Rubber and tin from Malaya, oil from Indonesia, rice and food staples from several countries, all disappeared toward Japan. The economic block outlined in the Greater East Asia Co-Prosperity Sphere that was to cut out both economic and political domination of the West, was quickly turned into a vast supply area for the Japanese population, the insatiable Japanese war machine, and the industry that produced for it.

On the whole, not surprisingly, the peoples of conquered lands were not deceived by Japanese propaganda and promises. Some nationalist leaders were deceived, and yet others saw in the Japanese occupation the possibility of furthering their cause in various ways. For one thing, those who were optimistic hoped the occupation would not last forever. For another, it formed a focal point of unrest and a very credible rallying ground to unite progressive and nationalist forces within their countries. In this, such leaders proved correct, for when Japan was thrown out of its wartime conquests the tide of nationalism in each occupied land was infinitely stronger than it had been before. And in most, strong nationalist forces soon removed the former colonists when they returned after the war. So, whatever its disastrous short-term consequences, we can reasonably see Japanese actions in East Asia and Southeast Asia as the catalyst that hastened the pace of change and independence. But that was not intended.

There was no other benefit in what for the most part was a brutal, inhuman, and cold-blooded rape of the occupied lands. Japanese troops as a whole, and in particular the *kempeitai*—the military police—were sadistically brutal, and memories of their rule of terror in many places are unlikely to be effaced until the generation that suffered under them has died out.

'On one occasion the village of Ting Hsien...was suddenly attacked by the Japanese. All the people were driven into a large compound, the Japanese pulled one young man out and asked him who the district chairman was. "I don't know," was the reply. The young man was decapitated there and then. The Japanese then asked a woman, and got the same reply, "I don't know." They bayonetted her through the breast. They asked a boy of eleven and got the same answer. The boy was cut to pieces. When they were about to bully an old man, someone cried out, "I am the district chairman." The whole crowd echoed him, crying, "I am the district chairman." The Japanese finally found the chairman and dragged him away. In the night— the best time for guerrilla activities—the people found the place where he was held and rescued him....'

Stuart Gelder: *The Chinese Communists*. 1947

In general, there were campaigns to encourage the conquered peoples to learn Japanese and to respect Japanese culture. These were carried on vigorously on radio, in the newspapers, and by films. The Japanese set up 'national' governments in many territories, promoted whichever religion was dominant in any particular country, and made a great show of leading the people toward 'independence'. The pace of such activities increased in 1943 when the tide of war was turning against the Japanese and the Allies were on the offensive instead of the defensive. Japan then needed the active support of the conquered peoples to help in its fight to retain territories it had conquered so easily.

On August 1, 1943, conquered Burma was granted 'independence' under a Burmese nationalist lawyer Dr. Ba Maw, who had in fact been head of a nationalist administration in the country since August of the year before. But by spring of 1944, when a Japanese attempt at invading India had failed the nationalists made a pact with Britain, and the Anti-Fascist People's Freedom League (AFPFL) was formed. In late March, 1945, when the ten thousand men of the Burma National Army turned on the Japanese and materially helped in their defeat, the AFPFL was in a strong position. The British administration, when it returned, was therefore confronted, among the ruins left by the Japanese and their conquest, with a problem that can be taken as typical of the problem confronting other returning colonial governments, such as the Dutch in Indonesia. A strong nationalist movement had to be reckoned with, and never again could the clock be turned back to the days, only a few years before, when nationalism could be contained.

Resistance groups were active in most of the occupied countries and guerrilla warfare was carried on by them in several of these countries.

The initial Japanese successes caused wild enthusiasm in Japan and great self-confidence among Japanese armed forces. There were several reasons why for some time the Allies were unable to counter Japanese offensives. Britain had her hands full in Europe and the Japanese had sunk her two biggest ships in the East. America, initially shocked, was not geared industrially to support an all-out war on both Western and Eastern sectors, and while her war potential grew far faster than the Japanese could possibly have expected, it was some time before that potential became an operational fact.

The Tide of War Turns

Meanwhile Japan attempted to expand her Pacific perimeter and was rapidly warned by small bombing raids on the occupied Marshall and Gilbert Islands and on New Guinea, that the United States did not intend to remain passive. There was even a daring, strategically useless, air raid on Tokyo on April 18, 1942. This was a morale-booster for the Allied forces.

Japanese extension included the capture of part of the Aleutian Island chain, but their advance in New Guinea was halted. The final check was administered as they attempted to cut the sea link between America and Australia. In the Battle of the Coral Sea (May 7-8, 1942) the Japanese were for the first time defeated by American and Australian ships. Each side lost an aircraft carrier and had equal damage, but the occupation of Port Moresby was prevented and any hope of a Japanese advance on Australia was then out of the question.

In the following month, June, 1942, a Japanese fleet of four aircraft carriers and supporting ships attempted to seize the American Island of Midway. All Japanese carriers were sunk with their planes and crews for the loss of one American carrier. Japanese cruisers, battleships, and lighter craft were severely damaged. Admiral Nimitz, who commanded the American action, had succeeded in this 'Trafalgar of the Pacific' in blunting Japanese offensive power, and the initiative now lay with the Allies.

The Allied Pacific Counter-Offensive

1942	June 4–7	The Battle of Midway
	August	American landings on Guadalcanal, Solomon Islands
1943	February	American victory at Guadalcanal
	May, August	Attu and Kiska in the Aleutians retaken
	November	Tarawa in the Gilbert Islands retaken
1944	June	Battle of the Philippines Sea. 16 Japanese ships sunk or damaged, 400 Japanese planes destroyed. Okinawa retaken
	July	Saipan (Marianas Islands) retaken, bringing Tokyo within American bombing range
	September	New Britain, New Guinea, the Palau group, Morotai (in the Moluccas) re-occupied by the Allies
	October 20	American landing on Leyte (Philippines). First use by Japanese of *kamikaze* planes
	October 23	Battle of Leyte Gulf. Japanese naval and air-power almost completely destroyed
1945	February	Americans enter Manila, Philippines freed

The Allied Counter-Offensive

The keys to Japan's defeat lay in the two-pronged island-hopping offensives which in the end cut off Japan from her 'empire' and therefore from her sources of vital supplies; and in the devastating bombing of Japan itself when the Americans got within bombing range.

The arduous land battles on the Asian continent, although fought with great tenacity on both sides, proved less important in the grand strategy of defeat.

One of the two prongs started with the capture of Guadalcanal. From there, General MacArthur moved on in the following year after a bitter struggle for the island that lasted five months, bypassing Japanese garrisons that were not dangerous or in the direct line which he wished to pursue. American forces with the help of Australians retook New Britain, New Guinea, Peleliu in the Palau group of islands, and Morotai in the Moluccas. From this point they were soon in a position to launch the attack on the Philippines.

Meanwhile, the second prong of the offensive, which began with the retaking of Tarawa in the Gilbert Islands, progressed to the Marshalls, the Carolines, and the Marianas. It was during fighting in the Marianas that another blow of great severity

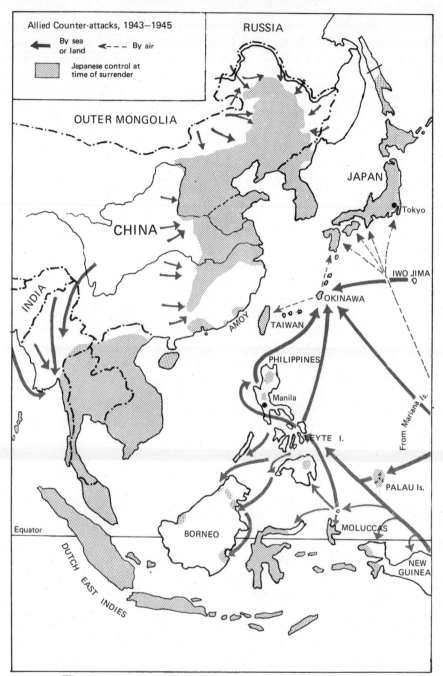

The strategy that defeated the Japanese in World War II

was struck at Japan's sea and air forces with the crippling or sinking of sixteen
Japanese ships (including three aircraft carriers) and the destruction of four hundred
planes. This was the Battle of the Philippines Sea, in June, 1944.

The fall of Saipan in the Mariana Islands brought Tokyo and other centres in
Japan within range of heavy United States bombers. Iwo Jimo to the north of the
Mariana Islands fell. The Island of Okinawa fell in June; and in October, 1944, the
two prongs of the offensive converged on the Philippines with Americans landing

at Leyte on October 20. The Japanese for the first time sent their suicide planes, which they called *kamikaze*, against ships landing American troops. Each plane was manned by a pilot who had pledged himself to use his machine loaded with bombs and explosives as a guided missile. The pilot dived on the selected target and died in the resulting crash. The word *kamikaze* means 'divine wind' and was used to describe the typhoon that blew away the invading Mongol armada from the shores of Japan long ago.

On October 23, what was perhaps the greatest naval battle of the war took place. On the American side were Admiral Halsey's Third Fleet, Vice Admiral Mitscher's fast groups of carriers, and the Seventh Fleet under Admiral Kinkaid. This formidable force engaged the remains of Japan's once enormous fleet. Japan lost in this fierce battle practically all that remained of her navy. Nothing could then stop the Americans from retaking the Philippines, which they did in February, 1945. The end of the Pacific war was in sight.

The war so far had been fought for mostly tiny specks of land in the vast ocean, but in terms of loss of life and of 'hardware' such as ships and planes and guns, it was probably the most destructive of all aspects of the war. By the end of the hostilities all but 1.8 million tons of mostly small wooden coastal Japanese ships were at the bottom of the ocean. Eighty-five percent of the Japanese defenders of tiny Okinawa alone were killed either by the Allies or by their own suicide. On the Allied side there were over 49,000 casualties, most at sea and caused by the massed *kamikaze* attacks that sank 34 ships and damaged 368 others.

The destruction of Japan's merchant and naval fleets was now all but complete, as was that of her naval air-power. She was almost wholly severed from effective communication with the colonies she had so easily taken a few years before.

The other part of the Pacific offensive, air raids on Japan itself, began during the latter half of 1944. These raids, in which explosive and also fire-bombs were dropped, mounted in number and intensity until eventually there were flights of a thousand planes. The destruction they caused not only to Japan's industrial plant, but to the generally flimsy wood and paper-window, tinder-dry housing, was widespread. One example tells the story. On March 10, 1945, one hundred and thirty bombers made sorties across Tokyo dropping incendiary bombs. The death toll, mostly from fire, was 100,000 persons. The total civilian casualties in Japan were 668,000 dead, and almost two and a half million homes were destroyed.

The whole economy of Japan began to crumble. The railways ceased to function, the mines stopped, industrial production almost ceased, oil reserves were almost used up. The ordinary person was living on a very low diet of less than 1,500 calories per day.

But defeated Japan would not give in.

Taking Back Japan's Land Empire

We have already seen that it was Allied island-hopping, the sinking of Japan's fleets, the destruction of her planes, and the consequent severance of the country from its sources of supply, and the crippling of Japanese offensive power that were the deciding factors in Japanese defeat. But it would be both grossly unfair to the tireless efforts, the incredible bravery and tenacity of the soldiers of both the Allied and Japanese armies to omit an account of what they did on land. It would also falsify the picture of what occurred later as a result of these land battles in Asian countries.

There were several major objectives in warfare on the Asian continent. One was to tie down large numbers of Japanese soldiers who could otherwise be used else-where. The second was to launch attacks from air-bases inside Free China on the Japanese mainland itself. Originally, too, it was hoped to develop bases in China from which the ground war could be carried to the shores of China, and from there to attack Japan by a massive invasion such as took place across the English Channel to France. This last plan was given up in 1944 in favour of the more direct and successful island-hopping we have just followed. China was to play a leading role in the achievement of victory over Japan. She was the country which had suffered most (for many years before war was declared at all), so it was only fitting that she should have the status of one of the big four powers—with Britain, America, and Russia.

The United States were the prime movers in this, President Roosevelt being particularly insistent on having China as one of the Big Four. The Chungking government was given a loan (US $500,000,000) in 1942, and Chiang Kai-shek was appointed Allied Commander-in-Chief in the China theatre of operations. General Joseph Stilwell was his Chief of Staff.

After the overrunning of Burma by the Japanese, Stilwell went to train Chinese who had been forced into India, with a view to retaking upper Burma. And when, toward the end of 1943, the Inter-Allied Southeast Asian Command was formed to co-ordinate operations in the whole region, Stilwell became deputy to Admiral Louis Mountbatten, the Supreme Allied Commander.

The only supplies that China got from India and the outside world, came by plane with the now legendary American flights 'over the hump'—that is, over the Himalayas from Assam in northeast India to Kunming, the capital of the southern Chinese province of Yunnan.

Air support from bases within China was supplied by what were formerly Chennault's 'Flying Tigers' which had been incorporated into the Fourteenth United States Air Force, and which also operated from Southern China. They were also active in minimizing the indiscriminate Japanese bombing of Chinese cities and played a role in crippling coastal Japanese shipping and harrassing Japanese military positions.

Morale in China was understandably poor. The Chiang administration was corrupt and inefficient, riddled with nepotism, and wasteful. An effort to boost morale was made by Britain and America in 1943 with the signing, on January 11, of treaties abolishing the long humiliation of their extraterritoriality. The treaties also returned to China international concessions in Shanghai and Amoy, and the British concessions at Canton and Tientsin. At last, after almost a hundred years, the system of unequal treaties that had contributed so much to China's sad plight was abolished as other Western nations followed the British and American lead. America went further and repealed the law preventing Chinese immigration, permitting one hundred and five Chinese to go there every year—a small gesture but much appreciated. Only Hong Kong and Portuguese Macau were left (and still exist) as reminders of an age of Western greed unparalleled in the history of the world until the rise of Nazi Germany and its rape of Europe.

In April, 1944, Japan launched her first offensive in China since 1938, having in mind to finish off Chinese forces before they could be heavily supplied. The possibility of the re-opening of the Burma road would soon have made this practicable. Japan was also concerned with the use of China as the base for air attacks on shipping and military installations. Raids on southern Japan in June, 1944 added fuel to the fire. Finally, Japan hoped she could keep open the land routes through occupied China to Southeast Asian countries. If she could overrun all China it could be made into a huge base for Japanese offensives against all enemies—on the old and correct Chinese theory that China is a land that cannot be conquered complete.

To achieve these ends the Japanese had to advance westward and conquer the heart of central and western China. So they started moving in that direction from Kwangtung province and along railway lines from Hangkow.

They met with considerable success. By the end of 1944 they had driven Chennault's Fourteenth Air Force from its bases in southwestern China, and had firmly established a line of communication from Indo-China to Manchukuo.

The China, Burma, and India war areas in World War II

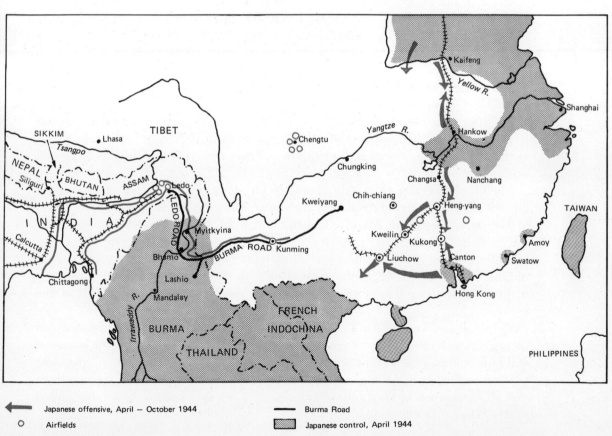

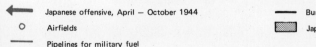

Japanese offensive, April — October 1944   Burma Road

Airfields   Japanese control, April 1944

Pipelines for military fuel

At this juncture, the fortunate coincidence of German surrender in Europe (Victory in Europe Day, May 8, 1945) released the Allied Powers from the burden of their commitments in the West and allowed concentration of men, supplies, and brains in the effort to get rid of the Japanese from the Asian continent once and for all. By August, 1945, the Japanese in China were in full and disordered retreat.

We should not forget the epic battles of Burma. In early 1944, a Japanese offensive began toward India from the Burmese frontier, its aim being to seize the airfields from which troublesome sorties were flown against them and from which supplies went over the 'hump' to Free China. The avowed goal was to free India from British colonial rule. The Indian nationalist Subas Chandra Bose with his Indian National Army (who were Japanese) assisted in this campaign. A British and Indian army finally defeated this force in the long battle of Kohima-Imphal, in the jungles of that incredibly difficult terrain in the summer of 1944. By the end of the year the Japanese were driven back to northern Burma. The special forces under General Stilwell, expert jungle fighters under such men as Wingate (the Wingate Raiders) and Merrill (Merrill's Marauders) were in action behind Japanese lines in exploits of thrilling daring and extreme danger. This episode of the War has rightly been much written about and constitutes, like some of the American assaults on the Pacific islands, one of the more heroic chapters in the story of both Allied and Japanese warfare.

By the beginning of 1945, Stilwell's Ledo Road from Assam to Burma was linked with the old Burma Road and the land route for supplies reopened. Most of Burma was in Allied hands by the end of the war.

The Diplomacy of the War with Japan

So far we have looked at the fighting and the military picture of one of the most ferocious parts of the most ferocious war in world history. Now we must take a look at the men, and the moves and countermoves they directed, that won and lost that war.

The list of conferences, meetings, and declarations tells something of the story of diplomatic moves during the course of the war, but it should be amplified in detail.

The signature of the Atlantic Charter laid a foundation on which a post-war international organization could be built into (it was hoped) an effective world body for keeping the peace between all nations. The Grand Alliance of twenty-six nations of January, 1942, demonstrated to both Allied and Axis powers that the majority of the world was united on at least one principle—their defeat of the aggressors.

Churchill and Roosevelt at Casablanca (Jan. 1943) and later at Quebec concerned themselves with the strategy of the Pacific war, aid to China, envisaging the intrusion of Russia against Japan eventually. The Moscow Conference of October in the same year, went further in calling on the Axis powers to surrender, and went one more step along the road of laying down principles for a world body. China later agreed to this Moscow Declaration.

There were problems at these meetings, for Japan and Russia were not at war, and the Soviet-Japanese Neutrality pact of 1941 prevented Chiang Kai-shek from

Conferences, Decisions, and Agreements of World War II

The Atlantic Charter, August, 1941. Drawn up by Winston Churchill and Theodore Roosevelt when they met at sea, and described by Churchill as a 'rough and ready wartime statement' of the aims of Britain and the United States. Although it did not mention Pacific problems since America was not yet at war with Japan, it was the first step toward what eventually became the United Nations.

The Grand Alliance, Washington, January 1, 1942. A meeting of twenty-six nations involved in the war with the Axis powers signed a declaration to co-ordinate war efforts and not to make a separate peace with any enemy. This was signed by Roosevelt, Churchill, Litvinov (Russia), and Soong (China).

Casablanca Conference of January, 1943. Meeting between Roosevelt and Churchill to discover the best means of carrying on the war.

Quebec Conference of August 1943. Roosevelt and Churchill discussed (among other matters) greater aid to China, and military strategy in the Pacific and Asia. The possibility of Russian participation in the war with Japan was touched on.

Moscow Conference of Foreign Ministers, October 19–30, 1943. Foreign ministers of America, Britain, and Russia signed the Moscow Pact which demanded immediate unconditional surrender of the Axis powers, and agreed on the post-war formation of a body to replace the League of Nations, and to be effective as the League had not been.

The Cairo Conference of November 22–26, 1943. Churchill and Roosevelt met Chiang Kai-shek and agreed on the eventual independence of Korea.

The Teheran Conference. This conference resulted in the Cairo Declaration of December 1, 1943. Churchill and Roosevelt met Stalin on December 2–7, 1943. Roosevelt got a promise from Stalin that the Soviet Union would declare war on Japan within three months of the defeat of Germany.

The Yalta Conference, February, 1945. Between Roosevelt, Churchill, and Stalin. Dealt with post-war Asia. (See details in the text.)

The Potsdam Conference, July 17–August 2, 1945. Britain, the United States, and Russia issued the Potsdam Declaration calling on Japan to surrender unconditionally or face 'prompt and utter destruction'.

Sino-Soviet Treaty of Friendship and Alliance, August 14, 1945. Acknowledged China's full sovereignty over Manchuria.

meeting Stalin. Britain and America had therefore had to confer separately with Stalin and with Chiang at the Cairo and Teheran Conferences. Chiang was also not present at the Yalta Conference.

The Cairo conference resulted in a Declaration:

'The Three Great Allies are fighting this war to restrain and punish the aggression of Japan.... It is their purpose that Japan shall be stripped of all the islands in the Pacific...seized or occupied since the beginning of the First World War in 1914, and that all the territories Japan has stolen from the Chinese, such as Manchuria, Formosa, and the Pescadores, shall be restored to the Republic of China. Japan will also be expelled from all other territories which she has taken by violence and greed. The aforesaid three great powers...are determined that...Korea shall become free and independent.

With these objects in view the three Allies...will continue to persevere in the serious and prolonged operations necessary to procure the unconditional surrender of Japan.'

At the Cairo Conference in 1943, Chiang Kai-shek, on the left, talks to President Roosevelt of the United States, while Winston Churchill is engaged in conversation with Chiang's wife

Japan ignored the declaration. But in it China was formally recognized as one of the Three Great Allies in the struggle against Japan, and at the following Teheran Conference China's great power status was insisted upon in the future United Nations, when eventually she took her place as one of the four great powers in the Security Council.

Russia agreed to fight Japan after Germany's fall, and in April, 1945, she refused to renew the Soviet-Japanese Neutrality Pact, facing Japan with Russian entry into the war when the pact expired in 1946. Japanese did not know of the Russian promise to act against them after Germany's fall, which formed part of the Yalta agreement. The contents of the Yalta Conference agreements as they referred to the East were:

> The *status quo* in Outer Mongolia (the Mongolian People's Republic) shall be preserved.
> The former rights of Russia violated by the treacherous attack of Japan in 1904 shall be restored, viz:
  a) The southern part of Sakhalin as well as all the islands adjacent to it shall be returned to the Soviet Union.
  b) The commercial port of Dairen shall be internationalized, the pre-eminent interests of the Soviet Union in this port being safeguarded and the lease of Port Arthur as a naval base of the U.S.S.R. being restored.
  c) The Chinese Eastern Railroad which provides an outlet to Dairen shall be jointly operated by the establishment of a joint Soviet-Chinese company, it being understood that the pre-eminent interests of the Soviet Union shall be safeguarded and that China will retain full sovereignty in Manchuria.

> The Kuril Islands shall be handed over to the Soviet Union.
> ...For its part the Soviet Union expresses its readiness to conclude with the National Government of China a pact of friendship and alliance between the U.S.S.R. and China in order to render assistance to China with its armed forces for the purpose of liberating China from the Japanese yoke.

Japan, 1941–1945: The Internal Situation

The preceding sections have told the story of what Japan's military machine did in World War II, and what was done by the Allies both in battle and in the conference rooms to counter Japanese aggression. Before looking at Japan as the war ended in her utter defeat, it is necessary to look first at what happened inside Japan during the war, and also at what happened in China during the same period. In this way we shall more easily be able to understand the meaning of defeat to Japan and of victory to China and her allies, and liberation to the victims of Japanese aggression round East and Southeast Asia.

Japan

The premier, Tojo Hideki at the war's commencement, remained throughout until 1944 in a strong position. He was a general on active duty and acted as his own minister of the armed forces, thus being in a position to oversee both civil and military matters. In 1944 he even took on another job, Chief of the General Staff co-ordinating command and administration in the army. The election of 1942 had secured his position with a pro-Tojo Diet. Yet Tojo was not a Hitler, a Mussolini, or a Franco. His position was not that of a dictator but of the first among a number of generals and admirals who were the ruling élite of Japan in wartime. Tojo was responsible to the emperor, and since the emperor was surrounded by the *juishin* (elder statesmen), to them too. The *juishin* were such former premiers as Konoe, the president on the Privy Council, and others.

General Tojo Hideki who led Japan into war. He always accepted full responsibility for this, but he insisted after the war was over that he was never informed of plans to attack Pearl Harbour. The navy had prepared and carried out its own plan of battle without consulting the army, even when its chief happened also to be prime minister

Japan's initial strategy was to wait until the United States tired of war, and to negotiate a peace. But from 1943, when the war was apparently turning against Japan, imperial advisers such as the *juishin* favoured immediate negotiations before Japan lost all she had gained. But such was the acute militaristic atmosphere in Japan in wartime that their discussions and conclusions were not revealed. There was a very real fear of assassination from military fanatics.

In economic matters the military wanted to take complete control of the *zaibatsu*, but this was fiercely resisted. And although some control was instituted, it was not until the *zaibatsu* themselves agreed to national control that this came in January, 1944, under a minister of munitions.

Food shortages, rationing of textiles and basic necessities, all these were borne stoically by the Japanese as long as they were still convinced Japan was winning the war. The media spoke only of victories. But when Japan was increasingly bombed, its homes and industries ruined, the truth dawned on the people and resentment set in.

It was the fall of Saipan in July, 1944, which caused the fall of Tojo. General Koiso was appointed. His cabinet lasted from July to March of the following year, 1945, when it fell with the fall of Okinawa. This brought to power a retired admiral and former premier, Suzuki Kantaro. He had Togo Shigenori as his foreign minister, a man who favoured a quick peace. But in the face of Allied demands for unconditional surrender, and the uncertain fate of the emperor, neither he nor anyone else could accept peace.

The first atomic bomb used in war explodes at Hiroshima on August 6, 1945

The July declaration of Potsdam offered Japan unconditional surrender or 'utter destruction'. The implication behind the statement (although Japanese did not know it) was the atom bomb. Japanese continued to 'press forward resolutely'. The United States, faced with an invasion of Japan that would certainly have cost her huge casualties, decided to use the bomb, and the decision was almost uncontested among the Allies.

Hiroshima was obliterated by one bomb on August 6, 1945. Russia declared war on Japan two days later. And on August 9, the second bomb destroyed Nagasaki.

The Japanese military were not moved by the bombs. It was the emperor in an Imperial Conference who commanded those advising surrender to do so. The one condition was that 'sovereign rule' should continue. The Allies rejected this. At a further Imperial Conference on August 14, opinion was split. The emperor, saying that 'the unendurable must be endured', gave his assent.

August 17 saw the formation of a cabinet under Prince Higashikuni to represent Japan at the surrender. General Douglas MacArthur and his troops moved into Tokyo and the signature of the Instrument of Surrender took place aboard the U.S.S. Missouri in Tokyo Bay on September 2, 1945.

Japanese surrender being signed aboard U.S.S. Missouri on September 2, 1945

China, Wartime Internal Situation

Occupied China consisted of a broad swathe of land stretching from Manchuria right down the coast to Indo-China and as far west as Hankow on the Yangtze. The capital at Nanking was the seat of a Japanese puppet government headed by Wang Ching-wei. About 200 million Chinese were under his 'rule'. Trade between occupied China and Japan was brisk, and much to China's detriment.

Wang declared war on Britain and the United States on January 9, 1943, during a visit to Tokyo, and in return the Japanese granted favours to the puppet state, returning her own concessions in Hankow, Shashih, Soochow, Hangchow, and Tientsin, besides her rights in the Shanghai International Settlement. Vichy France did likewise, surrendering her privileges in Shanghai, Hankow, and Canton. Italy renounced its place in Tientsin.

Britain and the United States had agreed with Chiang to return all that they had in China.

Japanese surrender of territories and extraterritorial rights in occupied China was an empty fiction. Her control of all the industrial and other Japanese undertakings continued as before. Such companies as the Central China Promotion Company and the North China Development Company, which were monopolistic and controlled the basic economic activity of occupied China, were still run by the Japanese—but in theory they now belonged to China. The Tokyo-Nanking treaty of alliance signed on October 30, 1943, pledged China to work with Japan toward the aims of the Greater East Asia Co-Prosperity Sphere.

Government was only nominally in Chinese hands, and when the fact that Japan was losing the war became evident in occupied China, that government disintegrated. Wang died in 1944 and was succeeded by another figurehead, Chen Kung-po who, with other leading collaborators, was later executed as a traitor by the Nationalists.

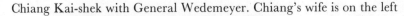

Chiang Kai-shek with General Wedemeyer. Chiang's wife is on the left

In the part of China not occupied by Japan there were several factors simultaneously at work. The failure of the Nationalist government to develop industrialization or to increase agricultural production; the inadequacy of its economic policy and planning leading to colossal inflation; unchecked corruption at all levels leading to low army and civilian morale (added to which was the Honan famine of 1942–1943 in which about 3 million people died); the brutality of the Nationalist army toward the civilian populace; the persistence of Chiang in letting his allies do all the fighting whenever possible.

This list of what was wrong with Free China during the war may seem in retrospect a harsh indictment of the Nationalists. But there are plenty of reliable first-hand sources that bear out every particular.

'I never heard Chiang Kai-shek say a single thing that indicated gratitude to the President or to our country for the help we were extending to him.... Invariably, he would complain about the small amount of material that was being furnished. He would make comparisons between the huge amounts of Lend-Lease supplies going to Great Britain and Russia with the meagre trickle going to China. He would complain that the Chinese had been fighting for six or seven years and yet we gave them practically nothing. It would of course have been undiplomatic to go into the nature of the military effort Chiang Kai-shek had made since 1938. It was practically zero....

'I have faith in Chinese soldiers and Chinese people: fundamentally great, democratic, misgoverned. No bars of caste or religion.... Honest, frugal, industrious, cheerful, independent, tolerant, friendly, courteous.

I judge the Kuomintang and the Kungchantang [Communist Party] by what I saw: [Kuomintang] Corruption, neglect, chaos.... Hoarding, black market, trading with the enemy.

Communist programme...reduce taxes, rents, interest. Raise production, and standard of living. Participate in government, practise what they preach.'

General Stilwell: *The Stilwell Papers*. 1948

General Albert C. Wedemeyer, Stilwell's successor in 1944, wrote:

'I have received many reports that the conscription of men for military purposes is not being carried on honestly or efficiently...as in taxation, the peasants are expected to bear the brunt of conscription, although in the cities there are thousands of able-bodied men, who should...be eligible for military service. Rich men's sons by the payment of money avoid conscription...and are being sent to school abroad instead of remaining here to help their country in time of great crisis.'

The General's harsh words are borne out by many others who worked with the Nationalists in wartime Free China. Chiang's own book *China's Destiny*, gives a picture of what sort of a man he was and what sort of ideas inspired him. It was published in 1943 as an answer to Mao Tse-tung's *On the New Democracy* (published in 1940). Its aim was to win support for the KMT. Although most of the book was written by secretaries, the ideas and the final approval were Chiang's. He put the blame for China's plight on Western imperialism, and his plan for reconstruction of China really embodied basically the old Confucian ideas that had been exploded and discarded years before. He tried to revive the essence of the New Life Movement which was based on the same theories, and which had also failed. It was all extremely reminiscent of nineteenth century scholarly reform, and as such so completely out of gear with the times that it had no effect at all in China. Abroad, where ignorance of conditions in China prevailed and Chiang was thought of as a popular hero, it was highly commended.

Nationalist influence in China weakened, while that of the Communists increased. In the countryside they had much broader support than the KMT, and managed from the very beginning of the war in the Pacific to get into Japanese-occupied areas of China where they established numerous bases. By the end of the Pacific war, the Communists probably controlled by far the larger part of the Japanese-occupied territories in China, at least between Manchukuo and the lower Yangtze.

In 1941, Mao Tse-tung made a key speech on the subject of fighting the Japanese, a speech that contains much else of importance as well:

'China's heroic war of resistance has already continued for more than four years... under the leadership of Generalissimo Chiang Kai-shek, and is supported by the co-operation of the Kuomintang and the Chinese Communist Party, and the co-operation of all classes, all parties, and all nationalities.... Only when the Three People's Principles [a reference to Sun Yat-sen's theories] are put into operation can victory be attained.'

He asks: why the Three People's Principles and not Communism?

'In present-day China conditions still do not exist for its implementation.... Nothing has been established and no practical problem solved that goes beyond the Three People's Principles.'

And he goes on to stress that the class struggle must be subordinated to the task of winning the war against Japan. He sees Communist theory as a logical extension of Sun Yat-sen's Three People's Principles.

A year before this, Mao's book *On the New Democracy* had appeared, mapping out the political, social, and economic plans of the CCP. In the book the essential nature of the leadership of the Chinese revolution was stated. That leadership must be a combination of peasants and workers but must also involve the participation of other classes—the intellectuals and the capitalists. So his speech in 1941 was a reaffirmation of this doctrine of forming a democratic state with joint dictatorship of all revolutionary elements.

The mechanism consisted of regional congresses, and smaller groups in definite areas and in villages, which were elected. Their membership was to be one-third CCP members, one-third non-Party members from the political left, and one-third centrists. These bodies contained a high proportion of students who in turn aroused the enthusiasm of their fellows. The sole area in which the CCP would not permit sharing of power was the army, whose officers were almost all CCP members.

This formed the political section of the programme. The economic part envisaged nationalization of banks and industries, while the land programme was to return the land to the peasant who tilled it. This was a policy difficult to carry out with the zeal of earlier times since in taking land from the landowners this class was alienated. For the time being the CCP could not afford to alienate anyone who could possibly be drawn into the fold. Private enterprise was allowed, although co-operative efforts were favoured. The main thing was to increase all types of food production. The playing down of the ultimate aims of Communism—class levelling, the extinction of capitalism, the dictatorship of the workers—was kept at very low key.

Mao's book had a far greater influence on literate China (still not a very large segment of a largely illiterate community, but an influential one) than did Chiang's *China's Destiny*. But even more influential in the end, was probably the trust the Communists showed in the peasants by arming them. Such was the confidence the Party had in the loyalty of the peasants, and the admiration peasants had for the Communist armies, that a national people's struggle became a reality. The KMT never succeeded in this. Communist policies in the country began to show the peasantry in a small way how order, reason, equality, unheard-of opportunities for help in distress, in sickness, and in gaining what, to all Chinese, has always been a yearning—education—could become realities. The response was vivid.

To paint such a picture (and it has been painted by responsible observers such as Edgar Snow) is not to say there was no harshness to be discovered in these communist-controlled areas. Mao once said:

'A revolution is not a dinner party, or writing an essay, or painting a picture, or doing embroidery. It cannot be so refined, so leisurely and gentle, so temperate, kind, courteous, restrained and magnanimous. A revolution is an insurrection, an act of violence by which one class overthrows another.'

Left, Mao Tse-tung making a speech in 1943. Right, in China, the tradition of woodcuts was used in war-time for propaganda. The title of this one is: 'Support our common people's own army'. The upper part shows peasants bringing in flocks for food, and other animals for transport, and welcoming soldiers with music and a banner. They stand guard (lower down, right), assist the wounded and send off new recruits with warmth. Below, an army building is the centre of attention and service

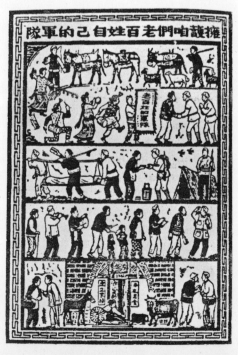

It is reckoned that the CCP in 1945 was active in 250,000 square miles of China—its communications by foot, by animal, and by radio. From a membership of 40,000 in 1937, it now had 1,200,000 members who were mainly from student and peasant background. Party schools in Yenan, in that strange stronghold in the arm of the Yellow River, living and working as the peasants of that *löess* land had done since the prehistory of China—party schools processed thousands of students. As numbers grew the *cheng-feng* movement (correcting unorthodox tendencies) was started, and thoughts, personal relationships (both in and out of the Party), speech, and written material came under review. Long self-criticism sessions and public repentances became normal procedure. The jargon used is inclined to be baffling (subjectivism, sectarianism, formalism, for example). But the effort was to re-educate and discipline new members and adherents, so that they got rid of their old way of thinking tied to the old Confucian morality.

In Yenan the Russian-orientated groups finally lost out to Mao and the realists who said that Communism in China must be brought about in conformity with the realities of China's past and present—not by rigid adherence to Russian dogma. This became the basis of what came to be called Maoism. The achievement of Maoism was to demonstrate that a Leninist party must in China be built on a peasant base, and that (quite contrary to its own theoretical statements) the CCP was independent of the urban proletariat. Mao once said:

> 'After Chiang Kai-shek's *coup* in Shanghai, we scattered. As you know, I decided to go back to my village. Two miles outside it there were trees without a scrap of bark left on them up to a height of twelve feet: starving people had eaten it. We could make better fighters out of men who were forced to eat bark than out of the stokers of Shanghai or even the coolies. . . .
> 'And there is no such thing as abstract Marxism, but only concrete Marxism, adapted to the concrete realities of China. . . . Revolution is a drama of passion; we did not win the people over by appealing to reason but by developing hope, trust and fraternity. In the face of famine, the will to equality takes on a religious force.'
> Quoted by André Malraux: *Antimémoires*

At the end of the war the Communists had nearly a million regular troops and over two million militia.

Wartime saw the continued avowals of both KMT and CCP that they would stick together and seek political and not military solutions to their differences. In 1943, a crisis brought a conference in which the CCP demanded a bigger Red Army and legal recognition. This was refused by Chiang. The following year, in May, 1944, the Communists demanded a coalition government. This was also refused.

The mediation of United States Vice-President Wallace, who offered American help in composing CCP-KMT differences, ended by Chiang's accepting the American offer to act as go-between for Chiang and the Soviet Union. Chiang hoped in this way to prevent any Soviet assistance to the Communists after the war. Mediation continued in August, 1944, with General Hurley as President Roosevelt's emissary. He arrived in China via Moscow where he was told by the Russian Foreign Minister Molotov that they regarded Chinese Communists as mere 'agrarian reformers'.

Hurley arrived in Yenan in November, 1944, to see Mao, who again demanded a coalition government and legal recognition of the CCP. He also wanted CCP representation on the United Nations Military Council, civil and political liberties throughout China, and unification of all armies in China under all-party command.

Chiang refused a coalition, and would have liked all the armies integrated with his own forces; and deadlock ensued. It continued to the end of the war against Japan.

Reasons for Japanese Defeat in World War II

In August, 1945, the spectacle of Japan was a sorry one. The Japanese were physically on their last legs. There was little food, and a sort of numbness from the shattering blow to their pride overtook them. The cities were destroyed in large part by bombing, Hiroshima and Nagasaki had been obliterated by a new and deadly type of weapon that was hardly understood by the people at large, except that its effects were terrible in terms of physical ruin and human disease. Industry was destroyed by bombs and fires, railways were torn up and falling to pieces.

Probably worst of all for the average Japanese was that he had had an intense national pride instilled in him or her from childhood. In this form of education there was no precedent for a military defeat. It had never happened before. When the

Central Tokyo at the time of the Japanese surrender. Bombing and fires had destroyed large segments of the city. Tokyo had yet another chance to rebuild

emperor's speech of surrender was broadcast, people in Japan were training with wooden spears for what they felt was the inevitable do-or-die 'battle of Japan' which they, the civilians, would fight against the invaders.

Their defeat was the result of many misjudgements by their leaders. The first misjudgement was a fundamental one—Japanese opinion that America and Britain were so fully occupied in the West that they had no energy to spare to combat Japan. Allied to this was the opinion that after Pearl Harbour America would not have the fighting spirit for war in the Pacific, and that her war industry could not expand rapidly enough to make such a war possible, and therefore that the United States would negotiate for peace.

Naval and army rivalry within Japan caused a fatal lack of co-ordinated policies (the Navy wanted to fortify and make impregnable the Pacific island conquests, while the army wanted to invade the rich field of India). This rivalry was even more disastrous tactically when the one service did not support the other in actual combat, as happened now and again.

The situation we have already examined in wartime Japan whereby civil government was really taken over by the military did not lead to mature policies. There was deep distrust between Japan and Germany (over their respective claims to racial superiority) and consultation between them was slight and poor.

When the Allied island-hopping counter-offensive began, the Japanese high command seems to have been unable to alter its strategy to cope with an enemy strategy they had not envisaged as possible. They had no contingency plans for this, and when the Allies destroyed their shipping and naval support, Japan was virtually severed from its sources of supply in the conquered lands of Southeast Asia. This at once lowered the possible output of military and other materials. And the heavy aerial bombing very rapidly diminished factory output even further.

Japanese troops had, for years before the outbreak of World War II, been tied down in huge numbers in China, and even more were then committed to occupied lands during the war. These troops never gained the confidence of the local people, and the economies of all the conquered lands ran down to near zero as a result of Japanese depredations and the totally unco-operative attitude of the people. Not even the beginnings of the much-advertised Co-Prosperity Sphere ever came into being. The Japanese lived in their conquered lands as military parasites surrounded by an atmosphere of active hostility caused in large part by their own brutality to the people.

20 Japan: from Occupation to Economic Upsurge, 1945–1952

J APAN, as we have seen, emerged from the war that she had made in Asia, in defeat, in chaos, in despair. The authoritarian quality of much history in Japan—both under the shogunate and the Meiji constitution—was such that the people as a whole expected a harsh authoritarian occupation by the Americans as agents of the Allied Powers. The sense of submission that had always been fundamental and extremely strong in all Japanese social systems now led the population to anticipate that the victors, as they took their spoils of victory, would treat Japan in the manner their own armies had treated the peoples they had conquered. It was therefore a tremendous surprise, and a great relief to them when the Japanese discovered not retribution but a constructive if severe approach to the occupation of their country.

The majority of the Occupation forces in Japan were American, although token forces from other countries were also present. But the operation was, theoretically at least, internationally directed by a thirteen-nation Far Eastern Commission sitting in Washington, advised by the four-power Allied Council in Tokyo. The title of Supreme Commander for the Allied Powers, shortened to SCAP, was given to General MacArthur.

The twelve-page document, Initial Post-Surrender Policies sent to SCAP by the joint Chiefs of Staff, formed the basis for future policies very largely designed by General MacArthur himself and was wholly carried out in Japan by his staff of American and some British troops.

Premiers of Japan, 1945–1954	
Prince Higashikune	August—October, 1945
Shidehara Kijuro	October, 1945—April, 1946
Yoshida Shigeru	May, 1946—May, 1947
Katayama Tetsu	June, 1947—February, 1948
Ashida Hitoshi	February—October, 1948
Yoshida Shigeru	October, 1948—December, 1954

The Initial Post-Surrender Policy for Japan, of August 29, 1945, contained the following major points:

> To ensure that Japan will not again become a menace to the United States or to the peace and security of the world.

> To bring about the eventual establishment of a peaceful and responsible government which will respect the rights of other states and will support the

objectives of the United States as reflected in the ideas and principles of the Charter of the United Nations. The United States desires that this government should conform as closely as may be to principles of democratic self-government, but it is not the responsibility of the Allied Powers to impose upon Japan any form of government not supported by the freely expressed will of the people. . . .

The Occupation, in spite of its internationally composed Far Eastern Commission, and in spite of the American, Russian, Chinese, and British Allied Council in Tokyo, was really an American affair. America decided what had to be done in basic terms, and its decisions were 'approved' by the Far East Commission. MacArthur's staff were mostly American. The general himself was a man of strong personality with very definite views on the Occupation and what its aims ought to be. He was virtual ruler of Japan.

Unlike the occupation of Germany, the Occupation in Japan was not direct rule. The decisions of the Occupation authorities were passed on to the Japanese government who then carried them out. SCAP headquarters contained several sections roughly paralleled by ministries in the Japanese government to which they communicated policies, at first via a Liaison Office staffed by Japanese foreign ministry personnel, later directly. This was criticized on the grounds that the same bureaucracy that had so slavishly agreed to carry out the policies of the Japanese militarists was now carrying out those of SCAP. But in fact the influence of the military decreased rapidly. By now, all Japan knew only too well what a brutal and moreover totally unsuccessful job of ruling Japan and conducting the war, the military had made.

General MacArthur photographed with the Emperor on September 27, 1945. MacArthur was a brilliant but easily angered man with a capacity for long hours of hard work. He never toured conquered Japan during the six years that he virtually ruled it. He lived in the American embassy in Tokyo, commuting each day to his office opposite the palace moat. His vanity caused stories to be told of him. One of these said that if you got up very early in the morning you might just be lucky enough to see General MacArthur walking on the waters of the palace moat. The allusion was to Christ, and reflected the god-like attitude of the general

Demilitarization

The first phase of the Occupation consisted in the abolition of the Japanese military apparatus and the enactment of democratic reforms imposed by SCAP. This must be the only example of democracy imposed by a conqueror which in the end proved more or less successful. All Japanese outside Japan were brought back, all military organizations were disbanded, and all ultra-nationalist or para-military groups also dissolved. The Shinto cult was declared no longer the official religion. The ministry responsible for police and local government was put out of action. Police power was cut, and the police were deprived of any authority to regulate free speech. Factories engaged in armament manufacture were dismantled. War crimes trials punished those responsible for wartime atrocities—seven of the war-time leaders including Tojo were hanged in December, 1948, and most of the rest were given long prison sentences. Curiously enough, the Japanese populace took little interest in these trials—for them the war was over and a new phase of life had begun.

The other aspect of getting rid of undesirable persons was the purge of 200,000 people 'to cleanse the government of elements which by their acts or associations participated in Japanese expansion'. This, broadly, led to the disappearance from office of the 'old guard' and its replacement by men who were not very different in outlook but were younger and more malleable, more liable to bend to the new democratic forms.

The crucial act of the early Occupation was the proclamation of a new constitution in 1947. Whereas the old Meiji constitution had stated firmly that whatever rights the Japanese enjoyed under it were a gift from a line of imperial rulers, the new constitution began:

'We, the Japanese people, acting through our duly elected representatives in the National Diet, determined that we shall secure for ourselves and our posterity the fruits of peaceful co-operation with all nations and the blessings of liberty throughout this land, and resolved that never again shall we be visited with the horrors of war through the action of government, do proclaim that sovereign power resides with the people and do firmly establish this Constitution.'

A decisive change had taken place. The formerly divine emperor was stripped of all 'powers relating to government', and became 'a symbol of the state and of the unity of the people, deriving his position from the will of the people with whom resides sovereign power.' What this *might* mean is uncertain, but what it certainly did mean was that imperial rule was at an end.

The major alterations in the new constitution were:

> The abolition of pre-war élites—armed services, Privy Council, and other officials close to the emperor—and those not abolished were to be strictly under cabinet control. The relationship between cabinet and Diet was to be a relaionship on the British pattern, the cabinet being a top committee of the ruling party in the Diet.

> Both upper and lower Diet Houses became fully elective by an electorate

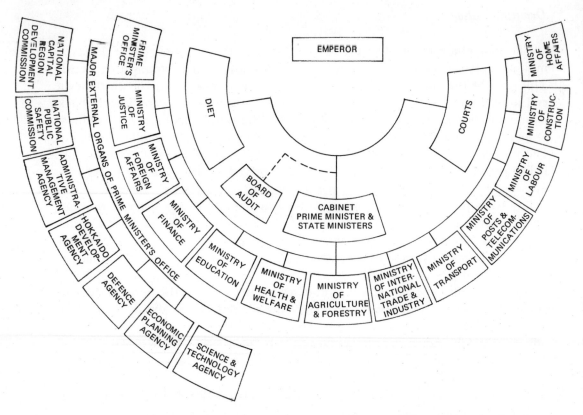

The structure of political power and governmental responsibility under the Japanese constitution of 1947

composed of all men and women over 20 years of age. The House of Representatives was to be chosen by the 118 electoral districts which would elect its 467 members. The House of Councillors (the upper House) was to be chosen partly by the electorate at large and partly by the prefectures. The judiciary was made independent, the Supreme Court having the power to rule on the constitutionality of Diet legislation. The higher local government offices were made elective. Human rights were guaranteed—classic Western eighteenth century rights such as life, liberty, equality, the pursuit of happiness—a curiously un-Japanese mixture. But also 'the right to maintain the minimum standards of wholesome and cultural living' (whatever these may be construed to be in Japan), 'academic freedom', and the right of workers to bargain collectively.

The new constitution thus attempted to bury the pre-war cult of the emperor as the divine head of the great Japanese family whose morality derived from the obligations of the people to the emperor and divinely given state rule. The new generation of Japanese view the emperor as something more approaching a celebrity.

Japanese acceptance of American supervision through SCAP was in many ways remarkably willing—perhaps a result of their long history of submission to authority. Demilitarization was fairly rapidly performed, and the trial and conviction of war criminals also. The scrapping of the 200,000 officials, and their replacement, took a little longer, and the programme of democratic reform including the new constitution (described by a Japanese journalist as 'by Japanese literary standards... quaintly and exotically American') took time also, and the land reforms even longer.

Land and Economic Reform

At the war's end, forty-six percent of Japan's cultivated land was tilled by peasants who paid seventy-five percent of their rent in kind. They were socially and economically subjects of their landlords, and therefore tended also to be politically aligned with the landlords. This block was a semi-feudal factor. SCAP pushed through legislation dispossessing absentee landlords by government purchase of their lands, and purchasing all other land except for ten acres to each family. The percentage of tenants had dropped from sixty-four to ten at the end of the reform, and there were almost no payments of rent in kind. There emerged a pattern of small independent farmers who were the base for social, political, and other changes in the country.

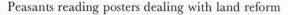

Peasants reading posters dealing with land reform

On the economic front, reform was aimed first at eliminating the vast *zaibatsu* whose internal organization had had a big hand in the rise of militarism in pre-war Japan. In the first reforms, 83 *zaibatsu* holding-companies were dissolved and the assets of the owning families frozen. Then, by a capital levy, most of this capital was removed from them altogether. Anti-monopoly laws prevented the re-forming of combines, and inheritance tax and other forms of income tax aided this same process.

It was unfortunate that at this time, late 1947 and onward, deterioration in American-Russian relations, and the situation in China, tended to turn the policies of the Occupation away from total reform toward rapid reconstruction. The end result of this may be seen today when, in a somewhat different form, what are essentially *zaibatsu* organizations have once again become the core of Japanese industry. However, the links of these combines are these days generally through the big banks in Japan—the banks being extremely powerful. And there are many examples of non-*zaibatsu*-type companies also.

'*Zaibatsu*-busting', as it was popularly called in SCAP, was accompanied by alteration in labour laws. The Trade Union Law of 1945 gave workers strike, bargaining, and organization rights. A further Labour Relations Adjustment Law (1946) and a Labour Standards Law (1947) encouraged the rise of unions, which stood at 6.5 million members in 1949 and nearly 9 millions in 1962. Expressed as a proportion of the total labour force, Japanese membership is a little less than that in Great Britain, and a little more than in the United States.

The unions tended toward leftish policies, and the Occupation (being essentially conservative by nature) forbade a railway strike in 1947, taking the view that wage increase had to await production increase. The crackdown on the Left in unions continued in tougher labour laws passed in 1949 and in the 'red purge' of the Communist leaders in 1950—all of this reflecting American opinion on, and American fears of Communism. Japanese unions, not unnaturally, have ever since been deeply suspicious of American interest in and policies toward their country.

Democratization

In the Imperial Rescript of January 1, 1946, when the emperor renounced (or denied, if it may be put that way—after all, not many people have had to do this, so the terms are ambiguous) his 'divinity', he was also at pains to tell the Japanese that they were not superior to other peoples. (The Germans had to learn the same unpalatable fact.)

SCAP encouraged the emerging new political parties in an effort to attain a true party government on the national level. In the first post-war election in April, 1946, there were four parties:

> The Liberal Party (which won) composed of conservative politicians who had escaped involvement in the purge of the 200,000.
> The Democratic Party (of the same approximate composition).
> The Social Democratic Party (moderates and socialists).
> The Communist Party.

Right, the leader of the Liberal Party, Yoshida Shigeru, who became first premier after the end of the occupation

Below, women were permitted to vote after the war. Here they are voting to elect the Mayor of Tokyo, in April, 1946

The Liberal leader was Yoshida Shigeru (born 1878) who had been a diplomat and now ruled with great strength—so much so that he has been accused of 'one-man government'. His first term lasted from May, 1946, to May, 1947: but he was to be premier again from October, 1948 to the end of 1954. Since his time, no Japanese premier has been able to put together so strong a faction, and later ministers have had in general to form coalitions. When the new constitution came into effect it was his successor, Katayama Tetsu (also born in 1878), who held office, and was the first Christian and the first socialist premier of Japan.

The new constitution came into effect on May 3, 1947. The bureaucracy and its functions and the interrelations of the departments can best be seen in diagrammatic form (see p. 322), and we may compare the new form of bureaucratic relations and institutions with that of the Meiji era (see p. 141).

Educational Reform

Education of one kind and another is of course at the root of what people think about everything—from their grandmothers to their political parties and their gods. Reform in Japan was crucial, since previous education had permitted the opinion of the Japanese as a whole to allow military men to make one of history's most terrible wars.

Various means were employed to eradicate past attitudes to education and to bring it more into line with educational methods and educational ideas and ideals prevailing in the United States. (Had the Occupation been by British personnel we would doubtless see British-style education in Japan today.) The portraits of the emperor that used to hang in every classroom were removed. The very narrow channels of pre-war days in education, each one of which, once chosen, led to vocational training, to technical schooling, or to university, were altered. The student who, pre-war, once embarked on his course had found it almost impossible to change direction, could now do so. Completing the work in any school meant that the next part of a pupil's education could be started in any other.

Compulsory education was lengthened from six to nine years (three years in secondary school), and great efforts were made to end learning by memorizing facts, and to promote learning that made the pupils think for themselves. A university was set up in each prefecture, but in early years of the Occupation there was an acute shortage of qualified teachers who had no stigma of nationalism from former days. The standards were therefore fairly low in educational terms.

Textbooks that had any nationalistic leanings were likewise replaced. Students were encouraged to question statements and to become independent in their thinking. All of this was to the good.

What the SCAP authorities did not foresee was that real freedom of thought for students leads to leftish tendencies in most young people—not just in Japan but in other countries also. And in fact the whole process in Japan of democratization took political thought toward the left. The SCAP-directed Japanese government action against Communism and left-wing organizations, and the Trade Unions Act of 1949 placing restrictions on workers' political activities, were some of the reactions.

Reparations and their Repercussions

The first feeling among the Allies was that Japan should pay for the damage she had caused by her aggression. But Japan's industries had been largely dismantled because many of them contributed to war potential. The aim of SCAP was to make the country economically viable in the shortest possible time (among other matters), but this aim was in contradiction with the policy of destroying war potential. After about 1948 there was a shift in SCAP policy in favour of economic reconstruction.

Problems of deciding how much each of the Allies should get delayed the reparations question. The American government decided in 1947 to make thirty percent of Japan's surplus industrial and other plants available for reparations. 'Surplus' meant material usable for military purposes. But this led to another anomaly. The United States was sending huge quantities of aid to Japan while at the same time removing from Japan in industrial reparations a large quantity of material that could bolster the Japanese economy if used there. America abandoned its reparations claims, and in 1949 stopped removals for reparations although other allies did not agree. In fact only one fifteenth of the material planned to be shipped out actually left Japan.

Territorially, China regained Taiwan, Manchuria, and the Pescadores Islands. The United States occupied the formerly Mandated Islands and the Ryukyu and Bonin Islands, while Russia took over South Sakhalin and the Kuril Islands.

The Occupation Ends

The United States was of the opinion that by the end of 1947 the Occupation had completed the major role assigned to it. By the terms of the Potsdam Declaration, Allied forces should then be withdrawn, the objectives having been achieved. Even General MacArthur, who was more powerful than any shogun or emperor had ever been, thought the Occupation should not be longer than three years. An independent Japan, started off on what seemed to the Western world a more or less suitable democratic course, would be a greater asset to the world than one perpetually in the tutelage stage and unable to stretch its wings freely. The Soviet Union, however, was against an early end to the Occupation, and it dragged on for several years.

When the 'cold war' between the West and the Soviet bloc began in 1947, American attitudes to the Occupation changed. And by the time in mid-1948 when it was clear that Communist forces in China were on the winning side, Japan seemed to the United States a land in a different and more important position. 'The foe of 1945 became the friend of 1948', as the American historian Reischauer succinctly puts the matter. American Occupation turned from radical reform to rapid reconstruction—a process only accelerated by the outbreak of the Korean war in 1950. Japan was made into a base for American fighting units on their way there and back, and into a factory and workshop for their machines.

General MacArthur commanded American forces in Korea, as well as heading the Occupation in Japan until he was dismissed by President Truman over differences of policy in April 1951. He was replaced in SCAP by General Matthew Ridgeway who was in command during the final stage of Occupation.

In 1951 the United States and Great Britain asked all those nations who had taken part in the war with Japan (but not Communist or Nationalist China) to the San Francisco Peace Conference. Forty-seven nations signed the treaty which had been largely drafted before the Conference began, but not before great troubles had been overcome.

Copies of a draft treaty were sent to India, Burma, and Yugoslavia, as they were to all participating countries. But these three refused to attend. The opposition of New Zealand and Australia was only overcome after the United States signed with them a mutual security pact (called the ANZUS Pact) on September 1, 1951. And similar opposition from the Philippines was overcome in a similar way—a mutual defence pact with the United States signed on August 30, 1951.

The final treaty was the result of the work of the fifty-one nations attending the conference, but was signed by forty-eight only. The abstainers were Russia, Poland, and Czechoslovakia. India signed a separate treaty with Japan shortly afterward, and so did the Nationalist Chinese Taiwan government. Diplomatic relations with Russia came only in 1956.

The San Francisco Treaty of September 8, 1951 ended the war with Japan, which accepted and agreed to the following articles:

> Her intention to apply for membership of the United Nations, and a promise of conformity to its Charter. (She became a member in 1956.)
> Recognition of the independence of Korea.
> United States trusteeship of the former Mandated Islands, and of the Ryukyu, Bonin, and Volcano Islands.
> To settle disputes with other nations peacefully and not to use force or threat of force against others for any reason.
> To pay reparations within her limited powers to the Allies.
> To renounce all her rights and former interests in China.
> To renounce all rights to the Kurils, South Sakhalin, Taiwan, the Pescadores, Spratly, and Paracel Islands.

Japan recovered full sovereignty over her own home islands.

The Americans signed with Japan on the same day as the San Francisco Treaty a bilateral security pact giving the United States the right to maintain its forces in Japan indefinitely, and guaranteeing Japan's security from foreign invasion. American forces staying on in Japan were then regarded as security forces. In February 1952, an Administrative Agreement was signed between America and Japan laying down the conditions under which Americans and their dependants might remain in Japan.

According to the 1947 constitution, Japan pledged in Article 9 to 'forever renounce war as a sovereign right of the nation', and never to maintain 'land, sea, and air forces', or other 'war potential'. But by 1950 a 'National Police Reserve' of 75,000 men was established, sea and air forces were added, and by the 1960s Japan possessed a 'National Defence Force' of 200,000 men equipped with more than 1,000 planes, with tanks, destroyers, and artillery.

Above, the prime minister of Japan, Yoshida Shigeru, signing the Treaty of Peace at San Francisco on September 8, 1951

Below, Japan's iron and steel industry has grown since the war to the position of third biggest in the world

Above, the ship building industry in Japan, and also its fleet of merchant ships, are among the world's largest

Below, scene in heavy industry—the huge end of part of a 100,000 kw turbine

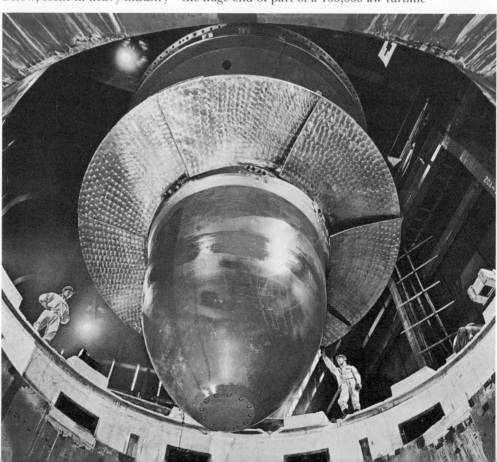

Japan's leading chemical fertilizer manufacturer, the Toyo Koatsu plant at Osaka

Japanese economic recovery began with the four billion US dollars procurement for material for the Korean war placed in Japan by America. The Korean war boom in Japan was followed by the recession of 1953–1954, and by another boom in 1955–1957. By the 1960s Japan, partly by good fortune, partly due to the processes of the Occupation, and very largely by her own skills and dedication to hard work and intelligent development, had recovered a pre-eminent position in commercial Asia. Whether she has succeeded in allaying the suspicions of Asian countries is another matter. The ominous words 'economic imperialism' are heard in the 1970s with increasing frequency in relation to Japanese trade in East and Southeast Asia.

21 China: Civil War and Revolution, 1945–1949

THE deterioration of Nationalist-Communist relations during the second half of World War II, and the fact that by the end of that war much territory nominally occupied by the Japanese and ruled by puppets such as the turncoat Wang Ching-wei, was actually administered by the Communists—these were potent factors in what happened after the Japanese defeat.

China came out of World War II with a position (more theoretical than real at that time) as one of the big four powers. But in fact China was a country ravaged by wars, deeply divided about who should control her destinies. General MacArthur's orders on the Japanese surrender in China typify that dilemma. He ordained that all Japanese forces in China should surrender to Chiang Kai-shek, with the sole exception of those in Manchuria. Yet in fact large areas of Japanese-occupied China were controlled by the Communists.

For the Nationalists, Japanese defeat came much sooner than they imagined it would. But the Chinese Communists, anticipating the defeat when Russia entered the war against Japan, were much better prepared. They were also better placed, as we have seen, existing in strength inside formerly Japanese-occupied areas.

The Japanese Commander-in-Chief in China, Okamura Yasuji, surrendered, as ordered, to Chiang. This resulted in Chiang's regaining control of many central and southern cities and areas of the country. In the summer of 1945, the Nationalist capital was removed from its wartime base at Chungking back to Nanking. Communist forces gained control over huge areas north of the Yangtze River.

The Japanese puppet state of Manchukuo, formerly Manchuria, had already been re-occupied by the Russians and posed a difficult problem for everyone—Chinese, Americans, and Russians. By the terms of the Sino-Soviet Treaty of Friendship and Alliance, dated August 14, 1945, Russia had agreed to respect the rights of Nationalist China in Manchuria, and there was unwritten agreement that Soviet forces would be withdrawn from the area by three months after Japan's defeat. The problem for Russia then arose, at the Japanese surrender, that it was not Nationalists but Communists who were in control there. Stalin, his ideas on Chinese Communism almost consistently wrong since he and the Russian government first took a hand in the formation of the Chinese Communist Party long ago, paradoxically had no wish to see the Communists take over Manchuria. He did not withdraw Russian troops until May, 1946.

Neither had the Americans any wish to see Mao in Manchuria. The Japanese surrender of August, 1945 was at once followed by the massive American airlift and sea-transportation of about half a million Nationalist troops to the coastal cities of China and to Manchuria.

The advance of Communist power in China, 1937–1950

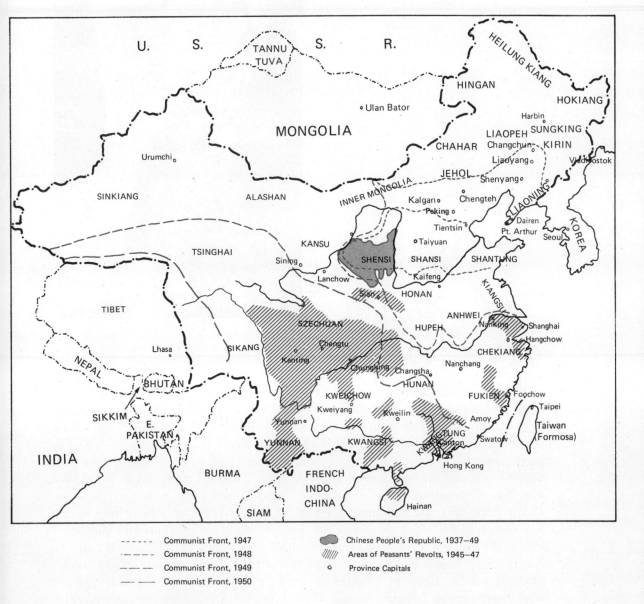

----- Communist Front, 1947	⬤ Chinese People's Republic, 1937–49
---- Communist Front, 1948	▨ Areas of Peasants' Revolts, 1945–47
--- Communist Front, 1949	○ Province Capitals
— Communist Front, 1950	

Civil War and Mediation

The Communists meanwhile strove hard to re-occupy first as many Japanese-held cities as they could before the Nationalists got there. Mao still insisted that a coalition of CCP and KMT should rule China, and Chiang refused to have the Red Army under any command but his own. The immediate transport of Nationalist troops to the liberated areas by the Americans was widely interpreted as a direct intervention in what was really now to all intents and purposes a Chinese civil war.

Chiang Kai-shek photographed during the
Civil War

But the Americans did continue efforts to bring about some form of conciliation between the two sides. At the end of August, 1945, Mao Tse-tung went, in company with the American ambassador, to Chungking where Chiang still was, and where forty days of talks were held. On the Double Tenth (October 10, 1945) an agreement was announced that gave legality to all political parties, promised the release of political prisoners and the breaking up of secret police organizations. The agreement also promised a People's Consultative Conference, pledging that both Communists and Nationalists would seek under Chiang's direction to avoid civil war. The Communist forces were to be reduced from forty to twenty divisions.

Any hope that this document might have had of being translated into reality was destroyed by what the American general Wedemeyer (Stilwell's successor) called 'the greatest air and sea transportation in history', of Nationalists and also American troops moving into dozens of Chinese cities. The Communists were under physical attack. Even in Chungking itself—a Nationalist stronghold—protests were heard and a League Against Civil War was formed in November, 1945; and in Kunming 30,000 students were demonstrating in the streets against Americans.

In December, 1945, America made a further attempt by sending General George Marshall to bring about a truce in the civil war. Such a truce was signed (Chou En-lai representing the Communist side) on January 10, 1946, and the People's Consultative Conference began a three-week session. One of its resolutions was that a National Assembly should meet in May and draft a constitution, and that government should be administered by a State Council, half of whose members would be Nationalists.

Right, Chou En-
lai, Mao Tse-
tung, and Chu Teh
on Yenan airfield

Below, General
Marshall and Mao
Tse-tung at Yenan

In reality, the intention of the Communists was that their armed forces should never come under the direction of Chiang's Nationalists; and the intention of Chiang was that his 'supervision' by means of parliamentary government should never be allowed to become a Communist-led 'new democracy'.

'It is impossible not to agree with General Stilwell that his [Chiang's] ignorance of the science of administration rendered him incapable of an intelligent use of power at such a juncture. His ignorance was buttressed after the defeat of Japan by an overwhelming stubbornness and self-confidence, for he assumed that in the last resort the United States would never fail to support him. Added to this was the lamentable state of the Kuomintang, which...had fallen more and more into the hands of the most reactionary or corrupt. To their dismay, the industrialists and businessmen of Shanghai, once the backbone of the party, found that the main areas of the economy were...to be run by government monopolies over which the Four Great Families exercised undisputed hegemony....'

Henry McAleavy: *The Modern History of China*

The centre of conflict was now Manchuria. The Russians, reluctant to leave until they had stripped every last industrial plant of its machinery (which they did with unparalleled thoroughness), lingered on in Manchuria until five months after the date set, only leaving in May, 1946. What they took with them has been estimated as worth 2,000 million US dollars.

General Wedemeyer strongly recommended that in the face of Communist resistance to his landings of Nationalist and American troops in Manchuria, the operation be dropped. But Chiang insisted. He had his way.

Chinese guerrillas active in anti-Japanese days and also in the Civil War. Here, in a setting of boats on a lotus-covered lake, they are being briefed on an operation

Chinese cavalry during the Civil War crossing a river on the way to Taipaishan on the Shensi-Kansu border

Nationalist troops landed and slowly dislodged the Communists. By June 17, 1946, the Nationalist Government ordered the Red Army to withdraw unconditionally from a long list of its liberated areas—all the way from Manchuria to the Yangtze. Henry Pu-i, the Japanese puppet emperor of Manchukuo, unfortunate and unprincipled to the last, found himself handed over to the Communists—eventually to emerge as a common Chinese citizen of the People's Republic of China in 1959.

Until the summer of 1947, Chiang's armies went from victory to victory, even capturing Yenan, the Communist stronghold for eleven years.

The reaction of a peasant leader of a village (Liu Ling) near Yenan to the Nationalist overrunning of the land is interesting and typical of peasant reaction all over the areas in which the Communists had had time to carry out land reform and peasant organization:

'In June 1935 we divided up the land... according to the size of each family and the quality of the land. Everyone got a paper with a stamp on it saying he owned the land.... In the next ten years things got better.... Our prosperity just increased. New caves [the people in this area live in caves scooped from the compact *loëss* earth], new land brought into cultivation. More and more families moved here.... Everybody had enough to eat.... But then came General Hu Tsung-nan [the Nationalist commander of the drive in that area] at the turn of 1946–7....

It took a whole month for us to remove our store of goods. Then we buried what was left and fled into the hills.... Hu Tsung-nan's troops ate up everything there was in the district. The rest they destroyed. People said: "What are we to do? We have nothing to live for any longer." So, when I came down from the hills during the occupation and saw that everything had been destroyed and that there were Hu Tsung-nan's troops everywhere, there was no working in the co-operative association any longer for me. Instead, I began to work politically. I became a guerrilla....'

General Marshall, having made his sincere and strenuous effort for peace, packed his bags and left China in January, 1947, his mission a total failure.

The Consultative Conference, eventually called at the beginning of 1946, was a farce—no Communist attended and the sole other large party (the Democratic League) was declared illegal soon after, leaving Chiang in total control.

But the Communists were not beaten. Their strength was, as ever, in their understanding of, and co-operation with the peasants, and in guerrilla tactics. In 1945, Mao had written:

'...the victory of the war of resistance has been won by the people with bloodshed and sacrifice. It should be the victory of the people and it is to the people that the fruits of the war of resistance should go. As for Chiang Kai-shek, he was passive in resisting Japan but active in anti-communism. He was a stumbling-block. Now this stumbling-block is coming forward to monopolize the fruits of victory. We will not tolerate this. This gives rise to struggle. Comrades, it is a most serious struggle.'

He was right. It was both serious and ferocious. The result was not finally to appear until four years later.

Chiang, in mid-1946, was confident that in renewal of the civil war his battery of modern armament would prove his armies superior to anything the Communists could put into the field. The Nationalists were about three million strong at the beginning of the civil war, their opponents only one million. With numerical strength and most of the aid in material that the United States had sent to China during the Second World War, and was still sending (it was said to amount in total to three and a half billion dollars between 1941 and 1948), it was hardly surprising that Nationalist forces spread out rapidly. But the width of that spread, the lack of control of military by civil authorities with the result that no sound economic base was established, was their undoing. Their strategy, too, was bankrupt. The general aim of establishing themselves strongly in this and that strategic

The People's Liberation Army artillery in 1946

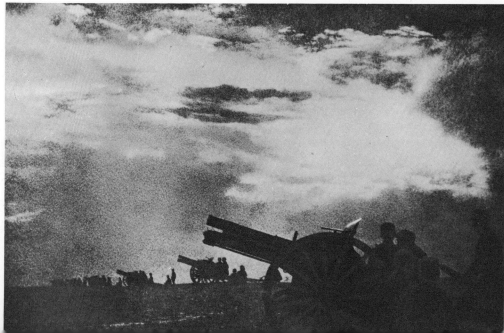

Communist forces attack Shenyang in Manchuria in 1948

place, hoarding supplies, and awaiting Communist attack in the knowledge that with superior weaponry the enemy could then be defeated, was not a forward-looking one. Corruption, desertion of their forces, and general demoralization, along with the distrust of the peasantry, did not assist them.

As the Nationalist commanders (Chiang included) might well have learned years ago (having had ample opportunity in the field to do so), Communist strategy did not play into their hands. The Communists moved about in the countryside, recruiting massively from the peasants, destroying Nationalist communications (railways, telegraph lines, roads) and avoiding at all costs direct confrontations in battle. Their arms improved in quality and number from captured Japanese stocks and from Nationalist defectors. By June, 1948, the Communist forces probably equalled in numbers those of Chiang, and equalled his armament in their various acquisitions. They cut off the Nationalist Manchurian garrisons from the rest of the country and in October that year took their surrender. More than 300,000 men surrendered at that time.

Another factor in Nationalist defeat was the bungling of its finances both during and after World War II. Revenue in 1941 provided only fifteen percent of expenditure, and the government fed its bureaucracy on salaries in kind—on rice from the land tax in kind that it had taken over. By the end of the Japanese war the bank note issue was 465 times that of mid-July, 1937. Between the beginning of 1946 and August, 1948, prices doubled no fewer than 67 times, and in the following six months they rose 85,000 times. Not even city dwellers felt much remnant enthusiasm for a Nationalist government that could permit this explosive inflation that wiped out the value of their capital and made nonsense of incomes in terms of buying power.

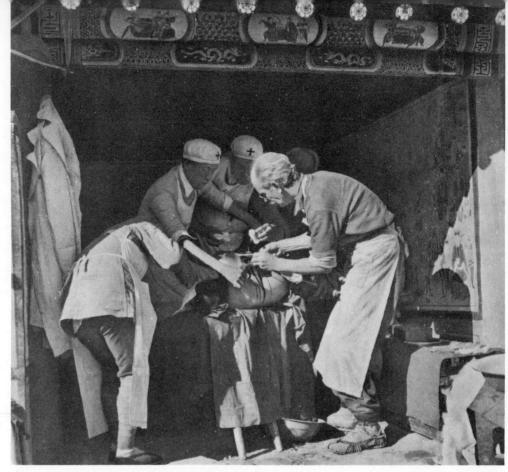

Above, Dr. Norman Bethune, a Canadian who served with the Communist forces in the Civil War. Working in the most primitive conditions, he saved many lives before dying of an infection caused by a cut when his knife slipped during an operation

Below, a Communist attack in the Huai-Hai battle of 1948

At the same time the Nationalists lost much of what intellectual backing they had. Agitation among teachers and professors as well as students for peace and an end to civil war led to the Kunming assassination in 1946 of Professor Wen I-to (1899–1946)—poet and patriotic Chinese intellectual. In the late 1920s he had expressed the hopeless situation of China in one of the most brilliant of the poems in the still new vernacular style:

The Dead Water

This is a ditch of hopelessly dead water.
No clear breeze can raise half a ripple on it.
Why not throw in some rusty metal scraps,
Or even some of your leftover food and soup?

Perhaps the copper will turn its green patina into jade,
And on the tin can rust will bloom into peach blossoms;
Then let grease weave a layer of silk brocade,
And germs brew out coloured clouds. . . .

The Huai-Hai Battle

But that mood had passed during the civil war. The mood of the whole country was to end war, to finish with the old order of things, to be rid of the ceaseless strife that had continued longer than anyone living could now remember.

The decisive battle of the civil war lasted for two months and was fought in the area where, almost a hundred years before, the Nien rebellion had raged—the Huai River basin. The battle has been called the Battle of Huai-Hai (from Huai River and Lung-Hai Railway).

Against the advice of his staff, Chiang had 50 divisions of his remaining 200 deployed on the plains round Hsüchow, about 175 miles north of Nanking. The Communists, however, controlled villages, and as they moved they put back into use the railways they had previously destroyed. Thus they were able to deploy large forces and to surround the Nationalist divisions. In the middle of November, 1948, there were four separate Nationalist army groups surrounded on the Hsüchow plains—about 340,000 men who were now completely cut off. By the end of the year another sixteen Nationalist divisions had been brought up and the remaining 130,000 Nationalist troops who had survived were herded into an area six miles square and surrounded by 300,000 men of the People's Liberation Army. On January 10, 1949, they surrendered. About 200,000 Nationalist troops died in this great battle of the war, and about 325,000 were captured or surrendered.

With Manchuria in their hands, with this desperate Nationalist loss and re-markable Communist victory of Huai-Hai, Peking and Tientsin were cut off, and they surrendered in January, 1949. By April the Communists had moved across the Yangtze. The month of May saw them in Shanghai, October in Canton, November in Chungking.

Chiang Kai-shek resigned as president in January, 1949, but retained command of the remnant Nationalist armies. The acting president, Li Tsung-jen, attempted

Mao Tse-tung inspecting from a jeep the People's Liberation Army at West Peking Airport in 1949

to negotiate with the Communists but was ignored. The Nationalist 'government' was driven down to Canton, from where Chiang and the Nationalists fled to Chungking, and from there onward to Taiwan on December 8, 1949.

Mao Tse-tung, confident that complete victory was his, had already announced the setting up of the People's Republic of China on October 1, in Peking, now renamed and once more the capital of a united China.

Why the Nationalists Failed

Put briefly, the causes of Nationalist failure to unify China under their lead were several. Perhaps the most important was that the majority of the Chinese people did not give Chiang or the KMT their real support. They did not do so for a variety of reasons. Everyone could see the corruption of Nationalist officials and Nationalist officers, most of whom managed even in the worst days to live very well while the people around them were starving or near to it. The treatment meted out to ordinary people by the Nationalists was that of unfeeling conquerors. Their contempt for everyone but their own kind aroused the anger and resentment of millions everywhere they went.

This was in marked contrast to the treatment of people by the Communist authorities and armies. While the character of the Communists was seen as something people could join with, that of the Nationalists was seen as yet another form of warlordism. The frugality of the Communist armies and authorities, their

The proclamation of the People's Republic of China by Mao Tse-tung on the balcony of Tien An Men in 1949

honesty, their prolonged attempts to reorganize life for the ordinary people in ways that showed at once marked improvements on the old ways, are not matters of Communist propaganda but are attested by sober Chinese, non-Chinese, and even anti-Communist observers.

As far back as 1943, the American embassy staff at Chungking (Chiang's capital) kept Washington informed of the signs of Nationalist breakdown, and of the virtual civil war American field officials saw with their own eyes as they travelled the interior of China. They reported troubles in Szechuan, uncontrolled bandits in Kansu, a famine in Honan and another in Kwangtung about which the Nationalist government did nothing, revolts against the Chungking government here and there, widespread resentment everywhere. Inflation, they reported, 'was eating the heart out of China, guerrilla activity against the Japanese was non-existent.' 'In the occupied areas the Japanese with a few hundred troops are able to sit behind their elaborate fortifications and contain thousands if not hundreds of thousands of idle Chinese troops.' This was the picture of Chiang's fight against the major aggressors in China, of all he did to avenge the Japanese brutalities that everyone cried out against. Those statements could be multiplied from a hundred sources.

The inflation that we have already mentioned got steadily worse. A 'currency reform' of 1948 by which the old paper currency was replaced by a new one supposedly backed by gold, led to the demand that all privately held gold be exchanged for the new paper currency. Controls were introduced. But in a very short time the whole operation (which was really a governmental swindle) collapsed, and the middle and upper classes who were the losers withdrew their support for Chiang.

Nationalist advantage at the start of the civil war was considerable, but as we saw in the classic process of Communist strategy in Manchuria and on the Hsüchow plains, ill-armed but skilfully used troops (troops, moreover, who believed in what they were fighting for) could defeat, surround, starve out, demoralize, and finally win, against armies several times their size who were much better equipped. The Nationalists never found the answer to Communist military strategy and tactical manoeuvring. Nor did they ever find, or seriously seek, a good answer to the peasants' longing for stability and safety.

Yet one more reason for Chiang's defeat was his own opinion that, whatever happened, America would bail him out. To believe this was not all fancy on his part. The sobering reports of American diplomats and military observers in China were consistently ignored by President Roosevelt who held firmly to the Nationalist propaganda cleverly put about by Chiang and his wife (the latter in lecture tours of the States) that Chiang was the saviour of China, and the KMT the sole force that could reform and unify the suffering country. But one American ambassador (among many other dissident American voices in China) thought and wrote to the Secretary of State in Washington quite otherwise. Clarence E. .Gauss had thirty-five years experience in China.

'Chiang and the Chinese have been "built up" in the United States to a point where Americans have been made to believe that China has been "fighting" the Japanese for five years, and that the Generalissimo [Chiang], a great leader, has been directing the energetic resistance of China to Japan and is a world hero. Looking the cold facts in the face one could only dismiss this report as "rot". [Chiang seems] to have lost his direct and active interest in military affairs in recent years and to have acquired a touch of unreality derived from a somewhat grandiose or "ivory tower" conception of his and China's role in world affairs.

His demands for lend-lease were insatiable and he kept brandishing the threat of a separate peace with Japan in order to have them fulfilled—pure blackmail, and bluff. 'Even the Communist leaders...tell us that it is a bluff and we should "call it" '

But the American government, hoping against hope, living in a world of apparently wilful fantasy about what the Nationalists and the KMT meant in China, went on supplying arms and money and advisers. In this way they unintentionally dragged out the civil war, and in the end with the 'stumbling-block' of Chiang's ineptitude in both military and administrative affairs, they were left with what they had most resolutely tried to avoid—a Communist China.

But the reason the Nationalists finally lost China was basically because the great mass of the Chinese people did not want them.

Why the Communists Succeeded

Nationalist resistance in small areas continued for some time but had no hope of resurgence or even of survival, and was eventually wiped out in 1950.

China at last was one country again. Only Taiwan, where the Government of the Republic of China had been set up by Chiang Kai-shek under American protection, was divorced physically from the great sub-continent of China. But more than that—for the first time since the signing of the first unequal treaty and the first loss of complete Chinese sovereignty just over one hundred years before—China was now her own master again and free from foreign presence on her own soil (apart from Taiwan). Once more there was a central government whose orders were obeyed. The population of China was at that time about 550,000,000, rising to 656,630,000 by 1957 at the census.

A task of unparalleled magnitude faced the government, how to make order in a country which for a century had been in disorder of various kinds, and for perhaps a century before that had suffered the effects of gradual weakening of the government. The ingredients of Communist Chinese rule are not by any means all derived from what is loosely called modernization, or from Marxist-Leninist principles and ways of organizing massive populations. There are many traditional elements among them.

For century upon century, Chinese governments have ruled from Peking, evolving highly skilled means of imposing centralized military, ideological, and social control, and organizing a vast bureaucracy in the provinces. This was one tradition of great importance inherited by the Communist government in Peking.

The other major factor in favour of Communist success in its nation-building was the country-wide craving for release from the seemingly eternal turmoil of so many decades, for an end to warlord armies rampaging over the country and living off the land, an end to devastation of the crops from battles and skirmishes, an end to the lawless brigands, to the brutalities of the Japanese occupation. And not least, an end to the corruption of the past that had slowly eaten into the very fabric of Chinese life.

The experience of local control over large areas of the country, acquired by the Communists in the long years since the days of the Kiangsi Soviet and broadened in Yenan and elsewhere, had taught them much about how Chinese are best organized. And much had been learned from the Reform Movement which failed in almost everything but the establishment of a university, and from the later Ch'ing reforms, abortive though they mostly were. Much also had been learned from mission schooling, from the Western introduction of technology, from small but important things such as simple hygiene measures, getting rid of flies, and rudimentary preventive medicine. Much, too, had come intellectually from Liang Ch'i-ch'ao's ideas on citizenship, from Sun Yat-sen's ideas for the welfare of the people.

It has been plausibly suggested that the first achievements of the People's Republic of China ruling from Peking after 1949, were very largely in knowing how to put all sorts of existing pieces, such as those, together in a rational and workable manner. But this was made possible by their Marxist-Leninist disciplines.

The revolution in China was immediate in many of its effects. Later, as time passed and the problems of making a thorough revolution in the face of the hostility of most of the world and the desertion of the single great ally, Soviet Russia, had to be confronted, the new China was miraculously to survive. Today, secure in its position in the United Nations, the picture of that China with which we began this history has vastly altered. China, in Mao Tse-tung's words, 'has stood up'.

The picture of Japan, too, has changed quite as deeply, and the picture of East Asia as a whole is now one in which the colonialism of a hundred years ago has all but ended, and in which East Asian countries stand on their own feet as once, long before the West first arrived in the East, they had been accustomed to do.

The events of that century now ended in the East have fundamentally altered the picture of the whole world. The centuries of Western dominance in Asia are finished. China has emerged once again as a great nation, a great power, with the capacity to lead as she did before for many, many centuries. Japan, militarism firmly put down, has turned into one of the world's great manufacturers while retaining much of her old genius. Southeast Asia as a whole has gained independence. Even in Vietnam, where a pitiless war with at first the returning French colonists and later the Americans supporting the régime in the south lasted for a generation that can never be erased from the national memory—even there the Vietnamese are now once more in complete control of their country. Only, perhaps, over Korea where the division between the Communist north and the large southern portion of the peninsula actively supported by the United States, does a question mark hang.

But East Asia, after a century of foreign interference and of internal strife has, broadly, now moved from bondage to liberation.

List of Chinese Names & Terms

A
Aigun	瑷珲
Amoy	厦门
Anhwei	
Anhwei, province	安徽
Anking	安庆
Annam	
Annam, Macao	澳门

B
Ba-kua chiao	八卦教
Boxer (Fists of Righteous Harmony, see Plum)	
Bethel, Town of the	伯特利城
Bethual, LMS	伯特利会

C
Cantonese Kwangchow	
Chahar (province)	
Chang	
Changsha (modern Sha)	长沙
Changchun (or Kuan)	长春
Chang Chien	张謇
Chang Chih-tung	张之洞
Chang Hsueh-liang	张学良
Chane Kuo-tao	张国焘
Changsha	长沙
Chang Tso-lin	张作霖
Chekiang (province)	浙江省
Chekiang, province	浙江(省)

List of Chinese Names & Terms

A   Aigun   璦琿

Amoy   廈門

Amur   黑龍江

Anhwei (province)   安徽

Anking   安慶

Annam   安南

Ao-men (Macau)   澳門

B   Ba-kua chiao   八卦招

Bocca Tigris (Tiger's Mouth):
  see Humen

Bogue, Treaty of the   虎門善後條約

Balkhash, Lake   巴爾喀什湖

C   Canton: see Kwangchow

Chahar (province)   察哈爾（省）

ch'an   禪

Ch'ang-an (modern Sian)   長安（西安）

Chang-chia-k'ou (Kalgan)   張家口

Chang Chien   張謇

Chang Chih-tung   張之洞

Chang Hsüeh-liang   張學良

Chang Kuo-t'ao   張國燾

Chang-sha   長沙

Chang Tso-lin   張作霖

Chefoo Convention   煙台條約

Chekiang (province)   浙江（省）

Chen Kung-po	陳公博
Ch'en Lan-pin	陳蘭彬
Ch'en Tu-hsiu	陳獨秀
Cheng-feng yün-tung	整風運動
Cheng Kuan-ying	鄭觀應
Ch'eng-te (Jehol)	承德（熱河）
Ch'i-shan (Kishan, Keshen)	琦善
Chiang Kai-shek	蔣介石
Chiang-nan Chi-ch'i chih tsao chü	江南機器製造局
Chiao-chou wan (Kiaochow Bay)	膠州灣
Chih-kang	志剛
Ch'ih-wai-fa-ch'uan (extraterritoriality)	治外法權
Chihli	直隸（河北省）
Ch'in (dynasty)	秦（朝）
Chin Shan	金山（於鎮江）
Ch'in Shih-huang-ti	秦始皇帝
China Revival Society: see Hua-hsing hui	
Ch'ing (Manchu) dynasty	清（朝）
Ching kang shan	井崗山
Chingkiang	鎮江
Ching-tê-chen	景德鎮
Chü-chiang (Pearl River)	珠江
Chu Hsi	朱熹
Chu Teh	朱德
Chuang-yüan	狀元
Chuenpi	穿鼻
Ch'ung-hou	崇厚
Chung, hsin, tu, ching	忠、信、篤、敬
Chung-hsüeh wei-t'i, hsi-hsüeh wei-yung	中學爲體，西學爲用
Chung-san (Sun Yat-sen)	中山（孫逸仙）
Chungking	重慶
Chusan Island	舟山羣島

Co-hong 公行

Confucius: see K'ung Fu-tzŭ

D   Darien 大連

democracy: see min-ch'uan chu-i

E   Eight-legged Essay: see Pa ku wen

Eight Trigrams Society:
   see Pa-hua chiao

Extraterritoriality:
   see Ch'ih-wai-fa-ch'uan

Empress Dowager: see Tz'u-hsi

Empress Dowager Lung Yu 龍如太后

F   Fan kwei 番鬼

Feng Kuei-fen 馮桂芬

feng-shui 風水

Fengtien 奉天

Feng Yü-hsiang 馮玉祥

Foochow 福州

Fukien (province) 福建（省）

G   Greater East Asia Co-Prosperity
   Sphere: see Ta Tung-ya Kung-yung
   Ch'üan

H   Hainan Island 海南島

Hai Ts'an Wei (Vladivostock) 海參威

Han (dynasty) 漢（朝）

Han-yeh-p'ing 漢冶平

Hangkow 漢口

Hanlin Academy 翰林院

Hanyang 漢陽

Heavenly Capital: see T'ien-ching

Heavenly King: see T'ien-wang

Heavenly Kingdom of Great Peace:
   see T'ai p'ing t'ien-kuo

Heilungkiang (province)   黑龍江（省）

Ho Ju-chang   何如璋

Ho Shen   和珅

Honam Island   河南島

Hong Kong   香港

Hoppo: see Yueh-hai-kuan-pu

Hsiang Braves: see Hsiang yung

Hsiang-shan   香山

Hsiang yung (Hsiang Braves)   湘勇

Hsing-chung hui   興中會

Hsiung-ti   兄弟

Hsüchow   徐州

Hu Shih   胡適

Hu-men (Bocca Tigris)   虎門

Hua-hsing hui (China Revival Society)   華興會

Huai Braves: see Huai yung

Huai-Hai Battle   淮海之役（淮河，
                           隴海鐵路）

Huai-ho   淮河

Huai River: see Huai-ho

Huai yung (Huai Braves)   淮勇

Huang-ho (Yellow River)   黃河

Huang Hsing   黃興

Huang-hua Kang   黃花崗

Huang Tsun-hsien   黃遵憲

Hui   回族

Hunan (province)   湖南（省）

Hundred Days' Reform:
   see Wu Hsü Wei-hsin

Hung Hsiu-ch'üan   洪秀全

Hung Jen-kan   洪仁玕

Hupeh (province)   湖北（省）

I Ichang 宜昌

I-ho ch'uan 義和拳

I-ho t'uan 義和團

Ili 伊犂

J Jehol: see Ch'eng-te

Jen-ching hua-bao 前清畫報

Jui-ch'eng 瑞澂

Jui chin 瑞集

Jung-lu 榮祿

K Kaifeng 開封

Kaiping Coal Mines:
  see K'ai-p'ing mei-k'uang

K'ai-p'ing mei-k'uang 開平煤礦

Kalgan: see Chang-chia-k'ou

K'ang-teh 康德

K'ang Yu-wei 康有爲

Kansu (province) 甘肅（省）

Keshen: see Ch'i-shan

Kiaochow (Chia-Chow) Bay:
  see Chiao-chou wan

Kiakhta 恰克圖

Kiangnan Arsenal: see Chiang-nan
  Chi-ch'i chih tsao chü

Kirin (province) 吉林（省）

Kishan: see Ch'i-shan

Kiukiang 九江

Koo, V.K. Wellington 顧維鈞

Korea 朝鮮

Kowloon 九龍

kowtow 叩頭

kuan-tu shang-pan 官督商辦

Kuang-fu hui 光復會

kung (artisan)	工
Kungchantang	共產黨
Kung-ch'in (Prince Kung)	恭親王
K'ung Fu-tzŭ (Confucius)	孔夫子
Kuo Mo-jo	郭沫若
Kuo Sung-tao	郭嵩燾
Kwangchow (Canton)	廣州
Kwangchow Bay	廣洲灣
Kwangsi (province)	廣西 (省)
Kwangtung (province)	廣東 (省)
Kwantung Peninsula (Liaotung Peninsula): see Kuan-tung pan-tao	
Kweichow (province)	貴州 (省)

L

Lao Fo-yeh (Old Buddha)	老佛爺
Li Chi	禮記
Li-fan-yuan	理藩院
Li-Fournier Convention: see Chien ming ho-yüeh	
Li Hsiu-ch'eng (Loyal King)	李秀成 (忠王)
Li Hung-chang	李鴻章
Li Li-san	李立三
Li Lien-ying	李蓮英
Li Ta-chao	李大釗
Li Tsung-yen	李宗仁
Li Yuan-hung	黎元洪
Liang Ch'i-ch'ao	梁啓超
Liaotung Peninsula: see Liao-tung pan-tao	
Liaoyang	遼陽
likin (tax)	釐金
Lin Tse-hsü	林則徐
Lin Wei-hsi	林維喜
Liu-ch'iu Islands (Ryukyu)	琉球羣島
Liu Hsi-hung	劉錫鴻

	Liu K'un-i	劉坤一
	Loukouchiao (Marco Polo Bridge)	蘆溝橋
	Loyang	洛陽
	Lu Chen-hsiang	陸徵祥
	Lu Hsün	魯迅
	Lung-chang Papermill	倫章造紙廠
	Lung-hai Railway: see Lung-hai t'ieh-lu	
	Lung-hai t'ieh-lu	隴海鐵路
	Lushunkow	旅順口
	Luting Bridge	瀘定橋
M	Ma Chien-chung	馬建中
	Macau (Ao-men)	澳門
	Manchu: see Ch'ing	
	Manchukuo	滿州國
	Manchuria: see Manchou	
	Manchou (Manchuria)	滿州
	Mao Tse-tung	毛澤東
	Marco Polo Bridge: see Loukouchiao	
	Matteo Ricci	利瑪竇
	men-hu kai-fang cheng-ts'e (Open Door Policy)	門戶開放政策
	min-ch'uan chu-i (democracy)	民權主義
	min-sheng chu-i (socialism)	民生主義
	min-tsu chu-i (nationalism)	民族主義
	Ming (dynasty)	明（朝）
	Miao	苗族
	Moho Goldmine	漠河金礦(在吉林)
	'most-favoured-nation': see tsui-hui- kuo	
N	Nanking	南京
	Nantung	南通
	nationalism: see min-tsu chu-i	

National Peking University:
   see Pei-ching Ta-hsüeh

Nien Fei (rebellion)   撚匪（之亂）

Ningpo   寧波

Nippon (Japan)   日本

nung (peasant)   農

O   Old Buddha: see Lao Fo-yeh

Open Door Policy:
    see men-hu kai- fang cheng-ts'e

P   Pa ku wen (Eight-legged Essay)   八股文

Pa-kua chiao (Eight Trigrams Society)   八卦教

Pakhoi   北海

pai hua   白話

Paoting   保定

Pao-huang hui (Emperor Protection
    Society)   保皇會

Pearl River: see chü-chiang

Pei-ching Ta-hsüeh (Pei-ta)   北京大學（北大）

Peiho   白河

Peiping   北平

Pei T'ang   北堂

Peiyang Fleet   北洋海軍

Pin-ch'un   斌椿

Port Arthur: see Lushunkow

Prince Ch'un   醇親王

Prince Kung: see Kung-ch'in

Pu-i (Pu-yi)   傅儀

R   Ryukyu Islands: see Liu-ch'iu Islands

S   san min chu-i (Three Principles of the   三民主義
      People)

Self-strengthening: see tzu-ch'iang

shang (merchant)	商
Shanghai	上海
Shansi (province)	山西（省）
Shantung (province)	山東（省）
Shashih	沙市
Sheng Hsüan-huai	盛宣懷
Shen-yang (Mukden)	瀋陽
Shensi (province)	陝西（省）
shih (scholar)	士
Shun (Shen) Pao	申報

Sian: see Ch'ang-an

Sikkim	錫金
Sinkiang (province)	新疆（省）

socialism: see min-sheng chui-i

Soochow	蘇州
Soong Ching-ling	宋慶齡
Soong, T.V.	宋子文
Su-pao	蘇報
Su Sung	蘇頌
Suiyüan (province)	綏遠（省）
Sun Chiah-ku	孫家穀
Sun Yat-sen, Dr. (see also: Chung-shan)	孫逸仙
Sung Chiao-jen	宋教仁
Szechuan (province)	四川（省）

T	Ta-t'ung shu	大同書
	Ta Tung-ya Kung-yung Ch'üan (Greater East Asia Co-Prosperity Sphere)	大東亞共榮圈
	Taierchuang	台兒莊
	Taipaishan	大白山
	T'aip'ing	太平
	T'ai-p'ing T'ien-kuo (The Heavenly Kingdom of Great Peace)	太平天國

Taiwan	台灣
Taku (Forts)	大沽口
T'ang (dynasty)	唐（朝）
Tangku Truce	塘沽停戰協定
Tatu River	大渡河
T'ien-ching (Heavenly Capital)	天京
Tien-an Men	天安門
Tien-tê	天德
T'ien-wang (The Heavenly King)	天王
Tientsin	天津
Tonkin	東京（安南北部）
tribute	貢禮
Ts'ai Yuan-p'ei	蔡元培
Tsêng Chi-tse (son of Tsêng Kuo-fan)	曾紀澤（曾國藩之子）
Tsêng Kuo-fan	曾國藩
Tsingtao	青島
Tsingtao-Tsinan Railway	青島濟南鐵路
Tso Tsung-t'ang	左宗棠
Tsui-hui-kuo ('most-favoured-nation')	最惠國
Tsung-li ko-kuo shih-wu ya-men (Tsungli yamen)	總理各國事務衙門（總理衙門）
Tsun-yi	遵義
Tuan Ch'i-jui	段其瑞
T'ung-chih Restoration	同治中興
Tungchow	同洲
Tung-hua-lu	東華錄
T'ung-meng hui (United League)	同盟會
Tung Pi-wu	董必武
T'ung-wen Kuan	同文館
Tunhuang	敦煌
Tz'u-an	慈安
tzu-ch'iang yün-tung (Self-strengthening)	自強運動
Tz'u-hsi (Empress Dowager)	慈禧太后

U   United League: see T'ung-meng hui

           Ussuri River   烏蘇里江

V   Vladivostock: see Hai Ts'an Wei

W   Wang, C.T.   王正廷

           Wang Ching-wei   汪精衞

           Wanghsia   望厦

           Wan-li   萬曆

           Wei Chêng   韋昌

           Weihaiwei   威海衞

           Wei-wu Pu   衞護部

           Wenchow   溫州

           Wen-hsiang   文祥

           Wen I-to   聞一多

           Wo-jen   倭仁

           Wu Hsü Wei-hsin (Hundred Day's   戊戌維新
           Reform)

           Wu P'ei-fu   吳佩孚

           wu-su   武術

           Wuchang   武昌

           Wuhu   蕪湖

Y   Yangchou   揚州

           Yalu River   鴨綠江

           Yeh Ming-chin   葉名琛

           Yellow River: see Huang-ho

           Yen Fu   嚴復

           Yen Hsi-shan   閻錫山

           Yenan   延安

           Yi (Barbarian)   夷

           Yin-ping-shih-ho-chi   飲冰室合集

           yüan   院

           Yüan (dynasty)   元 (朝)

Yuan-ming-yuan	圓明園
Yüan Shih-k'ai	袁世凱
Yüeh	粤
Yüeh-hai-kuan-pu (Hoppo)	粤海關部
yung	勇
Yung-an	永安（現廣西蒙山）
Yung Wing	容閎
Yunnan (province)	雲南（省）

Glossary of Japanese Terms

Aikoku Koto	— 'The Public Party of Patriots'—a political party
bakufu	— 'army headquarters'. Under the shogunate the word came to mean the government
bakumatsu	— 'the end (*matsu*) of the shogunate government (*bakufu*)'
bangaku	— 'barbarian learning', meaning study of Western books
buke	— the warrior class
bushido	— 'The Way of the Warrior'. The military code of behaviour
chonin	— the townspeople
daimyo	— a feudal lord
Daishin-in	— The Supreme Court
Dajokan	— 'The Council of State'—set up under the Charter Oath as the supreme organ of government
genro	— the men who led the movement culminating in the Meiji Restoration
Genro-in	— The Chamber of Elders
goshi	— peasants who were used part-time in armies
han	— a feudal domain belonging to a *daimyo*
heimin	— the common people
jiyu minken undo	— 'movement for freedom and people's rights'
Jiyuto	— 'Liberty Party' formerly *Kokkai Kisei Domei*, a reorganized political party
jushin	— elder statesmen
kamikaze	— 'the divine wind'—later used to mean suicide planes in World War II
kana	— the general term for cursive signs in written Japanese. There are two main categories, *hiragana* and *katakana*, derived by abbreviation of Chinese characters.
kazoku	— former court nobles together with former *daimyo*
kempeitai	— military police
ken	— a prefecture, one of the forty-three divisions of the country, formerly feudal land
Kenseikai	— a political party
kobu-gattai	— union between emperor and *bakufu* advocated by Satsuma clansmen

Kokkai Kisei Domei	—	'The League for Establishing a National Assembly', formerly called *Aikoku Koto*
kuge	—	court nobles
Kurai tanima	—	'the dark valley'—the decade in Japan ending in 1941
Meiji	—	the reign-title of the Emperor Mutsuhito (reigned 1867–1912)
metsuke	—	secret police whose main function was to check on *daimyo* activities
Minseito	—	a political party (formerly *Kenseikai*)
mon	—	family crest, later used by merchants as a business symbol
rangaku	—	a polite term for *bangaku*. *Rangaku* means 'Dutch learning', and was introduced in the eighteenth century
Rikken Kaishinto	—	'The Constitutional Progressive Party'—a political party
Risshisha	—	'The Society to Establish One's Moral Will'—a political party
Sa-in	—	'the Left Chamber' of the Council of State
sakoku-seisaku	—	'the closed country'. A period of self-imposed isolation in the seventeenth century
samurai	—	'those who serve'. Feudal warriors in the service of the *daimyo*
sankin-kotai	—	'attendance by turn'. The system intended to keep the *daimyo* under strict control by forcing them to reside in Edo every alternate year
Sei-in	—	'the Central Chamber' of the Council of State
Seiyukai	—	A political party
Shinto	—	'The Way of the Gods'. The original Japanese religious cult
shizoku	—	former *samurai*
shogun	—	Originally '*seii-tai-shogun*', meaning 'barbarian-quelling generalissimo'. The term was shortened to shogun and meant the military ruler of Japan
shuinjo	—	Permits stamped in vermilion, permitting Japanese mariners to go abroad to trade
sonno Jo-i	—	'support the emperor, expel the barbarians' movement
sumo	—	Japanese wrestling
U-in	—	'the Right Chamber' of the Council of State
zaibatsu	—	originally a 'financial group, or clique'. Later the word came to mean any large industrial combine
Zen	—	The Japanese name for what was originally the Chinese *Ch'an* sect of Buddhism

Appendix C

List of Illustrations

Appendix D

List of Maps & Diagrams

Bibliography

van Alstyne, Richard W. *The United States and East Asia*. Thames and Hudson, London, 1973.

Barr, Pat. *Foreign Devils: Westerners in the Far East*. Penguin, Harmondsworth, 1970.

de Bary, Wm. Theodore, Chan Wing-tsit, Watson, Burton, Tan, Chester. *Sources of Chinese Tradition*. 2 vols. Columbia University Press, 1960.

Beasley, W.G. *The Modern History of Japan*. Weidenfeld and Nicholson, London, 1969.

Brandt, C., Schwartz, B., Fairbank, John K. *A Documentary History of Chinese Communism*. Atheneum, New York, 1966.

Bye, Lucian W. *Warlord Politics. Conflict and Coalition in the Modernization of Republican China*. Praeger, New York, 1971.

Cary-Elwes, Columba. *China and the Cross*. Longmans Green, London, 1957.

Ch'en, Jerome. *Yuan Shih-K'ai, 1859–1916*. Allen and Unwin, London, 1961.

Cheng, J.C. *The Taiping Rebellion, 1850–1864*. Hong Kong University Press, 1963.

Chow Tse-tung. *The May Fourth Movement. Intellectual Revolution in Modern China*. Harward University Press, 1964.

Edwardes, Michael. *Asia in the European Age, 1498–1955*. Praeger, New York, 1962.

Fairbank, John K. *The United States and China*. Harvard University Press, 1962.

Fairbank, John K., Reischauer, Edwin O., Craig, Albert M. *East Asia: The Modern Transformation*. Houghton Mifflin, Boston, 1965. (Eighth printing 1973)

Fitzgerald, C.P. *The Birth of Communist China*. Penguin, Harmondsworth, 1968.

Fitzgerald, C.P. *The Chinese View of Their Place in the World*. Oxford University Press, 1964.

Fitzgerald, C.P. *China and Southeast Asia Since 1945*. Longman, Australia, 1973.

Hibbert, Christopher. *The Dragon Wakes: China and the West, 1793–1911*. Longman, London, 1970.

Liu Kwang-ching. *Americans and Chinese. A Historical Essay and a Bibliography*. Harvard University Press, 1963.

McAleavy, Henry. *The Modern History of China*. Weidenfeld and Nicholson, London, 1967.

Meyer, C., Allen, I. *Source Materials in Asian History*. Vol. 1, *China*. The Jacaranda Press, Australia, 1969.

Morse, Hosea B. *The International Relations of the Chinese Empire*. 3 vols. Longmans Green, London, 1910–1918.

Neill, Stephen. *A History of Christian Missions*. Penguin Books, Harmondsworth, 1964.

Reischauer, Edwin O. *Japan Past and Present*. Knopf, New York, 1964; Tuttle, Tokyo, 1973.

Reischauer, Edwin O., Fairbank, John K. *East Asia: The Great Tradition*. Houghton Mifflin, Boston, 1958. (Third printing 1966)

Rice, Edward E. *Mao's Way*. University of California Press, 1972.

Schurmann, F. and Schell, O. (Editors). *Republican China*. Pelican, Harmsworth, 1967.

Storry, Richard. *A History of Modern Japan*. Penguin, Harmondsworth, 1967.

Teng Ssu-yu, Fairbank, John K. *China's Response to the West: A Documentary Survey, 1839–1923*. Atheneum, New York, 1963. Originally published by Harvard University Press, 1954.

Tsunoda, Ryusaku, de Bary, Wm. Theodore, Keene, Donald. *Sources of Japanese Tradition*. 2 vols. Columbia University Press, 1958.

Woodcock, George. *The British in the Far East*. Weidenfeld and Nicholson, London, 1969.